39.95

D1083379

Scholars have long recognized that Chinese politics changed fundamentally in 1925, when the radical nationalism of the May Thirtieth Movement took political center stage and the Nationalist revolution began. This book explains that epochal development by showing the connection between that nationalistic upsurge and the introduction of modern World War I–style warfare to China. Its focus is the key year 1924, which saw a regional dispute about the status of Shanghai escalate into a massive civil war. Drawing on a wide range of newly available archival and other sources, this book shows how the war of 1924 opened the way for radical nationalism, deeply affecting the Chinese economy, society, politics, and foreign relations – and ultimately the ways Chinese thought about what was wrong with their society and how it should be changed. Like the author's well-received first book, *The Great Wall of China: From History to Myth*, this highly readable volume moves easily and persuasively from specifics of strategy and politics to the large and abiding issues of Chinese history and culture.

Cambridge Studies in Chinese History, Literature, and Institutions

General Editor, Denis Twitchett

FROM WAR TO NATIONALISM

From war to nationalism

China's turning point, 1924–1925

Arthur Waldron

U.S. Naval War College; Brown University

CAMBRIDGE UNIVERSITY PRESS

951.041
W16f

Published by the Press Syndicate of the University of Cambridge
The Pitt Building, Trumpington Street, Cambridge CB2 1RP
40 West 20th Street, New York, NY 10011-4211, USA
10 Stamford Road, Oakleigh, Melbourne 3166, Australia

© Cambridge University Press 1995

First published 1995

Printed in the United States of America

Library of Congress Cataloging-in-Publication Data
Waldron, Arthur.
From war to nationalism : China's turning point, 1924–1925 /
Arthur Waldron.
p.   cm. – (Cambridge studies in Chinese history, literature, and institutions)
Includes bibliographical references and index.
ISBN 0-521-47238-5
1. China – History – Warlord period, 1916–1928.   I. Title.
II. Series.
DS777.36.W34   1995
951.04′1 – dc20   94-40940
CIP

A catalog record for this book is available from the British Library.

ISBN 0-521-47238-5 Hardback

To my mother, Gertrude N. Waldron (1920–), and
my father, William A. Waldron (1913–)

University Libraries
Carnegie Mellon University
Pittsburgh PA 15213-3890

"War is the father of all things."
Heraclitus (535–475 B.C.)

Contents

Illustrations and maps

Photographs

Jacket

Modern warfare 1924, as imagined by a contemporary Chinese artist. (From *Jiazi ZhiFeng zhanshi*. Shanghai: Hongwen tushuguan, n.d.).

Following page 51

Infantry attack with air support near Shanghai.
The Chinese Parliament at Beijing, 1918.
Shanghai's War Memorial.
Members of the Shanghai Scottish Volunteer Company guarding the boundary of the international settlement, Shanghai, October 1924.
"The Old Firm," 1929.
Marshal Wu Peifu.
Kenkichi Yoshizawa, Japanese minister to Beijing, with his wife, 1932.
General Zhang Zuolin with his son Zhang Xueliang and Brigadier-General W. D. Connor, U.S.A.

Following page 90

Refugees fleeing Suzhou at the beginning of the Jiangsu–Zhejiang War, August 31, 1924.
Temple at Liuhezhen used as headquarters by Zhejiang defenders.
Zhejiang forces firing from trenches at Liuhezhen, August 30, 1924.
Camouflaged Zhejiang field-gun at Huangdu.

Following page 118

Fengtian aircraft.
Fengtian troops charge under cover of mortar fire.
Fengtian armored train in action.
Farmers press-ganged at Qinhuangdao to serve as munitions carriers for the Zhili forces.

ix

Wireless station on platform at Qinhuangdao station (now destroyed), next to "His Excellency" – Marshal Wu Peifu's train.

Zhili machine gun, posted on railway line to shoot stragglers and deserters.

Fortifications at Jiumenkou pass, eastern side.

One of Wu Peifu's armored cars, mounting a one-pounder gun.

Stokes mortar in use.

Wounded Zhili soldiers leaving the front.

Following page 207

General Feng Yuxiang.

After the Beijing coup d'état, Feng Yuxiang's men searched automobiles entering the Legation Quarter and prevented any from passing out and into the northern section of Beijing.

The Tianjin Conference, November 1924.

Sun Yat-sen, photographed shortly after his arrival in Tianjin.

Following page 262

The war as seen by the *New York American.*

Warlord fighting puppets and foreign puppeteers: cartoon from *Kladderadatsch* reproduced in *Dongfang zazhi.*

Soviet-influenced cartoon, prepared by Kuomintang First Army political department, 1926.

The May Thirtieth Movement: communist leader Li Lisan (1899–1967) addresses a crowd in Shanghai.

Maps

Following page 10

Distribution of Power, 1924
Theaters of War

Following page 71

The Jiangsu–Zhejiang War (General)
War in the Shanghai area
The Second Zhili–Fengtian War (General)
The Battle of Shanhaiguan

Page 240

Distribution of Power, 1926

Preface and acknowledgments

This book is about two wars fought in China in 1924. I have written it
because I believe they were extremely important, but to do so I have had
to open new scholarly territory. In Chinese, as in other histories, warfare
has been a neglected topic in recent years. Although a valuable literature
exists about what is usually called the warlord period in China, very
little of it in fact deals specifically with war or military questions.
Indeed, so little has actual fighting been studied that when this research
was begun, no modern book exclusively devoted to the wars treated here
existed even in Chinese. So my first debt of gratitude must be to those
who made sources available to me, above all to the National Second
Historical Archive of China in Nanjing, its director, Wan Renyuan, and
Liu Jingxiu, research archivist. I owe an equal debt to Chinese scholars
who shared their work with me: in particular to Professors Lai Xinxia
and Guo Jianlin, and Jiao Jingyi, of Nankai University, and Yang
Liqiang of Fudan University, as well as to my guides in the city
of Qinhuangdao and at the Shanhaiguan battlefield, Professor Qi
Qingchang and Sun Zhisheng. I also owe thanks to Professor Zhang
Kaiyuan of the Institute for Research on the 1911 Revolution at
Huazhong Normal University and to Professor Gu Xuejia and his colleagues in the History Department at Sichuan University, particularly
his student Yao Bo. In Taiwan I owe thanks to Professor Chen Tsun-
kung of the Academia Sinica, to Professor Tung-hua Li of National
Taiwan University, and above all to Professor Ling-ling Kuan of
Soochow University.

Although the most important research materials have come from
China, I have also relied a great deal on research collections in the
United States. During my years at Princeton, the staff of the University's
libraries went out of their way to help, and I would like to thank in
particular Diane Perushek, former Curator of the Gest Oriental Library,
and Chiu-kuei Wang and Martin Heijdra, the former and present

xi

Chinese bibliographers. I also owe special thanks to the library of the U.S. Naval War College, especially to Alice Juda and Marguerite Rauch and their superb colleagues in the reference department. I appreciate as well assistance from the Brown University Library, and in particular from Mrs. Kyong Hae Jin of the East Asian Collection, the Harvard–Yenching Library, the Oriental Library and Special Collections at Columbia University, the Yale Divinity School Library, and the Hoover Institution. Invaluable assistance with illustrations was provided by Peter Kolk, Nicholas Cull, now of the University of Birmingham, and the Imperial War Museum, London, as well as by Leslie Ann Eliet, Registrar of the Picker Art Gallery at Colgate University, and Edward Kasinec, Chief, Slavic and Baltic Division, New York Public Library.

The Mellon Seminar on Nationalism and Culture at Princeton University provided an initial academic setting for my work, and thanks are owed to the Andrew W. Mellon Foundation for making it possible. Similar gratitude is due the nationalism project of the Harry Frank Guggenheim Foundation. I am also grateful to my former colleagues in East Asian Studies and in History at Princeton University for their interest in my work, in particular to Marius Jansen, James T. C. Liu, Frederick Mote, Denis Twitchett, and Ying-shih Yü, and to my former graduate student, Allen Fung, and to Peter Paret of the Institute for Advanced Study, as well as to my current colleagues in Strategy and Policy at the U.S. Naval War College and in East Asian Studies at Brown University. For the most exacting criticisms and the greatest assistance I am indebted to Shiwei Chen, of Beijing University; Zhitian Luo, of Sichuan University; and Min Ma, of Huazhong Normal University; as well as to the late David Harrop, of Providence. Shuchi Chen, Amy Huang, and Chui Lau have been wonderful research assistants. For their generous publication subsidy, I am grateful to the Chiang Ching-Kuo Foundation for International Scholarly Exchange.

Finally, I would like to thank the Chinese scholar who confirmed me in my choice of topic by hearing out my argument in its rough form and agreeing with it in Beijing one day in 1986 while he showed me the few bits of his native city that remain from the 1920s; the Foreign Policy Research Institute in Philadelphia, which made it possible for me to complete the first draft of the manuscript during a very pleasant year spent as Hooper Fellow; and above all my wife, Xiaowei, to whom I owe the most: without her, the work would never have been completed.

Arthur Waldron
Providence, R.I.
June 30, 1993

Note on romanization

To minimize confusion, all Chinese personal and place names in the text have been rendered in Pinyin romanization. This has been done without the use of brackets to indicate modifications to the text, even in direct quotations, whether from primary or secondary sources, that use other systems. Thus Zhang Zuolin, for example, is never Chang Tso-lin, even when British minister Ronald Macleay spells his name that way. The only exceptions have been made for Chinese who had well-known foreign names, which are supplied in brackets at the first occurrence, as in "Gu Weijun [V. K. Wellington Koo]"; for Sun Yat-sen, Chiang Kai-shek, and the Kuomintang [Guomindang in Pinyin]; for certain non-Chinese place names such as Mukden; for nonstandard romanizations widely used at the time in trademarks and company names, as in the "Chee Sin Cement Works"; and in the bibliography and notes where original spellings are always followed.

Characters and chronology

The Main Characters

The Zhili Party (Beijing Central Government)

CAO KUN (1862–1938): President of the Republic of China.

WU PEIFU (1874–1939): "The Jade Marshal," Commander in Chief of central government armed forces; generally recognized as China's most gifted soldier.

FENG YUXIANG (1882–1948): "The Christian General," Commander of the crack 11th Division; a close collaborator of Wu Peifu, who ultimately betrayed him.

QI XIEYUAN (1897–1946): Governor of Jiangsu, Commander of the Zhili campaign against the Anfu Party in Zhejiang and Shanghai.

SUN CHUANFANG (1885–1935): Conqueror of Fujian, key collaborator in the campaign against the Anfu Party in Zhejiang and Shanghai.

The Fengtian Party (Mukden)

ZHANG ZUOLIN (1872–1928): "The Old Marshal," ruler of Manchuria as an independent kingdom but with ambitions to control China proper.

ZHANG ZONGCHANG (1881–1932): "The Dogmeat General," an uneducated caricature "warlord" who was Fengtian's best natural strategist; his polyglot army (Russians and Japanese as well as Chinese) repeatedly won critical victories.

The Anfu Party (Shanghai)

LU YONGXIANG (1867–1933): Governor of Zhejiang and Commander of Zhejiang and Shanghai against Jiangsu.

DUAN QIRUI (1865–1936): Senior leader of the Anfu party; former and future premier; when the wars begin he is in retirement in Tianjin, devoting himself to the study of Buddhism.

The Kuomintang or Nationalist Party (Guangdong)

SUN YAT-SEN (1866–1925): Long-time revolutionary leader and briefly provisional President of the Republic of China in 1912; a man of great personal prestige, but as the wars begin is in danger of losing even his foothold in Guangdong.

The Main Events

1920   **Zhili–Anfu War** drives Duan Qirui from premiership in Beijing; joint Zhili–Fengtian administration succeeds.

1922   **First Zhili–Fengtian War** pushes Fengtian forces back to Manchuria; Zhili takes unchallenged control of central administration.

1923   **Cao Kun** assumes presidency after bribing parliament; treaty guaranteeing **military neutrality of Shanghai area** prevents war in the Yangzi valley.

1924   JUNE: Defeated Anfu generals from Fujian arrive in Zhejiang, violating 1923 neutrality agreement; **war in Yangzi valley looks increasingly likely.**

AUGUST: **Financial panic** begins in anticipation of war.

SEPTEMBER 3: Zhili forces from Jiangsu and Fujian attack Zhejiang and Shanghai; **beginning of Jiangsu–Zhejiang War.**

SEPTEMBER 7: Fengtian declares war in support of Zhejiang.

SEPTEMBER 15: **Beginning of Second Zhili–Fengtian War,** fought in Manchurian–Chinese border areas north and northeast of Beijing.

SEPTEMBER 19: Anfu forces abandon Zhejiang; retreat to Shanghai perimeter.

OCTOBER 7: Fengtian forces break through Zhili lines at Jiumenkou, near Shanhaiguan.

OCTOBER 12: Anfu forces flee Shanghai; **Zhili victory in Jiangsu–Zhejiang War.**

OCTOBER 17: Fengtian forces break Zhili lines at Shimenzhai; after heavy fighting, Wu Peifu stabilizes the front.

OCTOBER 23: **Feng Yuxiang leaves the front to carry out coup d'état in Beijing.** Zhili position destroyed; Chinese politics thrown into confusion.

NOVEMBER 10: As chaotic fighting continues, Zhang Zuolin, Duan Qirui, and Feng Yuxiang begin **negotiations in Tianjin.**

NOVEMBER 24: **Duan Qirui** inaugurated as **Provisional Chief Executive** in Beijing.

DECEMBER 4: **Sun Yat-sen** arrives in Tianjin.

DECEMBER 13: **Duan Qirui** dissolves parliament and abolishes both the Provisional Constitution of 1913 and the Constitution of 1923, thus sweeping away all previous legal structure of Chinese government.

1924–1925   DECEMBER–JANUARY: Confused military **struggle for control of Shanghai.**

1925   FEBRUARY: **Strikes begin in Shanghai** textile factories.
MAY 30: **British police kill nine Chinese demonstrators in Shanghai;** disorder quickly spreads throughout the country. Effective beginning of Kuomintang-led Nationalist Revolution.

1926   Full civil war breaks out within the Northern Regime. Kuomintang begins **Northern Expedition.**

1927   Kuomintang establishes **new National government at Nanjing.**

1928   Last forces of the **Beijing government defeated** by the Kuomintang.

Abbreviations used in footnotes

BDRC	Boorman, Howard L., ed. *Biographical Dictionary of Republican China*. New York: Columbia University Press, 1967.
CB	*Chen Bao* [The Morning Post], Beijing.
CWR	The *China Weekly Review* [Mileshi Pinglunbao], Shanghai.
CYB	The *China Year Book* (annual). Edited by H. G. W. Woodhead. Peking and Tientsin: The Tientsin Press.
DZ	*Dongfang zazhi* [The Eastern Miscellany], Shanghai.
FO	Foreign Office General Correspondence, Far Eastern Department, F.O. 371 Series. Public Record Office, London.
FRUS	*Foreign Relations of the United States* (annual). Washington, D.C.: U.S. Government Printing Office.
JDBH	Rong Mengyuan and Zhang Baifeng, eds. *Jindai Baihai*. 13 vols. Chengdu: Sichuan renmin chubanshe, 1985.
MIR	U.S. Military Intelligence Reports, China 1911–1941. Edited by Paul Kesaris. Guide prepared by Robert Lester Microfilm. Frederick, Md.: University Publications of America, 1983.
NYT	The *New York Times*, New York.
SB	*Shenbao* [The Shun Pao], Shanghai.
SD	Records of the Department of State Relating to Political Relations of the United States with China, 1910–1929. (National Archives Microfilm Publications Microcopy No. 339); also Records of the Department of State Relating to Political Relations Between China and Other States, 1910–1929 (National Archives Microfilm Publications Microcopy No. 341).
YHZB	*Yinhang zhoubao* [Bankers' Weekly], Shanghai.

Introduction

In the early autumn of 1924 the central government in Beijing ordered a military mobilization that was unlike anything seen before in Chinese history. The hour had arrived for a showdown in its long-smoldering dispute with Zhang Zuolin, "the Old Marshal" [*dashuai*], whose quasi-independent military kingdom in Manchuria posed a growing threat to the security of North China and the Beijing government. Fighting between allies of Beijing and of the Old Marshal had already been going on for almost three weeks in the Shanghai area; now the struggle had spread north. A vast and potentially decisive battle was taking shape at the border between China proper and Manchuria, at Shanhaiguan, the famous "first gate under heaven" in the Ming defense line, that was popularly called the Great Wall.[1] The central government's commander in chief was China's ablest general, Wu Peifu, a classically educated soldier whose military brilliance had won him the admiring epithet *yushuai*, "Jade Marshal." Like his rival, Wu hastened to concentrate all available forces at the critical point. And as Wu's troops and materiel were drawn from all of China north of the Yangzi, they were funneled by the rail network through Tianjin, a little more than 100 miles south of the front.

The first of the central government's troop trains rolled through Tianjin Central Station in the dead of night, at 1:00 A.M. on September 17. Thirty-four cars long, it was carrying 1,000 officers and men of the 23rd Division from Langfang, on the southeast outskirts of Beijing, toward a staging area at Luanzhou, some 100 miles farther north. By 10:00 A.M. eight more military trains had cleared the station. Six had carried officers and men of the 23rd Division – roughly 3,200 in all – one had carried equipment and one had been a hospital train. At 5:00 P.M.

---

1. The rather misleading term is of Western origin. See Arthur Waldron, *The Great Wall of China: From History to Myth* (Cambridge, England: Cambridge University Press, 1990).

flatcars carrying an airplane squadron passed the station on their way north. By day's end fifteen military trains had cleared the station. Sixteen more trains followed on the eighteenth, twelve on the nineteenth, and eighteen each on the twentieth, twenty-first, and twenty-second. They were carrying field guns and ammunition, headquarters staff, airplanes, field kitchens, hospitals, cavalry, pack animals, coolies, and, above all, soldiers. The 23rd, 9th, and 13th Divisions and the 14th Mixed Brigade passed through Tianjin on the seventeenth, and seven trains of artillery alone on the twenty-first – parts of an unending stream.[2]

By September 26, 100,000 men, of an expected total of 200,000, had already been moved to the front, with the rest expected within a week. In all, nearly 300 trainloads of troops would go forward to the Manchurian frontier, moving an average of 300 miles each. To serve this mobilization, Wu Peifu placed transportation under military control and requisitioned almost the entire rolling stock of railways north of the Yangzi River. Crews worked double shifts, and discipline was enforced at gunpoint.[3]

To support these massive ground forces, Wu sent air and naval units north as well. The air force of the central government consisted of eighty-three planes, based in peacetime at Nanyuan, Baoding, and Luoyang. These were now deployed as four squadrons: one at Beijing, one at Tianjin, one at Changli, and one at Beidaihe.[4] The Bohai naval fleet commanded by Wen Shude had seven ships; these were now augmented by more vessels from the south. Among the fleet assembling from Nanjing, Shanghai, and Qingdao, were two cruisers, the *Haishen* and the *Chaohe*, the destroyer *Tongan*, and two gunboats, the *Yongxiang* and the *Chuyu*. On September 21 China's finest warship, the *Haiqi*, a second-class, steel-protected cruiser (built at Elswick in 1898) and armed with two 8-inch and ten 4.7-inch guns, sailed for the north. The fleet was gathering off the coast of Manchuria in preparation for a maneuver never before attempted in Chinese warfare: an amphibious landing, of the sort the Japanese had used against the Chinese in Korea thirty years earlier, to envelop Zhang Zuolin's forces from the rear.[5]

Foreign attachés, monitoring these developments closely, found no-

---

2. Headquarters U.S. Army Forces in China, Office G-2 Military Intelligence, Tientsin. Intelligence Bulletins nos. 2-11, September 22-26, 1924, in Military Intelligence Reports (hereafter cited as MIR).

3. J. E. Baker, "Chinese Military Rail Transport," CWR, December 20, 1924, pp. 73, 78; *New York Times* (hereafter cited as NYT), September 26, 1924, p. 23.

4. Li Tianmin, *Zhongguo hangkong zhanggu* (Taibei: Zhongguo de kongjun chubanshe, 1973), p. 42; Mao Jinling, "Beiyang zhixi jundui zhi yangjin" (Ph.D. dissertation, National Taiwan University, 1987), p. 111; NYT, September 20, 1924, p. 6; Anthony B. Chan, *Arming the Chinese: The Western Armaments Trade in Warlord China, 1920–1928* (Vancouver: University of British Columbia Press, 1982), p. 120.

5. Mao Jinling, p. 111; NYT, September 22, 1924, p. 1.

2

thing exotically East Asian about the armies they watched mobilizing. If anything, the Chinese forces moving in 1924 were uncannily reminiscent of the ones most of them had come to know well in the great European war that had begun just a decade before. All wore World War I–style uniforms; some had helmets with a battered French eagle on their crests.[6] Nor did the similarities end with uniforms and armaments. We will see how in China in 1924 – as in Europe of 1914 – a series of seemingly minor local conflicts triggered a great conflict the course and consequences of which would be far different from what any of the participants wanted or expected.

This seeming accident of history should perhaps not have been a surprise. The year 1924 was not just any year. It was what the Chinese call a *Jiazi* year, after the two characters that designate it – in the calendar used since ancient times – as beginning an entirely new cycle of sixty years.[7] By tradition such years brought change. So it was entirely fitting that it should have witnessed great wars whose impact was felt in every area of Chinese life; wars, indeed, that changed the course of modern Chinese history. This book tells their story.

Two major and related conflicts were fought in *Jiazi* year, each reflecting the rivalry between the party in control of the central government, usually called Zhili, after the province in which Beijing lay, and Zhang Zuolin, whose party was usually called Fengtian, after the name of the southernmost of the three provinces of Manchuria. The first of these conflicts was the Jiangsu–Zhejiang War (August 28–October 12). It was a contest for control of the pivotal area of the lower Yangzi valley, and Shanghai in particular, with its strategic position and unparalleled wealth. This first war ended with victory by regional forces aligned with the central government, and the Zhili party that controlled it. The high-stakes war in the Yangzi valley, however, sent tremors through the whole Chinese political system, which touched off the much larger Second Zhili–Fengtian War (September 17–October 23). It was fought directly between Zhili and Fengtian. Each side threw everything they had into it because, throughout, it seemed to promise a decisive victory for one or the other. It ended, however, in political and military chaos worse than anything seen since the abdication of the Qing dynasty a dozen years earlier.

6. Lawrence Impey, *The Chinese Army as a Military Force*, 2nd ed. (Tientsin: Tientsin Press, Ltd., 1926), illustration facing p. 22.
7. See, e.g., Gu Tiaosun, *Jiazi neiluan shimou jishi* (Shanghai: Zhonghua shuju, 1924); He Xiya, "Jiazi dazhanhou quanguo jundui zhi diaocha," *Dongfang zazhi* **22** (1925): no. 1, 103–12; no. 2, 34–57; no. 3, 69–83. Chinese commonly used cyclical characters to designate major events, but material from the time makes clear that the particular significance of the *Jiazi* year was not lost on them.

Militarily, these wars marked the arrival in China of fighting in the style of World War I in Europe, something new and deeply destabilizing. *Jiazi* year saw the first example in Chinese history of a new kind of war fighting: *liti zhan* – "three dimensional" or "combined arms warfare," in which operations by infantry, cavalry, ships, and aircraft were coordinated in the service of a single strategic plan. This in turn was the product of the technological revolution in warfare that had begun for Europe in the mid-nineteenth century. That same revolution had been at work in China at least since the establishment there of the first Western-style arsenal in 1861. Sixty-three years later the result was, for the first time in China, recognizably modern war.[8]

The combatants used machine guns, airplanes, barbed wire, and mines. "File closers" (to shoot deserters) followed the troops into battle. Half a million men were thrown into the fighting; nine provinces were engulfed in the war zones; and fourteen in all were directly affected. The wars more than absorbed the Beijing government's entire budget. The fighting was bloodier and more bitter than in any struggle since the nineteenth century.[9] True, the scale of the struggles was not remotely comparable to World War I in Europe. But in terms even of the recent Chinese past, they were absolutely unprecedented. Even foreigners were impressed.[10]

The wars of *Jiazi* year are little known today, even among specialists, and even in China. Still less do most people suspect their critical importance in the history of twentieth-century China. The standard works treat them but with extreme brevity and no sense of their implications. The classic textbook of Chinese history, *East Asia: The Modern Transformation*, devotes only four lines in reduced-size type to the events that are the subject of this book, dismissing them as meaningless "marching and countermarching."[11]

Yet the destructive and costly modern warfare that was unleashed on

---

8. I use the term advisedly. See Reid Mitchell, "The First Modern War, R.I.P." *Reviews in American History* (December 1989): 552–8.

9. Guo Jianlin, "Liang ci Zhi Feng zhanzheng zhi bijiao." *Lishi dangan* 1987: no. 3, 108–12; Hsi-sheng Ch'i, *Warlord Politics in China 1916–1928* (Stanford: Stanford University Press, 1976), pp. 137–8.

10. Ronald Macleay to Ramsay MacDonald, September 5, 1924, Foreign Office (FO) 371/10245.

11. John K. Fairbank, Edwin O. Reischauer, and Albert M. Craig, *East Asia: The Modern Transformation* (Boston: Houghton Mifflin, 1965), p. 657. Outside of the specialized literature to be cited below, probably the best accounts remain Li Chien-nung, *The Political History of China, 1840–1928*, trans. and ed. Ssu-yu Teng and Jeremy Ingalls (Stanford: Stanford University Press, 1956) and, for foreign relations, Hosea Ballou Morse and Harley Farnsworth MacNair, *Far Eastern International Relations* (Cambridge, Mass.: Houghton Mifflin, 1931).

China in 1924 brought with it a host of powerful and unanticipated effects and consequences. These ranged across society, politics, and economics, and ultimately had a great impact on thought and the arts. It is with these effects, as much as with the war itself, that this book is concerned. It is these effects, furthermore, that made the conflicts of 1924 a turning point – not only in Chinese warfare but also in the broad processes of the rise of nationalism and the emergence of revolution.

The wars of 1924 devastated the Chinese economy and visited a host of ills on society and politics. The Beijing government was bankrupted. Private finance, investment, and trade were shaken; the war caused many bankruptcies. Violence spread, and a sense of insecurity gradually became pervasive in society. Nor did the wars discussed here have physical impact only: their intangible effects can be detected in the intellectual and artistic realms. In China, as in Europe a decade earlier, modern war destroyed confidence in the status quo and led many to seek understanding of social change and cataclysm in ideas, mostly originating on the Left, whose influence had hitherto been limited. New questions were asked about Chinese society itself. What was wrong? Was the problem wars, or somehow War? If the latter, how was it caused? New words – such as *junfa* [warlord], indicative of a whole new way of thinking about violence – came into wide usage. New sensibilities and styles revealed themselves in areas from the novel to cartooning.

Nevertheless, I maintain that by far the most important consequence of the wars described was the rise of a nationalist and revolutionary movement that got under way a few months after the fighting had ended. It is in connection with this that I propose the most substantial modification in the way we think about the epochal changes that took place in the 1920s.

Most studies of early twentieth-century Chinese history skip from the May Fourth demonstration of 1919 to the May Thirtieth Movement of 1925 and the "great revolution" [*da geming*] that followed. Indeed, before the words "The Chinese Revolution" were transferred to mean the events of 1949, they referred to the fall of that regime that had ruled China since 1912 from Beijing and its replacement in 1927 by the government of the Kuomintang, or Nationalist Party, which ruled from Nanjing.[12]

In most narratives these are the events to which almost exclusive attention is paid. The political and economic events – indeed, even the

---

12. As in Harold Isaacs, *The Tragedy of the Chinese Revolution*, 1938, 2d rev. ed. (Stanford: Stanford University Press, reprint ed., 1961); Dorothy Borg, *American Policy and the Chinese Revolution, 1925–1928* (New York: American Institute of Pacific Relations, 1947; reprint ed., with new introduction by the author, New York: Octagon Books, 1968).

wars – that were at least their context and, I would argue, their permissive cause as well, are thoroughly neglected. Thus, the classic textbook mentioned restores a normal typeface when narration of the 1920s turns away from warfare to what is usually called China's "national revolution." First comes the incident of May 30, 1925, in Shanghai, when nine Chinese demonstrating against foreign privileges were shot dead by police as they threatened the Louza police station just off Nanjing Road in the International Settlement. Then follows the May Thirtieth Movement, which saw a tide of violent and uncontrollable demonstrations against foreign privilege sweep over the rest of the country. Next to be described is the Kuomintang's Northern Expedition, launched just a year later from Guangzhou by the charismatic general Chiang Kai-shek which, riding that tide, defeated armies controlled by Beijing and established a new National government at Nanjing in 1927. And finally the story arrives at that regime's decisive victory over the remnants of the Beijing government in the North in June of the following year.

The story of these events has been told many times but almost always without posing the most important questions. Why did the Beijing government fall at all? Given that it did fall, why did its crisis begin so suddenly – and as will be seen, so unexpectedly – in 1925? Why not in 1924, or even in 1919? None of these questions can be approached without a clear understanding of developments in the first four years of the decade of the 1920s. And unless the full impact of the wars of 1924 is taken into consideration, they cannot be answered satisfactorily at all.

But by and large the collapse of the Northern System of government and its replacement by the Nanjing administration have not seemed to most historians to demand much in the way of detailed explanation. The period from 1912 to 1927 when Beijing was the capital of the Chinese Republic is often still thought of in stereotyped terms; as a time of meaningless chaos and confusion; of "warlord domination" in the provinces and "comic opera government" in the capital.[13] Neither its politics nor its military affairs have been thoroughly studied (although we have some excellent studies of individual militarists).[14] That such a regime

13. "For over a decade now, imperial government has given way to comic opera government." Josef Washington Hall [Upton Close], *In the Land of the Laughing Buddha* (New York: Putnam, 1924), p. xvi.
14. Among the most important Western-language works on the topic are Jerome Ch'en, *The Military–Gentry Coalition: China Under the Warlords* (University of Toronto–York University Joint Centre on Modern East Asia Publications Series, vol. 1, no. 4 (Toronto: University of Toronto–York University Joint Centre on Modern East Asia, 1979); His-sheng Ch'i, *Warlord Politics in China 1916–1928* (Stanford: Stanford University Press, 1976); Donald G. Gillin, *Warlord: Yen Hsi-shan in Shansi Province 1911–1949* (Princeton, N.J.: Princeton University Press, 1967); Diana Lary, *Region and Nation: The Kwangsi Clique in Chinese Politics 1925–1937* (Cambridge, England: Cam-

should have been swept away seems scarcely surprising to most writers. So scholarly attention has focused not on the origins of this change but, rather, overwhelmingly on its effects: on society, economy, and above all on foreign relations.[15]

Such explanation as there is of the end of the Beijing regime focuses largely on the concept of nationalist revolution. The May Thirtieth Movement is depicted as part of a great nationalistic wave that swept all before it, propelling radical social change, and not only that of the Nationalists but that of the Communists as well.

The limitations of this approach, however, are beginning to become evident. The period from 1912 to 1927 is increasingly recognized as one of vigorous economic, social, and intellectual development. And far from being the "comic opera government" sometimes portrayed, the Beijing regime is being understood to have had real institutional and political strengths; enough in any case to make its ultimate military defeat and replacement by the Nationalist government of the Kuomintang far from inevitable. The Beijing government's control of China was limited but not perhaps more limited than would be Chiang Kai-shek's (in 1928 he exercised military control over 7% of China's provinces; by 1936 that figure had only risen to 25%).[16] The western Powers and Japan recognized Beijing as the government of China and expected it to continue to fill that role: that was one of the most basic premises of the Washington treaties of 1922, which in effect constituted a carefully hedged but nevertheless real vote of confidence in its future. And within China the Beijing government enjoyed a higher degree of legitimacy than is sometimes recognized: as Andrew Nathan notes in the *Cambridge History of China*, "until 1923, if not later, many leaders of public opinion,

bridge University Press, 1975); Gavan McCormack, *Chang Tso-lin in Northeast China, 1911–1928: China, Japan, and the Manchurian Ideal* (Folkestone, Kent, England: Dawson & Sons, 1977); Andrew J. Nathan, *Peking Politics 1918–1923: Factionalism and the Failure of Constitutionalism* (Berkeley: University of California Press, 1976); James L. Sheridan, *Chinese Warlord: The Career of Feng Yü-hsiang* (Stanford: Stanford University Press, 1966); Donald S. Sutton, *Provincial Militarism and the Chinese Republic: The Yunnan Army, 1905–25* (Ann Arbor: University of Michigan Press, 1980); Odoric Y. K. Wou, *Militarism in Modern China: The Career of Wu P'ei-Fu, 1916–39* (Folkestone, Kent, England: Dawson & Sons; also Canberra: Australian National University Press, 1978).

15. Among the most important works treating the impact of developments in China on international relations are Dorothy Borg, *American Policy and the Chinese Revolution, 1925–1928* (New York: American Institute of Pacific Relations, 1947; reprint ed., with new introduction by the author, New York: Octagon Books, 1968); Akira Iriye, *After Imperialism: The Search for a New Order in the Far East 1921–1931* (Cambridge, Mass.: Harvard University Press, 1965); Warren I. Cohen, *America's Response to China: An Interpretative History of Sino-American Relations*, 2d ed. (New York: Knopf, 1980); Katsumi Usui, *Nihon to Chūgoku: Taishō jidai* (Tokyo: Hara Shobō, 1972).

16. Hsi-sheng Ch'i, *Nationalist China at War: Military Defeats and Political Collapse, 1937–45* (Ann Arbor: University of Michigan Press, 1982), p. 23.

while deploring the feuding and corruption of politicians, voiced hope in the ultimate success of the constitutional order" on which it was theoretically based. Finally, despite retrospective condemnation by nationalistic writers, nowhere were the Beijing government's successes greater than in foreign policy: its Ministry of Foreign Affairs "had more power and independence, more continuity, better personnel, more positive policies and nationalistic motivations than most people realize." Yet, as Nathan observes, these achievements largely "remain to be studied."[17]

As for the rising tide of nationalism, there was a time earlier in this century when such an idea was easily accepted. It seemed so natural and intuitively comprehensible that scholars confronted with political or social change could simply invoke nationalism to explain them, and be finished – but no longer. Nationalism is now recognized as an elusive concept: It cannot be taken for granted as a self-sufficient explanatory tool but, rather, must itself be better understood. Invoking it explains very little; instead, it creates new problems.[18]

Taken together, empirical reexamination of the period of the Beijing government and theoretical reevaluation of China's national revolution bring us to a question. If the Beijing government was in fact far more than a mere interlude, then how are we to account for its decisive defeat by the Kuomintang, a force that at the start of the Northern Expedition was certainly far weaker in nearly every way one can measure? And in particular, if we cannot look to "nationalism" to solve the problem, then where can we find an answer? I insist that we must look to the potent agency of war.

Modern China, like nearly every other state, has been formed chiefly by war. War is a powerful and capricious historical actor that regularly confounds historians who try to tame it. It refuses to accept dependent status and follow easily along the contours of the economic, social, or intellectual developments that are usually considered primary. Rather, it cuts across other lines of causation, intervening to overturn and trans-

17. Andrew J. Nathan, "A Constitutional Republic: The Peking Government, 1916–28" in *The Cambridge History of China*, vol. 12, *Republican China 1912–1949, Part 1*, ed. John K. Fairbank (Cambridge, England: Cambridge University Press, 1983), pp. 266, 268, quoting Sow-theng Leong, *Sino-Soviet Diplomatic Relations, 1917–1926* (Honolulu: University of Hawaii Press, 1976), pp. 268, 294–5.
18. Such at least is the approach of an increasing number of scholars. See, for example, Benedict Anderson, *Imagined Communities: Reflections on the Origin and Spread of Nationalism* (London: Verso, 1983); Partha Chatterjee, *Nationalist Thought and the Colonial World – A Derivative Discourse?* (London: Zed Books for the United Nations University, 1986); and Miroslav Hroch, *Social Conditions of National Revival in Europe: A Comparative Analysis of the Social Composition of Patriotic Groups among the Smaller European Nations* (Cambridge, England: Cambridge University Press, 1985), as well as my review essay, "Theories of Nationalism and Historical Explanation," *World Politics* 37 (April 1985): no. 3, 416–33.

form human society in unexpected and inscrutable ways. And as it was with World War I in the West, the effects of the wars of 1924 on Chinese politics and society were largely unexpected and, frankly, often contrary to the intentions of the combatants. Yet these wars were perhaps the most crucial of all factors in causing the events of the 1920s with which all are familiar. The May Thirtieth Movement and the Northern Expedition could never have succeeded without the prior occurrence of multiple shifts in China's life: military, political, economic, social, and even intellectual. And if that is the case, then these wars were indeed a major turning point, for without the victory of the Kuomintang, for which they prepared the way, all that followed – even including the rise of the Communists to power – would have been different.

This book treats both the technical aspects of warfare and the larger considerations of its consequences. It begins with a general survey of China on the eve of the wars, under what I call the "Northern System." Then it examines the political origins of the military showdown and the strategies of the contenders. This is followed by analysis of resources, particularly weapons and their capabilities, an account of the fighting, and the unexpected denouement. This political and military narrative, however, is intended to serve a deeper purpose.

The spur to writing this book has come not from a fascination with the details of warfare but, rather, from a general interest in the phenomena of nationalism and revolution, and dissatisfaction with the way historians have treated both in China during the pivotal decade of the 1920s. Neither nationalism nor revolution is very useful as an explanatory concept. Quite the opposite: each is in itself a historical problem, and a very difficult one. Yet for China, nationalism in particular has been taken – until recently – to be a sort of universal explanatory concept, the prime mover of change (as will be seen in detail in the "Conclusion" of this book) from the nineteenth century to the present. Such an approach is intellectually unsatisfactory, for it takes what should be the problem – why the explosion of nationalism that transformed Chinese politics in the 1920s? – and makes it into the explanation: rising nationalism – a given – caused new politics (which then get all the attention).

Therefore, although the book is narrowly focused on a series of key events, the broader history of nationalism in China – and in many other countries – has always been in my mind as I have written it. My belief is that nationalism – and revolution too, with which it is often associated – are usually better analyzed as consequences than as causes. Both are often portrayed as powerful autonomous actors – in the forms of swelling national sentiment or mass revolutionary unrest – but in fact neither is commonly found except in association with other factors. Both tend to

9

appear in situations in which existing institutions are in crisis, and such crises, since the French Revolution, have often as not been military in their origins. To note this fact is not to argue that nationalist feelings or the desire for revolution are caused by war: their deeper roots in economic, social, and intellectual developments are generally recognized. But their moves to center stage and opportunities for success almost always occur as part of some other and unrelated change. Usually they can rise to dominance only after some other force has destroyed the hitherto existing order. This, I argue, is what happened in China during the 1920s. In these years war became a dominant fact of Chinese life, and within the sequence of wars, those of 1924 had a pivotal importance. Indeed, in their own way they were every bit as important to Chinese history as the May Fourth Movement.

The reason, however, is not intrinsic to the wars. It has to do with their broader effects – the possibilities they foreclosed, the structural changes they caused, and the intellectual and cultural transitions they spurred. The wars of 1924 had many secondary effects on society at large; these effects, treated in the second half of the text, are the key links in my analysis, for what the book is really about is how the wars changed China. It shows how they gravely undermined the political cohesion and military capacity of the Beijing government while strengthening its rivals for power. It demonstrates that new patterns of conflict and political alignment consequently arose and persisted through the 1930s and beyond. It discusses how the fighting brought chaos to trade and commerce in some of China's richest and economically most advanced regions while sending waves of panic through financial and credit markets.

The book reveals that war disrupted the lives of all Chinese, particularly those of the politically important urban merchants, students, and workers. Furthermore, war devastated the international policies toward China that had been worked out at the Washington Conference of 1921–2, and stimulated a shift in the way Chinese thought about their nation's problems. This in turn led at the war's end to a rapid adoption of the radical and revolutionary vocabulary of the Left and a new receptiveness to the politics of the Left. These developments all provide the indispensable background to the events of the year 1925 – and more broadly, for understanding what we call, usually without thinking about precisely what we mean, China's "National Revolution" of the 1920s.

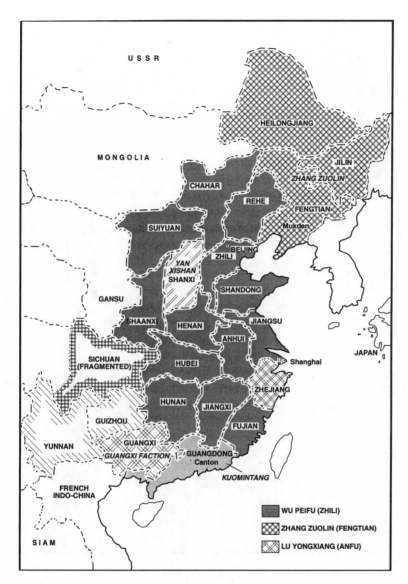

Distribution of Power, 1924

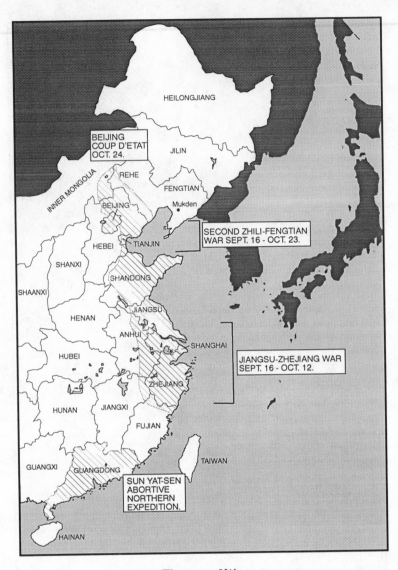

Theaters of War

1

China under the Northern System

Neither war nor revolution was much on the minds of either Chinese or foreigners in the fall of 1924. The American minister to Beijing, Jacob Gould Schurman (1854–1942), met President Calvin Coolidge in Washington on September 19, when the fighting around Shanghai was already approaching decision. His tone reflected firm optimism. "China is improving every day," he told the president. "Her finances are better. Her customs receipts are greater and the people generally are in a more prosperous condition than they were a year ago." When Coolidge asked about it, Schurman specifically minimized the potential importance of the war. It was "merely a fight between two governors of provinces," and meant "nothing to the people of China" for whom business went on "as if there was no struggle and no occasional shooting."[1]

Schurman's appraisal may strike us as strange today, accustomed as we are to thinking of the early and mid-1920s in China as a dark age of chaos. In this we have been greatly affected by the retrospective historiography of two revolutions: that of the Nationalists from 1925 to 1928 and that of the Communists from 1945 to 1949, both of which trace their earliest beginnings to this period, which for reasons of their own they paint as unfavorably as possible. The reality was somewhat different, and although Schurman failed to understand the devastation war would bring, he was nevertheless not far off in his other observations. A former president of Cornell University, Schurman showed himself to be a conscientious and sympathetic envoy to China. He traveled everywhere and met everyone, including individuals very much non grata with the Beijing administration to which he was accredited – most notably Dr. Sun Yat-sen (1866–1925), the revolutionary leader who, from his base in distant Guangdong, still dreamed of a return to the center of power.

1. *New York Times* (NYT), September 16, 1924, p. 25; see also Richard Clarke DeAngelis, "Jacob Gould Schurman and American Policy toward China, 1921–1925," Ph.D. dissertation, St. John's University, 1975, esp. pp. 304–5.

Schurman knew China about as well as a diplomat could, and he shared hopes for its future.

And in the autumn of 1924 few except perhaps the generals themselves expected any major change in either China's internal politics or its foreign relations. More than seventy years had elapsed since the mid-nineteenth-century wars between Britain and China had intensified interlocking internal and external crises that would eventually force the Qing dynasty's abdication in 1912. During those nearly three generations of struggle and cooperation between foreigners and Chinese, both sides had accumulated much knowledge and learned many lessons. Neither entirely accepted the other, but they had developed a way of working together that by the 1920s gave much cause for optimism. Within the imperfect structures they had evolved, China was clearly moving up to date in just about every area, from commerce to diplomacy to education and intellectual life. In this book the way in which the Chinese government and the Powers managed their relationship, well established by the 1920s, will be called the Northern System. And, as Schurman recognized when he spoke with Coolidge, the Northern System was not working badly and promised to work better.

One reason such optimism was possible was that scarcely anyone, Chinese or foreign, had yet understood the impact on China of the global revolution in military technology. So even as the first clouds of war gathered on the horizon, presaging the same cyclone that had devastated Europe, many Chinese paid little attention and got on with their lives, an approach very much in keeping with the immemorial Chinese devaluation – except among specialists – of the importance of things military. As for the foreigners, although the foundations of European power had been ruined by war, the structures of European primacy survived in much of Asia, and the hazy afternoon sun of European privilege and influence still shone on China.

This is not to say that China at this time was a colony. It is true that for foreigners, whether in Beijing's Legation Quarter, or in the concessions at Tianjin, Shanghai, Hankou, or any of a grand total of seventy-three treaty ports, large and small, life in China probably seemed not unlike life in a full-fledged European colony of the same time.[2] China had many of the superficial trappings of colonialism: the heat, the privilege, the boredom, and the alcohol were the same. It had its foreign settlements and foreign firms, and in Tianjin or Shanghai one found the same foreign soldiers and colonials, the same clubs, the same Sikh

2. Yen-p'ing Hao, "Treaty Ports," in *Encyclopedia of Asian History*, 4 vols., ed. Ainslie T. Embree (New York: Scribner's, 1988), vol. 4, pp. 131–3.

policemen, and the same expatriate burnt-out cases that one would have found in India or Africa. One might even be forgiven for thinking of the British or American minister, with his carriage, his military guard, and his proud bearing, as a sort of viceroy. That, however, would have been a mistake.

In China the elaborate paraphernalia of colonialism lacked real substance. In a colony the economy was supposed to serve the colonial power, and authority and security were supposed to be firmly controlled by foreign hands. But China in the 1920s, although deeply penetrated by foreign influences, nevertheless had a government, an economy, and an army of its own. True, this government was greatly circumscribed in its actions by the scores of agreements, major and minor, concluded with foreign powers, that since the Qing had constituted what was called the Treaty System. But, unlike a colonial government, the Chinese regime gave high priority to revision and eventual abolition of this system. It was true that foreign banks, merchant houses, and shipping lines were well established in China and enjoyed certain privileges. As was less often true in a colony, however, indigenous enterprises competitive with them were rapidly developing and doing not badly. Finally and most important, there was the army. The total number of men under arms in China in the autumn of 1924 was roughly 1,404,000.[3] Although they mostly fought one another, there was little doubt about their ultimate purpose. As a close observer put it at just this time, "Recent events in China seem to indicate that sooner or later there will be a definite clash between the military forces of the Republic and the armies of some foreign Power or Powers."[4] This point was underlined not so subtly by the way in which during this period China's annual military field maneuvers were held during anniversary weeks of the humiliating eight-power armed intervention against the Boxers in 1900.[5]

Such an intervention, however, was already close to impossible by the 1920s, when Europeans were becoming increasingly challenged just to keep the upper hand in territories where they alone had weapons and the people were totally disarmed – not to mention a place like China, where the foreign presence was far more limited. India is a good example. Its unambiguous status as part of the British Empire did little to secure rule; in the period after World War I the British army garrison of some

3. *China Year Book* (CYB), 1925, 1193.
4. Lawrence Impey, *The Chinese Army as a Military Force*, 2d ed., enl. (Tientsin: Tientsin Press, 1926), p. 9. European powers and the United States would probably have avoided confronting a modernized and competent Chinese army. However, Japanese policy throughout this period – and on into the 1930s – demonstrates a concern with the threat and repeated attempts to preempt it.
5. See *The Sphere: The Empire's Illustrated Weekly*, July 11, 1925, 52.

71,109 men, assisted by an Indian army of 161,711, was increasingly overstretched, despite the fact that ordinary Indians had no access to weapons.[6] Indeed, the biggest problem Gandhi's assassins faced in 1948 was obtaining a simple pistol.[7] That would have been no obstacle in China.

Nevertheless, neither the foreign nor the Chinese administration in China at this time was strong. Indeed, it could be said that each was weak because of the existence of the other. The Chinese government had been weakened in the nineteenth century by warfare with foreign powers and the treaties that followed. Although those treaties gave extensive privileges to the foreign powers, at least within the bits of territory turned over to their administration, the foreign powers never had the resources really to exert control. The Chinese government always retained more than enough autonomy to make it impossible for any foreign power or combination of powers actually to dominate China. The result was a situation in which the two sides had to work together. Beijing was the place where the structures of this Northern System of interdependence and cooperation were worked out by the early Republican government much as they had been by the late Qing. But the military revolution posed a grave threat to the system.

The late summer of quasi-imperial foreign domination lasted only so long as the Europeans maintained a decisive advantage in the means of coercion – roughly until World War I. At that point a combination of Western self-destruction and Chinese modernization began to shift the balance decisively the other way. We have seen that three days before Schurman and Coolidge chatted in the White House (because of the international date line Beijing is one day ahead of Washington) the first Zhili troop trains began to clear Tianjin's two stations – East and Central – on their way north. The relative modernity of those forces and the war they fought were an omen of things to come.

The city of Tianjin through which they passed is as good a place as any to begin to describe this China of the Northern System, today an almost entirely forgotten world. The city was hardly attractive. Built on the flatland along both banks of the Hai River, it was a turn-of-the-century boomtown that served as port for Beijing, 100 miles to the west. On the river's north bank were the Austrian, Belgian, Russian, and Italian concessions; on the south the German, French, and Japanese. Also on the south was the British concession, a plot of land about a mile

---

6. John Scott Keltie and M. Epstein, eds. *The Statesman's Year-book*, 1925 (London: Macmillan, 1925), p. 143.
7. See Larry Collins and Dominique Lapierre, *Freedom at Midnight* (New York: Avon Books, 1976), pp. 425–6, 437–8, 463–4, 489, 493.

wide and a mile long, where British law prevailed. There had once been an American concession, but it had been made over to the British. The Russian concession had been surrendered a few months before the war began.

Several thousand foreigners lived in Tianjin. Brian Power (b. 1918), who grew up there, recalls how his mother hated everything about it: "The oppressive summers, the icy winters, the dust and the flat treeless landscape with its stagnant creeks." And there was the Chinese population, more than 800,000 in 1922. "The hordes of coolies, surging along Dagu Road like a human river, made her uneasy." Tianjin's grand Western-style buildings – banks modeled on the Parthenon, "false Roman villas, imitations of medieval castles" – strangely juxtaposed, were tasteless even in their heyday. The city's rapid growth had been fueled by inland trade channeled through its port and by larger and larger manufacturing enterprises. Its real kindred were not Chinese inland cities but, rather, the other great nineteenth-century trading cities: Bombay, Singapore, even New York. By the 1960s, the seagoing trade having long since dwindled almost completely away, the city had become, in Simon Leys's memorable description, "a nightmare Disneyland, with old Belgian tramways shaking along the boulevards, everything tawdry, peeling, decrepit, ramshackle – a whole city with its walled-up windows, its blind and leprous facades."[8]

But in the 1920s Tianjin was challenging Beijing for the title of most important city in North China. In the days of the steamers, the port (inland from the sea, like Shanghai, along a carefully dredged river) was the Chinese capital's connection with the rest of the world. Proximity to the sea made Tianjin a center of commerce. It had been a treaty port since 1860; it boasted godowns, banks, lavish residential quarters, the French-built Cathedral of Notre Dame des Victoires and an Anglo-Chinese college, three English and three Japanese newspapers, and Kiessling and Bader's Cafe. In the city center, at Victoria and Meadows Roads, stood the Astor House hotel, where nearly everyone stayed, coming and going. The city was also a center of land transportation. It was the key junction in the networks of modernity – the railways and telegraph lines – which, passing through endless tracts of seemingly changeless agricultural countryside, linked the various outposts of modern China to one another. Trains from Shanghai to the south and Mukden to the north all passed through Tianjin on their way to the

---

8. Brian Power, *The Ford of Heaven* (London: Peter Owen, 1984), p. 28; CYB, 1925, 6; Westel W. Willoughby, *Foreign Rights and Interests in China* (Baltimore: Johns Hopkins Press, 1920), pp. 222–3; Pierre Ryckmans [Simon Leys], *Chinese Shadows* (New York: Viking Press, 1977), p. 65.

capital. It was in Tianjin that a young Owen Lattimore (1900–1989) learned the wool business, and from that city he set out in 1925 for Inner Asia with moral and, apparently, some financial support from his friend, the journalist H. G. W. Woodhead (1883–1959), to whom he dedicated *The Desert Road to Turkestan.*[9] In addition to trading houses, quite a number of mills and factories were located in Tianjin. Such important industrial enterprises as the Kaiping and Lanchow Coal Mining Companies, the Chee Sin Cement Works, and the Chiu Ta Salt Refining Company, as well as several of the largest carpet factories in China, the best known of which was the Jen Li Company, were all headquartered there. There were also banks, the Continental or Ta Lu, for example, that depended on North China and Tianjin for their shareholders and principal investments.[10]

Because of its proximity to the capital, Tianjin could scarcely avoid becoming a center of political intrigue. It was through Tianjin that arms were smuggled; to Tianjin that government ministers retired when coups occurred in the capital; it was to Tianjin that the last emperor, Puyi (1906–1967), was hustled by the Japanese in 1925; it was at Tianjin that Ataman Semenov and his White Russian forces negotiated with would-be employers; and in Tianjin that the Japanese Colonel Doihara Kenji (1883–1948), whom Woodhead called "the Lawrence of the East," based his operations.[11]

Tianjin had long been the administrative and political capital of the province of Zhili (now Hebei, which surrounds the capital), and in Qing times the posts of provincial governor-general [*Zhili zongdu*] and commissioner of trade for the northern ports [*Beiyang dachen*] were two of the pinnacles of the imperial service.[12] Li Hongzhang (1823–1901), the great northern power broker who held both positions, made Tianjin his base. There he founded in 1885 the German-staffed Tianjin Academy, later called the Kaiping Military Preparatory School. Marshal Wu Peifu (1874–1939), whose troop trains were passing through the city in September 1924, had gone to Tianjin in 1898 and attended the school for five months in 1900. But Wu's military education had been interrupted by the Boxer Rebellion.[13]

9. Owen Lattimore, *The Desert Road to Turkestan* (Boston: Little, Brown, 1930). Woodhead was the editor of the *Peking and Tientsin Times* and of the *China Yearbook* series.

10. O. D. Rasmussen, *Tientsin: An Illustrated Outline History* (Tianjin: Tientsin Press, 1925); *Guide to Tientsin*, presented by the Astor House Hotel, Ltd. (n.p., n.d. in collection of Brown University Library); W. W. Yen [Yan Huiqing], *East–West Kaleidoscope, 1877–1946: An Autobiography* (New York: St. John's University Press, 1974), p. 170.

11. Power, *Ford of Heaven*, p. 98.

12. Stephen R. MacKinnon, *Power and Politics in Late Imperial China: Yuan Shi-Kai in Beijing and Tianjin, 1901–1908* (Berkeley: University of California Press), p. 13.

13. For Wu, the basic sources are Odoric Y. K. Wou's fine English-language biography,

In 1900 the armies of the Boxers had occupied Tianjin, to be driven out in their turn by the forces of the eight Powers which landed there to relieve Beijing that summer. Tianjin had fallen after a bloody battle on July 14, and on July 30 the Powers had set up a provisional government. In the noonday of colonialism they might have stayed put, but those times were past, and although the Powers wanted access to Chinese trade, they feared the political and military responsibilities that would have been involved in actually administering it themselves. So the great Viceroy Li Hongzhang was wheeled out of retirement to negotiate a humiliating settlement. He died shortly thereafter, to be succeeded in both his posts by his protégé Yuan Shikai (1859–1916). Yuan was a skilled diplomat, and on August 15, 1902, the Powers' provisional government handed the city over to him. Adhering to the approach of his mentor, Yuan stressed concrete modernization. He repeatedly remarked that there were only two things that seemed important to him, "schools and the army."[14] Wu Peifu eventually graduated from one of the schools Yuan founded, the Baoding Military Academy, in 1903.[15] Under Yuan's administration the city passed through a brief convalescence. Then its economic health returned, and the boom resumed.[16]

Tianjin's dominant rival economically was Shanghai, some 830 miles to the south by rail; it was farther by sea around the Shandong peninsula. Already by the 1920s Shanghai was one of the world's great international cities.[17] The cliché every foreign newcomer learned was that whatever it might be, "Shanghai was not China." Certainly that was widely believed and was confirmed by the city's seeming immunity to the vagaries of Chinese war and politics. Whereas Tianjin was both a political and an economic center, Shanghai's importance was above all financial. Shanghai was home to the head offices of the great banks, both Chinese and foreign. What Lombard Street was in London, Wall Street in New York, or Marunouchi in Tokyo, in Shanghai was the twenty-

Militarism in Modern China; Guo Jianlin's path-breaking work in Chinese, *Wu Peifu da zhuan: yidai xiaoxiong* (Tianjin: Tianjin Daxue Chubanshe, 1991); and the Japanese account by Wu's adviser, Okano Masujirō, *Go Haifu* [Wu Peifu] (Tokyo: Banseikaku, 1939).

14. Charles D. Tenney to G. E. Morrison, letter dated February 21, 1904, in *The Correspondence of G. E. Morrison*. I: *1895–1912*, ed. Lo Hui-min (Cambridge, England: Cambridge University Press, 1976), p. 255. Quoted in Dali Yang, "Beiyang University, 1895–1912: Charles D. Tenney and the Politics of Educational Entrepreneurship," paper presented to the Workshop on the History of Christian Higher Education in China, Yale University, February 1990, p. 22.
15. MacKinnon, *Power and Politics*, p. 36; BDRC vol. III, 445.
16. Ibid., pp. 37–41.
17. Perhaps the best English-language evocation of Shanghai during this period is Nicholas R. Clifford, *Spoiled Children of Empire: Westerners in Shanghai and the Chinese Revolution of the 1920s* (Hanover, N.H.: Middlebury College Press, 1991).

block area of the International Settlement bounded by Beijing Road, Hankou Road, Shanxi Road, and Huangputan Road. The last of these was also called "the Bund," an Anglo-Indian word of Persian origin. On the Bund, which ran north–south closest to the river, were the headquarters of two major Chinese banks, the Zhongguo Jiaotong and the Zhongguo Tongshang, as well as the Chartered, Hong Kong and Shanghai, Mercantile of India, P. & O., Credit Foncier d'Extrême–Orient, Banque de l'Indochine, Yokohama Specie Bank, and Bank of Taiwan, among others. On Jiujiang Road nearby were other Chinese and foreign banks: the National City Bank, American Express, Sumitomo, Nederlandsche Indische Handelsbank, Italian Bank for China, as well as the *jinye jiaoyisuo*, or money exchange. The native banks, or *qianzhuang* – low-capitalization money shops of a type that long antedated Western-style banking in China and had greatly expanded their activities since the nineteenth century – were mostly on Ningbo, Tianjin, and Beijing roads.[18]

Shanghai was the entrepôt for the overseas trade of the whole vast Yangzi valley drainage and commercial network. In arcs around Shanghai lay the prosperous smaller cities of Jiangsu and Zhejiang, places such as Suzhou, Wuxi, Hangzhou, and Ningbo, all having long indigenous traditions of entrepreneurship and craftsmanship. But Shanghai was the focal point. It was also an ultimate refuge, the place where people and money fled when times became dangerous.

Tianjin and Shanghai were not China: the overwhelming majority of Chinese at this time were farmers, far from such cosmopolitan urban centers. The economic health of these cities, nevertheless, was connected to that of the nation as a whole, and for most of the 1910s and 1920s the picture was not bad. China's economy was growing steadily during most of this period, and the dynamism of port cities like Tianjin and Shanghai had influences and effects far inland.[19] Agricultural prices fluctuated somewhat, owing to warfare and other disasters, but by comparison with the period from 1926 until 1949, they were relatively stable. Both industrial and agricultural production showed upward trends. Production was steady; supply and demand for capital goods were in balance. Money was sound, for control of the money supply was out of political hands. The Beijing government never had the power to establish a dominant central bank, and the two banks over which the government

18. Yang Yinbo, *Shanghai jinrong zuzhi gaiyao* (Shanghai, n.p., ca. 1929), pp. 20–2. Also Jiaotong yinhang zong guanlichu, *Jinrong shichang lun* (Chongqing: Zhengzhong, 1945), pp. 74–5.
19. Thomas G. Rawski, *Economic Growth in Prewar China* (Berkeley: University of California Press, 1989).

had influence, the Jiaotong [Bank of Communications] and Zhongguo [Bank of China], nevertheless retained a certain degree of autonomy. As a result the price level at Shanghai, which reflected economic conditions in the entire country, enjoyed great stability during the period from 1912 to 1927.[20] The favorable expectations held for the future were perhaps expressed in the urban architecture of the time: solid, and built to last, as it has.[21]

Shanghai's only potential rival as the economic center of a region was Mukden. Shanghai was the new gateway to the Yangzi valley, which had long been the most prosperous part of China; Mukden by contrast was an old city which fed on the new wealth of Manchuria. The whole territory, which had been Chinese episodically in the past, was definitively brought into the empire by the Qing, for whose ruling Manchus it was homeland. In the 1920s Manchuria was growing rapidly, as Chinese immigrants poured in, along with smaller numbers of Koreans, Japanese, and Russians. Because of its strategic position and great economic potential, the territory was coveted by Moscow and Tokyo as well as by Beijing. Manchurian wealth came from natural resources and the industries based on them: the vast open-pit coal mines and the iron ore that supplied the Japanese-run iron and steel industry; the rich soil that produced abundant grain and food products such as edible oils; the other heavy industries; and the railroad connecting easily to the Japanese empire to the east and the Russian to the west, as well as to the fine ports of the Liaodong peninsula. Strategically, the Manchurian coast controlled the approaches by sea to Tianjin and thus to the Chinese capital, while on land Manchuria dominated the Beijing region as well. Strong military forces in Manchuria usually spilled out into China proper, and the 1920s were no exception. Further complicating all of this was the fact that Japan had secured for itself a special position in Manchuria, guaranteed by a host of treaties, giving it ownership or control of resources and infrastructure, as well as the right to station troops.

At the hub of this modernizing China was the ancient and seemingly timeless capital city of Beijing. Its Chinese inhabitants, whether living in courtyard houses or slums, had a distinct character which was

---

20. Zhongguo shehui kexue yuan Shanghai jingji yanjiusuo and Shanghai shehui kexue yuan jingji yanjiusuo, eds., *Shanghai jiefang qianhou wujia ziliao huibian* (Shanghai: Shanghai renmin chubanshe, 1958), pp. 4–8. In 1922 prices in Shanghai fell 5.7%, in 1923 rose 3.4%, in 1924 fell 4.0%, in 1925 rose 1.4%, and in 1926 rose 0.7%. ibid., 4.
21. Rasmussen, *Tientsin*, has excellent illustrations for that city; for Shanghai, see, among others, *Shanghai of To-day: A Souvenir Album of Fifty Vandyck Prints of "The Model Settlement,"* 2d. ed., enl. Introduction by O. M. Green (Shanghai: Kelly & Walsh, 1928).

manifested in everything from cuisine to colloquial speech. Tianjin, Shanghai, and Mukden were modern cities that had grown around ancient cores, many of whose Chinese inhabitants had moved there in the late nineteenth century or after; their ways of life blended the traditions of their original homes with the commercial and cosmopolitan mores of the new cities. Beijing, by contrast, with its ancient buildings and long traditions, had a relatively more rooted Chinese population than its economically more dynamic counterparts, and conveyed a far more powerful sense of both the magnificence and the subtlety of the Chinese civilization.

Perhaps for these reasons, Beijing had a particular attraction for certain foreigners. The city, "Old Style," as the future *New York Times* correspondent Hallett Abend (1884–1955) put it, could cast a powerful spell. Arriving there for the first time from Shanghai in 1926 on a "damp September evening, chill with gusty wind and drizzling rain," Abend felt what he called a miracle: "Everything I saw around me was unfamiliar, strange and alien, but never had I returned to any place where I had lived with such a deep sense of homecoming." He decided instantly that he would spend the rest of his life in Beijing; as it turned out he stayed a little more than a decade, leaving only when forced to by the Japanese occupation. Other foreigners made the same decision, and by the mid-1920s more than 1,000 Europeans and Americans had made the city their home.[22] Some foreigners tried to escape into a dream of the exotic: "Take care," warns a character in *Silhouettes of Peking* (1926), a novel by the French minister, Damien, comte de Martel (1872–1942), "you don't shortly become a Peking silhouette, one of those peculiar people who avoid Europeans like the plague, and isolate themselves in a temple in the Chinese quarter, seeking, alone the origin of some long forgotten hieroglyphics and, at nights, air their melancholy on the Tartar Wall . . . dreaming of the barbarous and splendid past related in the court annals."[23] Other foreign residents, however, were very much on the make.

Foreigners commonly reached Beijing by rail from Tianjin. During the Boxer Rebellion the railway line had been blocked, and Article IX of the Final Boxer Protocol of 1901 therefore secured the right of the Powers to station troops at Tianjin to keep the railway open and to send international trains regardless of the situation in China proper. The American

22. Hallett Abend, *My Life in China 1926–1941* (New York: Harcourt, Brace, 1943), p. 42; Alex. Ramsey, ed. *The Peking Who's Who 1922* (Peking: Tientsin Press, 1922), pp. 78–90.
23. D. de Martel and L. de Hoyer, *Silhouettes of Peking*, trans. D. de Warzee (Peking: China Booksellers, 1926), p. 18.

troops charged with this task formed the first headquarters of American military forces in China, in Tianjin. Furthermore, the Protocol provided that Beijing might not station or march troops within twenty Chinese *li* (six or seven miles) of the city, and that the forts guarding sea approaches to Tianjin at Dagu and elsewhere would be destroyed. The system seemed to work well. During the revolution of 1911–1912 the Powers divided control of the Beijing–Mukden railway among themselves. The crisis was weathered by the foreigners, and by 1920 they had reduced their control to a handful of posts.[24]

During the peaceful period that followed, visitors were likely to take the regular train service from Tianjin to the capital. The trip was a pleasant one. Willem-Jacob Oudendijk (1874–1953), the Dutch minister, describes it as it was in the early 1930s:

a luxurious train drawn by an eighty-ton locomotive, with a dining-car and a comfortable compartment fitted with blue window-panes against the violent sunshine, which lands one in a little over three hours at the spacious Chien-Mên railway station where porters are ready to take the luggage to the motor-bus of the palatial Hôtel de Pékin.[25]

For a diplomat, nowhere else in the world was quite like Beijing in the 1920s.

Tianjin or Shanghai might look and sound like transplanted Western metropolises, but Beijing remained what it had been without break since the Ming emperor Yongle (r. 1403–25) had made it his residence and capital in 1420: namely, the political center of a proud and distinct political and cultural world. The city still had its magnificent outer walls and gates. Mary O'Malley (1889–1974), the wife of Owen St. Clair O'Malley (1887–1974), British consul from 1925, in her prize-winning novel *Peking Picnic* (written under the pen name Ann Bridge) tried to evoke something of the city's magic. Her heroine Laura Leroy, also the wife of a British diplomat, found that

in the quiet Legation garden the confused noise of the city reached her, but it was a different quality of sound from the roar of traffic in a European city, the muffled drumming of soft feet on unpaved earth – bare or slippered human feet, the pads of camels, the light tapping of the small unshod feet of donkeys. In this low murmur other sounds stood out sharply, like loud notes in soft music – the hoot of a distant motor horn, the ringing of tram bells, a scream of a steam whistle and sounds of shunting from the railway station just outside the city wall.[26]

24. Willoughby, *Foreign Rights*, 221–3.
25. William J. Oudendyk, *Ways and By-Ways in Diplomacy* (London: Peter Davies, 1939), p. 20.
26. Ann Bridge [Mary O'Malley], *Peking Picnic* (Boston: Little, Brown, 1932), p. 39.

The British Legation was a substantial structure in the Legation Quarter, where the foreign community still lived behind walls with their own guards. Traces of it may be found just to the south of the present Beijing Hotel (itself the latest metamorphosis of the old Hôtel de Pékin). The Legation Quarter breathed permanence. Its walls and gates, its embassies and chancelleries, were constructed with the monumental solidity characteristic of European building at its turn-of-the-century peak (and they required liberal doses of explosive to be demolished, as many of them were, in the Cultural Revolution). The diplomatic body, with its long-established traditions and protocol, seemed similarly timeless and, in fact, it already had a considerable history. The Beijing corps had begun to come into existence more than two generations earlier, when permanent representatives of England, France, Russia, and the United States first took up residence in the Chinese capital in the aftermath of the Treaty of Tianjin of 1858.[27] From the signing of the Boxer Protocol in 1901 until 1931, the ministers of the foreign powers, nineteen in all, met at least once a month except in August, when chargés or counselors took over, their seniors having escaped to the seashore at Beidaihe or to the hills to the west.

In its glory days after 1901 and before World War I – in many ways a far more important event for foreigners in China than the abdication of the Qing in 1912 – the diplomatic body (or *corps diplomatique*), which conducted its business and kept its records in (rather anglicized) French, included every foreign representative. In China the ministers of all the Powers sat down incongruously together, as they did nowhere else in the world: the French with the German, the British with the Imperial Russian, the American with the Japanese, along with the Dutch, the Austro-Hungarian, the Brazilian, the Cuban, the Mexican, and a number of others. The Boxer Rebellion and the siege of the legations had defined a common interest for all of them even if none had existed before. For the Boxers, all foreigners were enemies so, in China at least, all foreigners became allies. At times of tension anyone with a foreign face could walk through the gate of the Legation Quarter without being challenged. By the period with which we are concerned the key players among these foreign diplomats formed an informal group which called itself the "the Old Firm" (in Japanese, *shinise*, "a long-established shop").[28]

27. Immanuel C. Y. Hsü, *China's Entrance into the Family of Nations: The Diplomatic Phase 1858–1880* (Cambridge, Mass.: Harvard University Press, 1960), esp. pp. 21–120.
28. See Daniele Varè, *Laughing Diplomat* (New York: Doubleday, Doran, 1938), where, pp. 298ff characteristically makes it "Ye Olde Firme"; Kenkichi Yoshizawa, *Gaikō rokujū nen* (Tokyo: Jiyū Ajiasha, 1959), p. 82, gives *shinise* and then adds parenthetically "Old

They were a fascinating and colorful group, this "Old Firm" – a nickname, of course, never a formal institution. Its members had common backgrounds and long acquaintance if not friendship. Most had been born in the 1880s and gone out to China for the first time by the teens. Most returned home around the time of World War I, only to find themselves together once again in Beijing as China suddenly moved to the foreground of world attention in the second half of the 1920s.

There was Daniele Varè (1880–1956), who had initially been posted in 1912 as first secretary to the Italian legation. With his wife and a child just over a year old, he had sailed from Genoa in September on the *Prinz Eitel Friedrich* of the German line, not to return to Italy for eight years. Like his French colleague de Martel, Varè was the author of books about old Beijing, either charming or precious and exoticizing, depending upon one's taste, of which the best known is *The Maker of Heavenly Trousers* (1936).[29] Less than a year after Varè's arrival, John V. A. MacMurray (1881–1960), who was a year younger than the Italian, would turn down the offer of the ministership in Siam [Thailand] in order to become secretary to the American Legation in Beijing. He held this post until 1919, when he returned to Washington as chief of the State Department's Division of Far Eastern Affairs.[30] There was Sir Ronald Macleay (1870–1943), educated at Charterhouse and Balliol, who learned his Chinese politics from Sir John Jordan (1852–1925). He was succeeded by Sir Miles Lampson (1880–1964), first Baron Killearn, who had served as second secretary in Tokyo from 1908 to 1910, and first secretary in Beijing from 1916 to 1919. Over six feet five inches tall and weighing eighteen stone (252 pounds), Lampson, educated at Eton, was "in some ways a figure out of another century"; nevertheless he proved effective both as a leader within "the Firm" and a realist as he steered the Powers away from confrontation in the post-1925 period.[31] The Dutch were represented by Willem-Jacob Oudendijk, longtime dean of the *corps diplomatique*, a man of impressive linguistic abilities (his English was of native fluency, and in addition to the diplomat's usual collection of

firm." For the definition quoted see Nelson's *Japanese–English Character Dictionary*, 2d. ed., s.v.

29. Varè, *Laughing Diplomat*; idem, *The Maker of Heavenly Trousers* (New York: Doubleday, Doran, 1936).
30. Wilson to MacMurray, August 518, 1913, MacMurray papers; see also Janet Sue Collester, "J. V. A. MacMurray, American Minister to China, 1925–1929: The Failure of a Mission" (Ph.D. dissertation, Indiana University, 1977), p. 33.
31. For Macleay, Obituary, *The Times* (London), March 8, 1943; for Lampson, E. T. Williams and C. S. Nicholls, eds., *The Dictionary of National Biography 1961–1970* (Oxford University Press, 1981), pp. 627–8; Obituary, *The Times* (London), September 19, 1964.

European languages, he also had Russian, and Chinese "à merveille").[32] Oudendijk (who anglicized his name as William Oudendyk) had gone to China as a young man in 1894. Like the others, he left China on the eve of World War I, first for Persia and then The Hague.[33]

Japan was represented by Yoshizawa Kenkichi (1874–1965), whose knowledge of China probably surpassed that of any of the others. After graduating from the Imperial University of Tokyo and entering the diplomatic service in 1899, he served in Xiamen, Shanghai, Yingkou, and Hong Kong; he was also first secretary in London and director of the Bureau of Asiatic Affairs in Tokyo before returning to Beijing as minister in 1923. His marriage to the daughter of Inukai Tsuyoshi (1855–1932) brought him connections at the highest levels of Japanese politics.[34]

The group of diplomats who could count substantial China experience before World War I was small, and they were indeed what Varè signed himself under the extracts from his China diary, published in the *Giornale d'Italia* – "O.C.H." or "Old China Hand[s]."[35] For them the war would serve as the punctuation between junior service in the last glow of genuinely self-confident European imperialism, and return at a senior rank thereafter.

The presence of so skilled a group of diplomats was a reminder that for all its ubiquitous remnants of antiquity, Beijing was also a city of rapid change. Ambitious foreign service officers generally were eager to serve there. They felt invigorated by a sense of China's dynamism and promise and expected their own careers to be propelled forward with it. China was changing, waking up; a posting to the Chinese capital was a great coup. Furthermore, whether trader, remittance man, or diplomat, one lived with a certain style in Beijing. As American minister from 1925 to 1929, MacMurray had a generous staff of cooks, valets, grooms, gardeners, houseboys, and other assorted servants, and moved in

32. Académie Diplomatique Internationale, *Dictionnaire Diplomatique comprenant les Biographies des Diplomates du Moyen Age à nos jours, constituant un traité d'Histoire Diplomatique sur six siècles* (Publié sous la direction de M. A.–F. Frangulis. Paris and Geneva: Académie Diplomatique Internationale, n.d.), p. 794.
33. Oudendyk was made minister to Persia in 1910, and given leave from diplomacy in 1914. He had a cottage near Beijing, and attempted to make his way back there. William J. Oudendyk, *Ways and By-Ways in Diplomacy* (London: Peter Davies, 1939), pp. 158, 200–1.
34. Barbara J. Brooks, "China Experts in the Gaimushō, 1895–1937," in *The Japanese Informal Empire in China 1895–1937*, ed. Peter Duus, Ramon H. Myers, and Mark R. Peattie (Princeton: Princeton University Press, 1989), pp. 386–7; Carroll Lunt, ed., *The China Who's Who 1926 (Foreign): A Biographical Dictionary* (Shanghai: Kelly & Walsh, 1926), p. 296.
35. Varè, *Laughing Diplomat*, p. vii.

diplomatic circles where the full protocol of the pre–World War I world was still punctiliously observed.

Like the foreign establishment, the Chinese government during the period of the Northern System had a long tradition and an aura of permanence. The Beijing government had originated when Yuan Shikai, commander in chief of the Qing army, turned against the dynasty and allied himself with the southern republican movement long enough to get himself installed as president, a post he exercised with a relatively high degree of success until his unexpected death from uremia in 1916. Under the terms of the abdication Yuan Shikai forced on the Qing imperial house – the so-called *youdai Qingshi tiaojian* or "articles of favorable treatment for the Qing house" – the former imperial family was permitted to live and reign within the walls of the Forbidden City. Through these arrangements, according to the Italian minister, Count Carlo Sforza (1873–1952), Yuan hoped to duplicate the "masterpiece of wisdom" whereby the Italians accommodated two sovereigns – pope and king – in the single capital of Rome.[36] The result was that as the wars of 1924 broke out, the last of the Qing emperors, Puyi, was still ensconced in the Forbidden City, off-limits to the *corps diplomatique* (who recognized only the Republic), his numinous aura not yet entirely vanished, living in fading splendor with his wives, retainers, and palace ladies. Meanwhile, beginning with President Yuan Shikai, the neighboring walled compound at Zhongnanhai had become the customary residence and office of republican heads of state.

Both palace complexes were in the heart of Beijing, which in those days still had its twenty-four miles of outer walls. The Forbidden City, where Puyi resided, had been built by the Mongol Yuan dynasty and restored by Yongle of the Ming. Zhongnanhai lay just to the west of it and was known for the more informal lakes and gardens to which the same Ming emperor had devoted particular attention. These, in the words of Juliet Bredon, were quite different from the monumental vastnesses of the Forbidden City. They had the charm of informality, for "like the builders of Versailles, Yongle knew instinctively how to compose a landscape. He understood the charm of surprise and contrast, the value of artificial hills in a flat landscape and of artificial water on a dry plain."[37] Yongle had created three artificial lakes, and near them built palaces that in the early years of the Republic formed part of the headquarters of government.

36. Carlo Sforza, *Makers of Modern Europe: Portraits and Personal Impressions and Recollections* (London: Elkin Mathews & Marrot, 1930), p. 381.
37. Juliet Bredon, *Peking: A Historical and Intimate Description of Its Chief Places of Interest* (Shanghai: Kelly and Walsh, 1931), pp. 133–4.

Visitors, whether on business or attending a garden party, would enter Zhongnanhai through the Xinhuamen, erected by Qianlong (r. 1736–96). Today this is the heavily guarded gate to the residences of China's Communist rulers. Once inside, however, visitors would find the ensemble of government buildings mostly built by Yuan Shikai. Standing on the southern edge of the southernmost of the three lakes, the visitor would survey an ensemble of covered gangways, stone kiosks, and the new and old official buildings of the government. These included the presidential palace, the offices of the various ministries, the headquarters of the chief of protocol, as well as the Juren tang, former throne room of the Empress dowager Cixi (1835–1908) where Yuan Shikai had died, and the Huairen tang, used for entertaining.

Beijing's foreign community saw this government compound at the regular garden parties hosted by the republican presidents and ministers. Opinion was divided about its beauty. E. S. Fischer was "impressed by the beauty of nature combined with the artistic ideal of Chinese landscape engineers and architects," whereas Juliet Bredon complained of the "the ugly, red, foreign-style buildings put up by Yuan Shikai and used by him as Presidential offices."[38] After tea and refreshments around the lakes, the high point of such receptions would often be a visit to the so-called Mongol Throne Hall to view the collection of imperial portraits.[39] Even after Yuan Shikai's death in 1916, his successors – several of whom emerged from the system of modern armies he had created – maintained the tradition, thus representing a thread of continuity between the late Qing and early Republic, broken only in 1925.

At the head of the government administration was the president. Like that of the Qing or Ming emperor before him, the republican president's day usually began before dawn. Yuan Shikai generally called a minister or other official to his breakfast table to discuss urgent matters. Yan Huiqing [W. W. Yen] (1877–1950) recalled being summoned many times to see President Xu Shichang (1855–1939) in winter at an hour when most of the inhabitants of Beijing were still asleep but the "lights were burning brightly in all the rooms" in the palace.[40]

China's presidents were chosen by the parliament. This, in theory, had two chambers, a senate, whose members were elected to six-year terms by the provincial assemblies, and a house of representatives, chosen for three-year terms by a two-stage system of voting at the level

---

38. E. S. Fischer, *Guide to Peking and Its Environs Near and Far*, rev. ed. (Tientsin and Peking: Tientsin Press, 1924), pp. 2, 61–2; Bredon, *Peking*, pp. 137, 145.
39. Bredon, *Peking*, pp. 137, 145.
40. W. W. Yen, *East–West Kaleidoscope, 1877–1946: An Autobiography* (New York: St. John's University Press, 1974), p. 128.

of the *xian*, or county. Its buildings had been constructed by Yuan Shikai on the site of the *xiangfang*, or elephant stables, of the Ming, just west of the Shunzhimen gate along the inner south wall of the Tartar city, the second of Beijing's three concentric sets of walls. Neither architecture nor institution was much respected by the 1920s. L. C. Arlington's guide (he was an American from Kansas who had lived in Beijing since 1879) described the buildings as "uninteresting, modern types" where "the first Chinese parliament held its interminable, turbulent, and futile sessions . . . until its natural death in 1924, or thereabouts."[41]

The parliament indeed had a chequered history. Originally chosen in 1913 as required by the provisional constitution adopted in 1912, in an election that was generally accepted as legitimate, it was then repeatedly purged, dissolved, or dismissed in the years following, although all or part of it kept on meeting outside of the capital. Yuan Shikai had attempted to replace it with a nominated assembly under his constitutional compact of 1914, but this did not outlive him, and in 1917 his successor, President Li Yuanhong (1864–1928), had restored the provisional constitution and reconvened the 1913 parliament. Scarcely was this done when pressure from Prime Minister Duan Qirui forced him to dissolve it. Then followed Duan's attempt to secure his own power by means of yet another constitution, which ended when he was defeated in the Zhili–Anfu War of 1920. President Xu Shichang then held elections for an entirely new parliament, although because only eleven provinces participated, its legitimacy was not universally recognized. In 1922 Li Yuanhong, again president, sought to restore governmental legitimacy by recalling the 1913 parliament once more.

President Li's action may reflect the degree to which the idea of constitutional government, despite its patent difficulty in practice, had struck root in China, and it nearly succeeded. But unfortunately not all the parliamentarians heeded his call to reconvene in Beijing. Die-hard Kuomintang partisans remained in Guangzhou with Sun Yat-sen and his rival government. Had they returned, what many considered the most disgraceful episode in the whole history of the parliament might not have taken place: this was the election, in 1923, of the man who was China's president (*da zongtong*) in 1924, Cao Kun (1862–1938).[42]

Cao Kun was the leader of the most powerful political faction at the time, that called Zhili, after the capital district, as we have already

41. L. C. Arlington and William Lewisohn, *In Search of Old Peking: City of Palaces and Temples* (Peking: Henri Vetch, 1935), p. 164.
42. See William L. Tung, *The Political Institutions of Modern China* (The Hague: Martinus Nijhoff, 1964), pp. 1–90; Ch'ien Tuan-sheng, *The Government and Politics of China* (Cambridge, Mass.: Harvard University Press, 1950), pp. 60–9.

mentioned. He was an old soldier, a friend of Yuan Shikai, and like him, a veteran of the war with Japan in 1894–5. The "presidential bug" [*zongtong yin*, literally "addiction"] bit him after his Zhili forces defeated those of Zhang Zuolin (1872–1928) and his Fengtian faction in the First Zhili–Fengtian War of 1922.[43] President at the time was Li Yuanhong, in 1911 the brigade commander who proclaimed the anti-Manchu uprising in Wuhan, and thus possessing a certain political stature. But Cao's ambition was not to be frustrated. He and his associates first forced Li to flee from the capital to Tianjin (among other things, they cut off light and water to the palace). That done, they established an office in the capital from which 8,000 to 10,000 yuan per vote, cash up front, was paid to parliamentarians in order to secure Cao's election as president. When ballots were counted, Cao seemed to have won with 480, and success was duly proclaimed. But because only 539 representatives had in fact been present, while a quorum required 583, Cao's election never filled even the basic formal requirements.[44] Nor did Cao redeem himself when he secured the ratification by parliament of the constitution of 1923, considered by Qian Duansheng to be "perhaps the best drafted" of the five such documents promulgated up to the end of the period of Northern rule in 1928.[45]

Cao's assumption of the presidency on October 10, 1923 – Double Ten, the anniversary of beginning of the anti-Manchu revolt a dozen years earlier – was marked by carefully orchestrated rejoicing, and even more carefully arranged security. Beijing was festooned with lights, flags, and banners, but as the inaugural procession passed, its safety was ensured by double police lines (officers back to back, one rank facing the street while the other surveyed the pavement), tirelessly shuttling mounted sentries, patrol cars, and plainclothesmen.[46]

Cao was served by five prime ministers [*guowu zongli*] during his year in office, and an examination of them tells us a good deal about the complex nature of the Northern System.[47]

The first of Cao Kun's prime ministers, Gao Lingwei (1868–1943),

43. Guo Jianlin, *Wu Peifu dazhuan: yidai xiaoxiong* (Tianjin: Tianjin Daxue Chubanshe, 1991), vol. 2, p. 486.
44. Guo Jianlin, *Wu Peifu*, vol. 2, p. 495. But William L. Tung records Cao's election as conforming to the election law of 1913, stating that 593 members were present and 590 cast votes, which would make the 480 that went to Cao more than the required three-quarters. William L. Tung, *The Political Institutions of Modern China* (The Hague: Martinus Nijhoff, 1964), pp. 63, 70, note 1.
45. Ch'ien, *Government and Politics of China*, pp. 63, 70.
46. Guo Jianlin, *Wu Peifu*, vol. 2, p. 495.
47. For a table of government officials under the Northern government, Qian Shifu, ed., *Beiyang zhengfu zhiguan nianbiao* (Shanghai: Huadong Shifan Daxue Chubanshe, 1991); Xie Benshu, "Beiyang junfa tongzhi shiqi Beijing zhengquan yuanshou, guowuzongli

was born in Tianjin. After passing the imperial examinations he became a protégé of Zhang Zhidong (1837–1909), the great viceroy of Hunan and Hubei, whom he assisted in his ambitious projects of self-strengthening: arsenals, industrial plants, modern schools, and a modern monetary system. After the Qing abdication he had retired to Tianjin, where he continued to devote his energy to the modernization of Chinese banking but subsequently returned to government service as finance minister or minister of the interior in a series of cabinets. In January of 1924 he was appointed director general of the customs administration, replacing the newly designated prime minister, Sun Baoqi (1867–1931).[48]

Sun was also a man of outstanding education. Born in Hangzhou, he was the son of the imperial tutor of the Xianfeng emperor (r. 1851–62) and was related by marriage to the former imperial family, which he had served as minister in France and Germany, although he subsequently acquiesced in their ouster. Later he served as assistant director of the Tianjin–Pukou railway, director general of the customs administration, minister of foreign affairs, minister of finance, and director of the famine relief commission. His cabinet was similarly distinguished.[49] Gu Weijun [V. K. Wellington Koo] (1887–1985), his foreign minister, was perhaps the most brilliant of all the Beiyang government officials. His Ph.D. was from Columbia University, and he had already published a learned book, *The Status of Aliens in China*.[50] Cheng Ke (1878–1936), minister of the interior and chairman of the law codification commission, had graduated from the law faculty of Tokyo Imperial University and joined the revolution on his return. Having become associated with another leading member of the Zhili faction, General Feng Yuxiang (1882–1948) in Henan in 1922, he served the government and was designated acting minister of justice in 1923.[51] The minister of finance and director general of the salt administration, Wang Kemin (1873–1945) was a provincial

gengxuan biao," *Lishi jiaoxue* (1962), no. 6, 51–2; also Ch'i Hsi-sheng, *Warlord Politics in China*, p. 243.

48. M. C. Powell, ed. *Who's Who in China*, 3rd ed. (Shanghai: China Weekly Review, 1925), pp. 406–7.

49. Powell, *Who's Who in China*, pp. 684–5; BDRC, vol. 3, pp. 169–70.

50. BDRC, vol. 2, pp. 255–9; Obituary, NYT, November 16, 1985, Section 1, 34; V. K. Wellington Koo, "The Status of Aliens in China." *Studies in History, Economics and Public Law*, edited by the Faculty of Political Science of Columbia University, vol. 50, no. 2 (New York: Columbia University Press, 1912). Gu's memoirs, available in original English typescript in the rare books and manuscripts room, Columbia University, have been translated and published in Chinese: *Gu Weijun huiyilu* (Beijing: Zhonghua shuju, 1983). The best study is Pao-chin Chu, *V. K. Wellington Koo: A Case Study of China's Diplomat and Diplomacy of Nationalism, 1912–1966* (Hong Kong: Chinese University Press, 1981).

51. *Who's Who in China*, 4th ed. (Shanghai: China Weekly Review, 1931), pp. 70–1.

degree holder [*juren*] from Hangzhou who had studied in Japan. He was
first appointed governor of the Bank of China in 1917 after successfully
serving as the Chinese managing director of the Banque Industrielle de
Chine.[52] Yan Huiqing, Sun's son-in-law, served as minister of commerce
and agriculture.

In July 1924, Sun resigned because of friction with Wang Kemin, and
Cao nominated Yan as his successor. Parliament, however, withheld
approval until September 24, and in the meantime Gu Weijun served as
acting prime minister. Sun refused appointments as director general of
the newly created special administrative area of Shanghai and as
ambassador to the Soviet Union, instead becoming president of the
Hanyehping Iron and Steel Company and of the China Merchants'
Steam Navigation Company.

By any measure, these men were an impressive group whose personal
connections ramified throughout China and abroad. At a time when
China itself was not, by then-prevailing European standards, in any
sense the national equal of the West or even of Japan, most of these men
were in every respect – education, professional competence, command of
languages, even wealth – the personal equals of the members of the
foreign elites with whom they dealt. Indeed, they were probably the
most impressive group of officials to serve China at any time in this
century. By and large they pursued a reforming and nationalistic agenda,
in area after area laying down the policies and approaches their successors would follow; indeed, their traces are visible right down to the
present. These men were scarcely hidebound reactionaries; rather, if
anything was striking about China a little more than twenty years after
the catastrophe of the Boxer uprising, it was the extent to which government had passed into the hands of a technically competent and forward-
looking generation.[53] Nevertheless, they and their foreign counterparts,
with whom by and large they enjoyed easy working relationships,
faced formidable and interlocking problems: financial, military, and
diplomatic.

China in the early 1920s was poised to enter either an ascending or a
descending spiral of development. The European-centered world order
was effectively finished, which meant that the old Northern System with
its Chinese–foreign interdependence was on its way out. It had been a

52. BDRC, vol. 3, 386–8.
53. Some may object to this characterization, noting that certain important Northern
    government officials – Wang Kemin, for example – collaborated with the Japanese in
    World War II. (Others, such as Wu Peifu, absolutely refused to do so.) I hold no brief
    for collaborators but would note that the issue can be extremely complex, as the better
    known case of Wang Jingwei (1883–1944) demonstrates. Allowing it to color history
    retrospectively can do intellectual damage.

product of the nineteenth century, when China was weak and the West was close to the all-time apogee of its world power. Not surprisingly, the treaties that followed the wars of the nineteenth century had therefore been extremely one-sided, loading China with obligations and the Powers with privileges. But the system in that form was effectively a snapshot of a momentarily unequal constellation of power, one that shifted rapidly as China's economy developed, its government reformed itself, and its military power modernized and grew. Even before Europe's astonishing suicide as the center of world power in World War I had made it untenable, the system was widely admitted to be archaic. With the Western collapse in the early teens, however, the need to create new international structures to accommodate China and the rest of Asia became even more pressing.

For Asia generally the 1910s had been a difficult decade, repeatedly plagued by friction between China and Japan. In November of 1921 there convened in great splendor at the Pan American Union Building in the American capital, the Washington Conference, a meeting that created what most believed was a new order for Asia. The treaties approved at Washington provided an international framework for reconciling the interests of the Powers in China, including those of Japan, with the maintenance and restoration of Chinese sovereignty and international equality. As the great statesmen of the time – Charles Evans Hughes (1862–1948), Aristide Briand (1862–1932), Arthur James Balfour (1848–1930), Shidehara Kijūrō (1872–1951), and others – left the United States when the conference ended in February of the following year, they believed that they had raised the curtain on a new era, one that would see the end of the archaic structures that had governed foreign relations with China since the wars of the nineteenth century, and usher in a new period of peace, progress, and international cooperation. After 1922 it was widely assumed that the Washington System would gradually take the place of the Northern System within China. The provisions of the Washington treaties would have turned over to China a larger share of customs revenue. This would have strengthened the central government and begun the process of dismantling foreign privilege, thus meeting nationalistic grievances. The Powers would have been committed to a cooperative rather than an adversarial relationship. Had the treaties been put into effect at once, an ascending spiral could have begun, with China gradually regaining financial and political health, a strengthening central government moving to unify the country, and tension with the Powers diminishing proportionally. But by 1924 the implementation of the Washington treaties had been delayed for more than two years, and both China and the Powers were beginning to be tugged instead into a descending spiral toward chaos and hostility. One cause was the wars of that year. The possibility of conflicts on such a large scale had not even been considered at Washington. But there were other problems as well.

One of these problems had long been within the ability of the Powers to resolve. This was something called the "gold franc dispute," which, by starving the central Chinese government of funds, had greatly improved the odds for military challenges to its authority. The origins of the dispute went back to China's entry into World War I on the allied side on December 1, 1917. At that time, Boxer indemnity payments had been suspended for five years. Thereafter some powers remitted the payments entirely, but when the period of grace expired, France, with the support of Italy, Belgium, and Spain, insisted its share of the indemnity be resumed, with payments to be made in gold specie rather than in the depreciated francs then being used in France itself. Gu Weijun was adamant that China would not accept such terms and argued his case with great persuasiveness. France, in retaliation, refused to ratify the Washington treaties, which meant that the process of tariff revision was frozen. This caused severe financial problems for the Beijing government.

It also led to disillusion among those Chinese who had genuinely believed in a new Washington Conference order, Yan Huiqing for one. He and his colleagues had "hoped so much to give a new lease of life to China, during which she should put her house in order and gradually arrive at her rightful place in the family of nations," but by 1922 he had "grown pessimistic about the political situation and saw no immediate prospect of putting into execution the decisions of the Washington Conference." As a result, he went into semiretirement and devoted his time to a thorough study of China's finances in preparation for the eventual opening of the international conferences.[54] For a time, his Commission for the Readjustment of Finance had its offices in the beautiful "round city" at the end of a marble bridge on the south bank of the northernmost of the three lakes in Zhongnanhai; later he and his assistants would work in the Yingtai, the melancholy palace on an island in the midst of the southernmost lake where the reforming emperor Guangxu (1871–1908) had been imprisoned for the last thirteen years of his life. Yan and his colleagues devoted themselves to the first comprehensive inventory of China's debt and its status, and to proposals for ameliorating the situation once the Powers should agree to come to the table.[55]

54. Yen, *East–West Kaleidoscope*, p. 131.   55. Ibid.; Fischer, p. 49.

The inability of the Europeans to come to terms even over the gold franc underlined a larger problem: namely, the future role of foreign powers in China under the Washington System. The Washington treaties had envisioned a gradual reduction in foreign privilege as China resumed full sovereignty by increments. Nibbling away of foreign privilege in China had already begun under Yuan Shikai who, in classic Chinese fashion, cultivated the strong but distant powers Britain and the United States to counterbalance the nearby threats posed by Japan and to a lesser extent Russia. Yuan had shown how effective this strategy could be when he used it to blunt the Japanese attempt to make China effectively a protectorate, through the Twenty-one Demands in 1915.[56] The real payoff of this approach came only after World War I. The losers in that conflict returned to China shorn of all privileges. The German minister rejoined the meetings of the diplomatic body after the war, but he no longer represented a treaty Power. There were no longer any German concessions, and Germans no longer enjoyed personal extraterritoriality. Austria–Hungary had disappeared during the war; so too did its leased territories and diplomatic position. The Washington treaties promised further concessions, notably in the area of extraterritoriality. The failure to ratify, however, exacerbated China's sense of grievance.

Nor did the Chinese react passively. Antiforeign feeling bubbled up from time to time, and the government pursued a hard-line nationalistic foreign policy. Perhaps the best example in this period was Chinese diplomacy toward the USSR. Imperial Russia continued to be represented in the immediate postwar period, but that soon changed. The Russian diplomatic properties were placed under the trusteeship of the diplomatic body, and in May 1924 Beijing and the Soviet government established diplomatic relations. Lev Karakhan (1889–1937), a Bolshevik of Armenian origin, arrived and assumed (as the only full ambassador – the others were only ministers) the post of dean of the *corps diplomatique*. It was not an easy situation for "the Old Firm": the Powers continued their private meetings without the Soviet representative, but had to change their title to the "Group of Powers with Common Interests." The shift in the position of the Russians and the end of blanket privilege for all European foreigners gave the Chinese room to maneuver, and denied the Powers the advantages of a fully united approach. By and large, however, the Powers took this with a certain good grace as an inevitability that they all recognized and sought only to manage and guide. The

56. See Madeleine Chi, *China Diplomacy, 1914–1918*. Harvard East Asian Monographs, no. 31 (Cambridge, Mass.: East Asian Research Center, Harvard University, 1970).

exception was Japan, whose stake in China was far larger than that of any of the other Powers, and which therefore found any shift in the foreign position in China deeply worrying.

The Washington System and the Northern System might have worked together to stabilize China had it not been for the gold franc dispute and the 1924 wars. They might even have worked in this way if the wars had yielded a clear victor with a mandate to negotiate and the authority to make promises. Without such an outcome, however, the wars could only prove destructive. They would pose a major challenge, not only to the Northern System and the political and financial stability of China domestically but also to the whole map of the Chinese and Asian diplomatic and security future agreed on at Washington.

The consequences of the wars of 1924 were major. As is often the case with such conflicts, their immediate origins were extremely obscure.

2
How the wars began

It is a rare book of Chinese history that contains the names of Generals Zang Zhiping (b. 1867) and Yang Huazhao. They were two minor militarists who briefly controlled parts of Fujian province until their defeat in March 1924 after a year of sometimes hard fighting by Sun Chuanfang (1885–1935), the new military governor named by the central government. We will hear more of Sun, an able general whom the central government was counting upon to extend its control into the chaotic southeast. He was a Shandong native, trained at the Beiyang Military College in Tianjin and the Shikan Gakkō [Officers School] in Japan. By the mid-1920s he had become one of the most powerful military and political figures of China south of the Yangzi and the Shanghai area, known as "a skilful strategist with a genius for swift action" and an "efficient ruler" as well.[1]

By contrast, neither Zang nor Yang was a man of any particular importance. As members of the Anfu political faction, they had been more or less on their own since its loss of national power in 1920. Thus, mentioning their defeat in a routine report to London the British minister, Sir Ronald Macleay, called them "filibusters" – from the Spanish word for the banditlike independent military adventurers who stirred up trouble in Latin America.[2] Nor was Fujian, where they had briefly held sway, a place of much importance on the political map of China. Lying on the southeast coast, surrounded by mountains and without railway connections to the rest of the country, it was inhabited by speakers of the *Min* dialects, unintelligible elsewhere, who looked for

1. Howard L. Boorman, ed., *Biographical Dictionary of Republican China* (BDRC), 4 vols. (New York: Columbia University Press, 1967), vol. 3, pp. 160–2; quotations are from C. A. Macartney, *Survey of International Affairs 1925* (London: Oxford University Press, 1928), vol. 2, p. 325.
2. Foreign Office (FO) General Correspondence, Far Eastern Department, File 371, Ronald Macleay to Ramsay MacDonald, September 11, 1924. F3074/19/10.

35

their livelihoods not inland but to the sea: to trade, smuggling, and piracy.

When Zang and Yang fled into Fujian's remote and inaccessible northwest and eventually escaped into Zhejiang through mountainous country where bandits had long taken refuge, they ought by all rights to have disappeared from the historical horizon.[3] But in a *Jiazi* year things worked differently: instead, they set off China's greatest modern war so far. In Minister Macleay's words, they provided "the spark that . . . fired the train" leading to war, and eventually to the great revolution of the 1920s.[4] How did they do it? The answer begins in Shanghai.

China in 1924 was, as already mentioned, a country dominated politically by competition among factions – sometimes, and perhaps preferably, called "parties" – composed of military leaders, parliamentarians, and other influential persons.[5] At this time two were actively contesting power. The three provinces of the northeast, then known as Manchuria, were controlled by Zhang Zuolin's Fengtian faction, based in Mukden. Their adversary, the Zhili group, controlled eleven of the eighteen provinces of China proper plus three in what today is Inner Mongolia as well as the central government at Beijing, of which Cao Kun was the president. But Shanghai, the greatest city of China, and Zhejiang, the province bordering it to the south, belonged to neither group. Because Shanghai could prove decisive in a showdown, how to deal with it was a major strategic concern of both factions.

The anomalous status of Shanghai had its origins a decade earlier, when President Yuan Shikai feared that his colleague and rival, Feng Guozhang (1859–1919), who had been the military governor of Jiangsu since 1914, would grow too strong if the city of Shanghai remained under the jurisdiction of Jiangsu province. So Yuan divided Feng Guozhang's domain, leaving him as governor of Jiangsu but creating a new post, the defense commissioner of Songjiang and Shanghai [*Song-Hu hujunshi*] to control the city and its neighbor, Songjiang. He gave this position to the Anfu faction, so-called after the location of the meeting from which it emerged – at an address in Beijing's Anfu *hutong* [lane] – summoned

---

3. On these obscure events, see Zhang Yichun, "Zang Zhiping, Yang Huazhao zi Min tuwei ru Zhe ji" *Wenshi ziliao xuanji* (1960–) no. 35, 56–66.
4. Ronald Macleay to Ramsay MacDonald, September 5, 1924, FO 371/10245.
5. Most modern writers call these groups "factions" or "cliques"; Qihong Lin [Jermyn Chi-Hung Lynn], however, opts for "party." See *Political Parties in China* (Peking: Henry Vetch, 1930). The Chinese word usually used today is *xi*, "system," not *dang*, which is the usual translation for "party." Groups such as Zhili and Anfu lacked fully formalized organizations and programmatic platforms. Nevertheless, they behaved in many ways like full-fledged parties.

by Duan Qirui in 1917.[6] With Feng Guozhang's Zhili faction holding Jiangsu, while its Anfu rivals held Shanghai and part of its hinterland, a delicate balance of power was created in the lower Yangzi valley. The arrangement continued long after both Yuan Shikai and Feng Guozhang were dead. The Anfu faction naturally supported this arrangement and held on to its control of Shanghai even after military defeat by Zhili broke its national power in 1920.[7]

So it was that in 1924 Shanghai was under the effective control of two Anfu holdovers: Lu Yongxiang (1867–1933), *dujun* [literally, "supervisor of military affairs"] of Zhejiang, and his ally in the Anfu faction, He Fenglin (1873–1945), defense commissioner for Shanghai and Songjiang. Lu and He were both Shandong natives, like Wu Peifu, and both had trained in the North: He Fenglin at Beiyang Military College, Lu Yongxiang at Shanhaiguan Military Academy. Both had been protégés of Yuan Shikai, who sent them to the Yangzi valley in the early teens, to expand and consolidate his authority there. When Yuan's followers formed factions after his death in 1916, they cast their lots with the Anfu group. Lu and He remained in power through the period of Anfu ascendancy at Beijing, and when the faction fell in 1920, they stayed on – among the handful of Anfu group members to keep their posts.[8] But by 1924 their separate administration of Zhejiang and Shanghai was an anomaly. In particular, the city of Shanghai was politically isolated and alone, cut off from much of its traditional hinterland, with Zhejiang a last territorial reminder of the domain of the once-powerful Anfu faction.

The long-simmering issue of Shanghai came to the fore in 1924 because the process of military contention over who should control the central government in Beijing seemed to be approaching decision. It is a mistake to think of that government as being either powerless or the simple creature of one military commander or another. Just as the parliament contained representatives of a variety of political tendencies, so the government usually accommodated political rivals. Indeed, that was part of its function. China is too big to rule at the point of a gun: some sort of civilian authority, able to reconcile or balance competing policies and regional interests, is absolutely essential. The Beijing government played such a role during this period. Furthermore, through its authority

6. Tian Ziyu, Liu Dejun, eds. *Zhongguo jindai junfashi cidian* (Beijing: Dangan chubanshe, 1989), pp. 216–17.
7. Mao Jinling, "Beiyang Zhixi jundui zhi yanjiu (Minguo yuannian–16 nian). Ph.D. dissertation, National Taiwan University, 1987, p. 103.
8. Lai Xinxia, Guo Jianlin, and Jiao Jingyi, *Beiyang junfa shigao* (Hubei renmin chubanshe, 1983), p. 398; Yu Jianxin, "Song Hu hujunshi Lu Yongxiang," in Yang Hao and Ye Lan, eds. *Jiu Shanghai fengyun renwu* (Shanghai: Shanghai renmin chubanshe, 1989), pp. 135–43; *Who's Who in China* (3rd. ed.), pp. 281–2, 582–3.

and financial power, it exerted substantial control over the Chinese military. Although historical stereotype often makes it sound as if military commanders during this period operated independently of the government, in control of territorially based private and personal armies, this was far from the truth. We will find repeated examples of Beijing starving a general of funds, or removing him from command against his will, and replacing him with someone else.

Nevertheless, political authority in China was strongly contested during the period after the death of Yuan Shikai in 1916. Yuan had run a China that was substantially unified. The contest for power was chiefly among people who had all originally been subordinates of Yuan, and therefore members of the same group. Only gradually after his death did their cohesion begin to break, although it never vanished completely, for to the end all continued to attribute some form of legitimacy to the central government in Beijing. The struggle was furthermore extremely complex – which is one of the reasons it is little studied – carried on in parallel in both the military and political arenas. As it became more acute, resorts to military force, and eventually civil war, accompanied it. During the years after Yuan Shikai's death, two short and decisive wars, between Anfu and Zhili in 1920 and Fengtian and Zhili in 1922, had given Zhili military paramountcy in China proper. These military successes were matched by Zhili assumption of control of the central administration in Beijing, capped by Cao Kun's assumption of the presidency in 1923. So by 1924 Zhili was unquestionably the strongest political power and looked set to assume a relatively stable and uncontested control of China.

Much of Zhili's success was the result of its military prowess, which was embodied in Marshal Wu Peifu. Wu had been born into a poor Shandong family in 1874, but he was educated, having attained the status of *shengyuan* under the examination system before changing to the military career in which, under the tutelage of Yuan Shikai, he had risen by 1912 to the rank of chief adjutant of the modern and therefore critically important 3rd Division. This command had been a stepping-stone to power for the senior Anfu leader Duan Qirui (1865–1936), who held it from 1904 to 1906; for the current president, Cao Kun, who held it from 1906 to 1918; and for Wu, who replaced Cao.[9] Politically, Wu was an implacable foe of foreign influence in China, and after 1923 a strong believer in the use of force rather than negotiations to unify

---

9. Odoric Y. K. Wou, *Militarism in Modern China: The Career of Wu P'ei-fu, 1916–39* (Folkestone, Kent, England: Dawson & Sons, also Canberra: Australian National University Press, 1978), pp. 17, 27.

China, as his slogan – *wuli tongyi* – proclaimed.[10] His faction's rise to power seemed a textbook example of the carefully calculated resort to force, always in support of a political strategy, repeated when necessary until the goal was within sight.

Thus Wu had frustrated Premier Duan Qirui's attempt to bring the South under full control in 1918, by halting his own victorious troops at Hengyang and calling for peace talks. This action brought into the open the split, among Yuan Shikai's followers, between the emerging Anfu and Zhili groups. Two years later Wu had brought down the Anfu-dominated administration at Beijing by means of the brief Zhili–Anfu War, fought from July 14 to July 19 of 1920. Two years after that he had devastated his one remaining military challenger, Zhang Zuolin, in the First Zhili–Fengtian War, fought from April 28 to May 4, 1922. Each of these cases demonstrated Wu's remarkable ability to combine military efficiency with sound political calculation, so that a minimum but decisive application of force produced a substantial political benefit. Neither war had bogged down in attrition; rather, Wu had in each case literally routed his opponents by surprise, maneuver, and strategic originality. Now in 1924 Zhili's advance toward uncontested power was reaching its climax. The final challenge was to solve the two related problems of Shanghai and Manchuria.

The Fengtian faction in Manchuria, relying on the abundant economic resources of its base area as well as a close military and political relationship with Japan, had been reforming and reconstructing its army ever since the 1922 defeat. The remnants of Anfu power in Shanghai and Zhejiang, by contrast, were little more than a nuisance. It was true that Shanghai was potentially a powerful asset, but it was not a serious threat in itself. The danger came from the fact that it had aligned itself with Fengtian and with the other outsider in Chinese politics of the time, Sun Yat-sen's regime in Guangzhou, in a defensive "triangular alliance" [*sanjiao lianmeng*]. This meant that any war with the Anfu remnant could draw in other, more important, players.

Wu Peifu believed that war would eventually be required to deal with Zhang Zuolin in Manchuria. But, cognizant of the risks, he strongly opposed any war over Shanghai. His hope was to bring the Anfu remnants and the rich territories of Zhejiang and Shanghai into the Zhili coalition by peaceful means. Thus, in 1923, when Cao Kun bribed the parliament into electing him president (a move which Wu had opposed), Marshal Wu argued strongly that Cao should give the vice-presidency

10. Guo Jianlin, *Wu Peifu dazhuan: yidai xiaoxiong* (Tianjin: Tianjin Daxue Chubanshe, 1991), vol. 1, p. 378.

either to Duan Qirui, the senior leader of the Anfu faction, or to Lu Yongxiang. Had Lu or Duan been thus accommodated in 1923, war would almost certainly not have broken out in 1924 when, as will be seen, Zhili was not fully prepared but, rather, at a moment that Wu Peifu chose. Other members of the Zhili faction, however, were not willing to accept Wu's strategy, with the result that war broke out over Shanghai in the late summer of 1924.[11]

The difficulty Wu had in securing acceptance of his strategy reflected broader problems for the Zhili group that had begun in earnest with the the faction's first serious misstep, the bribed presidential election of 1923. The initial Zhili victory in 1922 had been accompanied by the return to the presidential residence of Li Yuanhong, who as we have mentioned commanded a good deal of legitimacy and prestige as a result of his role in the overthrow of the Qing. Li's return won a certain amount of public goodwill for Zhili as well. Furthermore, in the year following that victory, Wu Peifu had skillfully nobbled Zhili's potential rivals for power: Sun Yat-sen, who occasionally showed signs of life in Guangdong, was harried by Chen Jiongming (1878–1933), whom Wu supported; Lu Yongxiang in Shanghai was checked by Qi Xieyuan in Jiangsu, while the greatest threat, Zhang Zuolin in Manchuria, was deterred by Wu Peifu himself. But when Cao disgraced himself in the presidential election, things began to change. Wu became unpopular along with Cao. Beijing's die-hard opponents among the revolutionaries in Guangzhou gained new spirit. Lu Yongxiang began to think about moving back onto the national stage – perhaps by breaking out from Shanghai and taking the city of Bengbu in Anhui to secure control of the Tianjin–Pukou railway. Zhang Zuolin also stirred. The Anfu leader Duan Qirui, who had ostentatiously abandoned politics to devote himself to the study of Buddhism at his home in Tianjin, now came out of "retirement" to speak movingly against the evils of the Cao Kun government. Divisions within the Zhili faction were further exacerbated when some of Wu Peifu's rivals considered uniting with Zhang Zuolin against Wu; the shame brought to the faction by Cao Kun further discouraged would-be collaborators from other factions while ambitious members of the faction itself increasingly looked to their own personal interests.[12]

One of these last was Qi Xieyuan (1879–1946), Zhili governor of Jiangsu, Shanghai's neighboring province to the west, to which territory the city had traditionally belonged administratively. In 1924 Qi was still in his forties. A native of Ningbo, he was intelligent, highly educated (both a *shengyuan* under the traditional examination system and a dis-

11. Ibid., vol. 2, pp. 496–7.   12. Ibid., vol. 2, pp. 494, 496.

tinguished graduate of the Beiyang Military Academy), and ambitious.[13] Above all, he was frustrated by the anomalous status of Shanghai. Without it, Qi looked destined to remain a provincial governor, important to be sure but firmly relegated to the second rank of power. With it by contrast he could become a major player for the very highest stakes. So whatever the Zhili leaders in Beijing thought, Qi wanted to reassert his province's control of Shanghai, a goal best accomplished by defeating Zhejiang and Lu Yongxiang, its military governor since 1919.

Qi Xieyuan had already nearly invaded Zhejiang twice before, once in August and September of 1923, after the bribed presidential election (for which he had provided substantial funds),[14] when Qi had been outraged at the assistance Lu Yongxiang provided to anti-Zhili members of parliament who had fled to the city from Beijing, and again in November of that year, when the Shanghai police commissioner, Xu Guoliang, a Zhili loyalist, was assassinated at the order of the Lu's ally, Defense Commissioner He Fenglin. Both times, however, his allies in Beijing – and Wu Peifu in particular – had pressured Qi not to act. They feared a two-front war in which Mukden would move when fighting broke out around Shanghai; they were also reluctant to see Qi himself grow too strong.[15]

Public opinion also helped to avert war in 1923 in the Shanghai area. Large-scale conflict threatened disaster for the commerce of the city and the whole Yangzi valley. After much formal and informal lobbying and mediation both by diplomats and chambers of commerce, the rival generals Qi and Lu had accepted a series of measures designed to banish the specter of war by guaranteeing Shanghai's neutrality. The city authorities concluded bilateral non-aggression treaties with Hubei, Anhui, and Jiangxi. Most importantly, Qi and Lu together signed a treaty in August 1923, which provided that neither general would enter into alliances with other provinces, nor would he permit military forces from other provinces to pass through his territory, nor would he augment his own forces.[16]

It was in connection with the last provision that Generals Zang Zhiping and Yang Huazhao, whom we met at the beginning of this

13. BDRC, vol. 1, pp. 297–9.
14. Guo Jianlin, *Wu Peifu*, vol. 2, p. 543.
15. Ibid., vol. 2, pp. 543–5; Mao Jinling, "Beiyang," pp. 104–5; Walter E. Smith (vice-consul, Nanjing) to State Department, August 20, 1924, in Records of the Department of State Relating to Political Relations of the United States with China (National Archives Microfilm Publications Microcopy No. 339) 893.00/5560 (hereafter cited as SD followed by file number).
16. Mao Jinling, 104–5; *Dongfang zazhi* 20 (August 10, 1923), no. 15, 2–4 (hereafter cited as DZ); DZ 20.23 (December 12, 1923), 2–4; *North-China Herald*, August 25, 1923, quoted in A. M. Kotenev, *Shanghai: Its Municipality and the Chinese* (Shanghai: North-China Daily News & Herald, 1927), p. 22.

chapter fleeing Fujian, made their brief but extremely important contribution to the course of twentieth-century Chinese history. South to north, Fujian abuts Zhejiang, which in turn borders Shanghai. When eventually the two generals straggled out of the mountains into Zhejiang with perhaps 7,000 troops, Lu Yongxiang happily incorporated them, on June 8, 1924, into his own none-too-numerous forces.[17] But by doing this Lu had clearly violated the treaty of 1923, which had guaranteed Shanghai's neutrality. The flight of the two generals and their adherence to the Zhejiang cause put a match to the fuse. The delicate balance of military power in the lower Yangzi had been gravely disturbed. Qi Xieyuan now had a clear *casus belli*, and despite the remonstrances of his northern allies he lost no time in moving.

Qi began a full mobilization of his Jiangsu troops, called for reinforcements from the North, and began making deployments clearly designed to overthrow the Anfu administration in Zhejiang and to take Shanghai.[18] In response, Lu Yongxiang issued mobilization orders to his forces in Zhejiang and Shanghai. When Jiangsu began the fight, with an artillery barrage at Huangdu, west of Shanghai, the fateful provisions of the defensive triangular alliance came into effect, and both Zhang Zuolin in Mukden and Sun Yat-sen in Guangzhou declared their support for Lu. With that, Zhili's hand was forced. Zhang Zuolin would now mobilize, and unless Zhili preempted him, quickly secure a position of overwhelming advantage in a two-front war. Although it was more a pretext for war than its actual cause, the violation of the 1923 Shanghai neutrality treaty by Zang, Yang, and Lu had proven to be a fateful step. The city of Shanghai, long immune to the effects of Chinese politics, was finally in military play. And as interlocking alliances, guarantees, agreements, and understandings among potential combatants were unexpectedly activated, China – rather like Europe just a decade earlier – found itself abruptly thrust on the road to large-scale war.[19]

The risk that general war might break out in just this way had long been understood by military observers. On August 28, 1924, before any fighting had begun, Brigadier General William D. Connor (1874–1960) had arrived in Mukden, the city that had been the capital of the Manchu Qing dynasty before the conquest of China proper in 1644 and that was now headquarters of the Fengtian group. (Mukden was the city's Manchu name; today it is called Shenyang.) Connor was the commander of the United States Army forces in China, headquartered in Tianjin.

17. Mao Jinling, p. 102.
18. Ibid., p. 105.
19. *New York Times*, September 17, 1924, 25 (hereafter cited as NYT).

(Later he would serve as superintendent of the United States Military Academy at West Point from 1932 to 1938.) In Mukden he met the leader of the Fengtian group, Zhang Zuolin, "the Old Marshal," who gave a dinner in Connor's honor on August 30.

Zhang was physically a slight man. Photographs show him faintly ridiculous in his military regalia, overshadowed both by Chinese colleagues and by his many foreign advisers. He was born in 1873 to a poor peasant family in Fengtian, enlisted in the military before he was twenty, and fought in the Sino-Japanese War. Later, with his irregular (sometimes called *honghuzi*, literally "redbeards," or bandit) forces, he fought – characteristically – for both sides in the Russo-Japanese War from 1904 to 1905. Renowned for his cunning, he took control of Manchuria in 1916 when Beijing was in an uproar over the attempt by Yuan Shikai to proclaim himself emperor. Zhang drove out Duan Zhigui, the Fengtian *dujun* whom Yuan had named, assumed the job himself, and then – amazingly – secured Yuan's approval for the move.[20] In style of life he was the prototypical warlord. The coach and chassis of his Rolls-Royce "were certainly armour-plated and the windows had bullet-proof shields" while "the interior was lavishly gilded and the fittings were of solid gold."[21] But with the assistance of a gifted group of advisers and backing from Tokyo, Zhang managed Manchuria with considerable success as his own independent kingdom.[22]

On this occasion his analysis of the immediate situation proved prescient. Looking into the future, Zhang told General Connor before his departure that war between Zhejiang and Jiangsu was inevitable, and added that all provinces would eventually become involved in the fighting. Indeed, the Old Marshal believed that what was coming was no less than "a period of disorder similar to that following 'the year of the First Revolution (1911)'"; one that would affect not only China but also the foreign countries that had interests there.[23] Zhang did not add that he had long been preparing himself to emerge victorious from that period of chaos. His ambition had never been simply to be a regional magnate. Rather, he intended – like the Manchus who founded the Qing dynasty – to use Manchuria as a stepping-stone to power in China proper. He had made such an attempt two years earlier, but as we have

20. BDRC, vol. 1, pp. 115–22; Macartney, *Survey*, p. 324; Gavan McCormack, *Chang Tso-lin in Northeast China, 1911–1928: China, Japan, and the Manchurian Idea* (Folkestone, Kent, England: Dawson and Sons, 1977), pp. 15–44.
21. Charles Drage, *General of Fortune: The Story of One-Arm Sutton* (London: Heinemann, 1963), p. 170.
22. BDRC, vol. 1, p. 115; Drage, *General of Fortune*, 170.
23. R. P. Tenney, American Consul in Charge, Mukden, to Secretary of State, August 31, 1924, SD 893.00/5556.

seen, he was defeated decisively in the First Zhili–Fengtian War in 1922. Since that time everyone in China had been expecting a rematch.[24] When the first shots were fired at Huangdu, Zhang's moment of opportunity had arrived.

On September 4, the day after the fighting in the South began, Marshal Zhang summoned all his military staff above brigade commander [*lüzhang*] to his residence for urgent consultations. The situation was clear: Qi Xieyuan's mobilization threatened Zhang's best foothold in China proper. The defeat of Lu Yongxiang in Zhejiang and the addition of Shanghai to the territory of Qi and his Northern allies would unacceptably strengthen the Beijing government and, by consolidating its hold on central China, free its military resources for operations against Manchuria. Zhang and his advisers did not doubt that the crisis in the Shanghai area called for only one response: an immediate full-scale Fengtian mobilization and rapid advance directly against the heart of Zhili power at Beijing. Martial law was proclaimed in the area between Mukden and Tianjin on September 11, and all normal traffic on the Beijing–Mukden railway was suspended two days later. On September 15 Fengtian's formidable and well-equipped forces began deploying southward.[25]

In response to this mobilization, Zhili in turn prepared for war. On hearing of Zhang's actions, Marshal Wu Peifu left his base at Luoyang with some 2,000 bodyguards and arrived in Beijing – after delays en route – at 3:25 A.M. on Wednesday, September 17. Despite the late hour he was greeted in person at the station by Generals Feng Yuxiang (1882–1948) and Wang Huaiqing (1876–1953), as well as the chief cabinet secretary, Sun Runyu (1880–1960), representing the premier, Yan Huiqing (no admirer of Marshal Wu, whom he called "The Chinese Ludendorff").[26] Wu was promptly escorted to the presidential palace, the Yanqing lou, which would be his headquarters, and the government moved immediately into emergency session with military commanders and all cabinet ministers present.[27] War was agreed on; President Cao Kun declared Zhang Zuolin a rebel and, later on the same morning,

24. The First Zhili–Fengtian War, April 28–May 4, 1922. See Lai et al., *Beiyang junfa shigao*, pp. 268–73.

25. Ding Wenjiang, ed., *Minguo junshi jinji* (reprint ed., Taibei: Wenhai chubanshe, n.d.), pp. 35–41, 47–52; Lai et al., *Beiyang junfa shigao*, 299–301; Fu Xingpei, "Di er ci Zhi Feng zhanzheng jishi," *Wenshi ziliao xuanji* No. 4 (1960), 34; Li Taifen, *Guominjun shigao* (Taibei: Wenhai, n.d.), p. 162; "Zhi Feng bingli zhi bijiao," *DZ* 21.19 (1924), 152–62.

26. Yen, *East–West Kaleidoscope*, 119.

27. *China Weekly Review*, September 27, 1924, 133 (hereafter cited as CWR); Yen, *East–West Kaleidoscope*, pp. 146–7.

September 17, issued an order to crush him, Presidential Mandate No. 1409 [the so-called *taofa mingling*], over both his own signature and that of Premier Yan.[28]

President Cao was a former cloth peddler from Tianjin who had become an early friend and drinking companion of the first president of the Chinese Republic, Yuan Shikai, joined the army, studied and later taught at the Tianjin Military Academy, and fought bravely in Manchuria and Korea against the Japanese from 1894 to 1895. After the turn of the century he rose quickly in Yuan's service, becoming commander of the 3rd Division, which was then at Changchun, in 1906. After Yuan's death, he became one of the original members of the Zhili faction.[29]

Cao's prime minister, Yan Huiqing, could scarcely have been more different. Yan was an experienced civilian politician who had held a variety of ministerial portfolios. He was the son of an Episcopal minister, a Phi Beta Kappa graduate of the University of Virginia, and a third-degree Mason who had served as professor of English at St. John's University in Shanghai.[30] Yan, furthermore, reflected the opinions of many in his private opposition to the war. He believed that the complete political unification of China and its rise to international power could be accomplished only gradually and by peaceful means. His comparison of Wu Peifu to the imperial German general and politician Erich Ludendorff (1865–1937) suggested both a general understanding of the lessons of Germany's unification by force and the danger of drawing in foreign intervention, as well as the sure knowledge that a Kapp or Beer Hall Putsch in Beijing would terminate China's already precarious constitutional development. (It must be said, however, that Wu seems to have been an altogether more humane and sympathetic person than Ludendorff.)

At one meeting with the president and his military commander Yan "impressed on all the danger of inviting Japanese intervention if the war should be carried into Manchuria, and of the insuperable difficulty of overcoming Marshal Zhang Zuolin and his armies, as they could always retreat northward in case of defeat." To Yan's astonishment, "the Chinese president and his military commander [Wu Peifu] expressed themselves determined to settle Zhang's fate once and for all and to pursue him if necessary as far as Harbin." These were not idle boasts. "The Parliament," Yan noted, "which in normal times made itself

---

28. *Beiyang Zhengfu Gongbao*, ed. Zhongguo di er lishidanganguan (Shanghai: Shanghai shudian, n.d.) 212.271–6.
29. Lai et al., 447; BDRC vol. 3, pp. 302–5.
30. BDRC, vol. 4, pp. 50–2; also Yen, *East–West Kaleidoscope*.

obnoxious by its vociferous and obstructive methods, was as silent as the grave in the face of the oncoming trial of arms of the two great warlords. They knew the defeat of one of the parties might involve them in personal danger."[31] Other conflicts between militarists had been opposed, or at least deplored, by the Beijing government. The presidential mandate, however, meant that the war now taking shape on the northern border would have the full official sanction of the legal Chinese government.[32]

The commander of the punitive expedition [*taonijun*] against Zhang was naturally Wu Peifu. General Connor had visited Wu as well, in June 1924, at his headquarters in Luoyang, an ancient city in Henan, south of the Yellow River. It was a former capital of the Tang (618–907), among other dynasties. He had been impressed. The brick barracks, built by Yuan Shikai more than a decade earlier, were well kept, the men drilled and rode well, and although their equipment was poorer than American, it was excellent by Chinese standards. All learned patriotic songs, "and the impression created by several thousand men marching away from the drill fields at about half time, all singing at the tops of their voices, was very good."[33] Some described Wu as an absolutely typical stouthearted man of Shandong [*Shandong haohan*], while others detected a non-Chinese cast in his features: his "close-cropped hair had a distinctly brownish tinge," his "alert, wide-open eyes were light brown in colour," and his "flowing military moustache might almost have been described as ginger." But there could be no doubt about his strongly nationalistic sentiments. His proclaimed policy was never to set foot in a treaty port and to rely neither on foreign money nor on foreign alliances in his quest to unify China. Wu "had the reputation of being a sound Chinese classical scholar and a good soldier, but a poor judge of men and an inefficient statesman."[34]

Personally a considerate man – he provided railway cars to evacuate civilians from the neighborhood of battlefields[35] – Wu nevertheless stirred envy and resentment among some who worked with him. Combining a bit of the hauteur of the traditional Chinese man of learning with the

---

31. Yen, *East–West Kaleidoscope*, p. 147.
32. Two years earlier President Xu Shichang had refused to sanction Wu Peifu's action against Zhang Zuolin in the First Zhili–Fengtian War, and had ordered both sides to withdraw. See *Zhengful gongbao*, No. 2209, April 27, 1922.
33. "Notes on a Visit to Wu Pei Fu's Hdqrs" in *U.S. Military Intelligence Reports, China 1911–1941*, ed. Paul Kesaris (Microfilm. Frederick, Md.: University Publications of America, 1983), June 4, 1924 (hereafter cited as MIR).
34. Guo Jianlin, personal communication; Wou, *Militarism*, pp. 12–19; Drage, *General of Fortune*, 131; Macartney, *Survey*, 326.
35. Impey, *The Chinese Army*, illustration facing p. 10.

self-assurance of the master of strategic command, Wu clearly felt himself the man of destiny. And he was aware of fitting the classic type, described in the *Yijing* or *Book of Changes*, of the *kanglong* – the proud or arrogant dragon, poised to soar to the heights of power. Indeed, at one point he discussed with his friend and fellow provincial Qin Dequn (1893–1963) the rather ominous implications of the ancient classic's dictum: *kanglong you hui*, "the arrogant dragon will have cause to repent."[36]

As Fengtian mobilized, Wu and his staff began to coordinate the despatch northward of troops and materiel for what they too believed would be the decisive struggle for control of China.[37] Carried by an endless shuttle of railway trains, Wu Peifu's armies converged on Shanhaiguan, his air force moved north, and his navy gathered off the Manchurian coast. Meanwhile, his most important ally, the "Christian general" Feng Yuxiang, prepared to advance northward along the road to Rehe – or Chengde, the strategic place in the mountains eighty miles northeast of Beijing, where the Qing court had its summer palace – toward which Fengtian forces had started out a few days earlier. Feng is one of the most enigmatic figures of twentieth-century Chinese history. The son of a minor military officer, he had attended school for perhaps fifteen months as a child before joining the army. He was a big, strong man of seemingly passionate convictions and mercurial temperament; a professed Christian, inclined to revolutionary causes, and, depending on one's perspective, an idealist manqué or a total opportunist.[38] Feng and Wu were not close, but they had worked together effectively in the defeat of Zhang two years earlier and, if all went well this time, there would be plenty of spoils to cement the relationship again.

On September 18 the people of Beijing watched the colorful spectacle of Feng's armies marching north. In good order, they were dressed in faded blue cotton uniforms and each carried "a bedding roll, an extra pair of cloth shoes, a tin cup, a rifle, an ammunition belt and a Chinese umbrella wrapped in a neat cloth cover and slung over his shoulder." They wore red cloth armbands, presumably to distinguish them from General Wu's forces. Machine guns and field pieces were carried or

36. *Qian* hexagram; see *The I Ching or Book of Changes*. The Richard Wilhelm Translation Rendered into English by Cary F. Baynes. Foreword by C. G. Jung (New York: Pantheon Books, 1950), v. 2.16. Guo Jianlin, *Wu Peifu*, vol. 2, p. 579.
37. The Chargé in China (Bell) to the Secretary of State, September 18, 1924, *Foreign Relations of the United States 1924*, 2 vols. (Washington, D.C.: U.S. Government Printing Office, 1939) vol. 1, pp. 378–9 (hereafter cited as FRUS, with year); NYT, September 18, 1924, 25.
38. BDRC, vol. 1, pp. 37–43.

hauled by mules, and more than 1,000 camels were commandeered to carry supplies. Fatefully, with Feng's army went most of Zhili's best artillery.[39]

The whole strategic and political map of China was now suddenly in flux, and the stakes were the very highest. The next three chapters will examine armament and military operations in detail. Before turning to those, it is important to understand the logic of the struggle and its many implications beyond the military realm.

On logic, it is important to understand that warfare in China has usually been internal, and as such has necessarily had a more complex political dimension than is found in the wars between discrete nations. China is also very large, and this has meant, and continues to mean that the country cannot strictly speaking be conquered by purely military means and certainly not by attrition. On a nationwide scale, the ability of regions to defend themselves will almost always be greater than the capacity of any region or even the central government to conquer them. So Chinese warfare has placed a premium on the bold strategic maneuver that succeeds not only militarily but also psychologically. Repeatedly in periods of disunion in Chinese history, and never more strikingly than in the twentieth century, holders of local military power have kept themselves back from the struggle at the national level until a certain momentum of victory has built up. Once an outcome becomes clear or even plausible, however, they begin to place their bets, declaring neutrality or joining the side they expect to win – and by doing so increasing its chances of success – a phenomenon political scientists call "bandwagoning." Momentum may build and success be achieved. If so it brings with it the need – faced classically by the Song founder Zhao Kuangyin (927–976) – somehow to disperse the armed coalition that brought the winner to power. If the bid fails, the main protagonists often fall for good from the national stage, while the lesser players return to their base areas, husband their resources, and try together to keep any one player from becoming too strong – behavior not unlike that which political scientists call "balancing."[40]

39. NYT, September 18, 1924, 25; Lawrence Impey, "Chinese Advances in the Art of War," CWR (December 27, 1924), 101.
40. Nearly every student of Chinese military politics has recognized these phenomena, even if they have not used this terminology. The best introduction, although it deals with a later period, is Avery Goldstein, *From Bandwagon to Balance-of-Power Politics: Structural Constraints and Politics in China, 1949–1978* (Stanford: Stanford University Press, 1991). See also Hsi-sheng Ch'i, *Warlord Politics in China 1916–1928* (Stanford: Stanford University Press, 1976); Andrew J. Nathan, *Peking Politics 1918–1923: Factionalism and the Failure of Constitutionalism* (Berkeley: University of

To put it another way, China has had two military states or phases: one is coalescence into unity, spurred by military victory and the expectation of more; the other is withdrawal into local base areas, the result of failed attempts at unity. Stated in its most basic form, the challenge facing the various generals who took to the field in the period of disunion in the 1920s was to create the momentum of victory – to shock the military situation from the second phase into the first. Even more than in Europe, then, warfare in China was – and is – a matter of psychology. As will be seen, when we examine how the wars were fought, this factor was fundamental to the war plans of all the participants.

As for implications, at the outset the most important seemed to involve foreign affairs. Foreigners viewed the mobilization and the fighting first with detachment, then with interest, and finally with deep concern. They felt that Chinese wars were none of their business, and in the past such struggles had impinged remarkably little on the major foreign settlements. Except for a few nervous days during the attempt to overthrow Yuan Shikai in 1913, called the "Second Revolution," Shanghai had effectively been spared conflict since the end of the Taiping rebellion in the previous century; Beijing and Tianjin had last seen serious fighting at the time of the Boxer Rebellion. The Boxer Protocol imposed in 1901 at the end of that war included a host of provisions to ensure that foreign settlements would be off limits in future Chinese wars: the railroad from Tianjin to Beijing, for example, was theoretically controlled not by Chinese troops but by Western soldiers whose authority extended for two miles on either side of the railbed. Foreign guards were stationed in the major treaty ports, and foreign gunboats patrolled not only China's coastal but its inland waterways as well. The Chinese were forbidden to place troops or construct fortifications at such strategic places as Dagu on the approach to Tianjin. There was something ominous about this mobilization unfolding in China with a mechanical logic as treaty provision engaged treaty provision.

The looming possibility of large-scale war clouded and threatened the pleasant prospects, laid out at the Washington Conference, with which the decade of the 1920s had begun in China. At first people tried to put a good face on events. We have seen already that Jacob Gould Schurman

California Press, 1976); Lucien W. Pye, *Warlord Politics: Conflict and Coalition in the Modernization of Republican China* (New York: Praeger, 1971); James E. Sheridan, *China in Disintegration: The Republican Era in Chinese History, 1912–1949* (New York: Free Press, 1975). For a general statement of the concepts, and a review of the literature, see Stephen M. Walt, "Alliance Formation and the Balance of Power," *International Security* 9 (Spring 1985), no. 4, 3–43.

was upbeat. A brief editorial in the *New York Times* was optimistic as well but for a different reason. Attempts to put into effect the agreements made at the Washington Conference had been plagued by China's disunity and consequent inability to negotiate with one voice. The coming war, the editorial explained, was the culmination of a campaign carried out by Beijing, whose "aim [was] to lift China out of a condition of chaos by beating down in turn the two most formidable opponents of the Central Government."[41] If unity resulted, that would be a good thing. Initially, diplomatic opinion was similar. With the exception of Japan, the Powers very much wanted to see China united. On August 28, 1924, British minister Macleay wired the Foreign Office his opinion that "it is an open question whether not only foreign interests but China as a whole will not, in the long run, benefit if Zhili factions are given a fair chance to eject their opponents from Shanghai and Zhejiang and thus recover those regions for the central government."[42]

The sheer scale of the firepower and the fighting was troublesome. Chinese soldiers were not yet strictly comparable to European, but they were unmistakably modern. Their organization was European in style. Their weapons too were of recent vintage, mostly the same sorts of arms used by Europeans in World War I. Both sides had air forces of close to 100 planes (on the eve of World War I the largest European air force, that of Germany, numbered 384[43]), and Zhili had a substantial navy as well.

Worries abounded. As the contest got underway, the *Literary Digest* asked: "Will China's civil war flame up into the greatest conflict that has ever been waged in that country?"[44] As it turned out, it did. Would it involve other powers? Here worries focused on Japan. Foreign minister Shidehara was a convinced internationalist who had repeatedly proclaimed his policy of noninterference in China's internal politics [*naisei fukanshō*]. The cabinet of Katō Takaaki (June 11, 1924–August 2, 1925) was already shaky, and if it genuinely did nothing then it ran the risk of seeing Fengtian defeated and Wu Peifu – who was widely expected, as a Russian newspaper put it, to "clean China of Japanese" – unite all of that country including Manchuria under Zhili control.[45] But the success

41. NYT, September 20, 1924, 14.
42. Macleay telegram, August 28, 1924, FO 371, F 2931/19/10.
43. Cyril Falls, *The Art of War from the Age of Napoleon to the Present Day* (New York: Oxford University Press, 1961), p. 159.
44. *Literary Digest*, October 3, 1924, 15–16.
45. *Tribuna* (Harbin), September 16, 1924. Translation in G. C. Hanson (American Consul, Harbin) to Secretary of State, September 23, 1924; in SD 893.00/5662. For Tokyo's fears, see also James L. Sheridan, *Chinese Warlord: The Career of Feng Yü-hsiang* (Stanford: Stanford University Press, 1966), pp. 140–1.

of direct Japanese military action was by no means assured, and it would in any case arouse the hostility of the other Washington Conference participants, with whom Japan had agreed "to respect the sovereignty, the independence and the territorial and administrative integrity of China."[46] Such considerations led the *Sacramento Union* to worry that if Japan should intervene, "The opening of a civil war in China might well presage the beginning of a world turmoil greater than that created by the World War."[47]

In spite of the substantial foreign economic and political interests in China, no Power was in fact eager to intervene. The whole rationale of the Washington Conference had been to put such intervention in the past. The Powers feared one another and understood that a new scramble for influence in China could be disastrous. They put their hope in law, diplomacy, and cooperation. As the war unfolded, the Powers limited their role to warning and pleading with the Chinese. There were formal notifications to the Chinese that violations of the treaty provisions that so far had kept foreign communities pretty well immune to Chinese warfare would bring down the gravest of consequences. But in the post–World War I period such threats carried less weight than they would have a decade earlier. Who really believed that any Power (except Japan) might care enough to commit large numbers of troops against Chinese forces? And even in Japan the popular mood was rather antimilitary, and there was no doubt about Shidehara's pacifistic convictions. So except for the journalists and attachés who accompanied the combatants, the foreigners hunkered down in their traditional sanctuaries, ready to let the storm rage around them.

46. Nine-Power Treaty, in *Conference on the Limitation of Armament, Washington, November 12, 1921–February 6, 1922* (Washington, D.C.: U.S. Government Printing Office, 1922), p. 1624.
47. *Literary Digest*, October 4, 1924, 15.

Infantry attack with air support near Shanghai, contemporary sketch. (From *JiangZhe zhanshi*. Shanghai: Hongwen tushuguan, 1924.)

(*Above*) Members of the Shanghai Scottish Volunteer Company guarding the boundary of the International Settlement, Shanghai, October 1924. (*The Sphere*, November 1, 1924, p. 126a; courtesy of the *Illustrated London News* Picture Library.)

(*Opposite, top*) The Chinese Parliament at Beijing, 1918. (Photo by Elmer L. Mattox; courtesy of the Hoover Institution, Stanford University.)

(*Opposite*) Shanghai's War Memorial, situated on the boundaries of the International Settlement and the French Concession. (From *Shanghai of To-day: A Souvenir Album of Fifty Vandyck Prints of "The Model Settlement,"* Introduction by O. M. Green, Editor of the North China Daily News, Second Edition: Enlarged. Shanghai: Kelly & Walsh Ltd., 1928.)

"The Old Firm," 1929. *Left to right*: Sir Miles Lampson (Britain); Comte de Martel (France); Willem Oudendijk (Netherlands); J. V. A. MacMurray (U.S.A.); Daniele Varè (Italy); only Yoshizawa is absent. (From William J. Oudendyk, *Ways and By-ways in Diplomacy*. London: Peter Davies, 1939, facing p. 352.)

Marshal Wu Peifu. (From Lawrence Impey, *The Chinese Army as a Military Force*. Third and enlarged edition. Tientsin: Tientsin Press, Ltd., 1926, frontispiece.)

Kenkichi Yoshizawa, Japanese minister to Beijing, with his wife
(1932). (From Kenkichi Yoshizawa. *Gaikō rokujū nen*. Tokyo: Jiyū
Ajiasha, 1959.)

General Zhang Zuolin, with his son Zhang Xueliang (*left*) and Brigadier-General W. D. Connor, U.S.A. (*Illustrated London News*, January 30, 1926; courtesy of the *Illustrated London News* Picture Library.)

3

Armament and tactics

As a rule, foreigners did not take fighting among the Chinese very seriously. Nevertheless, one was better safe than sorry, so as the crisis developed in the late summer of 1924, treaty-port residents took both routine – and not so routine – precautions. In Shanghai the Municipal Council declared a state of emergency on September 9.[1] A cordon was created around the city, and roads into the settlement were barricaded. The fear was not so much that the city would be invaded directly but, rather, that if Zhejiang should lose, thousands of its defeated troops might retreat back into the neutral territory.[2] The Shanghai Volunteer Corps was mobilized. Under the command of Colonel W. F. L. Gordon, it numbered 1,695 including reserves, with companies of Scots, Americans, Japanese, Portuguese, and Italians as well as Englishmen. They were armed with field howitzers, mountain guns, Lewis guns, six armored cars, and Vickers machine guns – all on loan from the British Army, and they would guard the city until October 24.[3]

In addition the council asked the Shanghai consular body to request landing parties from foreign warships off Shanghai. At the peak of the crisis these ships numbered thirty-one, with a total complement of more than 7,000 officers and men. There were three British, one American, two French, one Italian, and two Japanese cruisers, and gunboats from all of those Powers and Portugal as well. Among these were the American flagship *Isabel*, and the destroyers *Bori*, *Smith*, *Thompson*, *Tracey*, *John D. Edwards*, *Barker*, and *Whipple*; the British cruisers *Despatch* and *Durban*, and the gunboats *Bee* and *Cricket* of the celebrated "insect class," which

1. Municipal Council Proclamation, September 9, 1924. Cited in Anatoli M. Kotenev, *Shanghai: Its Municipality and the Chinese* (Shanghai: North-China Daily News & Herald, Ltd., 1927), p. 24.
2. Kotenev, *Shanghai: Its Municipality*, pp. 22–3.
3. H. G. W. Woodhead, ed. *The China Yearbook 1925–26* (Tientsin: Tientsin Press, 1925), 1207. (Hereafter cited as CYB with the year.)

patrolled China's inland waterways; and the French cruisers *Colmar* and *Jules Ferry*.[4] The naval landing party from this fleet totaled about 1,800 men. Similar precautions were taken in Tianjin.[5]

These preparations were more impressive than anything seen for some years. Nevertheless, they manifested an appraisal of Chinese warfare and military capacity that was fundamentally dismissive. At the level of policy, the assumption was that nothing that happened in a Chinese war could have much effect on anything of real importance – such as foreign interests. And at the level of operations, the assumption was that a few thousand disciplined and well-armed foreigners would be more than a match for any Chinese force. Both these views rested on a seemingly solid base: the fact of total Western military superiority nearly everywhere in the world for almost a century. But as the hostilities began around Shanghai, that base was already eroding. Chinese military capacities were growing in a way that fundamentally threatened Western dominance – although few, whether Chinese or foreigners, fully understood this fact or its implications.

Real war was considered a Western monopoly. Thus, just seven months before the fighting broke out around the city, on February 16, 1924, Shanghai had solemnly unveiled its war memorial. Placed on the Bund so as to be clearly visible from the harbor, it was "a beautiful piece of work, simple in construction and striking in general effect" representing the Angel of Victory with her hand upon the head of a little child, and bearing the inscription "*Ad mortuorum gloriam*." Of course it was a memorial to the European Great War, World War I.[6] In the minds of Shanghailanders and foreigners in general, that conflict defined war. The armed struggles of the Chinese, by contrast, were harder to name and received scarcely any notice, not to mention memorialization.

Chinese soldiers were simply not the genuine article. In 1925 a seemingly disbelieving British correspondent would describe some of Wu Peifu's men on maneuvers as moving "with the precision of real soldiers."[7] Chinese fighters seemed unmartial to Westerners; they were rarely threatening, often absurd. Foreigners could never accustom themselves, for example, to the way Chinese foot soldiers carried umbrellas into battle, although with intense sun and frequent downpours that made some sense. For Europeans this habit was simply confirmation of

4. Cunningham to Bell, September 3, 1924, SD 893.00/5561.
5. Kotenev, *Shanghai: Its Municipality*, p. 24.
6. F. L. Hawks Pott, *A Short History of Shanghai, Being an Account of the Growth and Development of the International Settlement* (Shanghai: Kelly and Walsh, Ltd., 1928), p. 275.
7. *The Sphere: The Empire's Illustrated Weekly*, July 11, 1925, p. 52.

what they had suspected all along. Chinese wars were poor jokes, a kind of "Celestial Opera Bouffe," in which, as a journalist put it in 1923, "one wonders whether one has not, somehow or other, fallen into the middle of a new Gilbert and Sullivan opera where presently the painted general will elope with the painted Mimi, and the soldiers will all march in with parasols over their heads and sing the chorus."[8]

The stereotype of Chinese warfare as farce was a powerful one, compounded partly from the contempt Europeans anywhere in the world felt at the time for "native" martiality, partly from Europe's own tradition of ridiculing warfare in genuine comic operas such as Jacques Offenbach's (1813–90) *La Grande Duchesse de Gérolstein* (1867).[9] As the various Chinese mobilizations got underway in the autumn of 1924 such stereotypes, rather than the memory of European war, framed initial reporting and reaction. The *China Weekly Review* would recall how in August and September, "Old time foreign residents of Shanghai had joked at first about the 1924 Chinese war preparations. They hoped both sides were well equipped with umbrellas, and only feared that the Jiangsu forces facing Shanghai would fire so high over the Zhejiang line that the bullets would fall into Shanghai as they did during the revolution, a dozen years ago." It was "confidently believed that one side or the other would retreat before fighting started, in consideration of a round sum for the commander, and a matter of $10 Mex. or so apiece for the soldiers."

The war shattered these stereotypes. As the *Review* added, "their dope was upset." There was "sufficient seriousness to the Zhejiang–Jiangsu scrap for even the veterans of the late European show-down to call it a war."[10] Something had happened since the time a decade or two earlier when a handful of well-equipped foreign soldiers had been more than a match for any number of "natives."

In the autumn of 1924 it was no longer possible to dismiss the armed forces at China's disposal. The Chinese Army itself was large and although by no means uniformly good, contained enough well-trained and well-equipped units to wage serious war. The oft-repeated adage that good iron was not made into nails, nor good men into soldiers, was only partially true. The fighting would show that there were plenty of

8. Ethel Andrews Murphy, "Celestial Opera Bouffe," *Travel Magazine* (Floral Park, N.Y.), 40 (April 1923), 15.
9. It portrayed "the amorous Grand Duchess of a joke German principality, embarking on a pointless war because its Chancellor, Baron Puck, needed a diversion. Its forces were led by a joke German general called Boum, as incapable as he was fearless, who invigorated himself with the smell of gunpowder by periodically firing off his pistol into the air." Alistair Horne, *The Fall of Paris: The Siege and the Commune, 1870–1871* (Harmondsworth, England: Penguin, 1981), pp. 27–8.
10. "This War," CWR 30 (September 27, 1924), no. 4, 104.

good soldiers on all sides. Furthermore, Chinese forces were increasingly self-sufficient, even in relatively sophisticated armaments. One of the most damaging misconceptions about China – damaging because it blinds us to a major transformative force – is the belief that until recently its arms industry was small and technically unsophisticated. In fact, military modernization has been perhaps the single most important engine of change in China since the nineteenth century. Certainly it was during the period we are considering, and it has rarely yielded that role since.

By 1924 the army of the Chinese central government had grown to thirty-five divisions and twenty-seven mixed brigades, not including regional forces.[11] Adding the regional units and gendarmerie to all the forces from regular divisions under the control of the central government yields a total for men under arms in China in 1924 of roughly 1,404,000.[12] To be sure, some of these units were little better than rabble. But others, the products of the sustained modernization effort begun in the nineteenth century, were comparable to what were found in European armies of the time.

By 1924, moreover, Chinese soldiers carried more than parasols. The entire Chinese Army was estimated to possess perhaps 1 million rifles, of which 80 percent were admittedly "antiquated, badly kept, or in poor condition."[13] Among European small arms commonly used were the Italian 6.5-mm Mannlicher–Carcano rifles and carbines, model 1891; the German model 1888 Commission rifle also known as the Mauser–Mannlicher model 88; the Mauser 6.8-mm rifle model 1918; and the Russian 7.62-mm Moisin–Nagant (or "Three Line Nagant") model 1891.[14] Japanese rifles were also widely used: the 7.9-mm rifles of the years 1887, 1889, 1895, and 1902, which were basically variations on the

11. He Xiya, "Jiazi dazhanhou quanguo jundui zhi diaocha," DZ 22.1 (1925), 102–12.
12. CYB, 1925, p. 1193.
13. CYB, 1924, p. 922.
14. For the Italian 6.5-mm Mannlicher–Carcano, model 1891, see William G. Dooly, Jr. *Great Weapons of World War I* (New York: Walker, 1969), p. 118; also George B. Johnson and Hans Bert Lockhoven, *International Armament With History, Data, Technical Information and Photographs of Over 400 Weapons* (Cologne: International Small Arms Publishers, 1965), vol. 1, pp. 317–24 [I have not seen these pages; they have been sliced out of Princeton's copy]; for the Mauser–Mannlicher Model 88, see Johnson and Lockhoven, pp. 291–6. About the 6.8-mm Mauser I am unclear: Zhongguo junshishi bianxiezu, ed. *Zhongguo junshishi*, juan 1, *bingqi* (Beijing: Jiefangjun chubanshe, 1983), p. 212, states that it was based on a 1904 Mauser model as yet unidentified. It would be tempting to identify it with the Model 1898 Mauser, which was "one of the most successful rifles in the history of firearms," used with variations in Europe well after World War I and manufactured in China, but that was a 7.9-mm weapon. See Johnson and Lockhoven, *International Armament*, vol. 1, pp. 386–403; for the Moisin–Nagant see Dooly, *Great Weapons*, p. 118. List is from CYB, 1924, p. 922.

7.9-mm Mauser rifle; also the so-called Arisaka rifles of 1897 and 1905. Named for the Japanese colonel who developed them, these were variations on the Mauser model 1893, but of 6.5-mm caliber, which remained standard in Japanese forces through World War II.[15] Among officers, bodyguards, and police, the German Parabellum (Lüger) 9-mm automatic pistol was the weapon of choice; the powerful American Browning–Colt .45-caliber automatic, "the most effective in the war," was scarce in China (as it had been, owing to production problems, among American troops in World War I as well).[16]

As for other guns, in 1923 the number of machine guns in China was estimated at 1,394; a year later the number was probably much greater, for this weapon, which had proved so decisive in colonial warfare, was very popular. The models used were in some cases obsolete: they included the original Maxim gun (introduced in 1889), the air-cooled and gas-operated Hotchkiss heavy machine gun, also useful against aircraft, the "German Pack," the "Rex," and the Japanese air-cooled gun, as well as more modern guns.[17] Among artillery, the most popular model was the Krupp 75-mm gun. The Gruson 57- and 75-mm guns, the Arisaka 75-mm gun, the Schneider–Creusot 75-mm gun, and the Hotchkiss 37-mm gun were also widely employed. Coastal artillery, almost all of Krupp manufacture, was in most cases thirty to thirty-five years old, and ranged in caliber up to the 10-inch guns below Fuzhou on the Min River. Although obsolete, many of these weapons were "known to be in good condition and have adequate supplies of fresh ammunition."[18]

Many of these weapons, as will be seen below, had been purchased abroad, often through the agency of the "sewing-machine salesmen" [arms merchants] ubiquitous at the time. But many were also of Chinese manufacture. Since the nineteenth century China's military had been rapidly modernizing itself, and by 1924 the process that William H. McNeill calls "the industrialization of warfare" had transformed fighting in China as well. It was no less than a military revolution: one that created an entirely new kind of war, and one that would have profound effects both on the Chinese combatants and on the Powers.[19]

15. Johnson and Lockhoven, *International Armament*, vol. 1, pp. 421–3.
16. CYB, 1924, p. 922; see also Johnson and Lockhoven, *International Armament*, pp. 81–92, 123–9; Dooly, *Great Weapons of World War I*, p. 114.
17. CYB, 1924, p. 922; Dooly, *Great Weapons*, pp. 73–6 for the Maxim gun, pp. 84–5 for the Hotchkiss.
18. CYB, 1924, pp. 922–3.
19. William H. McNeill, *The Pursuit of Power: Technology, Armed Force, and Society since A.D. 1000* (Chicago: The University of Chicago Press, 1982), 223 ff. The phrase "military revolution" was first used by Professor Michael Roberts in 1955 to describe changes in Europe during the period from 1560 to 1660. For a review see Geoffrey Parker, *The*

As in Europe, this military revolution had a number of manifestations. There was the rapid improvement of weapons, with consequent changes in strategy and tactics and, above all, the great increase in the power of the military in comparison with the rest of society. The Chinese always recognized that modernization had been forced on them in the first instance by gunfire, and military reform received a high priority.[20]

By 1924 China's modern military had developed substantially, building on reforms of the late Qing and first decade of Republican rule. The nominal strength of each of the thirty-five divisions in the Chinese Army in that year was 12,512 officers and men, but some were larger. Two such were Wu Peifu's 3rd and Feng Yuxiang's 11th Divisions, which probably exceeded 15,000 men each. A standard division consisted of two infantry brigades of two regiments each; one cavalry regiment of three battalions; one artillery regiment of three battalions, each having eighteen guns; one company of engineers; one transport company; four or more companies of machine guns, having from four to six guns each; military police; a sanitary detachment, a field hospital, and a band (consisting of twenty musicians and twenty-four apprentices). The authorized strengths were 748 officers, 10,436 enlisted men, and 1,328 coolies and camp followers. A mixed brigade [*hunchenglü*] consisted of two infantry regiments, one battalion of cavalry, one battalion of artillery, one company of engineers, one company of transport, and one or more companies of machine guns, while a mixed regiment [*hunchengtuan*] consisted of one regiment of infantry, one cavalry company, one artillery company, one or more companies of machine guns, and small artillery and transport detachments.[21]

To equip these increasingly modern forces, China developed its own military-industrial complex. The first modern arsenals and dockyards in China were established in the 1860s. The Qing built its first arsenals at Anqing, Shanghai, Nanjing and Fuzhou; others were later created at Hanyang in Hubei and at Dezhou in Shandong.[22] Nearly every provincial capital also had a factory of one sort or another able to turn out limited quantities of weapons and ammunition and there existed, in addition, numerous so-called arsenals, some of them workshops "little better than blacksmith's shops"; 134 in Sichuan alone according to one report.[23]

Military Revolution: Military Innovation and the Rise of the West, 1500–1800 (Cambridge, England: Cambridge University Press, 1988), pp. 1–44.
20. Monlin Chiang [Jiang Menglin], *Tides from the West* (New Haven: Yale University Press, 1947; Taipei: China Academy, 1974), pp. 3–4.
21. CYB, 1924, 920–1.
22. Zhongguo junshishi bianxiezu, ed., *bingqi*, pp. 208–10.
23. CYB, 1921–2, 532.

Constructing and operating these arsenals required Chinese to cope with modern knowledge, and therefore to change. The armament industry demanded complex organization, high levels of both technical knowledge and production skills, and mastery of modern machinery. Intricate procedures had to be carried out faultlessly and quality strictly maintained; high explosives, for example, were not forgiving of errors in preparation and handling. Driven by the demands of war, China had made substantial progress in all of these areas by the 1920s and had laid the foundation for the subsequent advances in military production of the 1930s under the Nationalists, and the 1950s and 1980s under the Communists.

In perhaps the best foreign survey of the topic for the 1920s, the U.S. military attaché, John Magruder (1887–1958), reported in 1927 that there were twenty major arsenals in China, in locations ranging from Hainan Island to Mukden. These had provided China with considerable military self-sufficiency. Seventy-nine hundred muzzle-loading, 11-mm-caliber Mausers had been turned out at the Jiangnan arsenal by 1871, when production was shifted to Remington breech-loading rifles at a rate of about twelve per day.[24] By the 1920s a wide variety of rifles was being manufactured in China. All were five-shot repeating models: by far the most widely produced and used was the 7.9-mm Mauser, manufactured at Hanyang. A 6.5-mm Japanese rifle, model 38, was made in Shanxi, but not widely used; a 6.8-mm rifle based on the 1904 Mauser was produced from 1912 to 1919 at Guangdong and Sichuan. In 1915 the Hanyang arsenal produced a 7.9-mm Mauser-type automatic rifle, but this was never put into full-scale production.[25] The first pistol manufactured in China was in 1913.[26]

The Chinese began developing light and heavy machine guns in the late Qing, but these went into mass production only after 1914. Between 1915 and 1924 Chinese-produced light machine guns included the Hotchkiss 9-mm model, the French Chauchat 8-mm gun, and a Japanese model 11 6.5-mm gun.[27] Chinese-made heavy machine guns were both air- and water-cooled. The air-cooled No. 13 machine gun was modeled on the Japanese type 3, while the water-cooled guns included versions of

24. Thomas L. Kennedy, *The Arms of Kiangnan: Modernization in the Chinese Ordnance Industry, 1860–1895* (Boulder, Colo.: Westview Press, 1978), pp. 64–5.
25. *Bingqi*, p. 212; CYB, 1924, 922, states that the Mauser–Mannlicher Model 88 was manufactured at the Hanyang and Guangzhou arsenals, and the Mauser 6.80mm at Hanyang, Guangzhou, Shanghai, and Henan.
26. Liu Xiangke, ed. *Zhongguo junshi zhi zuijianshuo* (Jinan: Shandong renmin chubanshe, 1989), p. 181; *bingqi*, p. 212.
27. *Bingqi*, p. 212. For the Hotchkiss gun, see Johnson and Lockhoven, *Internationae Armament*, vol. 2, pp. 416–23; for the Chauchat, ibid., pp. 275–81.

the Austrian 9.8-mm Schwartzlose machine gun, the Browning 1917 model, and the Maxim gun.[28] A Thompson-type submachine gun was manufactured in China in 1923.[29]

Artillery was also manufactured in the late Qing. A 75-mm Krupp-type artillery piece was first built, using Chinese steel, in Shanghai in 1905; later, Shanghai turned out mountain guns as well until 1920, as versions of the Krupp 75-mm gun. After 1920 Shanxi, Hanyang, and Mukden also produced copies of the Japanese model 38 75-mm gun and the model 6 75-mm mountain gun. In 1925 the Mukden Arsenal (detailed consideration of which will follow shortly) began to produce Austrian-type 77-mm and 105-mm cannon, Japanese-type 105-mm cannon, and a 150-mm howitzer. Mukden also produced a 37-mm antitank gun and a 75-mm antiaircraft gun. Both light and heavy mortars began to be manufactured in 1923: initially 82-mm, 76-mm, 57-mm, and 47-mm light models (later reduced to the 82-mm alone) and the heavy 150-mm mortar.[30]

Such guns required ammunition. The black powder needed for the Remingtons and other early rifles was manufactured at Longhua in Shanghai beginning in 1874. China first produced smokeless powder there as well – some 2,470,000 pounds per year – beginning in 1895, only nine years after it was first invented in France.[31] By 1922 China was manufacturing three kinds of high explosive: yellow powder, TNT, and nitroglycerine. The same year saw the first manufacture of hand grenades, initially of five different types, in China. At the same time 30-, 40-, 60-, and 120-pound high-explosive aerial bombs began to be produced.[32]

Balloons were used for military observation in the late Qing. China produced her own first airplane in 1910, and in 1913 the first Beijing government aviation school was established. The Nanyuan aviation complex was set up the following year, and at least one aircraft was produced there. In 1922 the Guangzhou administration created its own aircraft factory. In the 1920s the Fengtian, Shanxi, Jiangsu, Shandong, and Yunnan provincial military groups all imported airplanes, soon bringing the number of military aircraft in China to between 200 and 300. With these came antiaircraft guns. China also began to import and experiment with armored cars and light tanks.[33]

28. *Bingqi*, 212–13; for the Japanese type 3, see Johnson and Lockhoven, *International Armament*, vol. 2, pp. 452–1; for the Schwartzlose gun, ibid., pp. 424–30; for the Maxim, ibid., pp. 384–98.
29. Liu Xiangke, ed., *Zhongguo junshi zhi zuijianshuo*, p. 181.
30. Ibid., *bingqi*, p. 213.
31. Liu Xiangke, 180; Kennedy, *The Arms of Kiangnan*, pp. 64, 206.
32. Liu Xianke, p. 180; *bingqi*, p. 213.
33. *Bingqi*, pp. 212–13.

Such rapid development of military industry would not have been possible without an increasingly modern industrial base and knowledge and technical skills far beyond what most people instinctively imagine China possessed at this time. Although little studied, the rapid military modernization of the 1910s and the 1920s was clearly a development of cardinal importance.

Both the Zhili and Fengtian groups drew upon the new military-industrial complex. Zhang Zuolin depended on the main arsenal and a separate trench mortar works in Mukden, as well as on two arsenals in Jinan, while Wu Peifu manufactured weapons at the Hanyang, Jiangnan, Gongxian, and Beiyang arsenals.[34] The competition to develop arsenals accelerated the arms race already under way in China. In 1924 the Fengtian arsenals were superior technically to those controlled by the Zhili group; indeed, they were surpassed only when the Kuomintang began arming itself with Soviet assistance.

The arms race between Zhili and Fengtian had begun in earnest with the Zhili victory in the war of 1922. As soon as the war was over, the Old Marshal Zhang Zuolin focused attention on reorganizing his army. He purged his command and was reported to have employed former Russian officers, of whom there were hundreds in Harbin, to train his artillery, and Japanese as well.[35] And Zhang Zuolin imported weapons from Denmark, Japan, the United States, Germany, and Italy.[36]

The Old Marshal had no desire to be dependent on outside sources of supply, so he placed particular emphasis on armament production. Shortly after taking control of Manchuria, Zhang decided to reorganize the old Fengtian military machinery factory [*Fengtian junxiechang*] into an arsenal. Because the factory's site was so small, it was decided in 1919 to take over the land just outside the city wall used by the Eastern Pagoda Agricultural Experiment Station [*Dongta nongye shiyanchang*] and devote it to the new Three Provinces Arsenal [*Dongsansheng binggongchang*]. The head of the old machinery factory, Tao Zhiping, was initially put in charge of the project. Construction began at once on engineering works and a smokeless powder plant; these were followed by shops to produce rifle ammunition and rifles, and by administrative offices. A Danish firm (Wen De, i.e., Nielsen and Winther of Copenhagen) provided the initial

34. The others were Guangzhou (large and small), Fuzhou, Taiyuan, Nanjing, Kaifeng, Nanchang, Hainan, Zhangjiakou, Chengdu, Changsha, and Kunming. See Report No. 7082, June 30, 1927, in MIR.
35. "Report: Quotations form Reports in Criticism of Various Points in the Chihli–Fengtien Fight of 1922. August 14, 1922, 5, in MIR.
36. Gavan McCormack, *Chang Tso-lin in Northeast China, 1911–1928: China, Japan, and the Manchurian Ideal* (Folkestone, Kent, England: Dawson & Sons, 1977), 107.

equipment. It was an ambitious undertaking: the arsenal sought to create expertise with little regard for cost; it had its own training programs for employees, a printing plant, housing for workers, and its own hospital, as well as an elaborate administrative structure.

The arsenal employed some 20,000 workers, who appeared "to be well trained and industrious." Most of the mechanics came from Jiangsu and Zhejiang, some from Guangdong. Few Northerners appeared to have the required skills, though the arsenal ran classes for heads of departments and foremen. There were also perhaps 100 foreigners. Swedes helped with explosives, and in 1927 a German gas expert was on hand, presumably to help with the installation of a German chemical and gas plant. As for equipment, some British, American, and French machinery was in use at the arsenal, but the majority was Japanese, Danish, German, and Austrian, in roughly that order.[37]

Zhang regularly entrusted control of the arsenal to his closest confidants. When Tao resigned in 1923 he was replaced by Han Linchun (1888–1930), who was superseded in turn by Yang Yuting (1886–1929) in 1924. These directors continued ambitious expansion. In 1923 artillery shell production was added, and work was begun on an electrical generating plant to serve the workshops; Yang Yuting expanded the arsenal even more in 1924. All of this was extremely expensive. Building the arsenal cost something on the order of 300 million silver yuan, not including the Japanese-equipped rifle ammunition factory whose cost of 900,000 yuan was paid personally by Zhang Zuolin. Monthly operating expenses were about 2 million yuan, of which salaries accounted for 500,000.[38]

By the mid-1920s the main arsenal occupied nearly five square miles. John Magruder estimated that it produced about forty per day of the Japanese modified 7.9-mm Mauser rifle, the so-called Arisaka rifle, to which Zhang Zuolin's forces were gradually standardizing, and 400,000 rounds per day of ammunition to fit, as well as ammunition to fit the Russian rifles also widely employed. The Arisaka rifle, as mentioned above, was derived from the same series that produced the 1898 7.92-mm Mauser used by the German Army through World War I; the Japanese made it lighter, shorter, of smaller caliber, and with less range

37. See Shen Zhenrong, "Dong sansheng binggongchang," *Liaoning wenshi ziliao*, No. 8 (Shenyang: Liaoning renmin chubanshe, 1984), pp. 51–2; for Nielsen and Winther, see Anthony B. Chan, *Arming the Chinese: The Western Armaments Trade in Warlord China, 1920–1928* (Vancouver: University of British Columbia Press, 1982), pp. 89–90; "Capacity and Product of Main Arsenal, Mukden," U.S. Military Attaché report no. 5913, July 29, 1926; "The Mukden Arsenal,": U.S. Military Intelligence Report No. 4410, December 6, 1927, in MIR.
38. Shen, "Dong sansheng binggongchang," pp. 50, 55.

than its German equivalent. The 1905 version was standard in the Japanese Army through World War II.[39] The arsenal also produced field guns: about eight per month of a modern postwar Austrian 77-mm gun which fired very rapidly and was highly accurate and lightweight; also the 37-mm infantry howitzer which was also an antitank gun, at a rate of about thirty per month; and 37-mm and 75-mm combined field and mountain howitzers, 105-mm and 150-mm guns, at a rate of about 200 per year. About 1,200 to 1,300 artillery shells were produced each day. Mills-type hand grenades were produced in large numbers: these were variants on the British No. 5 grenade, introduced in 1915, the progenitor of a whole series up to the 36M grenade, which was standard in World War II, and the prototypical time-fused fragmentation bomb with cast-iron body, brass or zinc alloy fittings, finger lever, and safety pin; also 16-pound incendiary and 100-pound high-explosive bombs. Japanese modified Maxim guns were also thought to be produced either at the arsenal or at a separate workshop in Mukden city. Experimentation with poison gas shells was also underway, though none had yet been produced.[40]

At the time of the Second Zhili–Fengtian War the Mukden arsenal reached its highest capacity. The 300,000 rounds per day it produced in ordinary times were not enough, and it proved possible to raise the output to 400,000.[41] In early September Zhang ordered the arsenal to work thirteen hours per day. Cartridge production rose to between 700,000 and 800,000 per day; aerial bombs and fragmentation grenades were also produced in quantity. New machinery for field gun manufacture was imported from Germany. As the crisis grew worse in late September, Zhang ordered the arsenal to work around the clock, including holidays and weekends. Foreign and Chinese technicians received triple payment while ordinary workers received double for this overtime.[42] Zhang apparently hired many new personnel: according to one report 1,516 foreigners – mostly Russians and Germans, though the British were still in charge of casting. Daily cartridge production reached 800,000.[43]

Located at the Great North Camp outside the city was another installation just as important as the main arsenal. This was the Mukden Stokes Mortar and Ammunition Factory. The Stokes mortar is often reckoned one of three decisive weapons in World War I (the machine

39. Johnson and Lockhoven, *International Armament*, p. 421.
40. "Capacity and Product of Main Arsenal, Mukden," U.S. Military Attaché report No. 5913, July 29, 1926; "The Mukden Arsenal," U.S. Military Intelligence Report No. 4410, December 6, 1927, in MIR.
41. Shen, "binggongchang," 55.
42. CB, September 24, 1924, 2.
43. CB, September 25, 1924, 2.

gun and the tank are the other two) that Lloyd George's Ministry of Munitions saved from being pigeonholed by the bureaucrats of the War Office.[44] Mortars are short pieces of ordnance with a very wide, smooth bore which were first used in sieges because of their power to develop high-angle fire. In their early forms they were heavy and difficult to move. The Stokes mortar, however, was light and portable, and fired a variety of finned shells (high explosive, smoke, illuminating, etc.). It proved invaluable against machine-gun emplacements and other targets not easily destroyed by rifle fire, serving in effect as the infantry's own easily portable artillery.

Part of the success of the 3-inch Stokes mortar (which with variants continued to be used into World War II) was owed to improvements made by "General" Frank ("One-Arm") Sutton (1884–1944), an old Etonian and veteran of Gallipoli, who made a fortune as an arms smuggler and consultant in China.[45] Having obtained rights to the manufacture of the Stokes gun in North America and the Far East, Sutton eventually arrived at Wu Peifu's headquarters with a sample mortar and a variety of explosive and tear gas shells. Failing to reach terms with Wu, who deeply distrusted foreigners, Sutton had turned to Mukden where, with the support of the Old Marshal's son Zhang Xueliang, he landed a contract to produce 600 of his mortars and 60,000 projectiles, for a total of (U.S.) $125,000. The result was the Mukden Stokes Mortar and Ammunition Factory, by all accounts a first-class operation. "During my nineteen years in China," wrote a "reliable source" in 1923, "I have visited all workshops of any importance including those connected with the various railways, shipyards and general engineering works, but nowhere have I seen a plant so excellently kept and managed."[46]

Sutton also played a role in Zhang Zuolin's urgent program of long-term expansion. Priorities were set: the first was to develop the capacity to produce 200,000 rounds per day of rifle ammunition by the summer of 1924; next came production of rifles, light machine guns, heavy machine guns and hand grenades; and then a version of the long-tested 3-inch Stokes mortar, which Sutton intended to make the backbone of the Fengtian Army's firepower. An 8-inch mortar, designed as a "morale booster," was also produced in limited numbers, while heavy artillery was given low priority. A mountain gun that threw an 8-pound shell and could easily be broken down for mule or pack-horse transport was

44. Dooly, *Great Weapons of World War I*, p. 83.
45. The only study of Sutton is a popular one: Drage, *General of Fortune*, cited above.
46. "Stokes Mortar and Ammunition Factory – Mukden" Report No. 5206, November 20, 1923, in MIR; also Drage, *General of Fortune*, pp. 131–3, 170 ff.

another Sutton innovation; indeed, this slightly mad Englishman turned his attention to "every minor military requirement, from entrenching tools to field telephones." To work on aircraft, which Zhang desperately needed to counter Wu Peifu's maritime power, Sutton rounded up two more adventurers, an Englishman named Talbot-Lehman and a New Zealander of Scottish extraction called Mackenzie.

Soon all were involved in a major smuggling operation – what Sutton liked to call "the importation of special merchandise" – through Shandong ports, and under the dogged surveillance of the Chinese Maritime Customs Service, Preventive Branch. This intelligence organization, staffed largely by "efficient and absolutely incorruptible" Europeans, many of them British, was charged with enforcing the arms embargo.[47]

Smuggling was routed through Shandong because ports there were less closely watched than either Shanghai or those on the Manchurian coast. Shandong, however, was neutral or contested as the war began, although much of it would eventually come under the control of Zhang Zongchang (1881–1932), a member of the Fengtian group, including control of two of the province's arsenals, both in Jinan. The larger had old German and English equipment and about 1,500 employees. It produced about 2 million rounds of rifle ammunition per month and ten to fifteen trench mortar bombs per day. Certain raw materials were supplied by Zhang Zuolin, who imported the most important one, TNT, from the Norwegian firm of Nielsen. The smaller arsenal had old equipment moved from the arsenal at Dezhou. Employing only about 300 men, with foremen and watchmen all being White Russians, this arsenal produced 2,000 to 3,000 hand grenades of the Mills type per month, as well as airplane bombs and rifle grenades. A small powder factory was located near the arsenal.[48] Also in Shandong, the Dezhou arsenal coped with the demands of the war crisis by hiring 120 additional workers for a night shift, and buying 100,000 *jin* [one *jin* equals 0.5 kilograms] of niter from Tianjin, and 100,000 *jin* of sulphur from Qingdao. This arsenal also produced machine guns.[49] Other arsenals apparently got started as the war crisis began to develop – preparation for the establishment of one in Heilongjiang was reported in July.[50] Such were the primary sources of armament for the Fengtian group.

Compared to this, the Zhili military-industrial base was weak. It centered on a great industrial complex in what is today the city of

47. Drage, *General of Fortune*, pp. 174, 183, 137.
48. "Arsenals," Report No. 7082, June 30, 1927, in MIR.
49. CB, September 8, 1924, 3; CB, October 8, 1924, 5.
50. CB, July 1, 1924, 2.

Wuhan. The Hanyang Iron and Steel Works spread over 107 acres of land with a long frontage on both the Han and Yangzi rivers. With its four blast furnaces (two of British and two of German construction) the works produced 400 tons of steel per day, most of which was used for rails. To the west, however, lay the Hanyang arsenal, in 1924 under the direction of Yang Wenkai. This facility could produce 80,000 cartridges and 120 Mauser-type rifles per day, also four Maxim guns per month.[51] Earlier it had also produced Krupp field and mountain guns, but in 1919 the government had stopped making the latter, laying off all but fifty of the 200 workers originally employed to do so, and sending the machinery to the Gongxian arsenal.[52] Hanyang arsenal's older equipment was of German manufacture; the newer had been provided by Pratt and Whitney to Yuan Shikai in 1914. The arsenal produced smokeless powder as well, and had "well equipped chemical and mechanical laboratories" as well as a school for apprentices.[53]

When fighting began in the Northeast, Wu Peifu moved to increase the arsenal's capacity. New workers were hired and operations were carried on day and night. Production rose to 100,000 cartridges and 200 rifles per day. Wu also ordered that it produce fifty field guns, upon which work was begun.[54] Wu ordered that three quarters of this output be sent to Beijing, and the remainder to Jiangsu.[55] By mid-October the arsenal's production had risen to 200,000 cartridges and 400 rifles per day, sufficient to maintain three divisions.[56]

In addition to ordinary rifles and ammunition, the Hanyang arsenal produced light machine guns based on a German model, and an anti-aircraft gun. Dozens of the machine guns were shipped, and on October 17 four antiaircraft guns were sent to Beijing. These were reported to be smaller than field guns but with longer barrels. At Wu's order, the mountain-gun equipment was also moved back from Gongxian, and production was begun at the rate of one per month. The Hubei *dujun* Xiao Yaonan (1877–1926) also contributed 100,000 dollars (Chinese) to this project. By the end of the third week in October the Hanyang arsenal's adjusted production was 120,000 cartridges, 205 rifles, 12 machine guns, and 200 pistols.[57]

As for the arsenal at Gongxian in Henan, about thirty-five miles west of Zhengzhou, which Wu also controlled: It had been built by Yuan Shikai, so its equipment, provided originally by Pratt and Whitney, was about a dozen years old. Twenty workmen under the supervision of two

51. Ibid.   52. CB, October 18, 1924, 5.
53. "Arsenals," Report No. 7082, June 30, 1927, in MIR.
54. CB, September 24, 1924, 2.   55. CB, October 4, 1924, 2.
56. CB, October 14, 1924, 4.   57. CB, October 18, 1924, 5.

foreign-educated Chinese engineers produced ammunition there for mountain howitzers and 75-mm guns.[58] Wu had upgraded both facilities. In February 1922 equipment for the Gongxian arsenal arrived from Niles, Bement, and Dord of New York via Arnhold Karberg and Co. and Carlowitz and Co. in Shanghai, and in April of the same year Wu employed two French engineers to inspect the arsenals, with a view to beginning the manufacture of airplanes.[59] When war broke out, Wu ordered the Gongxian arsenal to work day and night producing ammunition. Rifle ammunition, however, was the Hanyang arsenal's specialty; Gongxian had specialized in artillery and artillery shells. So new machines had to be moved from Hanyang to Gongxian before cartridge production could begin. Twelve boxes of such machines were sent via Zhengzhou on the Beijing–Hankou railway on October 4, 1924.[60]

Other less important arsenals should also be noted. Perhaps the most important of these was the Jiangnan arsenal in Shanghai, located near the Longhua station on a spur of the Shanghai–Hangzhou railway leading to the Shanghai South Station. This arsenal, with old German equipment, was capable of producing 50,000 rifle cartridges per day, as well as the 1898 German Snyder rifle. Between 1919 and 1920 it had manufactured a total of about 100 Krupp field guns of unknown calibers. It employed about 1,000 workers. The Beiyang arsenal in Tianjin, located near the military commander's headquarters and supervised for many years by Colonel Zhang Mengling, produced bayonets and spare parts for rifles. It could repair 300 to 400 rifles and ten machine guns per month, as well as artillery and Stokes mortars. It employed some 500 workers.[61] In August of 1924 it was reported that Liu Cunhou (1885–1960) had begun to build an arsenal in Shaanxi despite opposition from Hu Jingyi. Machines for the arsenal would arrive from Hankou from July to November.[62] The Jiangxi *dujun* Cai Chengxun (1873–1946) also applied for and received permission to build an arsenal. Machinery came from Shanghai, and a German engineer was hired to take charge of production.[63] There was also an arsenal at Kaifeng, which Soviet military intelligence reported in November 1925 was able to produce 61,500 cartridges per day for German Mausers and Japanese rifles. It could also produce 140 to 150 German Mausers per month and repair five to six machine guns, as well as artillery. It employed about 1,150. In the

58. Ibid.
59. Chan, *Arming the Chinese*, p. 97.
60. CB, October 5, 1924, 5.
61. "Arsenals," Report No. 7082, June 30, 1927, in MIR.
62. CB, August 16, 1924, 4; CB, August 22, 1924, 4.
63. CB, September 20, 1924, 5.

railway shops at Kalgan [Zhangjiakou] arms manufacture was also carried on. Ten thousand rounds of rifle ammunition and twelve artillery shells, as well as several hundred hand grenades, were its daily quota. By 1925 Russians were thought to be involved there in explosives work.[64]

Taken in sum, China had developed a rather impressive military-industrial complex with considerable speed. It was not entirely self-sufficient. Although Sutton in Manchuria was impressed by the relative abundance of necessary materials in Mukden, certain key items still had to be imported: copper, phosphorus, percussion caps from Andong, TNT from Japan and Norway, ballistite from Norway, and some unfinished mortar barrels (labeled "hydraulic tubes" on ships' manifests) from Shanghai and England. Zhili was even less self-sufficient. Supply lines furthermore crossed and crisscrossed. The Hanyang Iron and Steel Works, which was Zhili's most important supplier, got its coal from Shandong, Manchuria, and Japan. Hanyang No. 1 pig iron, in return, provided 65 percent of the input for Sutton's Stokes mortar plant.[65] Nevertheless, by the summer of 1924, both the Zhili and the Fengtian forces had established strong and reasonably modern weapons manufacturing capabilities, which made it possible for them to support warfare of the early World War I–type independent of foreign suppliers.

Nevertheless, both also had to turn to the international arms market. The Powers were sufficiently worried about this possibility to impose a comprehensive arms embargo on China on May 5, 1919. But with World War I surplus weapons worth about £1,000 million in Britain alone, the incentives to break the embargo were strong. Initially the embargo seemed to have limited to some extent the Chinese military leaders' access to weapons and, therefore, the scale of warfare. But in the long run it may have proved destabilizing, adding urgency to China's desire to build up its own military manufacturing base, and driving contenders for power there into the arms of the countries (particularly Japan and then the USSR) willing to violate the embargo's provisions.[66]

Before the embargo took effect in 1919, the Italians had delivered a consignment of more than 4,000 tons of war materiel to Wu Peifu, including 30,000 rifles and 3 million rounds of ammunition, six batteries (four guns each) of 75-mm field guns, and fifty Fiat machine guns. Its

64. "Arsenals," Report No. 7082, June 30, 1927, in MIR.
65. "The Hanyang Iron and Steel Works," Report No. 5897 July 23, 1926; "Stokes Mortar and Ammunition Factory – Mukden," Report No. 5206. November 20, 1923, in MIR.
66. Chan, *Arming the Chinese*, p. 60; Chen Cungong, *Lieqiang dui Zhongguo de junhou jinyun Minguo ba nian – shiba nian*. Zhongyang yanjiu yuan jindaishi yanjiusuo zhuankan 47 (Taibei: Zhongyang yanjiu yuan, 1983). The relevant documents are reproduced in Chen, 263–6; value of British surplus is in Chan, p. 61.

arrival at Tianjin in eighty rail wagons was closely monitored by British intelligence.[67] In the years immediately before fighting broke out in 1924, Wu imported far more. In August of 1922 an Italian intermediary had arranged Wu's further purchase of rifles, field and machine guns, and accompanying ammunition, valued at (U.S.) $5.6 million. An American named Stevens was instrumental in bringing rifles, machine guns, and ammunition from an American ship that docked at Vladivostok to Wu at Luoyang, labeled as "fish." In 1922 Cao Kun purchased ten airplanes from a French agent in Shanghai, while another American, James Slevin, was reported to be selling airplanes to Wu in February 1923. In the same month White Russians arriving in Shanghai sold heavy artillery pieces, machine guns, telegraph equipment, and rifles to Wu's agent. An Italian agent in Tianjin sold another $5.5 million worth of arms and ammunition to Cao Kun in 1923. In the spring of 1924, Wu Peifu bought 40,000 rifles, 50 million rounds of ammunition, several 7-cm cannon with 50,000 shells, and six machine guns, again through Italy.[68]

As war broke out, the contestants proudly exhibited up-to-date modern weapons in their inventories. For Lu Yongxiang these were twenty armored cars looking rather like trucks, with armor so strong that cannon fire could not pierce it, each mounting three machine guns. Lu procured twenty of these in knocked-down form from Shanghai. Six were assembled and three sent to the front at Huangdu on October 1; the rest were ordered assembled within two days.[69] In the second week of November, Zhang Zuolin mounted an exhibition of modern weaponry at his Tianjin headquarters, the Cao Family Garden [*Caojia huayuan*]. On display were aircraft, mortars, wire entanglements, and high-explosive bombs. Military experts were on hand to explain these weapons to interested visitors.[70] Zhang was also actively importing aircraft: twenty of the latest from France including two large bombers of a type considered advanced even there. A French steamer delivered fifteen of the latest French and Belgian artillery to Zhang. Both aircraft and cannon were so advanced that no Chinese understood how to use them; therefore they were accompanied by thirty machinists, technicians, and military officers from France, Belgium, Russia, and the Netherlands.[71]

67. Chan, *Arming the Chinese*, p. 98.
68. Ibid., pp. 97, 98–9; Ding Wenjiang, *Minguo junshi jinji*, 1926 (Tabei: Wenhai chuban-she, n.d.), vol. 1, p. 27, cited by Chan, 97, note 130.
69. CB, October 2, 1924, 2.
70. CB, November 16, 1924, 3.
71. CB, November 17, 1924, 2.

The development of modern armies and weapon-producing ability and the importation of the latest armaments, however important, were but contributors to a larger change that was transforming warfare in China. By the 1920s the railroads had created a new strategic landscape, and the growth in wealth of the treaty ports had brought into being a new set of strategic objectives. A network of rail lines linked Mukden to Beijing through Tianjin, while the far greater distance between them and Wuhan and Shanghai – the key cities of Central China – were covered by the north-to-south Beijing–Hankou and Tianjin–Pukou lines. Railroad bridges and junctions became new strategic key points; for example, the bridge where the Tianjin–Pukou line crossed the Yellow River, or the city of Zhengzhou twenty-three miles farther south, where the line intersected with the east–west Longhai railroad. Along these strategic arteries men and materiel could be moved as fast in China as in Europe, and battles for key points thus brought new peaks in intensity and destructiveness.

Away from the railways, the situation was totally different. China was bigger by an order of magnitude larger than any European country except Russia, as the distances testify. From Mukden to Beijing was about 400 miles; Beijing to Wuhan almost twice as far again; from Wuhan to Guangzhou roughly another 500 miles. The grand total is three times the distance from Paris to Berlin, and close to that from Berlin to Moscow. Most movement through this vast strategic battlefield was not by rail but by the traditional means: camel, pony, or horse cart.

So in effect, two distinct battlefields came into being in China: Where the railways ran, modern mobile war was possible, but elsewhere coolies bore munitions and materiel at walking speed, so campaigning could be no faster. The result was a way of fighting reminiscent of what had been seen outside the European theater in World War I (in Africa, for example). Armies having modern weapons, well-trained (usually European) officers, and mostly locally recruited ranks fought in an environment where railroads connected a few developed centers across hundreds of miles of jungle. It was, as Brigadier General Edmund Howard Gorges described it, a "new-fangled jumpy kind of ambuscade warfare."[72]

The eve of the conflicts of 1924, then, found warfare in China in the midst of a qualitative transformation, both in capabilities and battlefields. To be sure, the transformation was not yet by any means complete, but it had already rendered obsolete the caricatures of Chinese soldiery and

---

72. Byron Farwell, *The Great War in Africa 1914–1918* (New York and London: Norton, 1986), p. 60.

warfare then still current among foreigners. By the 1920s the Chinese were showing themselves remarkably effective in importing, producing, and employing the weapons that had earlier transformed European warfare. The Chinese armies mobilizing in 1924 had most of the basic modern equipment of World War I, from machine guns and artillery to field telephones and aircraft. They fought on a battlefield that was similarly modernized: with trench lines and rail junctions the key objectives. Yet at the same time their warfare was not exactly like the European, and for two related reasons. One was the scale of China. No matter how stalemated fighting might be at one place, the size of the country was such that some sort of flanking maneuver or surprise deployment was always possible – as had not been true on the European Western front. The other was the ubiquity of attempts at deception, subversion, and psychological manipulation. They of course existed in the West as well. In China they were far more important, both because the ratio of soldiers to territory and population was so much smaller there, and also because the possibility of success was so much higher. The players, after all, understood one another. They were all Chinese, and their differences were far less elemental than those between, for example, the French and the Germans. The sum total of these factors was a Chinese style of modern warfare that both the ancient Chinese master strategist Sun Zi (fl. ca. 500 B.C.) and the British commander in World War I, Field Marshal Haig (1861–1928), would have found at least partially familiar. Sun Zi would have recognized the manuever, the intrigue, and the calculation. Haig would have found little novel in the shuttling of troop trains, the interminable shelling back and forth over stalemated lines, or the streams of horribly wounded casualties. The combination, however, was something radically new for China. And like such revolutionary new forms of warfare elsewhere, its appearance had consequences that would extend far beyond the battlefield.

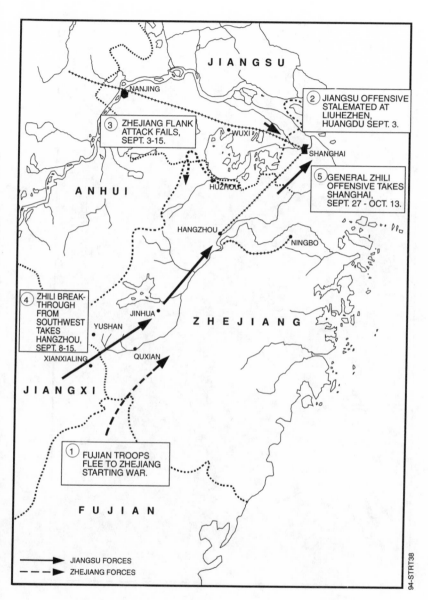

The Jiangsu–Zhejiang War (General)

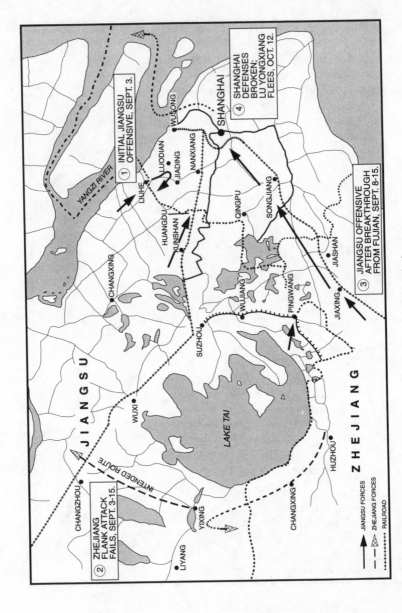

War in the Shanghai area

① INITIAL JIANGSU OFFENSIVE, SEPT. 3.

② ZHEJIANG FLANK ATTACK FAILS, SEPT. 3-15.

③ JIANGSU OFFENSIVE AFTER BREAKTHROUGH FROM FUJIAN, SEPT. 8-15.

④ SHANGHAI DEFENSES BROKEN; LU YONGXIANG FLEES, OCT. 12.

SHANGHAI

YANGZI RIVER

WUSONG
LUODIAN
JIADING
NANXIANG
LIUHE
HUANGDU
KUNSHAN
QINGPU
SONGJIANG
JIASHAN
JIAXING
PINGWANG
WUJIANG
SUZHOU
CHANGXING
WUXI

LAKE TAI

JIANGSU

ZHEJIANG

CHANGZHOU
INTENDED ROUTE
YIXING
LIYANG
HUZHOU
CHANGXING

JIANGSU FORCES
ZHEJIANG FORCES
RAILROAD

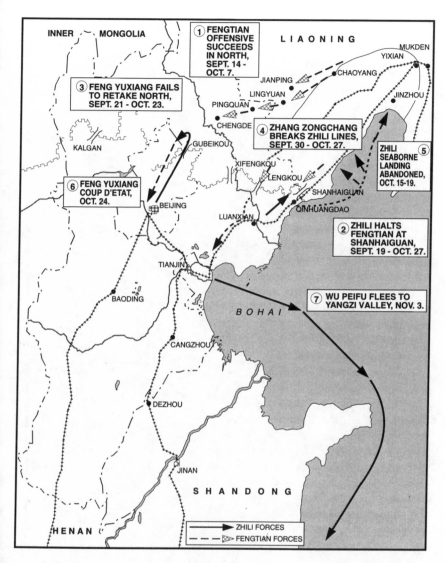

The Second Zhili–Fengtian War (General)

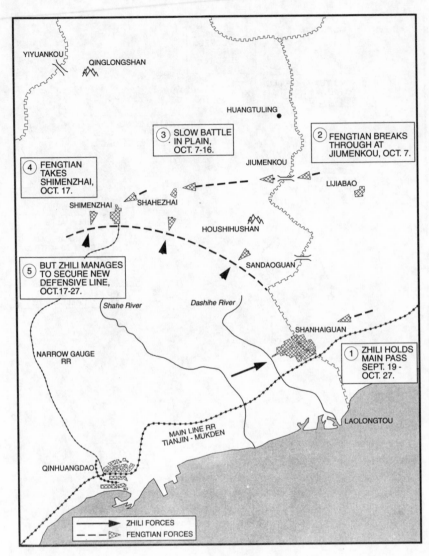

The Battle of Shanhaiguan

4

The war in the South

Jiangsu versus Zhejiang

The first of the wars of 1924 began at 10:00 A.M. on September 3 near the small railway depot at Huangdu just outside the Shanghai city limits. Jiangsu forces unleashed an artillery barrage; Zhejiang guns answered immediately; and the Jiangsu–Zhejiang War was under way.[1] This seemingly local conflict was linked potentially to the political struggle for China as a whole by the logic of power balance and alliance that we have already examined. Exactly how that possible larger role would take shape, however, depended on another and far narrower logic, which this chapter considers. This was the logic intrinsic to the actual fighting of war – the mysterious interplay of the factors of victory and defeat, including the wisdom of strategic choices, the weights of numbers and quality of equipment, and not least the imponderable fortuities of battle itself.

Even before the artillery barrages began, the military challenges facing Jiangsu and Zhejiang were very clear to all. Qi Xieyuan and the Jiangsu forces wanted to take Shanghai and, in order to minimize the possibility that Fengtian would mobilize and join the war, to do so as fast as possible. Their best strategy was therefore to strike rapidly with overwhelming force and break through the defensive lines – which would almost certainly lead to an immediate Zhejiang surrender. For Lu Yongxiang and the Zhejiang forces, the optimal strategy was just the opposite. They should seek protraction in order to draw their Fengtian allies down from the north and their Guangzhou allies up from the south. That would create a war on several fronts, which Zhili would be

---

1. Guo Jianlin, *Wu Peifu da zhuan* (Tianjin: Tianjin dexue chubanshe, 1991), vol. 2, p. 549; CB, September 5, 1924, p. 2; Cunningham to Secretary of State, September 3, 1924, SD 893.00/5489.

hard pressed to win, although it was superior to any of its adversaries taken singly. Which strategy would triumph, however, awaited the test of arms.

It was easy to miss both the scale and significance of this coming test. As "The War Cloud" – in the less-than-inspired phrase of the *North China Daily News* – was beginning to cast its shadow over Shanghai and foreigners in the city continued to joke nervously about how it would all fizzle out, a correspondent boarded a train for the front.[2] The journey up the line toward Suzhou would have taken an hour in normal times, but on this day it took three. And as he rode, it was "the scenes from the windows" that gradually forced on the journalist's attention "the reality of the situation" – so different from what it was imagined to be back in Shanghai clubland.

The countryside outside of Shanghai is mostly low lying, crisscrossed by waterways and dotted here and there by an occasional low hill or ridge. On this day the scene appeared superficially to be quite normal for the end of August. The late-summer fields were full of rich and luxuriant rice crops, but only one or two old women and an occasional boy were to be seen working among them. Closer inspection revealed that the civilian population of the countryside had vanished. Soldiers were the only people to be seen for miles; the military had taken full control of the railway, and every station, bridge, culvert, and embankment was guarded. The farther the train left Shanghai behind, the more each station platform appeared to be a huge ammunition dump.

Eventually the train passed Huangdu, the farthest point held by Zhejiang, and came to the place where the Suzhou Creek marked the unofficial beginning of Jiangsu territory, thirty-two miles from Shanghai. In peacetime this stretch of river was where foreigners came to row – they built a boat club, held their regattas there, and called it in Chinese "henli" (i.e., Henley). But now it was no-man's-land and almost entirely deserted – although two large British flags still flew: one over the club building, the other over a houseboat moored just below. After careful inspection by the Zhejiang military, the train was allowed to pass through the line to the Jiangsu side.

At the first station on the other side, military preparations seemed even tighter than within the Zhejiang lines. Around the station and on the platform were at least 5,000 soldiers "all well-armed, well-equipped, and well-dressed." They wore the same gray uniforms as their adversaries, but whereas Lu's soldiers were distinguished by caps "something like a baseball player's," Qi's men wore red armbands. Everywhere

2. *North-China Daily News*, August 24, 1924, in SD 893.00/5563.

ammunition boxes were piled high. Security was tight, and persons leaving the station were thoroughly searched and questioned. The railway station was connected by two telephones to the command headquarters, while in the city itself every street was under military control, with the best houses appropriated for officers' housing. All carried, pinned to their coats or gowns, a piece of cloth on which was stamped an official seal and the grade of their employment or exemption. "No-one has escaped the fine mesh drawn over the population." Even baggage required the official seal.[3]

Qi Xieyuan was gathering these troops for the main thrust of what was planned to be a rapid and multipronged advance against Zhejiang. By the look of things, moreover, it would probably be successful: by any index Qi Xieyuan was in the stronger position as war began. In his Jiangsu base he already had a formidable military establishment, and he was allied with the Zhili faction, the most powerful military force in China. He had good connections east and west on the Yangzi River, as well as north on the Long-hai and Tianjin–Pukou railways to Hubei and Henan. As hostilities began, he already had Zhejiang and Shanghai surrounded: Zhili controlled all the bordering provinces, and the Yangzi estuary as well. Lu Yongxiang, by contrast, was an Anfu leftover, whose only allies were distant, relatively weak, and probably unreliable. His forces were less numerous and less well equipped. At the same time, his challenge was more difficult. Qi had only to make one real breakthrough to win: Lu's territory was shallow enough that defense in depth was not practicable. Lu, however, had to stop him everywhere – along the perimeter of the city of Shanghai and the borders of Zhejiang province.

Qi had prepared his attack carefully. His capital was at Nanjing, and his headquarters at Changzhou in central Jiangsu, both well to the west of Shanghai, along the main railway line. In August, however, he had begun moving troops forward. His best division, the 6th, in which Qi himself had started out as a sergeant,[4] had been moved overland almost to the Shanghai border – to Kunshan, one station east of Suzhou on the main Shanghai–Nanjing railway. Here, only three miles from the main Zhejiang forces at Nanxiang, Jiangsu built up its largest concentration of forces. At the same time other Jiangsu forces were moving down the river. It was reported that the 4th Mixed Brigade, commanded by Wu Hengzan and for the previous ten years always stationed at Nanjing, was ready and awaiting orders for transfer to the fort at Jiangyin, the first port above Shanghai on the Yangzi. Twenty Chinese-style boats had

---

3. *Shanghai Times*, September 1, 1924, enclosed in SD 893.00/5566; Cunningham to Bell, September 3, 1924, enclosing *Shanghai Times*, September 2, 1924, SD 893.00/5561.
4. BDRC, vol. 1, p. 297.

already been requisitioned to assist with the operation, and all other boats, except ferryboats, were ordered to stay where they were and await possible use. Some large merchant vessels, previously the property of the Austrian Lloyd line, were requisitioned. At Kunshan 100 vessels were loaded with artillery pieces. Warships from the Yangzi fleet of Admiral Du Xigui (1875–1943) and the Fujian fleet of Admiral Yang Shuzhuang (1882–1934), numbering about thirty ships altogether, were assembling both on the Yangzi and in Lake Tai to support Jiangsu. And Qi had about thirty aircraft, recently arrived from the north.[5]

To move his forces, Qi commandeered all the rolling stock of the Nanjing–Shanghai railway. Six troop trains left Nanjing on the night of August 25, eight more on the twenty-sixth. Residents watched with alarm. Not since the two revolutions of 1911 and 1913, noted the *North China Daily News*, had Nanjing been so panic stricken.[6] On August 28 a correspondent described the city as "an armed camp." All was quiet and orderly; but brigade after brigade of soldiers passed through the streets. "Only a few buglers precede the soldiers, who soon get out of step. Each man carries, in addition to the usual implements of the soldier, a paper umbrella, together with extra straw sandals and other aids to comfort. During the war the rations of the troops are increased, the Northern soldiers being provided with plenty of bread, biscuits, and corned beef."[7]

As Qi's main forces moved against Shanghai, some by rail and others by ship along the river, Zhili forces that had been elsewhere moved to reinforce Nanjing. General Chen Diaoyuan (1886–1943), who had been in charge of bandit suppression in Jiangsu, Anhui, Shandong, and Henan, arrived to relieve the divisions sent to the front, while the forces of General Bai Baoshan (1878–1941) were moved to Xuzhou to replace General Chen's forces.[8]

In all Qi had at his immediate disposal the 6th and 19th National Army Divisions, the 1st, 2nd, and 3rd Jiangsu Divisions, and the 2nd, 3rd, 4th, 5th, and 7th Jiangsu Mixed Brigades, totaling about 60,000 men in all. The best of these were modern and quite well equipped; he

---

5. *Chen Bao* [*The Morning Post*, Beijing], August 26, 1924, p. 3 (hereafter cited as CB); CB, August 27, 1924, p. 3; Walter E. Smith to State Department, August 20, 1924, SD 893.00/5560, p. 3; CB, August 31, 1924, p. 4; September 2, 1924, p. 2; *Shanghai Times*, September 1, 1924, in 893.00/5566; Cunningham to Bell, September 3, 1924, 893.00/5561, enclosing *Shanghai Times*, September 2, 1924; *China Weekly Review*, 30.2 (September 13, 1924): 43; Mao Jinling, p. 106; *Jiang Zhe zhan shi*, v. 3.14.
6. *North-China Daily News*, August 28, 1924, enclosed in SD 893.00/5569.
7. Ibid., August 29, 1924, in SD 893.00/5567.
8. Ibid.

had, in addition, potential reserves from his Zhili allies in the provinces of Fujian, Jiangxi, and Anhui, all of which border Zhejiang.[9]

Qi was hoping for an early breakthrough directly into Shanghai. For this reason, he concentrated most of his forces at Kunshan, poised to move right down the railway line into the city, and at Pingwang, a town separated from Shanghai by a narrow strip of Zhejiang territory. This theater was entrusted to the Jiangsu First Army, commanded by Gong Bangduo (b. 1881) with Ma Yuren (1875–1940) as vice-commander. But Qi had to consider other contingencies as well, including the possibility of a spoiling flank attack by Zhejiang.

Jiangsu province, south of the main railway line, is effectively divided into two parts by Lake Tai, a body of water some forty miles across. As will be seen, Lu Yongxiang understood that Jiangsu's entire position might be made untenable by a thrust, first westward along the lake's southern shore, and then north to cut the railway that connected Nanjing and Changchou to the front line. If Shanghai's defenses held, such an attack could envelop the forward-deployed Jiangsu forces. So Qi placed the Jiangsu Second Army, under Chen Diaoyuan, along the western shore of Lake Tai, at the cities of Liyang and Yixing, west of the lake and just north of the Zhejiang border, to guard against such a move.

Finally, beyond Qi's ability to attack directly, but nevertheless of potentially decisive importance in the whole conflict, were the vulnerable western and southern frontiers of Zhejiang, on which Qi's Zhili allies from Fujian, Anhui, and Jiangxi were beginning to advance. The Third Army, under Wang Jin, was deployed from Guangde in Anhui to Lake Tai, while the Fourth Army, under Sun Chuanfang, attacked from Fujian and Jiangxi to the south. The Jiangsu provincial troops mobilized numbered about 60,000. Units came from other provinces as well – the Anhui 3rd and 5th Mixed Brigades; the National 2nd Division and the 10th and 24th Mixed Brigades, and the Fujian 1st Mixed Bridgade from Fujian; the Hubei 5th Mixed Brigade and one battalion of the Hubei 4th Mixed Brigade; and the Henan 3rd and 4th Mixed Brigades. These troops brought the total number mobilized by Jiangsu to over 100,000 men.[10]

Some observers believed that Marshal Qi was only "playing war." But correspondents' reports from the front told a different story. Jiangsu

9. Mao Jinling, pp. 105–6; Macleay to MacDonald, September 5, 1924, FO 371/10245; Ding Wenjiang, ed., *Minguo junshi jinji* (reprint ed., Taibei: Wenhai chubanshe, n.d.), pp. 160–8; *Jiang Zhe zhan shi* (Shanghai: Hongwen tushuguan, 1924), vol. 3, pp. 4–9; Lai Xinxia, Guo Jianlin, and Jaio Jingyi, comps., *Beiyang junfa shigao* (Hubei renmin chubanshe, 1983), pp. 296–9.
10. Mao Jinling, pp. 105–6; *Jiang Zhe zhan shi*, vol. 3, p. 18.

forces extended from a few miles outside Liuhe, on the Yangzi River, to Pingwang, just east of Lake Tai close to the Zhejiang border. At Kunshan he was thought to have 30,000 men; his line was "reinforced with modern artillery and machine guns of a type and manufacture date which would surprise those people who think he is relying on old stores." Among his aircraft were two big Vickers Vimys, and he had a group of pilots, mostly foreigners recruited in Shanghai, but including half a dozen Frenchmen who had come directly from Europe.[11]

Zhejiang, however, was by no means defeated before the first shots were fired. Lu Yongxiang was a well-trained and experienced soldier. At his direct disposal, as the fighting began, were the 4th and 10th National Divisions and the 1st and 2nd Zhejiang Divisions, as well as two mixed brigades and his personal bodyguard, which was reported to be roughly equal to a mixed brigade. In addition, Lu had the forces that generals Zang and Yang had brought from Fujian, now reequipped and augmented to about 20,000. There were also the garrison troops belonging to his ally, the Shanghai commander He Fenglin, which were stationed at Wusong (where the Huangpu River flows into the Yangzi from Shanghai) and in the city of Shanghai itself. Altogether these numbered perhaps 74,000 men. Lu also had about thirty aircraft, and when fighting began, some 600 coolies were building an airfield for them at Huzhou, just south of Lake Tai, to be ready in October. On the water, Zhejiang had six vessels in Admiral Lin Jianzhang's independent fleet. But Lu had no allies nearby or reliable transport routes for resupply.[12]

Lu Yongxiang's headquarters were at Hangzhou, once the capital of the Southern Song and still a city of surpassing beauty. Its strategic location about seventy miles southwest of Shanghai controlled one major route to the city. Lu himself was in overall charge of operations and in direct command of the Zhejiang southern front, which extended from the city proper along the southern shore of Lake Tai as far as Huzhou. That city was the headquarters of the Zhejiang Second Army, commanded by General Chen Leshan, with Yang Huazhao as deputy, which was charged with the flank attack along Lake Tai against Jiangsu positions around Yixing. Defense against attack from Jiangxi or Fujian was made the responsibility of the Third Army, under the command of two Zhejiang natives: Generals Zhang Zaiyang (b. 1873) and Pan Guoguang (b. 1882). Shanghai and its neighbor, Songjiang, were under the immediate

11. *Shanghai Times*, September 1, 1924, enclosed in SD 893.00/5566.
12. "Week of Hard Fighting Gives Little Advantage to Chekiang or Kiangsu" *China Weekly Review* 30 (September 13, 1924), no. 2, 43; Mao Jinling, 106; *Jiang Zhe zhan shi*, vol. 3. 14; Macleay to MacDonald, September 5, 1924, FO 371/10245.

command of Lu's close comrade, Defense Commissioner He Fenglin, whose headquarters were at Longhua, just outside the International Settlement.[13]

Today Longhua has been engulfed by the Shanghai urban area, but in the 1920s it was six miles from the city, a suburb beyond Xujiahui, that had grown up along the small Longhua River near its junction with the Huangpu. The settlement is dominated by the Longhua temple, whose origins tradition places in the period of the Three Kingdoms (238–50 A.D.), with its thin and angular pagoda painted strikingly brown and yellow. From the late Qing on, however, Longhua has also been known as the site of an arsenal. It was there, as we have seen, that smokeless powder was first manufactured in China. Had Yuan Shikai's troops not held it against pro–Sun Yat-sen forces in July 1913, the attempted "Second Revolution" might have succeeded. In the 1920s a regimental commander stationed there, named Zhang Muhan, raised money for the restoration of the temple (slated for demolition by the early Republican government) to something like its present form.[14] Today the Longhua River is gone, paved over to make way for a market, but the temple survives – as does the arsenal, now Chinese People's Liberation Army Factory No. 7315, at No. 2577 Longhua Road. In 1924 He Fenglin had 12,000 troops at Longhua, and more at the Wusong forts, the entrance to the Port of Shanghai, about ten miles up the Huangpu River from the city proper at the point where the Huangpu joins the Yangzi – the northernmost point held by Zhejiang.[15]

Stalemate on the Shanghai Perimeter

The war began with Jiangsu attempts to break through at two important Zhejiang outposts north of Shanghai. The first was the railway bridge at Huangdu, which controlled the way to the city itself; the second was

---

13. Mao Jinling, 106; CB, August 25, 1924, p. 3; CB, August 28, 1924; *North China Daily News*, August 25, 1924, enclosed in SD 893.00/5563; *Jiang Zhe zhan shi*, vol. 2, pp. 2–20.
14. Gao Zhennong, *Longhuasi* (Shanghai: Shanghai shehui kexueyuan chubanshe, 1989), pp. 1, 30; C. E. Darwent, *Shanghai: A Handbook for Travellers and Residents* (Shanghai: Kelly & Walsh, 1920), p. 100.
15. In addition to the *Chen Bao* [*Morning Post*], the narration that follows draws on the following sources: Ding Wenjiang, ed., *Minguo junshi jinji* (reprint ed., Taibei: Wenhai chubanshe, n.d.), pp. 169–74, 174–218;" Dongnan zhanshi de liaojie," DZ (1924), no. 19, pp. 1–6; Ma Baoxing, "Qi Lu zhi zhan jilue," *Wenshi ziliao xuanji* no. 35, pp. 41–55; Shi Yazhen, "Jiang Zhe zhi zhan," in *Zhongguo xiandaishi dashi jishi benmo (1919–1949)*, vol. 1, pp. 259–61, ed. Wang Weili (Ha-er-bin: Heilungjiang renmin chubanshe, 1987); Tao Juyin, *Beiyang junfa tongzhi shiqi shihua* (rev. ed.), 3 vols. (Beijing: Sanlian, 1983), vol. 3, p. 1345; Zhang Xianwen, ed, *Zhonghua Minguo shigang* (Henan renmin chubanshe, 1985), pp. 206–9.

Liuhezhen, a town of about 10,000 population, at the point where the Liuhe River, which marked the boundary between Shanghai municipality and Jiangsu province, flowed into the vast Yangzi estuary. Liuhezhen was strategically attractive because it stood "near the terminus of an excellent road from Shanghai"; the Zhejiang garrison there was "practically the only obstacle between Jiangsu and the Wusong Fort."[16] The Jiangsu first route army, commanded by Gong Bangduo and Ma Yuren, concentrated for the offensive at Kunshan, just across the provincial boundary and fifteen miles by rail from Shanghai.

The attack on Huangdu came first, with Jiangsu firing the first shots of the war at 10:00 A.M. on September 3, as has been mentioned, to be answered immediately by the Zhejiang commander, Zhu Shenguang. As the artillery exchanged fire, Gong Bangduo's Jiangsu infantry moved toward the small railway station at Huangdu, which was his objective number one.[17]

The following day, September 4, Ma Yuren's Jiangsu forces fell on Liuhezhen. Facing them was the Zhejiang 10th Division, 39th Brigade. One unit broke under the Jiangsu attack and fell back south on Luodian, opening part of the road to Shanghai. This was a pivotal moment in the war. Had this breakthrough been properly followed up, Jiangsu troops might have swept on to rapid victory, with all that would have implied for the big picture of Chinese politics. But Zhejiang realized its peril: the following day Yang Huazhao sent a relief force that recaptured Liuhezhen after bitter fighting. Two thousand Fujian troops, under Colonel Zhang Yisheng, arrived on September 5, in the nick of time. On September 6, a Jiangsu surprise attack in which troops were brought to the front in automobiles also just failed.[18]

Zhejiang could not settle simply for holding its own lines. Victory would require some sort of breakout. He Fenglin decided to follow up the success at Liuhezhen with a general offensive. Yang and He did not let Ma Yuren withdraw in peace: they pursued his forces. This led to a substantial Jiangsu counterattack on September 7, seeking the recapture of Liuhezhen, which failed with the loss to Jiangsu of 400 men. By the fourth day of the war a stalemate had developed at Liuhezhen, where Jiangsu and Zhejiang forces faced each other, entrenched on high ground on either side of the small Liuhe River. On September 9 and 10, and

16. "Week of Hard Fighting Gives Little Advantage to Chekiang or Kiangsu," *China Weekly Review* 30 (September 13, 1924), no. 2, 43.
17. Guo, *Wu Peifu*, vol. 2, p. 549; CB, September 5, 1924, p. 2; Cunningham to Secretary of State, September 3, 1924, SD 893.00/5489.
18. *China Weekly Review* 30.2 (September 13, 1924), 41.

again on September 15, Jiangsu undertook major attacks on Liuhezhen, but the Zhejiang lines held.[19]

The same pattern was apparent at Huangdu, a few miles to the west. The place was a minor stop on the railway from Shanghai to Nanjing. The railway station lay on high ground with creeks on either side: that on the west crossed by a three-span bridge known as No. 24, that on the east by the smaller No. 23 bridge. On the first day of the war Jiangsu troops, covered by heavy artillery barrage, had moved forward along the railway line from Kunshan. The Zhejiang troops had fought every inch of the way, before falling back into well-prepared defensive positions at Huangdu. Here, as at Liuhezhen, a stalemate developed. For the next six weeks, thousands of men would fight, World War I–style, back and forth for control of this patch of ground. Jiangsu had kept Huangdu under continuous artillery bombardment from September 3 to September 9. The "little railway station [was reduced to] a mass of ruins." But Jiangsu had difficulty accomplishing much more. Their forces were entrenched on the west side of bridge No. 24, and twice they managed to advance to Huangdu and briefly capture the station, "under terrible fire from the machine-guns of... the Zhejiang army." But each time this happened, the Zhejiang forces, in shallow trenches with well-deployed machine guns, managed to force them back and retake the station. Whole companies were mowed down as they charged across the partially destroyed bridge into the sandbagged trenches from which the Zhejiang forces fired their guns. It was "like a scythe in a cornfield" according to observers.[20] Qi was so worried by the carnage that he moved his base back from Kunshan to Suzhou, fearing that the Zhejiang forces might be reinforced from elsewhere on the line and actually break through. On Saturday, September 5, seven complete trains were kept ready at Kunshan station, as well as General Qi's own private train, in case retreat should prove necessary.

In the meantime, Qi brought thousands of reinforcements converging on the front at the three-span bridgehead. Two trainloads of troops were diverted from the Yixing sector to Kunshan, while from the north four or five trains a day arrived, bringing soldiers from as far as Xuzhou, Kaifeng, and Hubei. In Beijing, more than 700 miles to the north, two brigades of Feng Yuxiang's troops entrained for Kunshan. And three or four trains a day were carrying wounded away from the front. The military hospital at Kunshan was full; Red Cross and mission hospitals

19. Guo, *Wu Peifu*, vol. 2, pp. 549–50; Cunningham to Secretary of State, September 8, 1924, SD 893.00/5587.
20. *Shanghai Times*, September 11, 1924, enclosed with American Consul General in Shanghai (Cunningham) to Secretary of State, September 11, 1924, SD 893.00/5594.

at Suzhou were also full. Less serious cases were being sent to Changzhou and Nanjing.

Fighting raged elsewhere as well, on the water as well as on land. The Jiangsu front line stretched from Liuhe to Jiading, which was a mile from Huangdu, and then to within a few miles of Qingpu. On September 7, near Liuhe, the naval forces of the two sides fought an engagement: the Jiangsu navy under Du Xigui advanced as the Zhejiang navy of Admiral Lin Jianzhang immediately withdrew. Thereafter, the Jiangsu navy provided support to Jiangsu land forces in the Liuhezhen battle.[21] Inside Shanghai, there was concern. By September 11 the strength of Jiangsu seemed to be overwhelming. By the middle of the month artillery fire could be heard most of the night along the defensive cordon that was gradually drawing closer.[22]

This stalemate, however, was not what Jiangsu had planned at the beginning of the campaign. They enjoyed great superiority in numbers, on the Shanghai front perhaps two to one – and growing, for most of the units that arrived from other provinces joined the fight here. They had abundant resources and ammunition. Nevertheless, they pounded away at Huangdu, Liuhe, Jiading, and Qingpu at great cost and with little success. There were several reasons. One was that a large number of men created confusion as well as strength: as Jiangsu's forces swelled, orders got lost or garbled along improvised chains of command connecting units whose soldiers might speak mutually unintelligible dialects. The Zhejiang defenders, by contrast, knew one another well. Furthermore, Lu Yongxiang was able to concentrate his best men along a relatively short defensive perimeter, while Qi Xieyuan had to worry about flanking attacks from the south.[23]

Perhaps the most important reason for Zhejiang's impressive showing was its understanding of the machine gun. Jiangsu had the edge in artillery. A particularly effective weapon was an improvised armored train mounting two field guns on steel trucks. During the retreat toward Huangdu, this ran up and down the line dropping shells into the Zhejiang forces. Because it was mobile, the armored train could hit almost any target; for the same reason it was difficult for Zhejiang to attack. It was stopped only when Zhejiang disabled bridges Nos. 26 and 27 to the west of Huangdu. But Zhejiang was better at placing and using machine guns, and this skill kept Huangdu securely in its hands and Jiangsu forces along the rest of the front largely immobilized.

21. CB, September 9, 1924, p. 2; CB, September 10, 1924, p. 2; CB, September 24, 1924, p. 2.
22. CB, September 6 through September 16, 1924; page 2 in every case.
23. Mao Jinling, "Beiyang Zhixi jundui," p. 107.

Lu Yongxiang also knew how to take advantage of Qi's increasing commitment to attrition warfare along the front. As the stalemate developed around Shanghai, he launched a bold thrust that gravely threatened the Jiangsu rear. Chen Leshan's Second Army had begun to advance around the western side of Lake Tai as soon as the fighting had begun. The plan was first to enter Jiangsu from the south and occupy Yixing. Then he was to thrust north and cut Jiangsu's most important line of communication, the railway that connected the provincial capital at Nanjing and the military headquarters at Changzhou to the front on the outskirts of Shanghai. This move was risky but promising. At a minimum, it could disrupt the Jiangsu supply lines. A really powerful punch, however, could split the Jiangsu forces, and send them reeling east, where they could be cornered against the still-intact Zhejiang defensive line.

Initially, the plan looked to be working. On September 5, Chen moved from Huzhou, in northern Zhejiang, to Changxing, and from there entered Jiangsu. Chen's forces did well, helped perhaps by the presence on his staff of an officer named Ge Sun, who had received military higher education in Germany. By September 11 Chen's forces had advanced as far as Xushan, only two miles from the key city of Yixing, which controlled the road leading north to Qi's headquarters at Changzhou.

Accounts of the fighting at Yixing vary: Some describe full-scale fighting in which the Jiangsu forces ultimately withdrew; others describe a settlement negotiated by the local gentry and merchants [*shenshang*] who persuaded Jiangsu to withdraw, and Zhejiang not to use artillery against the city. Heavy rain on September 12 and 13 stopped fighting at most points on the front. But a week after the weather cleared, Qi's forces withdrew from Yixing on September 20. Chen reported the victory a day later. But Yixing proved to be as far as Chen got: his forces were not adequate for the planned northern thrust against the railway.[24] Furthermore, decisive changes were occurring elsewhere.

On September 17 the Zhili–Fengtian War got underway in China's north. This could only help Zhejiang, for it divided the Zhili military effort and forced Wu Peifu to fight on two fronts. That day artillery duels raged through the night on all fronts around Shanghai, and the Shanghai Volunteer Corps prepared to act if fighting should reach the city itself. Jiangsu was shifting its attention from Huangdu, where the day saw only artillery exchanges, to Liuhezhen, where one major attack had just failed and another was being prepared. At Jiading, midway between Liuhezhen

---

24. Account based on news reports collected in Beiyang Zhengfu Jingji weishu zongsilingbu dangan [Archive of the Beiyang Government office of the commander of the Metropolitan Defense Force], 1024.93; also Guo, *Wu Peifu*, vol. 2, p. 550.

and the railway, the firing was reported to have "subsided somewhat." There was fighting at Yixing as well, but in every case the Zhejiang line held.[25]

On September 18 came a lull after "two days and a night of continuous stubborn resistance" by the Zhejiang forces in Shanghai, with both sides looking with interest to the situation in the north. Reinforcements to the Zhejiang line were being brought in from Longhua. Meanwhile, fresh supplies of munitions were reaching both sides, with trench mortars of German manufacture in particular strengthening the Zhejiang front. According to the *New York Times*, the Zhejiang troops were being armed by the Germans, Japanese, and French, while the Jiangsu and Zhili forces got most of their supplies from the Italians.[26]

Breakthrough on the Fujian Front

The decisive battle of the war, however, would not be fought on the railway line or anywhere on the long front that surrounded Shanghai completely but, rather, more than 200 miles to the southwest, in the remote territory of Zhejiang's border with Fujian, the very area through which Generals Zang and Yang had passed three months earlier. When making his deployments at the start of the war, Lu Yongxiang had been least concerned about the possibility of attack from this direction. He believed that Sun Chuanfang's troops in Fujian were neither very strong nor particularly willing to fight. Furthermore, the Xianxia ridge that straddled the border was a strong natural defensive position requiring only an adequate garrison to be held. Lu secured it using Zhejiang local forces – a serious mistake as it turned out.

In early September Sun Chuanfang led the 2nd Division and the 10th Mixed Brigade from Fujian north into Jiangxi. From Yushan they crossed into Fujian, easily overcoming the resistance of local forces. At the same time, Jiangxi troops under General Yang Yilai moved northeast into Zhejiang, threatening the right flank of the 1st and 2nd Zhejiang Divisions, which Lu had charged with defense of the provincial borders. Sun's forces soon swept across the Xianxia ridge, taking Jiangshan and Quzhou in a swoop. At Xianxia ridge, Zhang Guowei, commander of an artillery regiment of the 2nd Zhejiang Division, went over to Jiangsu. On September 16 the 1st Zhejiang Division under Pan Guoguang was defeated at Jiangshan, which lies on the present-day rail line inside the border from Jiangxi, and began a retreat back on Shaoxing. Just as

25. NYT, September 17, 1924; Guo, *Wu Peifu*, vol. 2, pp. 549–50.
26. NYT, September 18, 1924, p. 25.

Chen's advance in Jiangsu threatened Qi's headquarters at Changzhou, so this defeat opened the road to Lu's Hangzhou headquarters to Sun Chuanfang, who aspired to succeed him in controlling the province.[27]

On September 18 Lu called a meeting of his officers, and the difficult decision was made to abandon the province of Zhejiang and concentrate all effort on holding the city of Shanghai. If Zhang Zuolin won in the north, things might still come right. But for the moment, Lu's forces began a withdrawal into a much narrower defense perimeter. Sun Chuanfang, in the meantime, was reaching agreements with some of the Zhejiang troops, who began to come over to his side. The Zhejiang civil administration split. Wu Peifu had taken the precaution of secretly contacting Xia Chao (1882–1926), chief of the constabulary in Zhejiang. Wu now proclaimed himself civil governor of the province while Zhang Zaiyang, the incumbent, cast his lot with Lu Yongxiang in the retreat to Shanghai. As a result of these defeats and Sun Chuanfang's powers of persuasion, the Zhejiang Third Army joined the invaders from Fujian, staged a sham battle, and then marched north on Hangzhou. On the night of Thursday, September 18, units of the rebellious army were reported parading in Hangzhou and Ningbo, the principal concentration centers in Northern Zhejiang for Lu's troops, bearing banners declaring their allegiance to the governor of Jiangsu. A "general retreat of the Zhejiang forces toward Shanghai" became "almost inevitable."[28]

So Lu Yongxiang abandoned Hangzhou, taking some troops away from the Yixing line to reinforce Songjiang; on September 19 he arrived at Longhua.[29] The only possible source of optimism for the Zhejiang forces was the war in the north. A telegram made public by the Longhua arsenal authorities indicated that Zhang Zuolin had moved his First and Second Armies twenty-five miles toward Shanhaiguan; this would prevent Wu from sending reinforcements to Jiangsu.[30]

On September 20, the *New York Times* reported on the front page that the Zhejiang command at Longhua arsenal had admitted that surrender of Shanghai to Jiangsu forces was a possibility, but maintained that Zhejiang soldiers had inflicted heavy losses on their opponents and captured many prisoners in heavy fighting. Renewed heavy artillery and machine-gun fire had started at about 2:30 in the morning along the whole front from Liuhe through Jiading and Huangdu to Qingpu. It was evident that "heavier artillery than that previously used had been

27. Guo, *Wu Peifu*, vol. 2, p. 550; Mao Jinling, "Beiyang," p. 107.
28. CB, September 20, 1924, p. 2; September 21, 1924, p. 2; Mao Jinling, p. 108; Guo, *Wu Peifu*, vol. 2, p. 551; NYT, September 19, 1924, p. 1.
29. Cunningham to Secretary of State, September 19, 1924, SD 893.00/5541.
30. NYT, September 17, 1924, p. 25.

brought up to aid the Jiangsu forces, together with strong reinforcements." Reports that the Jiangsu army had broken the Zhejiang army's lines at Huangdu and was marching on the city caused new alarm in outlying districts in the small hours of the morning. By late afternoon the sound of gunfire was coming nearer and nearer. An observer who managed to penetrate near Liuhe in the afternoon said that continuous firing could be heard. It appeared that the Zhejiang forces were stubbornly holding their lines there. But the defeats in southern Zhejiang and the revolt of the Zhejiang Third Army now threw the brunt of the battle squarely on Shanghai itself and on the Zhejiang First Army, commanded by He Fenglin.

Meanwhile, an observer who traveled by steamer to Zhenjiang and thence on a troop train from Changzhou to the Lake Tai sector of the front had returned to Shanghai. He reported that the Jiangsu positions were well prepared, with "batteries of 3-inch Schneiders, four or five guns to the battery... as well as a few 6-inch naval guns in position" near the Zhejiang line, making it impossible that the Zhejiang troops could break through. Artillery, machine-gun, and rifle firing was almost continuous.[31]

On September 21 the Zhejiang naval squadron, including the cruiser *Haichou* (built 1897, 2,954 tons), the gunboat *Yongji* (built 1915, 860 tons), and two torpedo boats, went over to the Jiangsu fleet at Liuhe, thus giving Admiral Du Xigui complete control of the waterways around Shanghai.[32] The following day, heavy gunfire from the directions of Jiading, Huangdu, and Longhua announced that the Jiangsu army had resumed its offensive. Reports of the mutiny in the Zhejiang army turned out to be exaggerated; the problem was confined to Hangzhou, but the situation was becoming grave. With the abandonment of Hangzhou, the Zhejiang forces to the west of Lake Tai were cut off, and it was admitted at Longhua that those unable to make their way back to reinforce the lines at Shanghai would be forced, sooner or later, to surrender.[33]

September 22 saw Hangzhou occupied officially for Jiangsu by detachments under Meng Zhaoyue and Lu Xiangting.[34] Three days later, just as Sun Chuanfang entered the city, the Thunder Peak Pagoda collapsed into a pile of rubble. This was considered a sinister omen: the pagoda had stood for nearly 1,000 years on the southern shore of the famous

---

31. NYT, September 20, 1924, p. 1.
32. CB, September 23, 1924, p. 2; September 25, 1924, p. 2; September 27, 1924, p. 2; September 29, 1924, p. 2; Cunningham to Secretary of State, September 21, 1924, SD 893.00/5572; NYT, September 22, 1924, p. 1.
33. Mao Jinling, p. 108.
34. Guo, *Wu Peifu*, vol. 2, p. 550.

West Lake, and the saying was that it would fall on the day the people lost their liberty.[35]

As Hangzhou was being occupied on September 22, the Jiangsu forces to the north apparently attempted a breakthrough on the Shanghai perimeter. The first artillery barrage began at 6:00 A.M., but it proved ineffectual. A second charge started at 8:00 A.M., followed by a lull until noon. At 2:00 P.M. there was a resumption of intense firing but without any marked change in position. All accounts agreed that the Jiangsu forces suffered heavily. Lu's machine guns were "skillfully disposed behind earthworks, which the Jiangsu artillery failed to locate."[36]

By this point the Zhejiang troops were holding almost entirely thanks to their machine guns. Foreign observers found the Jiangsu artillery "formidable in its noise," but its fire was not well directed and the timing of the fuses was poor. As a result, when the men of the Jiangsu infantry followed the standard World War I tactic of advancing after a heavy preliminary bombardment, they usually found "the machine gunners of their opponents as accurate as ever." Nevertheless, "all foreign correspondents with the Jiangsu army agreed that in equipment and numbers this army is so superior that it must ultimately break through."[37]

While this battle raged, a new offensive got underway against Zhejiang in the south, concentrating on the district near Qingpu. Zhejiang headquarters was reported to have ordered troops across the Huangpu River to establish a new defense line east of the city between the river and the East China Sea. At the same time, a general counteroffensive by Zhejiang forces was reported, spreading southward along the whole fighting line from Liuhe on the Yangzi coast to Qingpu in the low district east of Tai Lake. These two offensives combined to produce the bloodiest fighting of the southern phase of the war. The Beijing *Chen Bao* [*Morning Post*] reported "unprecedentedly severe fighting" on September 24, with the Jiangsu forces firing over 1,000 artillery rounds.[38]

The end of the war was now clearly in sight. Sun Chuanfang triumphantly entered Hangzhou on September 25. As ambitious as Qi, and his rival, Sun was riding the crest of a remarkable victory. Not only had he forced Lu Yongxiang to abandon Zhejiang without a real fight; he had greatly strengthened his own forces by incorporating five of the

35. Carl Crow, *Handbook for China*, (4th ed.). Shanghai: Carl Crow, 1925), pp. 158–9; E. H. Clayton, *Heaven Below* (New York: Prentice-Hall, 1944), p. 32.
36. CB, September 23, 1924, p. 2; September 25, 1924, p. 2; September 26, 1924, p. 2; September 27, 1924, p. 2; NYT, September 22, 1924, p. 1.
37. NYT, September 22, 1924, p. 8.
38. CB, September 25; NYT, September 28, 1924, p. 20.

surrendered divisions into them. Controlling Fujian, Jiangxi, and now Zhejiang, he was close to his goal of becoming *bawang* – hegemon – of the south. He threw his forces against the western defenses of Shanghai: Qingpu, Jiading, Songjiang.[39]

On September 27 Lu took personal control of a Zhejiang counteroffensive to straighten out a dangerous salient to the northeast, between Nanxiang on the railway and Jiading. Fighting was severe all day on September 29, with the Jiangsu earthworks proving very strong. Casualties on both sides were numerous: Lu lost an unknown number of dead, 1,700 wounded, and 2,000 missing on September 29, but by September 30 his troops gained their objective and dug in. Their casualties fell to 679 wounded on October 1 and 176 on October 2. At the same time, the Jiangsu forces began an offensive from Liuhe to the railway. It was accompanied by the heaviest artillery bombardment of the war and was carried out by a succession of infantry advances. The Jiangsu troops probably outnumbered the Zhejiang by four to one, but barbed wire and machine-gun nests made the difference. With Jiangsu artillery still poorly employed, Lu Yongxiang's men held their positions.[40]

More wounded reached Shanghai on September 30 than on any one day since the fighting started. Relief stations behind the front were full, while stretchers steadily brought more in. A "carrion odor" covered the front. Hospitals were overflowing and measures were reported to keep any more wounded from being sent to the foreign settlements.[41]

Zhejiang counterattacked in the teeth of Jiangsu's all-out push. The night of September 30 heard firing along the whole front, and saw hand-to-hand bayonet encounters near Huangdu, where Jiangsu made yet another attempt to break through. As before, however, machine-gun fire finally forced their retreat with heavy losses, leaving (according to Zhejiang sources) 400 dead on the field. Bombing of the Zhejiang headquarters at Nanxiang, however, prompted a withdrawal.[42]

While battles of attrition were being waged in the north and west, a strategic decision was approaching in the south. Like the Japanese in World War II, whose attack on Shanghai was stopped at great cost in the North but succeeded when a second front was opened at Hangzhou, the Jiangsu armies, stalemated to the north and northwest, were finally succeeding on the west and southwest. Sun Chuanfang was closing in on Songjiang, the city that controlled the approach to Shanghai from the

39. Guo, *Wu Peifu*, vol. 2, p. 551.
40. CB, October 1, 1924, p. 2; CB, October 2, 1924, p. 2; CB, October 3, 1924, p. 2.
41. CB, October 1, 1924, p. 2; CB, October 2, 1924, p. 2; CB, October 6, 1924, p. 2; NYT, September 30, 1924, p. 10.
42. NYT, October 1, 1924, p. 3.

southwest. The attackers numbered perhaps 20,000 against only 6,500 defenders. By October 4, the Zhejiang forces had been forced to retreat two miles to new positions after intensive night fighting in which both sides employed artillery. The railway station in Songjiang was "a bedlam of terrorized residents."[43] Meanwhile, Lu had exhausted his ammunition. According to the *Chen Bao*, all of it had been sent to the front, and none remained in his arsenals.[44] By October 8 the combined Jiangsu–Anhui–Fujian forces had nearly surrounded Songjiang and were blocking the escape of five Zhejiang trains from the main railway station. At the same time a coordinated advance by Jiangsu naval forces on the Huangpu River broke through Zhejiang defenses. But resistance was stubborn, and the Jiangsu forces were hampered by an order of Wu Peifu's, redirecting the flow of ammunition from the Hanyang Arsenal to the north, away from the Shanghai front. On October 9 heavy Jiangsu attacks were reported on the Shanghai–Hangzhou railway only fourteen miles from the Longhua arsenal. If the attack succeeded, it would cut off the Zhejiang troops at Songjiang and leave an open route to Shanghai for the Jiangsu forces. Songjiang was hard to reinforce, however. The line was swept by artillery fire and, although bonuses were offered to crews, only one train got through.

The October 9 attack succeeded. Sun Chuanfang managed to infiltrate troops around Songjiang's main defenses and take the city. This success broke the stalemate. Jiangsu advanced quickly, capturing Qingpu and Jiading between the tenth and the twelfth. Meanwhile, Chen Leshan, one of the key Zhejiang leaders, began to show sympathy for the Jiangsu cause. An urgent military conference was held at thier Longhua head-quarters by the Zhejiang leaders at midnight, October 12–13. Three of the leaders – Chen Leshan, Yang Huazhao, and Xia Zhaolin – expressed unwillingness to go on fighting. Shortly thereafter, Lu Yongxiang and He Fenglin disappeared. When this was learned, their soldiers raised the white flag and began to fall back on Shanghai.[45]

On October 13 a circular telegram from Lu Yongxiang announced his retirement from politics.[46] American Consul Cunningham reported that Lu Yongxiang and He Fenglin had embarked on the *Shanghai Maru* between 4:00 and 5:00 that morning and that the ship had sailed for

43. CB, October 4, 1924, p. 2; CB, October 5, 1924, p. 2; CB, October 7, 1924, p. 2; NYT, October 7, 1924, p. 25.
44. CB, October 6, 1924, p. 2.
45. CB, October 9, 1924, p. 2; CB, October 12, 1924, p. 2; CB, October 14, 1924, p. 2; CB, October 15, 1924, p. 2; Mao Jinling, pp. 108–9; Kotenev, *Shanghai: Its Municipality*, p. 23.
46. Guo, *Wu Peifu*, vol. 2, p. 551.

Nagasaki at 8:30 A.M. The consul mentioned only those two, but Zang Zhiping was with them as well. The former Zhejiang military head-quarters at Longhua was completely deserted, and it was said that mutineers from the front reached military headquarters about midnight, creating great confusion – which possibly was the immediate cause of the generals' departure.[47] At 6:00 P.M. Cunningham reported that "shortage of ammunition, dissension among troops, disloyalty of troops and apparent ultimate defeat by opponents" had led to the flight of Lu and He.[48] On October 14, Zhang Yunming arrived at Shanghai North Station with his Hubei troops and took control of the arsenal.[49] By the end of the month, Lu Yongxiang was reported to have taken refuge in Mukden.[50] With the arrival of the Jiangsu army, there was an entire change in personnel in the administrations of Zhejiang province and Shanghai. On September 20 Cao Kun had given Sun Chuanfang high military and civilian posts in Fujian, Zhejiang, and Jiangsu, which satisfied his ambitions, at least for the moment; the job of defense commissioner of Songjiang and Shanghai, awarded to Qi Xieyuan, had the same effect.[51] With Shanghai in their possession, the Zhili group had won one of the two victories it sought. Decision now moved to the North.

47. The Consul General at Shanghai (Cunningham) to the Secretary of State, October 13, 1924, 10 and 11 A.M. FRUS 1924, vol. 1, p. 381. Mao Jinling, p. 108.
48. The Consul General at Shanghai (Cunningham) to the Secretary of State, October 13, 1924, FRUS 1924, vol. 1, p. 382.
49. Guo, *Wu Peifu*, vol. 2, p. 551; Mao Jinling, p. 108.
50. McCormack, *Chang Tso-lin*, p. 130.
51. Guo, *Wu Peifu*, vol. 2, p. 551.

Refugees fleeing Suzhou at the beginning of the Jiangsu–Zhejiang War, August 31, 1924. (From *China Weekly Review* 30.1 September 6, 1925, p. 8.)

Temple at Liuhezhen used as headquarters by Zhejiang defenders. (*The Sphere*, November 1, 1924, p. 126a; courtesy of the *Illustrated London News* Picture Library.)

Zhejiang forces firing from trenches at Liuhezhen, August 30, 1924. (*Illustrated London News*, October 18, 1924, p. 722; courtesy of the *Illustrated London News* Picture Library.)

Camouflaged Zhejiang field gun at Huangdu. (*Illustrated London News*, October 18, 1924, p. 722; courtesy of *Illustrated London News* Picture Library.)

5
The war in the North

Zhili versus Fengtian

The Jiangsu–Zhejiang War was started intentionally by Qi Xieyuan. But the much larger conflict that it precipitated – the Second Zhili–Fengtian War – was, for Zhili at least, an unwanted struggle for which it was not well prepared. Wu Peifu's preferred strategy would have been peacefully to break the triangular alliance by luring the Anfu remnant in the lower Yangzi valley into some sort of cooperative arrangement with Beijing somehow – most likely by offering its leaders posts in the central government, economic concessions, and even bribes. Doing this would have eliminated the linkage between the political situation around Shanghai and that of China as a whole, which threatened Beijing with a multiple-front war. By isolating Sun Yat-sen completely and leaving Zhang Zuolin without the military foothold in China proper that Shanghai provided, Wu's approach would have greatly increased the central government's chances for success by permitting Beijing to concentrate on preparations for dealing with Mukden at a time of its own choosing, instead of being caught unprepared. The issue was forced by Anfu's violation of the Shanghai neutralization agreement of 1923, Qi Xieyuan's ambition, and the provisions of the still-intact triangular alliance. Mid-September 1924 found Zhili and Fengtian mobilizing at top speed, preparing to throw all the forces they had or could borrow into what looked to be their final and decisive showdown over who should rule China.

The theaters of this war could hardly have been more different from those in the south where the Jiangsu–Zhejiang War was still going on. The countryside around Shanghai was low and lush; trench lines were regularly flooded. Around Beijing it was chiefly dry and mountainous. The northern belt of mountains and semiarid plains, where Chinese had been encountering Inner Asian armies since before the unification of the state in the third century B.C., would be the setting for the fighting between Zhili and Fengtian. Dynasty after dynasty had fortified this territory: the Ming most recently, having planted ranks of walls and signal towers along its frontier to form the so-called Great Wall. This was a land of uncertain rainfall, on the edge of the steppe transition zone at the ecological limit of settled farming, good for one exiguous crop at best. The coarse and dirt-poor inhabitants contrasted sharply with the relatively prosperous farmers and merchants in the environs of Shanghai and the Yangzi delta, and Mongol horsemen with their long camel trains that carried goods to and from Inner Asia were still common sights in Beijing during the 1920s. Modernity was visible in the single-track railway that hugged the coast from Beijing to Mukden, but beyond it to the west and north lay only plains, mountains, and steep, treacherous roads through passes whose names evoked centuries of struggle. In autumn of 1924, heavy rains and flooding since late summer had caused mud and landslides that made the terrain more than usually impassable.

As they turned to the fight, both sides had similar strategies. That of Fengtian, carefully worked out and prepared in the period since the 1922 defeat, envisioned a war of rapid movement through this difficult territory. Its goal would be to destroy the main enemy forces and open the way to Tianjin and Beijing as soon as hostilities began, before the enemy forces were properly organized. At the outbreak of fighting, Fengtian's main forces would rush to seize the single most important strategic objective: Shanhaiguan, the elaborately fortified gate in the Great Wall, built by the Ming dynasty (1368–1644) and famous for its inscription, *Tianxia diyi guan*, or "First Barrier Under Heaven," that controlled the coastal road and the railway from Mukden to Beijing. At the same time, substantial armies would move inland to the north of the pass, to take control of the other routes from Manchuria to the capital, which passed through Rehe, now eastern Inner Mongolia. Infantry would be sent against Chaoyang, Jianping, and Chengde on the route to Lingyuan; cavalry forces against Chifeng.[1] Once that territory was under Fengtian control, a decisive move against Beijing from the northeast would be possible. Such a strategy would have menaced the capital, and the victory it would almost inevitably have produced would have quickly reestablished Zhang Zuolin as the dominant force in Chinese politics.

Wu Peifu was no less ambitious, and his strategy was almost a mirror

---

1. Fu Xingpei, "Di er ci Zhi Feng zhanzheng jishi," *Wenshi ziliao xuanji*, (1960–), no. 4, 29–37, at 31–3. Wen Gongzhi imputes the opposite strategy to Fengtian with respect to Shanhaiguan: holding it firmly while attacking strongly in Rehe. See Wen Gongzhi, *Zuijin sanshi nian Zhongguo junshi shi* (reprint ed., Taipei: Wenhai, n.d.), p. 191.

image of Zhang's, but with a few of his trademark touches. His goal was the conclusive destruction of Zhang Zuolin's power; but this would not be easy to attain, given that Manchuria is a natural fortress, virtually impossible to invade. Overland access to Manchuria was limited to the narrow corridor that the railway followed between mountains and the sea, and the folly of attacking there directly had already been clearly demonstrated by campaigns ever since the late Ming (although perhaps the most dramatic example was yet to come, in the 1945–49 civil war).[2] So Wu adopted an indirect approach. He would deploy major forces along the Ming walls at the Manchurian frontier and across the railway lines that passed through them. Their purpose, however, would be to pull Zhang Zuolin's armies forward and pin them.[3]

Victory would then be achieved, not by a frontal breakthrough but, rather, by the closing of a pincer movement. To the northwest of the Shanhaiguan front Feng Yuxiang's troops would move into the steppe transition zone, following the old road to the Qing summer palace at Chengde, and turn Zhang's right flank. To the east, Wu planned to land forces by sea along the Manchurian coast, thus turning the left flank as well. This was bolder than anything Wu. had ever tried before and may have been influenced by the successful use of sea landings by the Japanese.

Not all went according to plan. Wu's forces succeeded in taking Shanhaiguan ahead of Zhang's, thus immobilizing them at the very front where they had been counting on a breakthrough. Wu, however, proved unable to capitalize on this early advantage. A string of Fengtian victories in the Rehe sector climaxed in a breakthrough just west of Shanhaiguan at Jiumenkou. Had Fengtian been able fully to exploit this, they could have surrounded and defeated Wu's main forces at Shanhaiguan, thereby winning the war. This they did not achieve, but the strategic situation was reversed from what Wu Peifu had desired: Zhili became the force pinned and unable to maneuver, which meant that the Marshal's whole strategy began to unravel.[4]

2. On the latter, see in particular Donald G. Gillin and Ramon H. Myers, eds. *Last Chance in Manchuria: The Diary of Chang Kia-Ngau* (Stanford: Hoover Institution Press, 1989), 1–52.
3. Guo Jianlin, *Wu Peifu*, vol. 2, p. 557.
4. Sources for information about the war are numerous but often mutually contradictory. Among the most important are Bai Jianwu, "Di erci Zhi-Feng zhanzheng riji," *Jindaishi ziliao* (1982), no. 47, 100–12 (Bai was head of Wu Peifu's Political Administrative Department); Ding Wenjiang, ed. *Minguo junshi jinji* (reprint ed., Taibei: Wenhai chubanshe, n.d.), 25–62; Gu Tiaosun, *Jiazi neiluan shimou jishi* (Shanghai: Zhonghua shuju, 1924), in JDBH vol. 5, pp. 191–361; *Jia Zi Feng Zhi zhan shi* (Shanghai: Hongwen tushuguan, 1924); Lai Xinxia, Guo Jianlin, and Jaio Jingyi, comps., *Beiyang junfa shigao* (Hubei renmin chubanshe, 1983), pp. 299–307; Lou

Moves toward fighting in the north were precipitated on September 3 by the outbreak of the Jiangsu–Zhejiang War just examined; its protagonists were linked by both strategic interests and personal understandings to the contenders in the north: Qi Xieyuan to the Zhili faction, Lu Yongxiang through the triangular alliance to Fengtian. In the "Introduction" we mentioned the meeting of his military staff called by Zhang Zuolin on the evening of September 4 at his residence in Mukden, their decision immediately to send armies into the field against Cao Kun and Wu Peifu, and the mobilization that followed.[5]

As Fengtian moved, Zhili grew increasingly nervous. It had not been prepared for immediate mobilization. Most of its forces were not near the frontier, and its commanders were not yet chosen, let alone in the field. There was talk of moving immediately to take Chaoyang, but it came to nothing, although as the Fengtian First and Third Armies completed their concentration near Suizhong, on the coastal railroad just north of Qinhuangdao, small Zhili forces did manage to occupy the most advantageous ground at Shanhaiguan.[6]

The forces both sides mobilized were by far the largest yet seen in a modern Chinese war. Zhili had approximately thirteen divisions (including two regional divisions from Shaanxi), twenty-seven mixed brigades, two cavalry brigades, and eight mixed regiments, totaling about 130,000 men; Fengtian had three central divisions, twenty-seven mixed brigades, and five cavalry brigades, having a total strength of about 160,000 men.[7]

The Zhili First Army under the overall command of Peng Shouxin consisted of about 40,000 men in three regular divisions and three mixed brigades. It was in turn divided in three: Peng had direct command of the First Route Army, Wang Weicheng of the Second, and Dong Zhengguo of the Third. As mobilization began, these forces moved

xiangzhe, "Lun di er ci Zhi Feng zhanzheng" (Master's thesis, Nankai University, 1985); Mao Jinling, "Beiyang Zhixi jundui zhi yanjiu," Ph.D. dissertation, National Taiwan University, 1987; Tao Juyin, *Beiyang junfa tongzhi shiqi shihua*, rev. ed., 3 vols. (Beijing: Sanlian, 1983), vol. 3, pp. 1345–8; Wen Gongzhi, *Zuijin sanshi nian Zhongguo junshi shi* (reprint ed., Taibei: Wenhai, n.d.), pp. 180–97; Wu Liaozi, *Di er ci Zhi Feng de zhan ji* (Shanghai: Gonghe shuju, 1924); Xie Zongtao, "Di er ci Zhi Feng Zhanzheng suijun jianwen," in *Wenshi ziliao*, no. 41, 141–57 (Beijing: Wenshi ziliao chubanshe, 1963); Zhang Xianwen, ed., *Zhonghua Minguo shigang* (Henan renmin chubanshe, 1985), 209–11; Zhang Zisheng, *Feng Zhi zhanzheng jishi* (reprint ed., Taibei: Wenhai chubanshe, 1967). Because extensive censorship was immediately imposed (as had not been the case with the Jiangsu–Zhejiang War), the *Chen Bao* and other Chinese newspapers carried little war news. For this period, foreign papers are a better source.
5. Fu Xingpei, p. 34; Li Taifen, *Guominjun shigao* (Taibei: Wenhai, n.d.), p. 162.
6. Li Taifen, *Guominjun shigao*, p. 162; Fu Xingpei, "Zhi Feng zhanzheng," p. 34.
7. He Xiya, "Jiazi dazhanhou quanguo jundui zhi diaocha," pp. 102–12.

quickly up the railway lines toward the pass at Shanhaiguan. The Zhili Second Army, commanded by Wang Huaiqing (1876–1953) and Mi Zhenbiao (b. 1860), numbering about 23,000 men of varying origins and levels of training, was to be deployed at Chaoyang. The Zhili Third army was commanded by Feng Yuxiang and numbered about 25,000 first-rate soldiers in two divisions and two mixed brigades. It was divided in two: the First Route Army was commanded by Zhang Zhijiang (1882–1966); the Second by Li Mingzhong (b. 1886). They had an absolutely critical role in Zhili strategy: they were the mobile force that was to outflank the Fengtian forces pinned at Shanhaiguan. Their instructions were to go out of the pass at Gubeikou toward Rehe, which they should hold, and then move eastward, with the objective of occupying Kailu and Suidong farther to the north, and attacking Jinxi and Xingcheng, thus cutting Fengtian's western connections to Shanhaiguan. This would prepare the way for a massive Zhili breakthrough. Protection of the capital was placed in the hands of the 26th Division, under Cao Ying (1872–1926), and the 16th Mixed Brigade, under Cao Shijie. An independent strike force of cavalry was also organized in the north, under the command of Zhang Dianru, Tan Qinglin (b. 1878), Ding Changfa, and Ma Hongkui (1892–1970). Zhang Fulai (1871–1925) was in charge of reserves.[8]

On the Fengtian side, the First and Third Armies, commanded by Jiang Dengxuan (1882–1925) and the Old Marshal's son Zhang Xueliang (b. 1898), respectively, had a total strength of about 43,000 men in one regular division and seven mixed brigades. They would follow the route to Beijing taken by the conquering Manchus some 280 years earlier, from Mukden to Beijing via the pass at Shanhaiguan. The Fengtian Second Army, commanded by Li Jinglin (1885–1931) and numbering about 26,000 men in one regular division and four mixed brigades, moved farther west toward Chaoyang, on the road to Chengde, the old Qing summer capital, from which Beijing could be reached via the more difficult Gubeikou pass – in other words, the same route of march Feng Yuxiang was to take, but going the other way. Zhang hoped for a rapid advance along these two routes, culminating in the encirclement of Beijing.[9]

---

8. Ding Wenjiang, ed., *Minguo junshi jinji* (reprint ed., Taibei: Wenhai chubanshe, n.d.), pp. 28–35, 41–7; "Zhi Feng bingli zhi bijiao," DZ 21.19 (1924), pp. 152–62; Mao Jinling, pp. 110–11.
9. Ding Wenjiang, ed., *Minguo junshi jinji* (reprint ed., Taibei: Wenhai chubanshe, n.d.), pp. 35–41, 47–52; Lai et al., *Beiyang junfa shigao*, pp. 299–301; Fu Xingpei, "Di er ci Zhi Feng zhanzheng jishi," *Wenshi ziliao xuanji* (1960–), no. 4, 34; Li Taifen, *Guominjun shigao* (Taibei: Wenhai, n.d.), p. 162; "Zhi Feng bingli zhi bijiao," DZ 21 (1924), no. 19, 152–62.

So the fighting unfolded in two theaters. The first was to the northeast of Beijing: on the long border, running roughly southeast to northwest, that separated Zhili [today's Hebei] from Fengtian [today's Liaoning]. This was difficult, mountainous country with some important cities but no clear front. The second was almost directly to the east: around the clearly delimited and fortified area of Shanghaiguan. Today the battles in this second sector are still remembered, while those in the first have been almost entirely forgotten. Yet of the two theaters, the first was arguably of the most decisive importance to the outcome of the war.

The Chaoyang Front

The Chaoyang battle was part of the first major campaign of the war, getting underway even before the Zhili forces were entirely mobilized. Foreign press reports of the war, which – with some justice – blame Zhili losses here on cowardice, poor planning, and incompetence, nevertheless fail to grasp the details of this campaign. But the Beijing government understood very well the significance of the Chaoyang front.

In the First Zhili–Fengtian War in 1922, the decisive battle had been at Changxindian, an important railway junction near Beijing, Feng Yuxiang's troops had scored a dramatic breakthrough around the Fengtian flank, begun to roll up the line, and precipitated a rout of Zhang Zuolin's forces that did not end until they had escaped to the security of Manchuria, outside the pass at Shanhaiguan.[10] This humiliation taught Zhang Zuolin just how effective a flanking maneuver could be. Zhili understood that he had learned this lesson, and therefore calculated – correctly – that in the present war Fengtian would look for a way to turn their flank. The best plan would be to move troops to positions northeast of the main Zhili lines, along the little-used route between Mukden and Beijing that ran through Chengde. Troops thus placed could slash southward and cut lines of communication between Beijing and the most likely site of the main battle at Shanhaiguan. Intelligence reports on this possibility, and about Fengtian actions in the region, begin in August of 1922.[11]

---

10. For a brief discussion of this battle, see Guo Jianlin, "Liang ci Zhi Feng zhanzheng"; CYB, 1923, pp. 573–6. Documents are found in Guanyu di yi ci Zhifeng zhangzheng Zhijun shourong Feng fang Feng Cha liang jun kuei bing baogao [Report concerning the absorbtion by Zhili of defeated troops from the Fengtian and Chahar armies on the Fengtian side]. May 1922. Beiyang zhengfu bujun zongsiling yamen dangan [Archives of the Commander of Gendarmes] 1023.126.5.

11. Beiyang Zhengfu lujunbu dangan [Archives of the Beiyang Government Department of the Army], 26.160.

On September 11, 1922, Yin Gui in Chaoyang reported on the need to hold this northeastern area against Fengtian; another report from Mi Zhenbiao in Chengde made many of the same points.[12] Intelligence reports were also received concerning Fengtian military preparations in the area.[13] From March of 1923 Fengtian preparations were closely observed. On March 16 wires came from Peng Shouxin, commander of the 15th Division, and also from the *dujun* [military governor] of Jiangsu.[14] It was reported that Zhang was actively recruiting bandits into his forces.[15]

On March 12, 1924, Gong Hanzhi, the defense commissioner [*zhenshoushi*] at Chaoyang, sent wires to Cao Kun in the capital, to Wu Peifu in Luoyang, and to the commander in Tianjin, reporting that he had learned that Fengtian planned to invade the Suiyuan and Jinzhou areas. He reported that in the previous month Fengtian had sent eleven electric cars [*dian che*] to Xingcheng and Suizhong counties. On February 27 five large recruitment and training camps had been opened. These included camps devoted to electric cars, to military techniques, and to grenades. Gong had also learned that the commander of the 27th Division, Zhang Zuoxiang (1881–1942), was in Fengtian, where he had been meeting with the Heilongjiang and Jilin commanders. But he had not discovered what they had decided.[16] So for almost two years before the Second Zhili–Fengtian War began, there was steady concern with the area that would prove to be Beijing's Achilles' heel: namely, the Chaoyang front.

On September 10, 1924, Gong sent another telegram, to Wang Huaiqing, concerning conditions on this northeastern front. Chaoyang, said Gong, was the doorway to the eastern border of the entire Rehe area, but at the moment it was lightly held. Gong urged that Zhili should avoid taking an active attitude in the area unless Fengtian came directly across the border. If that happened, however, heavy forces would have to be used to defend Chaoyang. In any case, it was essential that Chaoyang be reinforced.[17]

When Zhili mobilized, Chaoyang was part of the territory assigned to the Second Army, commanded by Wang Huaiqing with Mi Zhenbiao as vice-commander. The town of Chaoyang lies on the Daling River about

---

12. Beiyang Zhengfu ReChaSui xuanyueshishu dangan [Archive of the Beiyang Government Inspector General of Rehe, Chahar, and Suiyuan], 1025.132.
13. Beiyang Zhenghfu jingji weishu zongsilingbu dangan, 1024.79, no. 133.
14. Beiyang Zhengfu ZhiLuYu xuanyueshishu dangan [Archives of the Beiyang Government Inspector of Zhili, Shandong, and Henan], 1020.30, March 16, 1923.
15. Beiyang Zhengfu ReChaSui xuanyehshishu dangan, 1025.132, no. 135.
16. Beiyang Zhengfu da zongtongfu dangan [Archive of the Beiyang Government Presidential Office], 1003.106.
17. Beiyang zhengfu ReChaSui Xuanyueshi dangan, 1025.131

160 miles west of Mukden. It was connected by a north-looping unpaved road to Jinzhou, where Zhang Zuolin had established his forward head-quarters. It was held by the 26th Brigade of the 13th Division, the 1st Rehe Mixed Brigade, and patrol troops – in all not more than 7,000 men, under the command of Gong Hanzhi. They had been instructed to defend themselves but not to assume the offensive. The Fengtian Second Army attacked from three directions. The 3rd Brigade, headed by Zhang Zongchang (1881–1932), took the Tongyu railway northward; a detach-ment under Li Shuangkai of Li Jinglin's 23rd Brigade came via the Jinzhou–Chaoyang road, while a detachment under Xing Shilian (1885–1954) from the 24th Mixed Brigade had occupied Fuxin enroute.[18]

The commander of the Zhili 26th Brigade, Liu Fuyou, was in Beijing when the battle began, returning only at the insistence of Wang Huaiqing. Gong Hanzhi had the command as a result of the influence of Cao's close associate and favorite Li Yanqing, who was involved in military procurement and was nothing if not corrupt. As for Gong, he is described by one writer as a "stupid coward, incapable of commanding an army." The roads between Jinzhou and Chaoyang had been blocked, indicating imminent action, but Gong did not concentrate his forces, instead leaving them dispersed guarding several passes. On September 14, Li Shuangkai crushed the Zhili front-line troops, and over the next few days the Fengtian forces just described closed in on the position.[19]

On September 18 a report came to the presidential office from a regimental commander, Ren Lianjia, concerning fierce battles on the approaches to Chaoyang, at Liangshuihe and Zihoushan. According to Ren, his Zhili "troops in the front line had been fighting very bloodily day and night for several days, and were already completely exhausted. Relief was urgently needed."[20]

On September 21, the Zhili Third Army under Feng Yuxiang headed north toward Gubeikou. The Third Army headquarters were at Nanyuan, near Beijing. On the morning of September 22 the first brigade of the Third Army and the National 7th Mixed Brigade were supposed to arrive at Gubeikou; at the same time the 25th Mixed Brigade should reach Miyun, and the 21st Mixed Brigade reach Gaoliying. Several independent brigades would also leave Nanyuan for Gubeikou, as would the Second Army with the 8th Mixed Brigade.[21] Had these forces arrived

---

18. Li Taifen, *Guominjun shigao*, pp. 162–3; NYT, September 17, 1924, 25.
19. Li Taifen, *Guominjun shigao*, p. 163.
20. Beiyang Zhengfu da zongtongfu junshichu dangan [Archive of the Beiyang Government Presidential Office Military Affairs Department], 1003.106.
21. Zhijun zai Shanhaiguan, Gubeikou, Luanzhou deng didai de jiangling guanyu cuibo dui Feng zuozhan junshi jiedian laidian [Telegrams from Zhili military commanders at

in time, the issue of battle would probably have been different. But as the fighting developed around Chaoyang, none of these troops had yet reached the front. Wang Huaiqing, who should have been in command, had gotten only as far as Lengkou, and had not yet taken command of the Zhili Second Army. Zhili transport was overtaxed and chaotic, and supplies were short. Soldiers did not yet have warm clothes and suffered from the cold. On September 22, the Fengtian Sixth Army's Mu brigade occupied Kailu.[22] At 6:00 A.M. on the following day, Chaoyang fell.[23]

A detailed report from Wang Huaiqing to Premier Yan Huiqing vividly describes the situation. The biggest problem came from railway delays. It had been clear from the start that new supplies would have to go out to Chaoyang, and these would have to go through Lengkou. But on the railway line leading east there were already four mixed brigades and the 23rd Division – at a minimum, 50,000 men in 1,000 railway cars (not coaches: the soldiers traveled in open boxcars). The railhead, furthermore, was some distance from the pass. As Wang put it to Yan, by the time the reinforcements had emerged from Lengkou, the battle for Chaoyang was already lost. Four thousand men withdrew from the Chaoyang debacle, in 100 railway cars.[24]

After the loss of Chaoyang, Gong Hanzhi and Liu Fuyou were dismissed and replaced. Zhili military efforts in the vast and amorphous northeastern front fell increasingly to the independent cavalry force under the command of Tan Qinglin and his colleagues, but they too suffered a setback in a hard-fought battle at Jianshanzi. On September 25, Zhili forces attempted a counterattack at Chaoyang, but this also failed.[25] Jianping fell to the Fengtian Sixth Army on September 29, after several days of maneuvering and fighting in which Zhili lost 2,000 men.[26] Zhang Zongchang reported the capture of 800 Beijing troops, as well as six field guns, eight machine guns, and 2,000 rifles.[27] Then Zhang attacked Lingyuan and defeated Dong Guozheng, who retreated southward to Xifengkou.[28]

Meanwhile, Feng Yuxiang was advancing but encountering difficulties and venting some of his resentments. On September 30 he reported to the presidential office concerning weaponry. "I have found," he wrote,

Shanahiguan, Gubeikou, Luanzhou, and other regions concerning the need to accelerate preparations for war against Fengtian, July–October 1924, 1003.108.
22. Li Taifen, *Guominjun shigao*, p. 162; Wen Gongzhi, *Zhongguo junshi shi*, p. 193.
23. Li Taifen, p. 162; Wen Gongzhi, p. 193; CYB, 1925, p. 1130. Sources disagree on date.
24. Beiyang Zhengfu Dangan [Archive of the Beiyang Government], 1002.300.
25. Wen Gongzhi, p. 193.
26. Ibid.; Li Taifen, p. 163.
27. NYT, September 24, 1924, 25.
28. Wen Gongzhi, p. 193.

"that the arms of the rebel Zhang [Zuolin] are excellent." The difference would clearly count in battle, and he asked for 200 more good rifles. The following day came word that Lingyuan had also been lost.[29]

The only prize remaining was Chifeng. This was the westernmost of the main positions controlling the front between Zhili and Fengtian, and it was hotly contested. The attack on it began at dawn on October 4. It was taken by Fengtian on October 7, and the Zhili forces that had held it retreated to Lengkou and Taolinkou. But Tan Qingling and Ding Changfa from Chahar [roughly eastern Inner Mongolia] to the west joined the Zhili forces, and it became impossible for the Fengtian army of Xu Langzhou (b. 1872) to hold the position.[30] The battle had begun when Wu Guangxin's (1881–1939) Fengtian cavalry had moved toward Chifeng and encountered Zhili forces at Molihe. Needing aid, they telegraphed to Li Jinglin, who sent them a very strong brigade [*tuan*] and they thus won the battle. The Second and Sixth Fengtian Armies then advanced together, but Zhili forces ambushed them near Chiefengkou Pass. Xu Lanzhou's forces then arrived and drove away the Zhili forces, and the now three Fengtian armies continued their advance.

Taking advantage of the exhaustion of the Fengtian forces, Wang Chengbin (b. 1873) launched a surprise attack at daybreak on October 7. Four hours of fierce fighting ensued, with neither army yielding and both sides suffering great losses. The stalemate was broken only when a Fengtian grenadier squad moved up under the Zhili fire to break the line. At 2:00 P.M. the Zhili forces abandoned Chifeng, and Fengtian captured more than 1,000 Zhili soldiers and two battalion commanders. This was a major victory, and Zhili's costly recapture of the position a week later came too late to affect the larger strategic situation.[31] On October 11 Wang Huaiqing again reported to Premier Yan. The Zhili front line had now been driven back to Pingquan, and Wang was concerned about supplies in the face of an evident enemy advance.[32]

These victories meant that the Fengtian forces had secured control of the northern route between Mukden and Beijing, the very route over which Feng Yuxiang was supposed, according to the Zhili plan, to advance into Manchuria. Feng's 11th Division had in fact left Beijing headed for Rehe on September 18. At the same time, Feng's ally, Hu Jingyi (1892–1925), was supposed to march northeastward toward

29. Beiyang Zhengfu da zongtongfu dangan 1003.108; Zhijun zai Shanhaiguan, Gubeikou, Luanzhou deng didai ge jiangling guanyu cuibo dui Feng zuozhan junshi jiedian laidian, 1003.103.
30. Li Taifen, p. 164.
31. Wen Gongzhi, pp. 193–4.
32. Beiyang Zhengfu dangan, 1002.300.

Pingquan from Xifengkou, the important pass where the Luan River flows through the Great Wall line, some 100 miles east of the capital.[33] Pingquan was on the route that ran to Mukden through Lingyuan, Jianping, and Chaoyang. The original Zhili strategy was that Feng and Hu's forces would initially secure the northeast approach to the capital. When the moment came, they would advance into Manchuria along the line, which had been held as far as Chaoyang and Fuxin when Feng began his march north.

The rapid Fengtian campaign meant that even before Feng's and Hu's forces were in place, the plan that would have ensured their share in a triumphant entry into Manchuria had already been frustrated. Hu Jingyi was particularly worried by developing problems at Pingquan. His own lines at Xifengkou were in order, and he was personally in command. But he urgently needed relief troops. He asked the center to order Wang Huaiqing to undertake a flanking maneuver. This could be done because the Fengtian troops attacking Pingquan were believed to be from Chifeng. If Feng Yuxiang could put together a small commando and move quickly from Chengde to attack Chifeng, then the enemy rear could be thrown into disorder. In spite of their difficulties with transport and supply, then, the Zhili generals were still thinking in terms of quick movement and bold maneuver. Hu added that his supplies of oil, salt, and other necessities were very low.[34]

But no supplies or reinforcements were forthcoming. These military facts, as much as political intrigues, led to a diminution in fighting on Feng Yuxiang's front, which ultimately hurt Zhili. Originally, Hu's and Feng's forces could have moved deep into Manchuria by simply reinforcing existing Zhili positions. The successful conclusion of such an operation would have brought the two generals to within less than 100 miles of Mukden itself. Now, if the battles at Chaoyang and Chifeng were any indication, their advance into Manchuria would be slow and extremely costly. Feng and Hu presumably grasped how different their campaign into Manchuria would now be from what they had expected – hence, a reported secret agreement between them to stay at Pingquan rather than advance. Fengtian in effect reciprocated: Li Jinglin was said to be concerned that his troops might not be willing to fight Feng and Hu, so he likewise declined battle with them, turning instead toward the south, where his forces greatly strengthened Zhang Zongchang when he

---

33. CYB, 1925, p. 1130.
34. Hu Jingyi baogao jiu "tao ni jun" yuanjun di er lu siling zhi bing qingyuan Pingquan weiji laidian [Hu Jingyi telegram reporting assumption of office of commander in chief of the second support brigade of the "anti-rebel army" and urgent reguest for relief of Pingquan] October 15, 1924, Beiyang Zhengfu da zongtong dangan, 1003.113.

attacked Lengkou – probably the single most important engagement in Zhili's defeat.[35]

Thus, in the period beginning with the Chaoyang battle on September 15, Fengtian scored a series of important victories in what was then Rehe province. The Second Army occupied Kailu in the north, then Chaoyang, and turned toward Lingyuan. Fengtian cavalry occupied Fuxin and Jianping. On October 7 Fengtian forces took Chifeng. Thus they had occupied all the important strategic cities in the region, and they had done so without committing their reserves. This gave Fengtian a great advantage, and proved to be a setback from which Zhili never fully recovered.[36]

Zhang Zuolin was delighted by these successes. When it was reported that his Second Army had put to flight a whole mixed brigade of the Zhili army near Rehe, and that Fengtian forces therefore controlled the entire railway line from Jinzhou to Chaoyang, the Old Marshal invited foreign consuls and residents to his headquarters in Mukden.[37] He warned them that he intended to push forward and to attack both Shanhaiguan and Qinhuangdao, the port city just to its southwest. There were gunboats of the Beijing navy off Qinhuangdao, and "his planes intended to bombard them." Meanwhile, one of his planes was reported to have been shot down over Chaoyang, and three companies of his troops to have deserted.[38]

Zhang had reason for his confidence. The Zhili front line in the northeast had been completely destroyed. Because of transportation chaos in rear areas, the reinforcements which were by now pouring into the Tianjin area could not be sent north with any effectiveness. With Lingyuan occupied, the Fengtian Second Army was in position to threaten the left flank of the Zhili First Army. And since neither Feng nor Hu was actively engaged in that theater, Wu Peifu had to detach 30,000 troops from his main army under Peng Shouxin simply to help Wang Huaiqing's thinly spread forces defend the passes north and east of the capital.[39] This unavoidably weakened him at the place where he still had the real possibility of achieving victory: namely, Shanhaiguan.

The Shanhaiguan Campaign

Shanhaiguan – where the whole issue of the war now focused – was a place full of history. Some 260 miles east of Beijing, in the narrow place

---

35. Li Taifen, p. 164.   36. Fu Xingpei, "Zhi Feng zhanzheng," pp. 34–5.
37. NYT, September 21, 1924, 25.   38. Ibid.; NYT, September 22, 1924, 1.
39. Li Taifen, p. 164; CYB, 1925, p. 1130.

where the road from the capital is squeezed between mountains and the sea, it is a complex of massive gates which permits the road from China proper to Manchuria to pass through the line of wall by means of which the Ming dynasty otherwise sealed the several-mile-wide strip of flat land that connects the two areas. In the east, end of the wall meets the sea at the "Old Dragon's Head" [*laolongtou*], a picturesque group of gates, pavilions, and temples that descend right down to the water; to the west the wall meets the mountains, along whose ridges it continues, but here the real fortification is supplied by the landscape itself, virtually impassable except where cut by a few deep and narrow passes.[40]

Wu Peifu concentrated his main forces at Shanhaiguan's main gate and along its flanks, with other units deployed to the rear, along the railway line. His purpose was to keep Zhang Zuolin safely bottled up on the other side. In all, Wu's forces numbered about 200,000 men, with four squadrons of airplanes, and the combined naval fleets of Nanjing, Shanghai, and Qingdao offshore. Like his rival Zhang, Wu exuded confidence of victory: he told the Associated Press that he expected "to put an end to Marshal Zhang Zuolin's reign in Manchuria within two months." Cold weather would be no problem, he said, as the troops were well equipped. Nor did he expect any trouble from Sun Yat-sen in the deep south. "General Wu said that the difficulty there was practically solved and that the Beijing Government expects to see its authority restored soon."[41]

The first clashes on this eastern front were reported on September 19. Fighting was reported at Huangjiatun, some six miles north of Shanhaiguan, as well as at the pass itself.[42] At 8:30 A.M. planes from Zhang's air force appeared over the city of Shanhaiguan, which had a population of about 30,000, and began dropping bombs.[43] Wu's air force was moved to the city, and general Wang Huaiqing, commander of the Zhili Second Army, departed for the front.[44] On September 21, elements of the Zhili fleet, including the *Hai Qi*, sailed for Shanhaiguan. Wu's 3rd Division began to move north, through Tianjin, clogging railway lines from the capital to the front.[45]

A stalemate appeared to be taking shape along the fortified line at Shanhaiguan: As the *Peking and Tientsin Times* predicted, "unless the Zhili forces secure an immediate and decisive victory over General Zhang the war will outlast the Winter." This would cause great civilian suffering, for it would cut off food supplies from Manchuria for the victims of the

40. For references on Shanhaiguan, see Waldron, *The Great Wall*, pp. 160–4.
41. NYT, September 21, 1924, 25.   42. NYT, September 18, 1924, 25.
43. NYT, September 19, 1924, 6.   44. NYT, September 20, 1924, 6.
45. NYT, September 22, 1924, 1, 8.

floods of the last few months. It would furthermore hurt General Wu, because it would give "time in which the anti-Zhili elements will be able to organize for a Spring campaign."[46]

On September 25 it was reported that Zhang's air force had destroyed the hotel in Shanhaiguan where the Zhili headquarters were located, and also a train arriving from Beijing, wounding several passengers. Near Shanhaiguan itself, the Fengtian Fifth Army drove back government forces. On the diplomatic front, Zhang was also doing well. He had reached agreement with the Soviets that the Chinese Eastern Railway would not be used against him, and his adviser, Colonel Takeo Machino, arrived in Tokyo, presumably to request positive aid from Japan.[47]

The *New York Times* for September 26 carried dispatches that confirmed the large scale of the warfare now taking shape. Wu Peifu had concentrated 120,000 of an expected 200,000 men already on the Shanhaiguan front, and the rest would arrive within a week. Private freight on the railways had stopped, and only a precarious minimum of mail and passenger traffic was maintained. There was great confusion at the concentration points, and the empty trains often were not sent back.[48] Cavalry was also being sent northward to counter the Mongols in General Zhang's service.[49] Obviously preparing for a long struggle, General Wu extended his mobilization.

The hard fighting that began in earnest at Shanhaiguan only about September 29 was concentrated on the fortified line itself.[50] The Zhili forces already commanded the strategically important points, and were unchallenged in the large plain which lay within the passes, separated from Manchuria by an arc of mountains. Peng Shouxin had reported the occupation of Yiyuankou and other minor passes along this arc to Cao Kun on September 28. So when the Fengtian 2nd Mixed Brigade under the command of Guo Songling (1883–1925) and the 6th Mixed Brigade under the command of Song Jiuling attacked the main pass, the Zhili 15th Division, under Peng Shouxin, managed to hold the position.[51] The Fengtian First and Third Armies also had difficulties advancing.[52] But at the end of the first week of October, this stalemate began to weaken.

46. Ibid.
47. NYT, 25.
48. NYT, September 26, 1924, 23.
49. NYT, September 30, 1924, 10.
50. On the battle, see Li Zaolin, "Er ci ZhiFeng zhanzheng zhong Shanhaiguan zhanyi qinliji," *Wenshi ziliao xuanji*, no. 4, 38–53 (Beijing: Wenshi ziliao chubanshe, 1960); Guo Xipeng, "Wo sui Fengjun sanjia Nankou zhanyi zhi huiyi," in *Wenshi ziliao xuanji* no. 51, 114–22 (Beijing: Wenshi ziliao chubanshe, 1962); "Yuguan dazhan," DZ 21 (1924), no. 19, 6–9.
51. Beiyang Zhengfu dangan, 1003.100.
52. Fu Xingpei, "Zhi Feng zhanzheng," p. 35.

Following twenty-four hours of artillery bombardment, at dawn on October 7 Zhang's aircraft appeared and rained bombs on Shanhaiguan. Apparently the Fengtian commander was attempting to break through, right at the main gate itself. Fighting was reported to be furious at 11:00 A.M., with the Fengtian troops trying to take the pass but finally retreating, unable to withstand the withering fire of the Zhili forces.[53]

At the end of the first week of October, however, developments farther west along the arc of mountains made the situation for Zhili forces at the main pass more difficult. Lengkou is a secondary passage through the mountains and the Ming wall, about fifty miles west of Shanhaiguan. It should be relatively easy to hold. Defending it for Zhili were both forces sent specifically for the purpose, and others that had been defeated beyond the frontier and had now fallen back: Yan Zhitang's 20th Division and Dong Zhengguo's 9th Division (Dong had been defeated earlier at Lingyuan and initially retreated to Xifengkou). Nearby were Wang Weicheng's 23rd Division close to Jielingkou, another minor pass east of Lengkou, and Hu Jingyi's Shaanxi 1st Division, which was near Qiananxian, slightly to the rear. But Hu Jingyi and Wang Chengbin (who had been defeated earlier at Chifeng) had already made a secret agreement with Feng Yuxiang not to exert themselves in fighting; there was discord as well between Yan Zhitang and Dong Zhengguo. Seeing the opportunity to cut Wu Peifu off from the rear by breaking through at Lengkou, Zhang Zongchang moved his army forward.

Of all the militarists of this period, Zhang Zongchang is perhaps the one most generally held in contempt. Known to his troops as "the dogmeat general" [*gourou jiangjun*] (dogmeat is a well-known Chinese "tonic"), Zhang was a "veritable bear," over six feet tall, born in poverty in Shandong, never educated, and notorious for his concupiscence, wealth, and general lack of polish. He was a brilliant instinctive fighter, nevertheless.[54] As he moved his mixed cavalry forces of Chinese, Japanese, and Russians south, he was joined by Li Jinglin. Li left a small detachment at Chengde and took his main force forward as well. These deployments were risky. Had the Zhili forces of Feng Yuxiang and his associates chosen to move at this moment, they could have cut Zhang and Li off from their bases, and crushed them against the line of the Great Wall. But Zhang Zongchang had – characteristically – made a

---

53. NYT, October 8, 1924, 21.
54. BDRC, vol. 1, pp. 122–7, "bear" is at 123. A good recent biography is Lü Weijun, *Zhang Zongchang* (Jinan: Shandong renmin chubanshe, 1980). Zhang's military prowess is rarely recognized, perhaps because he was despised by so many Chinese, intellectuals in particular, who saw him as the prototypical warlord. See Lin Yü-tang's bitter essay, "In Memoriam of the Dog-Meat General," in his collection, *With Love and Irony* (New York: John Day, 1940), pp. 195–8.

sharp-witted strategic judgment. As his forces drew near to the pass, both Yan Zhitang and Dong Zhengguo withdrew. Lengkou fell. This proved a decisive victory, one which began the process of turning Zhili's flank. For the moment, however, Zhang Zongchang and Li Jinglin did not dare to press their advantage home by advancing southward beyond the pass into the Zhili rear. There was always the danger that the Zhili forces they had left behind them might stir into action and cut them off.[55]

Breakthrough at Jiumenkou

The tenacity with which Zhili held the pass at Shanhaiguan had led Fengtian to shift their strategy, from one of breakthrough at the fortified gate itself to a more indirect approach of infiltration and flank attacks. Around the Shanhaiguan pass proper, fighting was fierce, and land changed hands several times. But the Zhili forces were on high ground and the Fengtian army had to attack uphill, leading to very heavy casualties. A vivid account by Wang Weicheng to Cao Kun describes how, in the early morning of October 6, the Fengtian forces attacked using two mixed brigades – perhaps more. The Zhili forces opened fire, but the enemy kept drawing closer and closer, with more and more reinforcements drawing up. Finally the Zhili forces "spent their last energy, with bullets and grenades flying, and closed to fight with bayonets, whereupon the enemy gradually weakened and withdrew." On October 8 Fengtian attacked again with "dare-to-die squads" (*gansidui*) of more than 1,000 men each. But Zhili had reserves and managed to hold and strengthen their position.[56] So after several days of inconclusive struggle at Shanhaiguan, Fengtian began to shift its attack away from the main gate.

West from the main pass at Shanhaiguan lie – in order – Sandaoguan, Jiumenkou, and Huangtuling. The first two are minor passes, the third a ridge. Having achieved nothing at Shanhaiguan, Fengtian now began to attack Huangtuling and Jiumenkou. On October 6, the Fengtian 16th Mixed Brigade, commanded by Qi Enming (b. 1877), attacked Huangtuling. The position was held by the Zhili 13th Mixed Brigade, under the command of Feng Yurong. Feng was not a particularly skilled soldier, nor was he particularly close to Cao Kun or Wu Peifu. Originally he had been a subordinate of Lu Jin (1879–1946), the minister of war. Because of his lack of personal connection with the men he was leading, they did not follow his commands. This problem, plus his own inepti-

---

55. Guo Jianlin, *Wu Peifu*, vol. 2, p. 565; Fu Xingpei, "Zhi Feng zhanzheng," p. 36.
56. Beiyang Zhengfu dangan, 1002.300.

tude, led to the loss of Huangtuling. The full force of Fengtian attack then shifted to Jiumenkou, which was initially attacked on October 7 by the Fengtian 10th Mixed Brigade, under the command of Sun Xuchang.[57]

The ways through the mountains at Jiumenkou (literally, nine gates pass) are far more difficult than at Shanhaiguan, some ten miles to the east. Shanhaiguan lies in a narrow plain that has been fortified on and off at least since Tang times. The nine-arched, Ming-dynasty gate that crosses the eastern opening of the defile at Jiumenkou (hence its name) by contrast seems almost superfluous, for the pass virtually fortifies itself. Several miles long, it is only a dozen feet or so wide in some places. It had furthermore been wired and mined by the Zhili forces defending it. Despite its difficulty, however, the pass is potentially of key strategic importance: the valley into which it opens intersects the valley in which Shanhaiguan lies, and then leads all the way to Qinhuangdao. Thus Jiumenkou can serve as a back door to the entire plain usually reached via Shanhaiguan; militarily, a breakthrough at Jiumenkou will threaten the rear of a force holding Shanhaiguan, and Qinhuangdao as well.[58]

Wu Peifu had assigned responsibility for holding Jiumenkou to one of the worst units in the Zhili army: the 26th Division, under the command of Cao Ying, "the president's incapable brother," of whom Lawrence Impey remarks that "it was madness to permit [him] to get any nearer to the front than some insignificant point in the lines of communication."[59] The only explanation for Wu's move (other than the entanglement with the Cao clan from which he could never entirely free himself) may be that he thought the position impossible for even Cao Ying to lose: "Anyone who has visited the spot will recognise that it is a position which is so strong as to be practically impregnable as long as the defending force's ammunition holds out."[60] But lose it Cao Ying did.

What seems to have happened is that a scheme of deception devised by Wu Peifu went wrong. Wu had originally instructed his officers to lure the enemy in at Jiumenkou, very deeply, and then to use heavy artillery to destroy them. It seems that this operation was undertaken as planned, with Feng Yurong leading a cavalry unit out of the pass to

57. Ding Wenjiang, *Mingguo junshi jinji* (reprint ed., Taibei: Wenhai chubanshe, n.d.), p. 57; Mao Jinling, p. 116.
58. Lawrence Impey, "Chinese Progress in the Art of War," *China Weekly Review* (December 27, 1924), p. 102. This strategic geography has not lost its importance. On a visit to the passes in 1991, the author learned that students had blocked military trains at Shanhaiguan during the period of the Tiananmen Massacre in 1989. The army broke the stalemate only by redirecting its forces through Jiumenkou, a route of which the students were unaware.
59. Impey, "Chinese Progress," p. 101.
60. Impey, *The Chinese Army*, p. 12.

attract the enemy. But in the smoke and confusion the Zhili artillery mistook their new forces for the enemy, and opened fire, killing most of the men. Then on October 8, the vice-commander of the Fengtian 1st Division, Han Linchun, took a dare-to-die squad of 3,000 into the defile. Tearing off his shirt, Han led the fight barechested. He touched off the mines Zhili had planted, and lost between 4,000 and 5,000 casualties from his men and their reinforcements. But he managed to secure the pass. Jiumenkou was lost to Zhili.[61]

With this brilliant stroke, Fengtian established a salient on the plain inside the Great Wall line that had hitherto been the exclusive preserve of Zhili. If they could expand it, they could cut the railway lines leading from Shanhaiguan back to Qinhuangdao, Tianjin, and Beijing; they might be able to divide the Zhili forces, capturing the huge deployments in front of Shanhaiguan. They might well win the war. Zhili reacted to the threat with near panic.

To stop the Fengtian breakthrough, the Zhili command dispatched artillery, but they had used up their shells firing at their own men. Then the battery and its entire accompanying battalion were destroyed by the powerful firing of the superior Fengtian batteries.[62] Zhili, alas, was short of the guns that could have turned the tide of battle, having given their best to Feng Yuxiang.[63] The breakthrough at Jiumenkou threatened to cause a Zhili rout, like that of the Fengtian forces at Changxindian two years earlier. Cao Ying fled, and most of his units disintegrated as well. Almost the whole 26th Division dissolved in panic. As the Zhili defenders fell back to the Liu River, Feng Yurong, who had lost Huangtuling, was reported to have taken poison and committed suicide (although rumors persist to this day that he was in fact shot at Wu Peifu's order).[64] A complete collapse of the Zhili line was only narrowly averted. Many officers behaved badly, but not all. Impey tells how "one, for instance, when Cao Ying's troops fled before Jiumen and seemed likely to involve his brigade in their rout, took a rifle from a soldier, and remarking that his men were at liberty to return to Henan and relate their disgrace to their wives if they pleased, started to walk up the valley toward the enemy. His soldiers hesitated for a moment and then followed him, with the result that the Fengtian advance was stemmed just when it seemed likely to overwhelm all the defenses and capture Qinhuangdao."[65]

61. Guo Jianlin, *Wu Peifu*, vol. 2, p. 563.
62. Wen Gongzhi, "junshishi," p. 194.
63. Impey, "Chinese Progress," p. 104.
64. Impey, *The Chinese Army*, pp. 12–13; Ding Wenjiang, *Minguo junshi*, p. 57; Mao Jinling, p. 116; Guo Jianlin, *Wu Peifu*, vol. 2, p. 563; author's personal information.
65. Impey, "Chinese Progress," p. 103.

With the breakthrough at Jiumenkou one of the turning points of the war had arrived. The victorious Fengtian forces had suffered heavy casualties: between 4,000 and 5,000 had been killed, and twenty-three railway cars were sent from Mukden for the wounded. The Japanese consul stated that the battle was the bloodiest yet fought, and General Zhang was reported to be sending two brigades of reinforcements to the front in twenty-one troop trains.[66] Loss of the pass was reported to Beijing by Peng Shouxin on October 8: the situation was critical.[67]

The whole shape of the battle at Shanhaiguan changed. Instead of being fought over a fortified wall line, or at mountain passes which should have been relatively easy to hold, it now moved into the level open country within those lines. Here the only important natural features were two small streams, the Dashihe and Shahe rivers, which flowed, parallel to one another, north to south across the plain into the sea. Parallel to them, beyond the Shahe River to the west, was a narrow-gauge rail line, used for hauling coal to Qinhuangdao from the mines in the neighborhood of the village of Shimenzhai. These relatively minor features now became the defining parts of the geography of the battle-field, as the Fengtian and Zhili forces lined up facing each other, with Fengtian looking for a decisive breakthrough, while Zhili tried desperately to hold on.

In short order after the victory at Jiumenkou, the Fengtian army moved forward to Wanggangzi, which they occupied on October 10, and then to Shahezi, just to the east of Wu Peifu's 3rd Division. Costly counterattacks by the Zhili 14th Division under Jin Yun'e (1881–1935) proved unsuccessful. The Fengtian army occupied high ground near Shimenzhai. The Zhili army was now menaced on its left at Jiumenkou and at its rear at Shimenzhai.[68]

But after the setbacks, Zhili appeared to be holding its own. On October 10 Zhou Mengxian, the commander at Qinhuangdao, reported on the fighting at Jiumenkou. He had arrived at 2:00 P.M. and met with Peng Shouxin, and found relief troops already arriving steadily in the Jiumenkou and Shanhaiguan areas. Reports indicated that most of the front was reasonably calm, but that fighting remained fierce inside Jiumenkou, at Gangouzhen, and at other points. So far, Jiumenkou had not been recovered, but Huangtuying had been, as well as Shahezhai. These gains had been by dint of bitter fighting. The Zhili forces had found that their hand grenades were extremely useful in hand-to-hand

---

66. NYT, October 10, 1924, 19.
67. Beiyang Zhengfu da zongtongfu dangan, 1003.100.
68. Fu Xingpei, "Zhi Feng zhanzheng," 35; NYT, October 9, 1924, 11.

fighting and had used them all up. Resupply was urgently requested.[69]

The situation was bad enough, however, to demand the presence at the front of Wu Peifu himself (who, as will be seen in the next chapter, remained in Beijing worrying about war finance). On October 11 Peng Shouxin sent an urgent telegram to the Marshal stating that battle in the Shanhaiguan plain had raged all night: the men were exhausted and the ammunition was used up. Reinforcement and resupply were essential; otherwise the entire war might be lost.[70]

On the same day Washington was informed that Marshal Wu Peifu had left early in the morning "to direct operations at the northern front." The U.S. Military Attaché Lieutenant-Colonel Joseph H. Barnard (1877–1945) and his colleague Army Captain Woodrow Woodbridge accompanied the Marshal as observers at his invitation. British, French, and Japanese officers also accompanied Wu in like capacity.[71] Lawrence Impey was aboard as well.[72]

Wu Peifu's trip to the front revealed one of the major problems besetting Zhili: Transport was in chaos. In spite of orders to clear the track for it, the Marshal's train – called "His Excellency" – took over thirty hours to arrive at Qinhuangdao. The Zhili military officers were by and large unwilling to cooperate with the civilian authorities. Impey recalls "several instances occurring where the station master and signalmen were cruelly ill-treated by soldiery just because they were unable satisfactorily to arrange for two trains travelling in opposite directions to pass one another on a single track." Trains were delayed, switches were blocked, desperately needed supplies were never unloaded. Even Wu Peifu's arrival at Qinhuangdao gravely interfered with necessary railway operations. The city had a large station "with up and down main line, main line loop, and fifteen to twenty sidings open at both ends, so that there was obviously ample room for railhead manipulation to be carried out." But first the Marshal's special train, with its string of thirty coaches, "took up its place on the down line, with its two engines with steam up, and there remained for the duration of the war. Next, General Cao Ying, having fled from Jiumen, arrived at Qinhuangdao and proceeded to park his private car and engine on the points controlling the

---

69. Beiyang Zhengfu da zongtongfu junshichu dangan, 1003.109.
70. Zhijun zongsiling Wu Peifu deng jiangling zai Qinhuangdao zhihui dui Feng zuozhan qingkuang ji youguan junwu laiwang wendian [Communications to and from the Zhili commander-in-chief Wu Peifu and others commanding Qinhuangdao concerning the battle with Fengtian and related military matters, October 11–23, 1924] 1003 (2).37; telegram of October 11, 1924, 6:30 A.M.
71. The Chargé in China (Bell) to the Secretary of State, October 11, 1924, FRUS 1924, vol. 1, p. 381.
72. Impey, "Chinese Progress," p. 102.

siding. . . . Then a trainload of artillery and another one with Citroen motor quickfirers and ammunition pulled onto the main line, and shunted about in its vicinity for the next fortnight, the bulk of the material they carried never being employed in the war at all."[73]

After arriving at Qinhuangdao on the evening of October 13, Wu immediately inspected the front line at Shanhaiguan with Peng Shouxin.[74] The chaos on the railways and his own train's contribution to it bespoke his defects as an administrator. But the Marshal was a superb leader of men and military tactician, and over the next week he labored mightily to restore the Zhili position. Wu had little fear; so little that his colleagues worried. "Since Wu Peifu arrived at the front," ran a telegram sent to Cao Kun by Shanhaiguan headquarters on October 21, "he has been leading and commanding at the very front of the line, most of the time under direct enemy fire, which is most dangerous. If he is hit, it will be a disaster for our whole war effort. But Marshal Wu does not listen to any of us, therefore, Your Excellency, please urge him, in the interest of our entire effort, not to go to the very most forward positions."[75] Wu's abilities and personal prestige were not lost on Fengtian either. As a general, according to Impey, Wu "was immeasurably superior to any of the Fengtian higher command. It was really almost comic to notice the awe with which Mukden regarded his strategic skill, always planning their coups on the sector of the front which was not being visited by Marshal Wu during that particular day, and ceasing their effort and attacking elsewhere as soon as the Generalissimo was known to be on the battlefield in person."[76]

During Wu's first visit to the front, which was now crammed with men and guns, the most active fighting was at Sandaoguan, another minor pass just west of Shanhaiguan. Wu ordered elements of his own 3rd Division and the 1st Mixed Brigade to reinforce that front. And a combined attack on Jiumenkou was ordered for the following morning, with a reward of 100,000 yuan posted for the unit that succeeded. After Wu had completed his inspection and rearrangement of lines by about 4:00 P.M., he would turn over responsibility to Peng, and prepare to set out to scout possibilities for a seaborne landing behind enemy lines.[77]

73. Ibid.
74. Fu Xingpei, 135; Beiyang zhengfu da zongtongfu junshichu dangan 1003.104.
75. Zhijun zongsiling Wu Peifu deng jiangling zai Qinhuangdao zhihui dui Feng zuozhan qingkuang ji youguan junwu laiwang wendian, 1003(2).37; telegram No. 18, received Beijing October 21, 1924, 1:00 P.M.
76. Impey, "Chinese Progress," p. 103.
77. Zhijun zongsiling Wu Peifu deng jiangling zai Qinhuangdao zhihui dui Feng zuozhan qingkuang ji youguan junwu laiwang wendian, 1003.(2).37, telegram No. 24, from Zhou Mengxian, commander at Qinhuangdao to Beijing, October 14, 1924, received 2:00 P.M.; Beiyang zhengfu da zongtongfu junshichu dangan, 1003.104.

Even while Wu was on the scene, however, the Fengtian forces pushed forward again. They advanced from Jiumenkou, first to Shahezhai and then to Shimenzhai, both positions lying almost directly in front of their original point of breakthrough, thus gravely threatening the left flank of the Zhili position. Another crisis was created. As Lawrence Impey describes it:

The Fengtian troops had pushed through the Jiumen pass so rapidly after its unexpected capture as to reach Shimenzhai before Marshal Wu was informed of the situation, and by the time that he reached Qinhuangdao Zhang Zuolin's troops had completed their southward march from Jiumen and were facing east on the immediate flank of the Zhili line of communications. This had created a threat to the strategy of the campaign which rendered any advance at Shanhaiguan both unlikely and dangerous until the Jiumen position could be regained.[78]

On October 14 Zhang Zhigong (b. 1881) reported to Wu about the fierce fighting at Shahezhai. He had arrived at Shimenzhai on October 13, where he had found the situation very tense. So at 8:00 A.M. he had gone to Shahezhai, where battle had raged all day. At 4:00 P.M. the enemy had suddenly broken through the lines, creating an extremely dangerous situation. But many of his troops sacrificed their lives in battle, and the line was recovered. Thirteen enemy soldiers and one officer from the Fengtian side were captured, along with ten rifles and twenty-six boxes of ammunition. Six Zhili regimental commanders and a number of officers had been injured. The battle had already lasted for more than a day and was not over yet.[79]

Nevertheless, the Fengtian breakthrough seemed contained for the moment, and the emerging situation was not unfavorable to Zhili. A war of attrition was shaping up, in which Wu's advantages looked likely to grow, particularly if he was able to draw on troops from Shanghai, where, as we have seen, his southern allies had finally achieved a decisive victory between October 9 and October 13 – not a minute too soon for Northern morale. But breaking the enemy position would probably be best done, not frontally but by turning his flank – either by breaking out through one of the passes, or more likely, by landing troops on the Manchurian coast.[80]

At 8:00 A.M. on October 15, Wu went to the waterfront at Qinhuangdao to board a cruiser. Fengtian planes immediately appeared and began dropping bombs very near the Marshal. Two laborers were wounded,

78. Impey, *The Chinese Army*, p. 15.
79. Beiyang Zhengfu da zongtongfu junshichu dangan, 1003.104.
80. Fu Xingpei, p. 36.

but Wu remained calm and called for Zhili aircraft. These arrived and chased away the Fengtian challengers.[81] Accompanied by two other warships, Wu's cruiser steamed for Huludao and Lianshanwan, both possible landing sites; the intention was to evaluate the suitability of Yingkou as well the following day. Command was left in the hands of Peng Shouxin and Cao Ying.[82]

As Wu was departing, Shimenzhai fell to the Fengtian forces. The Zhili garrison retreated, leaving their heavy artillery.[83] By the evening of October 17, the focus of the fighting had shifted to Jiaoshansi and Erlangmiao, the sites of the bitter final engagements of what was called "the battle of Yuguan [the archaic name of Shanhaiguan]" or "the battle of the Great Wall." These were both points originally behind the Zhili lines where the Zhili army had been concentrating artillery and machine gun troops to assist the forces farther to the north. Fengtian detachments attacked from the direction of the sea and fired heavily as they drove toward the railway station. The battle shifted back and forth, but by the evening of October 19, the Fengtian army had succeeded in taking Erlangmiao.[84]

The Marshal returned in time to prevent catastrophe. He eventually assembled five divisions and eight brigades to reoccupy Erlangmiao, and from October 19 to 24 heavy battles raged. Victory was denied to Fengtian.[85] But Wu's forces were now increasingly on the defensive, and stretched ever more thin. The First Army had started with a little more than 110,000 men, of which more than 30,000 had been sent to help the Second Army; the 13th Mixed Brigade and the 2nd Shaanxi Division, together about 12,000 men, had to be sent back to Luanzhou to recuperate after the disasters of Jiumen and Shimenzhai, and there had been more than 10,000 casualties. So the actual number that faced the enemy at Shanhaiguan in the month of October was fewer than 60,000 men. On the Fengtian side, the First, Third, and Fourth Armies consisted of 70,000 men, to which could be added the 1st and the 7th Mixed Brigades, after it was certain that Feng Yuxiang posed no threat.[86]

---

81. Zhijun zongsiling Wu Peifu deng jiangling zai Qinhuangdao zhihui dui Feng zuozhan qingkuang ji youguan junwu laiwang wendian, 1003.(2).37, telegram No. 46, October 14, 1924; from Cao Ying at Qinhuangdao to Cao Kun, Beijing.
82. Zhijun zongsiling Wu Peifu deng jiangling zai Qinhuangdao zhihui dui Feng zuozhan qingkuang ji youguan junwu laiwang wendian, 1003.(2).37, telegram No. 47, Wu Peifu to Cao Kun, Midnight, October 14, 1924; Beiyang Zhengfu da zongtongfu junshichu dangan, 1003.104; Fu Xingpei, p. 36.
83. Wen Gongzhi, p. 194.
84. Ibid., p. 195.
85. Wen Gongzhi, p. 195; Li Taifen, p. 165.
86. CYB, 1131.

Although the situation was difficult, Wu's immediate goal had to be the recapture of the Jiumenkou pass. He realized this after only ten minutes' conference with his generals at Shanhaiguan upon his return from his coastal reconnaissance, and he immediately withdrew the whole headquarters from that town back to Qinhuangdao. Fengtian troops were only fifteen or sixteen miles from there, their artillery was emplaced on the high ground at good vantage points, and their troops were poised to break down into the plain through which the Beijing–Mukden Railway runs. Wu assembled a counterattacking force, consisting of parts of the 3rd, 14th, and 24th Divisions. Given the terrain and dispositions, "direct frontal attack" was the only method available to them.[87]

This was not Wu's preferred method of operation. As we have seen, his original plan had been to tie down the Fengtian main forces at Shanhaiguan, and then use a naval flotilla to land the 14th Division behind them. He had prepared for such a maneuver by obtaining ten commercial transport vessels from Tianjin and Yantai, which he assembled on the sea at Tanggu. These embarked troops still at Beijing, Fengtai, and Changxindian north to Qinhuangdao: one brigade each of the 3rd and the 24th Divisions, and the entire 14th Division. These forces were then to await the order to land on the Manchurian coast. But after the Fengtian breakthrough at Shimenzhai, Wu was forced to abandon the idea of attacking the enemy rear, and orders were given for those units instead to disembark at Qinhuangdao to join the defensive struggle.[88]

The struggle along the rivers and narrow-gauge railway line in the valley drew in more and more forces. From October 13 until November 24 the Zhili units from Henan and Shaanxi that were commanded by Zhang Fulai mounted fierce attacks. Fengtian increased the troops of the First and Third Armies by three or more mixed brigades, and the senior commanders of the Fengtian First Army, Jiang Dengxuan and Han Linchun, directed the battle personally at the front lines. So powerful were the Zhili attacks, however, particularly in the vicinity of Heishanyao, that a brigade commander and many officers of lower rank died.[89]

Lawrence Impey, an eyewitness, gave his impressions of the struggle:

These three divisions on the Shihmenzhai front did push back a considerably superior force for some distance, and until the coup d'état in Beijing wrecked the whole campaign, it seemed more than likely that they would eventually succeed in regaining the Jiumen Pass. The bitter character of the fighting here was particularly noticeable during the night engagements of the 18th and 19th of

87. Impey, *The Chinese Army*, p. 16.
88. Mao Jinling, p. 117.
89. Fu Xingpei, p. 35.

October, the writer meeting a steady stream of casualties coming back from Shihmenzhai on the days following the engagements. The struggle was of a hand to hand character quite dissimilar to anything experienced in the campaign of 1922, and the writer noticed on the field a large number of rifles with broken butts and twisted barrels indicative of the bitter nature of the fight. The bulk of the casualties during the period, and they appeared to amount to about twenty per cent of the forces engaged, were bayonet wounds, bullet wounds, or machine gun wounds, the artillery seeming to have been comparatively harmless in its effects.[90]

Meanwhile, reinforcements were arriving. The situation was not easy at the Qinhuangdao harbor. Seven thousand Zhili troops were denied landing at Qinhuangdao on October 17 by order of the British garrison, citing a protocol of 1901.[91] But shortly thereafter, 30,000 troops intended for the landing on the Manchurian coast did manage to land there, and were thrown into the breach on the Shanhaiguan front.[92]

Given all this, it might have seemed that Fengtian was doing well, while Zhili seemed only barely to be holding on. But this assessment would have been misleading. In World War I–style battle, there is a big difference between a partial breakthrough, later contained, and one that leads to some strategically decisive military accomplishment. Zhang Zuolin had broken Wu Peifu's defensive line. But Wu had been able to withdraw, in reasonable order, to a new perimeter. He still had his lines of communications. Therefore, although Zhang Zuolin might seem to have been in a strong position, in fact his strategy was threatened by its apparent success. This was because in order to hold the new positions he had captured near Shanhaiguan, he had to withdraw troops from his flank positions at Rehe and Chifeng – and doing this would make him vulnerable to the sort of indirect attack at which Wu Peifu excelled. The possibility of a seaborne assault from the Zhili side could also not be completely discounted. The dilemma was well illustrated by the decisions Fengtian had been forced to make, just as its most dramatic break-throughs were being achieved.

The Fengtian forces had been mounting unsuccessful frontal attacks against Wu at Shanhaiguan for two days when the Japanese provided them with intelligence about the Zhili maritime strategy already mentioned, which the Japanese stated involved thirteen ships, which would transport three or four divisions from Dagu, near Tianjin, to Fengtian territory. But the intelligence sources did not know whether Huludao,

90. Impey, *The Chinese Army*, pp. 18–9.
91. NYT, October 17, 1924, 13.
92. NYT, October 19, 1924, 28.

directly behind the Fengtian lines, or Yingkou, at the head of the Liaodong bay, or some other place, would be the landing site.[93]

At this critical point some in the Fengtian headquarters suggested sending troops from the reserve army to Yingkou and Huludao. One staff officer argued that all the reserve should be kept at Jiumenkou and Shimenzhai. Zhang's chief of staff, Yang Yuting, did not agree, arguing that the pass was too narrow to accommodate so large an army. The Old Marshal himself had to intervene to resolve the argument. As his two advisers argued, he interrupted, saying "Please order that Zhang Zuoxiang's army should move quickly to Jiumenkou and join the final battle at Shimenzhai."[94] There they turned the tide – although Wu proved able to prevent the Fengtian tactical success at Shimenzhai from turning into a strategic victory.

In fact, even as the Fengtian forces moved forward, they were becoming overextended. And as Wu gradually solidified his position and moved up reserves, the possibility of further Fengtian breakthroughs receded. So Fengtian faced a double bind. Prudence demanded that they redeploy some forces back to Manchuria to deal with the flanking attack – from the sea or however – that Wu was bound to make. But if they did so, they would weaken their position in and around Shanhaiguan – thus increasing the likelihood that Wu would begin to win back lost ground, and even ultimately make a breakthrough of his own.

The situation at Shimenzhai, where the battle ebbed and flowed, was a particular strategic headache for Fengtian. To strengthen that position, Zhang Xueliang and Guo Songling decided secretly to withdraw eight regiments of three battalions from the front at the Shanhaiguan pass itself, as well as a major part of Guo Songling's artillery brigade, and to take them through Jiumenkou and use them to strengthen the Shimenzhai front line.[95] But there was disagreement within the command about this move, which – had Zhili discovered it – could have threatened the entire Fengtian position.

And, as on the Zhili side, personal rivalries repeatedly threatened Fengtian. Thus, in the midst of the most critical fighting, Han Linchun attempted to remove a commander of the artillery belonging to Guo Songling, an action that so enraged Guo that he marched eight regiments of his army away from the key position at Jiumenkou. Had Zhili known, they could have attacked and completely restored their position. But it was night, and they did not. In the meantime, the Old Marshal's son Zhang Xueliang hastened to the front and found Guo. Our source

93. Fu Xingpei, p. 35.
94. Ibid., pp. 35–6.   95. Ibid., p. 36.

tells how the two men fell tearfully into one another's arms, and how Guo was then persuaded to return to the front.[96]

From such drama, however, the "Battle of the Great Wall," as it is known, gradually settled down to a hard slog. Wu Peifu understood this development and realized that in the long run it could only favor him. Thus, once the defenses around Shanhaiguan had been secured, he showed no sign of taking any more risk than he had to. He no longer faced the imminent threat of a Fengtian breakthrough, so he could display the same sort of cold-blooded calculation the German General Erich von Falkenhayn (1861–1922) had when he entangled the French at Verdun. Falkenhayn had not planned actually to crush the French; only to bleed them white by forcing them to defend a position they could not, for reasons of pride, abandon. Likewise Wu. He had Fengtian where he had originally wanted them. They were pinned at Shanhaiguan, concentrating more and more of their forces there, hoping for a strategic breakthrough that was becoming more unlikely by the day. Only a bold maneuver – Wu's forte – could break the stalemate. The one he had originally planned – the seaborne landing – might have to be put aside for the moment. But time was on his side. He could hold the line at Shanhaiguan all winter if necessary and prepare his final stroke deliberately. In the meantime, he was content to make the Fengtian forces pay a high cost for their position.[97] This he did, with artillery bombardment from his lines, and from his navy along the Manchurian coast.[98]

According to American military intelligence, Wu Peifu's lines on October 22 were intact and his positions strongly held. In the opinion of foreign observers on the Shanhaiguan front, his army was "in the best condition since the mobilization started." Supplies and reserves were coming up to Qinhuangdao at a rapid rate, and of course the numbers were on Wu's side. Although Zhang Zuolin's main force concentrations made it difficult for Wu to advance, an offensive by Feng Yuxiang on the Fengtian flank could still have destroyed Zhang's position, enabled Wu to break through, and permitted "a victorious advance into Manchuria."[99]

Such an advance nearly happened: had the trends that were clear on October 22 continued, it most likely would have, with consequences that

---

96. Ibid.
97. NYT, October 19, 1924, 28; Alistair Horne, *The Price of Glory: Verdun 1916* (Harmondsworth, England: Penguin Books, 1964), p. 44.
98. NYT, October 21, 1924, 15.
99. Report: Situation Survey for the period of October 16th to December 31st 1924, pp. 1–2, in MIR.

are fascinating to consider. But it did not, because of what is usually called the *Beijing zhengbian* or "Beijing *coup d'état*" of General Feng Yuxiang. Just as victory seemed to be coming into Zhili's grasp, Wu's collaborator abruptly abandoned the front and made a surprise march on Beijing, where he took control of the city, put the president under house arrest, and proclaimed a new government. Feng's purpose was to make himself, at this critical turning point, the arbiter of Chinese politics. He fell far short of that goal, but he did succeed in throwing the Zhili position into chaos, ultimately forcing Wu Peifu to abandon the fight and flee to the Yangzi valley. The great showdown between Zhili and Fengtian thus ended with a whimper.

Just how and why Feng carried out his *coup d'état*, and more broadly why the war ended as it did, indirectly creating revolution in the process, are complex questions, and by no means purely military. They cannot be fully answered without more understanding of the economic, social, and diplomatic effects of the fighting we have just narrated. The next three chapters – 6, 7, and 8 – consider those effects in detail. The full story of Feng's *coup*, and its consequences for both war and politics in China, are told in Chapters 9 and 10.

Fengtian aircraft. (Still from "Modern Warfare in China in 1924–25: Struggle Between Mukden and Peking," evidently a Soviet-produced film, ostensibly documentary, of reconstructed dramatizations of scenes from the war and Zhang Zuolin's subsequent southward advance [1925]. Courtesy of Imperial War Museum, London.)

Fengtian troops charge under cover of mortar fire. (Still from "Modern Warfare in China"; courtesy of Imperial War Museum, London.)

Fengtian armored train in action. (Still from "Modern Warfare in China"; courtesy of Imperial War Museum, London.)

(*Opposite, top*) Farmers press-ganged at Qinhuangdao to serve as munitions carriers for the Zhili forces. Note the yokes from which munitions boxes will be hung. (From Impey, *The Chinese Army*, facing p. 32.)

(*Opposite*) Wireless station at on platform at Qinhuangdao station (now destroyed), next to "His Excellency" – Marshal Wu Peifu's train. (*The Sphere*, December 13, 1924, p. 309; courtesy of *Illustrated London News* Picture Library.)

Zhili machine gun, posted on railway line to shoot stragglers and deserters. (From Impey, *The Chinese Army*, facing p. 52.)

Fortifications at Jiumenkou pass, eastern side. (Photo: Author.)

One of Wu Peifu's armored cars, mounting a one-pounder gun. (*The Sphere*, December 13, 1924, p. 308; courtesy of *Illustrated London News* Picture Library.)

Stokes mortar in use. (From Impey, *The Chinese Army*, after p. 56.)

Wounded Zhili soldiers leaving the front. Most dead were buried in mass graves at the battlefield; only officers got coffins. (*The Sphere*, December 13, 1924, p. 309; courtesy of *Illustrated London News* Picture Library.)

6
The war and the economy

For more than twenty days at the beginning of the Zhili–Fengtian War, as decisive battles raged to the north, Wu Peifu remained in the capital. While his forces were being outmaneuvered on the western front and his lines broken in the east at Shanhaiguan, the Marshal's attention was focused above all on "the four–two loan"–an attempt to raise funds abroad on the security of customs revenue, so called because its face value would be $4,200,000 (Chinese). Wu needed all the money he could get. Unfortunately for the Marshal, Fengtian was financially in far better shape than Zhili. It was estimated that war on the scale unfolding would cost China something on the order of $20 million (Chinese) per month, a vast amount.[1] For both sides the ability to pay for the war looked likely to prove to be as important to its outcome as the skill and courage with which it was fought.

Equally, the economic impact of the war would turn out to be as important to China's future as the battles fought in its course. As we have noted, viewed over time and in aggregate, China did rather well during the decades of the 1910s and 1920s, with widening trade, stable prices, and more rapid economic growth than has usually been recognized.[2] But although prosperity and growth were real enough and widespread, they were also precarious and shallow-rooted. For Shanghai and Tianjin in particular, the 1920s were largely boom times, the product initially of the sudden boost that local industries received from World War I and sustained thereafter by the damping effects of the Chinese

1. NYT, October 7, 1924, 25. The Chinese monetary system at this time was extremely complex, and exchange rates were constantly in flux. However, *very roughly*, two Chinese dollars equaled one U.S. dollar. See CYB 1925, p. 699, which gives the tael exchange rate. The dollar was, very approximately, 64 percent of the tael. Unless otherwise noted, dollar means Chinese dollar in this chapter.
2. Thomas J. Rawski, *Economic Growth in Prewar China* (Berkeley: University of California Press, 1989).

silver standard on the world depression. In both cities, the boom created and was created by linkages to a hinterland: the Yangzi valley for Shanghai; the coal, iron, and other heavy industry of today's northeast and Hebei for Tianjin. Such largely untrammeled economic growth depended very much on the relative peace that had prevailed in Shanghai since the days of the Taipings and in Tianjin since the Boxer Rebellion. All that changed in 1924.[3] Even before the outbreak of fighting, financial panics spread through China, destabilizing both investment and commerce. As both sides borrowed at home and abroad, and imposed new taxes on commerce and property, they made the situation even worse. They commandeered and drafted the materiel and the men they would need for the battles to come, while the fighting itself destroyed property, threw transportation and commerce into disorder, separated buyers from sellers, and propelled waves of refugees and defeated soldiers into the hitherto calm treaty ports. The importance of such depredations can be and probably has been exaggerated: Thomas Rawski may well be correct when he observes that warfare in China had less of an aggregate effect on the economy than caricatures of the "warlord" period sometimes suggest.[4] But this is not to say that, at certain critical moments, the economic factors in the larger social and political equations were not very important. The wars of 1924 had a decisive impact on China's economy and society–the topics, respectively, of this and the following chapter.

Economically, Zhili and Fengtian were unevenly matched at the outset. In the 1920s the finances of Zhang's administration at Mukden were strong. The region's salt revenue belonged to him, and he enjoyed control as well of the railway from Mukden to Shanhaiguan. Yearly govenment revenues in Fengtian were over $30 million.[5] By the autumn of 1924, Wang Yongjiang (1871–1927), the brilliant scholar and industrialist whom Zhang had appointed as acting civil governor of Fengtian in 1992, had spent $20 million on preparations for the conflict with Zhili. When war broke out, he had already put aside sufficient funds to support six months' fighting.[6] Zhang also had plenty of money to help his allies. In the period before the war he made substantial advances to Lu Yongxiang, as well as to Sun Yat-sen, far away at Guangzhou,

---

3. See Yu Sun, "Jiang-Zhe jiufen zhong Hu bu jinrong zhi yice," *Yinhang zhoubao* 8 (September 9, 1924), no. 35, 5 (hereafter cited as YHZB).
4. Rawski, *Economic Growth*, 45–8.
5. Chen Yuguang, "Wang Yongjiang zhengtun Feng sheng caizheng zhi qianqian houhou," *Jilin wenshiziliao xuanji*, No. 4.
6. CB, November 1, 1924, cited in Lou Xiangzhe, "Lun di er ci Zhi Feng zhangzheng" (Master's thesis: Nankai University, 1985), 14, note 21.

who had seized upon the outbreak of fighting to announce an abortive Northern Expedition.[7]

Zhili, by contrast, faced a fiscal crisis even without the war: revenue-short and overborrowed, it would be hard pressed to pay for sustained military operations.[8] Prime Minister Yan Huiqing recalls a cabinet meeting as war was breaking at which Wu Peifu (who also served as minister of war), when asked how much money Zhili would need, replied that it would be "three *lakhs* [i.e., $300,000] (*per diem*)." When Wang Kemin, the minister of finance, was interrogated as to the possibility of finding the necessary funds, his reply was, "I will do my best, Sir."[9] Wang proved more than resourceful.

Finance was without question the most difficult ministerial portfolio in Beijing during these years, one that almost inevitably caught its holder in a complex crossfire, both domestic and foreign. Domestically, he would be torn between his duty to the president and to the cabinet. In theory a member of the cabinet, in fact the minister of finance was usually the president's man. The premier had no fixed financial allocation: provision even of the $50,000 per month required to run the cabinet secretariat was provided at the discretion of the minister of finance. So when premier and finance minister came into conflict – as Sun Baoqi and Wang Kemin did – it was usually the premier who resigned.[10] Beyond such domestic troubles, moreover, lay the issues of international borrowing; Chinese governments of the period always heard in the background the angry chorus of the Powers, demanding the payment of defaulted obligations.

The finance minister's predicament was thus difficult. But it would oversimplify to explain this as a matter of money alone. Wealth was not scarce in the China of the 1920s. Trade thrived, and even at the low rate at which internal and external customs duties were permitted to be levied, the yield was respectable – some Chinese $114,905,091 in 1924. The problem was getting these funds – theoretically the property of the central government – into the treasury. As it turned out, most of the sum just mentioned was not in fact available to the government. Once expenses of collection and so-called tonnage dues – amounts earmarked for harbor improvement and lighthouse maintenance – were deducted, the net customs revenue in 1924 was $93,586,889. Of this amount,

7. Beiyang Zhengfu da zongtongfu dangan 1003.31; Ye Jian xiansheng nianpu, 216–17; cited in Lou, "Zhi Feng," note 18.
8. CB, November 1, 1924, cited in Lou, "Zhi Feng," 14 note 21.
9. W. W. Yen, *East–West Kaleidoscope 1877–1946: An Autobiography* (New York: St. John's University Press, 1974), p. 147.
10. Ibid., 146.

however, $66,847,714 was set aside by the internationally supervised customs service for the service of foreign loans and indemnities.[11] This left the Beijing government with a theoretical income from customs of $26,737,175, not enough to cover the roughly $3.5 million of monthly government expenditure that was the minimum necessary at that time.[12] The result was a chronic deficit. From the abdication of the Manchus in 1912 until 1917, when Duan Qirui first took control of the government, the amount of money paid out by Beijing had approximately doubled. Government income, however, had not kept pace, and the difference was made up by internal and external borrowing.[13]

Because financial services had grown rapidly in China during the preceding decades, credit was initially not difficult to obtain. This situation changed, however, in the immediate post–World War I period. During the war, the government borrowed large amounts of money from Japan as well as domestically. By 1919 total internal loans amounted to approximately $400 million, but except for those having specific security, they were by and large in arrears.[14] Meanwhile, securing new funds became increasingly problematical, as the Powers attempted to systematize their financial dealings with China in a way that held both menace and promise. The threat to China came as the international banks increasingly cooperated to limit and regularize credit through the successive formation of two international banking consortiums.[15] But there was also the possibility of solving China's financial problems once and for all.

At the Washington Conference it had been recognized that the customs system as it stood was unfair to China. International treaties limited duty to 5 percent, and it was not even charged *ad valorem*; as prices rose the amounts paid to the Customs House remained the same.[16] So it was agreed that China shoud immediately be allowed a 2.5 percent surcharge on the customs revenue, pending a complete revamping of the system of financial administration. In addition, there was the possibility of further increasing customs levies in return for internal reforms in China. These

11. Stanley F. Wright, *China's Customs Revenue since the Revolution of 1911*, 3rd ed. (Shanghai: Inspectorate General of Customs, 1935), table on pp. 440–1. The amounts are given in HK taels and pounds sterling and converted to standard dollars at the rate of HK taels 100 = St. $155.80.
12. Yen, *East–West Kaleidoscope*, p. 145.
13. Gu Shiyi, *Minguo xu caizhengshi* (Shanghai: Shangwu, 1932), vol. 1, p. 53; cited by Lou, "Zhi Feng," p. 11.
14. Qian Jiaju, *Zhongguo de neizhai* (Shehui diaochasuo, 1933), p. 8; cited in Lou, "Zhi Feng," p. 11.
15. See Frederick V. Field, *American Participation in the China Consortiums* (Chicago: University of Chicago Press, 1931).
16. Yen, *East–West Kaleidoscope*, p. 158.

matters would be determined at a special conference on the Chinese customs tariff, which was set to open not more than three months after the ratification of the Washington treaties. As we have seen, however, this potential breakthrough was halted by the gold franc dispute.

In connection with that dispute and at the insistence of France, the inspector general of customs, Sir Francis Aglen (1869–1932), had drawn the contested amounts from the customs revenue and impounded them in an escrow account which by 1924 contained some $16 million – money that would otherwise have been available to the Beijing government.[17] The gold franc dispute furthermore prevented the levying of the increases in customs duties already promised by the Washington Conference, which would have totaled at least $46 million and would have reached $156 million once China abolished the system of internal transit taxes known as *lijin*.[18] Money in such amounts would greatly have ameliorated the Chinese government's financial problems. Without the fulfillment of the Washington Conference undertakings, however, the financial outlook was bleak.

In the interim, the Beijing government was forced to resort to ever more creative accounting to stay afloat. In 1920 the Columbia University–educated minister of finance, Zhou Ziqi (1871–1932), attempted to restore financial confidence by successfully redeeming discounted notes of the Bank of China and the Bank of Communications, and prepared a plan for consolidating internal dabt.[19] But in fact borrowing simply increased. In the two years before the Zhili group came to power in 1922, the Beijing government had floated seven internal loans having a total face value of $262,392,228 – so much that government credibility had hit rock bottom and bankers were unwilling to advance credit. Much the same was true of foreign loans. Between 1911 and 1924 Beijing had concluded some 352 foreign loan agreements having a face value of $1,123,651,157.[20] Service owed on foreign debts and indemnities in 1924 amounted to $66,752,025.[21]

In addition to this crushing burden of debt, the Zhili group faced other financial problems. The central government's most important revenues had traditionally come from two sources, the customs [*guanyu*] and the salt tax [*yanyu*]. The customs revenue was ordinarily used to

---

17. See Liu Yan, *Zuijin sanshi nian Zhongguo waijiaoshi* (Shanghai: Taipingyang shudian, 1932), p. 162, cited in Lou, "Zhi Feng," p. 12.
18. Stanley F. Wright, *China's Struggle for Tariff Autonomy* (Shanghai: Kelly & Walsh, 1938), pp. 447–8.
19. BDRC, vol. 1, p. 430; Yen, *East–West Kaleidoscope*, p. 112.
20. Lou, "Zhi Feng," appendix II, based on Zhongguo lianhe zhunbei yinhang, *Zhongguo neiwaizhai xiangbian*, table 1; also Lou, "Zhi Feng," p. 11.
21. Wright, *Tariff Autonomy*, pp. 440–1.

pay military costs, whereas the salt revenue guaranteed internal loans. We have seen that the customs revenue had effectively become unavailable to the government. At the same time, other sources of revenue that were earmarked for the central government were increasingly intercepted by local authorities. Thus, of the ordinary customs revenue, the so-called *changguanshui*, the central government was able to obtain only the proceeds from the taxes levied at the gates of Beijing itself–the *Chongwenmen jiandushu shui*, which amounted to less than $2 million.[22] This compared unfavorably with the amounts held back by local authorities. Lu Yongxiang and Ma Lianjia, for example, witheld $2 million in 1922 and $4 million in 1923.[23]

Taking office in 1922 after the First Zhili–Fengtian War, the initial Zhili administration adopted a policy of stringency that cut government expenditures drastically. No matter how it is measured, whether in number or value of loans, the period of Zhili administration from 1922 to 1924 saw Beijing's borrowing hit an all-time low. The amount borrowed in 1923, $39,697,735, was only a little more than 26 percent of the $149,585,917 borrowed by the Anfu government in 1918.[24] Military spending in 1924 had plummeted to the lowest level of any year during the period of the Northern System.[25] Nevertheless, by 1923 the Beijing government's income amounted to less than 10 percent of its expenditures, and by 1924 Prime Minister Yan Huiqing was speaking of a financial crisis that threatened the administration with collapse.[26]

The four–two loan was possible only because of China's recent and largely symbolic participation in World War I. Beijing's declaration of war on Germany and Austria in March 14, 1917, had meant the end of Chinese payments on those nations' shares of the Boxer indemnity. From that date those funds – which were deducted from the customs revenues – were no longer deposited in the Deutsch–Asiatische Bank on behalf of the Powers as previously, but instead became available to the Chinese government for certain purposes. With the agreement of the customs administration, these funds had already been used to service three existing internal loans, those of the third, fourth, and fifth years of the Republic. Once Aglen agreed in 1924 that they could be used to secure both principal and interest, there was no difficulty in floating what was

22. *Shenbao*, December 12, 1923 (hereafter cited as SB), cited in Lou, "Zhi Feng," p. 12.
23. SB, August 28, 1922 and May, 28, 1923, cited in Lou, "Zhi Feng," p. 12.
24. Xu Yisheng, *Zhongguo jindai waizhai tongji ziliao* (Zhonghua shuju, 1962), p. 240, table 3; Zhongguo lianhe zhunbei yinhang, *Zhongguo neiwaizhai xiangbian*, table 13, cited by Lou, "Zhi Feng," p. 11.
25. Lou, "Zhi Feng," p. 13.
26. SB, December 28, 1923; April 17, 1924, cited by Lou, "Zhi Feng," p. 13.

known as the Thirteenth Year Treasury Note Issue, or the four–two.[27] Authorized by presidential mandate on October 7, it was an issue of treasury notes having a face value of $4,200,000, bearing an interest rate of 8 percent, and fully redeemable by September 30, 1927. Issued at 94 – a figure, it should be noted, that suggests some degree of investor confidence – its total amount was immediately underwritten by the Beijing branches of the Bank of China, the Bank of Communications, the Salt Industrial Bank, and the Kincheng Banking Corporation.

The underwriters insisted, however, that the loan should be used not for military expenditures but, rather, to pay the costs of the civil government and the maintenance of order in the capital. For this reason they divided the payment into three monthly installments of $1,316,000 and went so far on two occasions as to hand over "the actual cash to the police authorities in the presence of Chinese and foreign witnesses." Wu, who had so agonized over the loan, ended up with less than $1,750,000.[28] Even so, Beijing's opponents, including Zhang Zuolin, Lu Yongxiang, and even Sun Yat-sen, all lodged vigorous protests with the *corps diplomatique*.[29]

Meanwhile, the other contestants in the wars were also raising money. As we have seen, the financial situation in Fengtian presented a sharp contrast to that in Beijing. Zhang Zuolin was rarely at a loss for funds, but even his reserves were not unlimited. He threatened to take control of the Manchurian customs revenues if the Powers permitted the four–two loan to go forward. This sufficiently worried the Japanese that they told the American ambassador in Tokyo that they would protect customs at both Dalian [Dairen] and Andong – though not at Ha-er-bin [Harbin] or Yingkou [Newchang] – unilaterally if necessary.[30]

Around Shanghai, meanwhile, a small storm began to brew when the provincial authorities of both Jiangsu and Zhejiang carried out an immediate – and by treaty quite illegal – seizure of all salt revenues – an amount that could reach $17 million – to be put to military purposes. Since this action threatened payment to foreign subscribers of the massive

27. Stanley F. Wright, *China's Customs Revenues Since the Revolution of 1911*, 3rd ed., rev. and enl. (Shanghai: Inspectorate General of Customs, 1935), pp. 195–6.
28. "Shishi shuping," DZ, 21.19, CB, November 10, 1924, cited by Lou, "Zhi Feng," p. 11; also Wright, *China's Customs Revenues*, pp. 272–3.
29. See Ferdinand Mayer to Secretary of State, November 5, 1924, to which is attached Dean Circular No. 277 of October 3, 1924 containing protests of Zhang Zuolin and Lu Yongxiang; Mayer to Secretary of State, November 22, 1924, to which is attached Senior Minister Circular No. 319 of November 3, 1924, which contains Sun Yat-sen's protest, transmitted by the senior Japanese consul in Guangzhou. SD 893.51/4738.
30. R. P. Tenney to Secretary of State, October 1, 1924 SD 893.51/4713; Edward Bell to Secretary of State, October 2, 1924 SD 893.51/4694; Caffery (Tokyo) to Secretary of State, October 18, 1924 SD 893.51/4697.

Reorganization Loan of 1913, British and other banking interests were immediately alarmed and began to lobby their governments to intervene.[31]

And in Beijing Wang Kemin continued to search for possible foreign support. There was a spate of rumors that in order to get hold of cash he had agreed to French terms for resolving the gold franc dispute; Yan Huiqing reported French attempts to bribe him for the same purpose. Although resolution of the dispute would have made Beijing's financial situation easier, and was almost certainly explored, the matter was a point of national pride and Gu Weijun clearly scotched any suggestion of capitulation.[32] Early in October the British group in the China consortium declined a Beijing request for an advance of £1 million, to be secured by complete control of the Tianjin–Pukou railway as well as German-issued Chinese railway bonds having face value of £2.2 million.[33] On October 21 the American consul in Qingdao reported an approach seeking a loan of several millions of dollars for Wu Peifu, to be secured by the revenues of the Qingdao wharves, though nothing came of it.[34]

The imbalance in resources between Zhili and Fengtian clearly affected the course of the war. Zhili's preparations were hampered by lack of funds. Lack of $2,400,000 forced postponement of essential overhauling of the warships that were crucial to Wu Peifu's strategy. Without money the Zhili airforce could not be properly constituted.[35] Lack of funds hampered Zhili weapons and ammunition production and affected quality as well. At the battle of Erlangmiao, Zhili forces outnumbering their Fengtian adversaries by two to one were defeated because their weapons were inferior. At the Jiaoshansi battle, the Zhili forces were unable to recover lost positions because of the ineffectiveness of their weapons. Bombing attacks by Fengtian aircraft several times forced Peng Shouxin and Wang Huaiqing to move their headquarters and greatly disrupted the Zhili forces during the Shanhaiguan battle. Experts at the time pointed out that the inferior quality of Zhili weaponry was an important reason for its defeat.[36]

The Zhili group's financial problems created real difficulties in morale.

31. See J. P. Morgan and Co. to Secretary of State, November 3, 1924, enclosing correspondence between Sir Charles Addis and C. F. Whigham.
32. Yen, *East–West Kaleidoscope*, pp. 127–8.
33. See Kellogg (American Ambassador, London) to Secretary of State, October 13, 1924 SD 893.51/4696; J. P. Morgan and Co. to the Secretary of State, October 20, 1924 SD 893.51/4700; Secretary of State to Bell, October 27, 1924 enclosing related telegrams from the American Embassy, London SD 893.51/4700.
34. Walter A. Adams to Secretary of State, October 21, 1924 SD 893.51/4721.
35. Okano Masujirō, *Go Haifu* [Wu Peifu] (Tokyo: Banseikaku, 1939), pp. 453–5, cited in Lou, "Zhi Feng," note 29; Zhao Hengti, ed., *Wu Peifu xiansheng ji* (1939; reprint ed., Taibei: Wenhai, n.d.), p. 318.
36. Lou, "Zhi Feng," p. 16, Impey, *Chinese Army*, p. 21.

In the summer before the war, the long-standing lack of military supplies had led Wang Chengbin and Feng Yuxiang, two of the leading Zhili commanders, to submit letters of resignation to President Cao Kun.[37] As his forces were setting out for the front, Wang Chengbin had asked Wu for funds. The Marshal flatly refused him and scolded him to his face. Although Wang did not show it, he was deeply upset by this incident, and Wu's move to deny him command of his 23rd Division did not improve relations between the two men.[38] Feng Yuxiang complained that payment of his troops was six months in arrears when the war began, and that clothing and provisions were deficient.[39] Feng's feelings cannot have been helped by the fact that Cao Kun impounded $2 million of his $6 million payment on setting out for battle [*chufafei*].[40] Indeed, Feng was enraged by the financial treatment he received at the hands of Cao and Wu.[41]

Morale problems extended to the troops as well. Wu instructed his units to acquire supplies locally. This meant that their food was often inadequate and that they lacked the padded jackets needed in the cold.[42] Soldiers, long unpaid, had a saying: "Fight as much war as there was money for" [*you duoshao qian bian da duoshao zhang*]. Troops of the 9th Division, sent to the front without provisions, considered that they had "done their job once they had fired one or two shots" [*daole qianxian, gei ta fang liang qiang, jiu suan duideqi ta*].[43] Indeed, the growing consensus among historians in China is that the economic imbalance between the two sides was probably the single most decisive factor in determining the military outcome of the war.[44]

The connection between economics and war was not limited simply to the verdict of the battlefield. The war and efforts to pay for it had deep effects on the politics and society of the time. Economic life in China was widely disrupted; confidence in government and the future was shaken; many people lost their homes or their money. Along with the fighting itself, the financial problems of the combatants sent wave after wave of

37. *Minguo ribao* May 4, 5, 7, 1924, cited by Lou, "Zhi Feng," pp. 14–15.
38. Lou, "Zhi Feng," p. 15.
39. *Feng Yuxiang riji*, shang, p. 72, cited by Lou, "Zhi Feng," note 25.
40. Jian Yuwen, "Feng Yuxiang zhuan," *Zhuanji wenxue* vol. 37, no. 2, cited in Lou, "Zhi Feng," p. 16, note 26.
41. Beiyang Zhengfu jingji weishu zongsilingbu dangan 1024.87 cited in Lou, "Zhi Feng," p. 15, note 27.
42. Lu Guangyu, *Minguo shiyao chuji*, p. 117, cited in Lou, "Zhi Feng," p. 15, note, 23; Ding Wenjiang, *Minguo junshi jinji*, shang, 53.
43. Wang Weicheng, "Zhixi de fenlie he er ci Zhi Feng zhanzheng Zhixi de shibai," in *Beiyang junfa shiliao xuanji* 2 vols., ed. Du Chunhe, Lin Binsheng, and Qiu Quanzheng (Beijing: Zhongguo shehui kexue chubanshe, 1981), vol. 2, pp. 92–105.
44. Lou is of this opinion: see "Zhi Feng," p. 16.

economic confusion crashing onto Chinese society, creating an instability that ramified, through market and financial networks, far beyond the actual theater of fighting.

Because adequate foreign financing was unavailable to any of the Chinese combatants, all were forced increasingly to seek out domestic sources. This meant that the cost of the war was met by native banks and provincial levies.[45] The attempt by the military to raise money was one of the causes of the economic crisis. The Beijing government was not rich in the best of times, and the demands of Wu Peifu's army led it to extreme measures. Not only were all government funds diverted to military uses; the government used extraordinary measures to force individuals, banks, and companies to extend credit to it. These measures directly and the impact of the fighting indirectly suddenly involved the lives and fortunes of China's still-emerging commercial and industrial class in war to an unprecedented degree.

Always sensitive to danger ahead, money and credit markets had registered the first signs of trouble even before the fighting began. In the Shanghai area, "commerce chambers and influential Chinese drafted peace terms," which were submitted to Generals Lu Yongxiang and Qi Xieyuan, to profuse thanks but without effect.[46] And as the opposing forces drew up their lines in the south, one of the most serious of Chinese financial panics up to that time began, starting in Shanghai and Beijing, and then spreading through the transport and trading networks to places as distant as Chongqing and Ha-er-bin. The economic impact of this panic did much to unsettle China's urban middle classes and prepare them psychologically for the revolutionary movement that would follow in a few months.

The first signs of the panic came in the Shanghai domestic money markets. Hard money in China at this time was mostly silver dollars of various kinds: for many years those of Mexico, Hong Kong, and the Straits Settlements, but increasingly replaced by the Chinese Sun Yat-sen dollars of 1912 and the Yuan Shikai dollars of 1914. The coinage was bimetallic – silver for large denominations and copper cash for smaller transactions. There were also numerous bank notes and government notes. In June and July alone the big Shanghai banks had issued 1 million yuan in paper.[47] Yuan, or "dollar," however, was a denomination: Value was measured, for purposes of reference and comparison, in terms of the dollar price of the *guiyuan*, a weight of silver of a certain

45. NYT, October 7, 1924, 25.
46. CWR, September 6, 1924, 28.
47. "Zuijin Shanghai jinrong shankuang zhi biandong," *Zhongwai jingji zhoukan* (1924), no. 81, 3.

purity. As one commentator observed, although the dollar might super-ficially be considered money, in fact it was no different from commercial goods because its exchange rate with the *tael* of silver, its parallel mone-tary unit, was determined by the market twice a day.[48] When demand for real silver coin was steady, that rate would be steady; if for some reason demand for coinage rose, the rate would rise. The rate was called the *yangli*: it was determined in the morning and at noon by two markets run by the Money Dealers' Association [*qianye gonghui*], one in north Shanghai, the other in the south.[49] At the beginning of August 1924 the price of the *guiyuan* was between 7.07 and 7.08, that is to say less than 7.1 [7 *qian* 1 *fen*], which indicated no unusual demand for specie.[50]

By the middle of the month, as the situation in the southeast became more anxious, the various note-issuing banks, expecting a rise in re-demptions, began secretly to buy silver coin; as a result, the price began to rise. By August 20, it had reached 7.2. This caused particular trouble for the *qianzhuang* and led to panic in the money market. Rumors began to fly. Many depositors began withdrawing their funds and changing paper money into specie. When the market opened on August 21, the price of silver soared to 7.4. By noon there were people bidding 8. Only intervention from bank administrations held the price at 7.4. Subsequent investigation showed that, despite the rise in price, the actual volume traded had been less than 10,000 yuan, which indicated that people were unwilling to sell specie. In the days following, the price moved up and down erratically, with fluctuations of 1 or 2 percent in a single day being common, ten times greater than what had previously been normal.

On August 27 transport between Ningbo and Shanghai was cut, and people became even more panicky. When the market opened, there were again bids of 8 or 7.9, but no sellers. The confusion was such that by 3:00 P.M. the market could not be sustained. Several foreign banks intervened, selling 5,000 yuan at a fixed price of 7.5, and the market was then closed. Without this forceful intervention the price would probably have risen above 8. But it then stabilized, not moving even when firing broke out on September 3, although it remained high.[51]

48. Yu Sun, "Jin yue Shanghai wujia zhisubiao zhi guancha," YHZB 8.41 (October 21, 1924), 7.
49. The *guiyuan* was a *liang* of silver having a purity of 916.666 thousandths. CYB 1925, 954–5; "Guiyuan zhi jieshi ji jisuanfa," YHZB, 8.35 (1924), 42–3; Wright, *China's Customs Revenue*, p. 11.
50. Zhongguo renmin yinhang, Shanghai branch, ed., *Shanghai qianzhuang shiliao* (Shanghai: Renmin chubanshe, 1960), p. 124.
51. YHZB, 8.33 (August 26, 1924), 3–5; 8.35 (September 9, 1924), 1–4, 5–6; *Shanghai qianzhuang shiliao*, 124–5.

The panic, however, had already produced serious effects. It involved the note-issuing banks in big losses. The June issue of 1 million yuan, for example, had been made at a time when the rate was 7.08; to redeem those notes at 7.25, which was where the price settled after the war broke out, meant a loss on exchange alone of 1.7 percent.[52] A large bank could absorb this, but the undercapitalized Chinese *qianzhuang* could not. In the days around August 20 seven of the major ones in Shanghai went bankrupt: the Baokang, Qingfeng, Yongchang, Deyu, Longyu, Yongchun, and Yufeng. Of these only the Baokang was ever able to reopen. These failures in turn led to the run on silver that caused the rise in price mentioned above. People began to crowd into banks to withdraw their savings. Hoarded bank notes were brought out to be redeemed. And the refugees who had come from elsewhere because of the war brought with them large quantities of paper money to be redeemed. Banks and money shops extended their hours and worked even on holidays, and sufficient silver was found to bring the situation under control.[53]

Financial collapse was averted only when the *qianye gonghui* introduced a series of temporary regulations designed to ease the pressure for redemption: long-term deposits could not be converted to short-term, short-term or bearer notes could be redeemed only with the approval of boards of directors, and short-term credit was in general not to be extended, even to prosperous merchants. The net effect was greatly to reduce the amount of liquid capital that the banks required in the short term, thus preventing the panic from growing worse. The measures worked. Firms that lacked specie were to report this to the head of the association; once he was assured that the bank actually had capital, he could raise funds for them from all the members of the association.[54]

With the banking crisis came a collapse in the market in government bonds. In mid-August, the Shanghai market suddenly dropped, throwing the economic situation into further difficulty. With the price of silver rising and some of the smaller banks in trouble, the prices of government bonds collapsed. Between August 14 and August 20, the most important financial bond [*jinrong*], having a face value of 100 yuan, fell from 91 to 78, while the 6 percent reorganization bond [*zheng liu*] declined from 80 to 65, and the long-defaulted 6 percent bond of 1910 [*jiuliu*] fell from 35 to 28. Trading could not be sustained, and the market was closed on August 20. When it reopened on the twenty-fifth it was still weak; on the

52. "Zuijin Shanghai," p. 3.
53. YHZB, 8.36 (September 16, 1924), 22–4; "Zuijin Shanghai," p. 2.
54. Yu Sun, "Hu bu qianye yingfu shibian zhi fengchao guan," HYZB, 8.33 (August 26, 1924), pp. 3–4; Yang Yinpu, *Shanghai jinrong zuzhi gaiyao*, pp. 68–9.

twenty-seventh, with rumors of fighting on the Huangdu front, prices fell about 10 yuan more, bringing on panic selling which led the authorities to close the exchange. When it was confirmed that there was indeed fighting, the *jinrong* bond fell to 71 yuan, the *zhengliu* to 57 yuan, and the *jiuliu* to 17 yuan. Even after fighting stopped, these prices did not recover. Investors and traders alike were seeing their money vanish.[55] Meanwhile, a similar panic had already hit Beijing, whose financial markets were more complex than those of Shanghai.

The characteristic problem in Beijing was that government officials, particularly members of parliament, were themselves deeply involved in financial transactions. "There were some *qianzhuang* whose business depended on their connections with the members of the parliament; there were also many members of parliament who themselves ran *qianzhuang*. Among the eight hundred parliamentarians in both houses, at least two hundred were involved in the government bond market." This situation led to another characteristic unique to Beijing: namely, that it was the *qianzhuang*, and not the commercial banks, that played the major role in the exchange of government bonds.[56]

In Beijing the prices of government bonds began to fall in early to mid-August, even earlier than they had in Shanghai. But the drop was not so serious as in Shanghai. On August 17–18 the price of the bonds in Beijing actually started to rise. But when on August 18 one *qianzhuang* suddenly sold 4 to 5 million of the 6 percent bonds, which it had probably just bought from Shanghai in an attempted arbitrage operation, a wave of selling was triggered, and the price fell rapidly, by almost exactly the same amount it had in Shanghai. The banks tried to save the situation, but failed. On August 20, after hearing the news of the several bankruptcies of the *qianzhuang* in Shanghai, the situation appeared so bad that the exchange suspended transactions.[57]

---

55. "Shu gongzhai baodie zhi yuanyin ji weiji zhaixin qingxing," and "Gongzhai shichang jubianhou zhi guancha," YHZB, 8.33 (August 26, 1924), 5–7, 8–11; "Shanghai gongzhai shimian tingshi qianhou zhi jingguo," YHZB 8.35 (September 9, 1924), 7–8; "Shiju jiufen zhong Shanghai jin zhou zhigongzhai shimian," YHZB, 8.36 (September 16, 1924), 14–16; "Gongzhai jiangluo yu shiju shi guanlian," YHZB 8.43 (November 4, 1924), 1–3.

56. YHZB 8.34 (September 2, 1924), 1.

57. The story of the government bond crisis may be traced from a fifty-page account by the famous columnist Shao Piaoping: "Beijing gongzhai shimian zhi baobian yuanyin ji qi yingfu qingxing (I–V)," in YHZB 8.34 (September 2, 1924), 1–16, 8.35 (September 9, 1924), 10–18; 8.36 (September 16, 1924), 17–22; 8.37 (September 23, 1924), 15–22; 8.38 (September 30, 1924), 18–28; also a shorter article probably also written by Shao, "Beijing gongzhai fengchao zhi yubo," YHZB 8.40 (October 14, 1924), 28–30 and 8.43 (November 4, 1924), 8–14. Note that only part II of the first article is in fact signed by Shao.

The crisis immediately involved both the central and local authorities. It was decided that any resolutions dealing with the aftermath of the crash would have to emerge from direct discussions among the ministries of finance, agriculture and commerce, and internal affairs. Minister of Finance Wang Kemin personally attended the crisis meeting of the Bankers' Association. (In Beijing the *yinhang gonghui* seems to have combined both commercial banks and *qianzhuang*, whereas in Shanghai bankers and owners of *qianzhuang* had their own organizations.) Suspecting corruption, the government sent officials to the market itself to investigate. The Daxing and Wanping county magistrates were summoned as part of an investigation headed by the chief of the Beijing City Bureau of Commerce. The Beijing police were also ordered to investigate possible manipulations of the money market. On August 24 the cabinet held a special meeting to try to deal with the crisis, which concluded by ordering the exchange to complete all business transactions on the following day – that is to say, to settle in cash all the transactions already concluded on paper.

The business of the exchange had been resumed on August 21, after cabinet intervention. But trading was limited to bonds that would mature in August or September. And those who wished to do business were required to pay an entrance fee of some 800 yuan. These decisions aroused discontent. The winners in the crash were eager to make their transactions final. But the losers, those who had bought the longer-term bonds only to see their prices collapse, were opposed to concluding the transactions. Many of these losers, it turned out, were members of parliament and government officials of some rank.

With losses of around 30 percent, the bondholders felt they had lost everything. Suspicion fell on the Beijing exchange [*zhengjuan jiaoyisuo*], which some believed was manipulating the market. There were widespread tales of market manipulation by Beijing bankers and brokers. Blame was placed on "money sharks, manipulators and rumor mongers."[58] Certainly there had been corruption, but the actual purpose of these accusations was not so much to root it out as to invalidate the disastrous deals made during the days of panic. The parliamentarians who had lost money had immediately organized a financial preservation association [*jinrong weichi hui*] so that they could act as a body. More than 150 parliamentarians went to the office of the Ministry of Agriculture and Commerce to see Yan Huiqing. They also pursued Yan to his home, demanding that the exchange be closed and then abolished. Thus they sought indirectly to invalidate all transactions made after Monday,

58. YHZB 8.34 (September 2, 1924), 1.

August 11, and to settle accounts on the basis of values as they had stood on Friday, August 9.

After the cabinet had ordered the completion of transactions, on August 25 crowds of parliamentarians surrounded the exchange, blocking access and shouting charges of corruption against it. Only after the intervention of the police were brokers able to enter the exchange and begin business. But trading was so weak that on August 27 the exchange closed again and by November it still had not reopened. On the same day there was a rush on the Industrial Development Bank of China, both in Beijing and Tianjin, for cash payment. In Tianjin $120,000 in specie was paid out in one day. Assistance of the bank's Beijing office and the Bankers' Association in Tianjin were required to restore normality. This particular panic appears to have been triggered by rumors that the bank's Nanjing branch had suffered serious losses as a result of the war in the south.[59]

The financial panic led to calls by parliamentarians for new laws to regulate the exchanges, so that if market prices fell too much, dealers would have to make up the difference. During mid-September, representatives of ten institutions, including cabinet ministries, Beijing city authorities, business associations, the city police department, and even the Beijing garrison command, met three times – on the fifteenth, the seventeenth, and the twentieth. They finally decided on a compromise: to complete, on September 24, business transactions of bonds that matured by September on the basis of the prices of August 23, which were higher than those that had obtained from the eighteenth to the twentieth. But the financial preservation association opposed this decision. It finally sued the exchange for doing business illegally and accused Wang Kemin, the minister of finance, of speculation.[60] The president of the exchange went into hiding when the police summoned him. By October 22, when the shareholders of the exchange held a reorganization meeting preparatory to reopening, none of the directors had appeared and the president of the exchange remained in hiding. Not surprisingly, the effort to reopen failed.[61]

Eventually the situations in both Shanghai and Beijing were temporarily stabilized. Bad as they were, the crises in the money and stock markets had chiefly involved paper gains and losses for individuals often in a position to absorb them. But the economic impact of the 1924 wars was not limited to the sometimes abstract-seeming world of arbitrage

59. "News from North China," CWR, September, 6, 1924, 20.
60. YHZB 8.41 (October 21, 1924), 22–3.
61. YHZB 8.41 (October 21, 1924), 22.

and investment. The crises in those areas were matched by the disastrous impact of war on commerce and trade. Thus, ripple effects of the financial crisis in Shanghai spread throughout the whole vast marketing network that converged on that city. The most important of these was the creation of an immediate liquidity crisis nearly everywhere else.

With the outbreak of war, business throughout Jiangsu was soon paralyzed, with Shanghai much affected. As a financial columnist observed at the time, the effects were what one would expect: the price of food went up, but the prices of industrial raw materials, including metals and cotton, went down as manufacturing and exporting activity slackened.[62] Money became tight; most Chinese would accept only silver or the notes of foreign banks, further aggravating the situation. Prices of staples went up very considerably, causing much suffering. The highly important cotton market was "pounded down" as a result of the military crisis, and business in the money exchanges was "effectively put to a stop" by the hostilities.[63]

The danger of war was enough to send silver flowing to the security of Shanghai, contributing to a shortage of silver and a rise in its price elsewhere. But silver was not the only problem. During the 1924 crisis the price of silver relative to copper also rose, for reasons that are not altogether clear (some believe war-induced demand for silver was the cause; others point to a large new issue of copper coin that would have depressed copper's price). These factors created a series of purely monetary obstacles to commercial transactions. Merchants would not part with what silver they had. The fall in the value of copper meant that prices expressed in it rose dramatically. As for paper, it was increasingly perceived to be worthless. China's traders found themselves without a medium of exchange. Add to this the severe impact of the war on transportation of goods, and the result was chaos in the entire commerce of the Yangzi valley, which involved the movement of cash crops and products through a whole series of primary and wholesale markets.

In Hankou, the greatest inland city of China, 600 miles upriver from Shanghai, the August panic was reproduced on the local silver exchange. Ready money was short, so to try to get commerce moving again the local *qianye gonghui* issued more than 1 million yuan in temporary notes called *liutongjuan*, which were backed by property, stocks, and bonds put

---

62. Yu Sun, "Jin yue Shanghai zhisubiao zhi guancha," YHZB 8.41 (October 21, 1924), 8–9; CWR, September 6, 1924, 34; for the fall of the cotton price, see also "Zuijin Shanghai jinrong shangkuang zhi biandong," *Zhongwai jingji zhoukan*, no. 81 (September 27, 1924), 10–11.
63. CWR, September 6, 1924, 28.

up by the association members issuing them.[64] Jiujiang was hit hard by Governor Cai Chengxun's ordering of a moratorium on notes issued by the government at Nanchang. As a result, notes of the Bank of China and the Bank of Communications at Nanchang were also discounted.[65]

In Nanchang, south of Hankou past the Boyang Lake and up the Gan River in Jiangxi, silver export had led to such a shortage of ready money by September that the provincial authorities ordered conversion temporarily suspended, and decreed that in markets local paper currency should be treated identically to specie. Widely credited rumors said that convertibility would be restored only on October 10. At Jingdezhen, the great porcelain-manufacturing center in the northeast corner of the same province, similar problems developed, leading the local merchants' association to meet and arrange for the issue of 200,000 yuan in paper currency. There was a run on the banks in Jinan, in central Shandong along the railway line, and 700,000 yuan were paid out. In the port of Qingdao it was observed that, because the city was only a short sea voyage from Shanghai, commerce between them was normally very active. But since the outbreak of war there had been a drop, followed by stagnation, as well as a shortage of exchange, which had led the local military authorities to ban the export of specie.[66] In Taiyuan, Shanxi, the Bank of China and the Provincial Bank were both well prepared and coped with the run. In Ha-er-bin rumors after the outbreak of the Jiangsu–Zhejiang War led to speculation, and the Jilin provincial government soon suspended trading at the bourse.[67] In Tianjin, floods had already greatly damaged trade; their effects were now compounded by those of war on the money supply. All business would be imperiled without a stable financial system, it was argued, so the Chinese Chamber of Commerce and other organizations began to hold urgent meetings with the bankers.[68]

During late summer and early autumn, copper coins poured into Beijing as a result of the war in the South, and the price of silver therefore rose. Pawnbrokers reduced the payments they were willing to make to the minimum, 10 percent of value, thus hoping to stay in business at a time when the spread between the prices of the copper in which they made their profits and the silver to which they converted

64. "Hu Han Yinhui zhi baodie ji qiantu," YHZB, 8.39 (1924), 7–9; "Shiju jiufenzhong gefu jinzhou zhi jinrong shimian (5)," YHZB, 8.40 (October 14, 1924), 14–15.
65. CWR, September 27, 1924, 114.
66. "Qingdao jinrong jingjin zhi yinguo," YHZB, 8.37 (September 23, 1924), 12–13.
67. "Ha-er-bin jinrongjie zhi jubian," YHZB 8:37 (1924), pp. 13–14; "Shiju," YHZB 8.39 (October 7, 1924), 17.
68. "Tianjin yinqian liangye gongye shi neirong," YHZB 8:37 (1924), 12; "Shiju," YHZB 8.39 (October 2, 1924), 14–17.

them was drastically reduced, cutting into their margins. By limiting credit, this decision hurt the lower-middle class in particular.[69]

In Beijing the police were sent to the money exchanges on October 10. On the one hand they were trying to halt trading, on the other somehow to restore trading losses. On the eleventh the police issued an announcement saying that because of military actions the silver price had soared and influenced many localities, affecting the lives of ordinary people. Therefore, to prevent the dealers from making profits or manipulating at such a moment, the police had to supervise the money markets. The new regulations required everyone to exchange according to the official rate, and ordered confiscation of secret or black market dealings. People involved in such activities would be arrested by military authorities and punished by military law.[70]

Gradually the financial crisis spread throughout the country. Monetary reserves were under pressure; bond markets everywhere were falling.[71] This financial crisis intertwined with and exacerbated problems in trade and commerce.

One of the most important commodities to be affected by the disruptions of war was rice. About 1 million Chinese lived in Shanghai at this time, and their numbers were swelled by refugees from the fighting. For nearly all, rice was the fundamental element in their diet. Shanghai itself did not produce rice: in normal times it imported most of its supply from Jiangsu. The rest came from Zhejiang, southern Anhui, the middle Yangzi area, and Southeast Asia. The war, however, changed all this. For one thing, the railways that connected Shanghai to Nanjing and Hangzhou were seized by the military and used to transport troops, as were many of the canal boats that ordinarily carried rice. Such measures affected the rice supply unintentionally and indirectly. So too did competition from other militarists collecting grain for their own troops: Wu Peifu was buying rice in Hunan, the Beijing military authorities were active in Anhui, and Fengtian representatives were buying flour in Shanghai, which increased the demand there for wheat.[72] But, as a Shanghai merchant observed, "In war grain is equal in importance to guns. The Jiangsu side will never assist its enemies on the Zhejiang side who have long controlled the city by permitting rice to reach the city." So General Qi Xieyuan also took active measures to cut off the city's food supply. Even when canal boats had not been seized for troop

69. CB, September 25, 1924, 6.
70. "Shiju," YHZB 8:41 (October 21, 1924), 17–18.
71. "Gongzhai fengchao yinguo ji zhipiao zhiben zhi fangzhen," YHZB 8:35 (1924), 15–17.
72. YHZB 8.40 (October 14, 1924), 8–9.

transport, they were forbidden to carry rice to Shanghai. By late August scarcely any rice boats from Jiangsu were arriving in Shanghai.[73] Furthermore, as it became clear that war was imminent, the owners of boats that had brought rice to Shanghai and were now empty did not dare bring them back. By the end of August more than 300 empty rice boats were waiting in Shanghai port for a safe time to return home.[74]

The constriction of the rice supply quickly affected prices. The price of rice was variable, usually moving a few *jiao* – which is to say less than 5 percent – weekly.[75] But on August 27, the price of rice began to rise. On that day the price per *dan* [one *dan* equals 2.838 bushels] rose about 25 percent, from the usual twelve yuan to fifteen yuan. The next day the price rose to seventeen or eighteen yuan per *dan*, making a total increase of almost 50 percent in two days, which caused panic. The city and district associations of rice and grain merchants and the Shanghai city and county chambers of commerce immediately convened meetings to try to remedy the situation. They adopted several measures: the highest sale price per *dan* of rice was fixed at fifteen yuan; petitions were submitted to the Zhejiang and Jiangsu authorities to permit the rice boats to move and the Red Cross was asked to protect them; customs authorities were asked to seize rice boats passing Shanghai; and proposals were made to send merchants to Vietnam and Thailand to buy rice. These petitions were of no use. Qi Xieyuan denied that he was in any way interfering with the rice supply. In reply to the merchants he explained that he had not conscripted any boats, though it was possible that some of the boat households [*chuanmin*] might have been alarmed by passing soldiers and fled. The situation should return to normal soon. The price ceiling seemed effective, if only because of falling demand: the common people had spent as much money as they had on rice, and as a result the price fell slightly in the middle of September.[76]

In September, rice that Shanghai merchants had bought in the middle Yangzi area was seized by Jiangsu authorities in Nanjing and Zhenjiang.[77] And General Lu, desperate for funds, slapped a special military supply tax [*junxu shanhou mi juan*] of one yuan per *dan* (or almost 7 percent of the controlled maximum price) on rice that was transported over county lines or imported from outside to be sold in the Shanghai area, a policy

73. YHZB 8.34 (September 2, 1924), 16, 21–22; the quotation is on p. 22.
74. YHZB 8.35 (September 9, 1924), 23.
75. YHZB 8.40 (October 14, 1924), 8.
76. YHZB 8.34 (September 2, 1924), 9–10, 17–25. The quotation from General Qi's telegram is on p. 24. Also, YHZB 8.35 (September 9, 1924), 9–10, 19–21, 23–5, 25–6; 8.36 (September 16, 1924), 7–8; 8.37 (September 23, 1924), 9–10; 8.38 (September 30, 1924), 9–10.
77. YHZB 8.41 (October 21, 1924), 8.

that simply accelerated the rise in price. The merchants' initial response to this was simply to stop selling: for two days no rice boats arrived in Shanghai. Then, their petition to have the tax cut by one half having failed, the merchants began to try to pass the tax on to buyers. But this they could not do within the officially set price ceiling. As a result, the actual price charged for rice had risen to as much as twenty yuan per *dan* in early October, almost double the prewar price.[78] Only after the war had ended in the area in mid-October did the price of rice begin to drop again, returning by the end of the month to the level of early August.[79] But the end of the war did not bring complete respite to the market. The victorious General Qi imposed his own special military tax [*junshi shanhou mi juan*] of one yuan per *dan* on all rice carried out of Jiangsu province.[80]

Later the same problems developed in Beijing. The capital usually imported its rice from Jiangsu, Zhejiang, and regions to the south, while wheat flour came from Zhili, Shandong, and Henan. When the Jiangsu–Zhejiang War broke out, most trains were taken over for military purposes, and grain transport along the Tianjin–Pukou and Beijing–Hankou railways had been greatly reduced. Grain from the north, however, had not been affected. But when war broke out in the North, the Beijing–Tianjin and Beijing–Suiyuan railways were also cut. With no outside source of food supply, Beijing citizens were thrown into panic. By mid-November, prices (as compared with mid-August) had risen 48 percent for rice and flour, and 40 percent for other grains.[81]

As the war around Shanghai developed, commerce in the whole upper Yangzi area was affected. With the autumn harvest upon them, merchants in Hankou were unable to handle the crops on the market because of the shortage of money. Most of the banks in Shanghai and Hankou were unwilling to let out silver and cash. The assets of most bank branches had been called back to the head offices in Shanghai. All lines of produce were waiting money to start business. Foreign firms were holding off orders in an effort to secure very low prices, and in most cases Chinese firms were being compelled to sacrifice.[82] One can speculate that by giving Westerners a financial edge and driving many Chinese traders to bankruptcy, these developments contributed to the antiforeign movement that exploded in Hankou the following year. By

78. YHZB 8.39 (October 7, 1924), 9–10, 28–33; 8.40 (October 14, 1924), 7–8, 9–10; 8.41 (October 21, 1924), 9–10.
79. YHZB 8.41 (October 21, 1924), 9–10; 8.42 (October 28, 1924), 11–12; 8.43 (November 4, 1924), 9–10.
80. YHZB 8.42 (October 28, 1924), 22–3; 8.44 (November 11, 1924), 7–9; 8.48 (December 9, 1924), 17–18.
81. CB, November 18, 1924, 7; CB, November 20, 1924, 7; CB, November 24, 1924, 7.
82. "News from Central China," CWR, October 11, 1924, 189–90, at 190.

late October, however, the tea market and wood and oil markets in Hankou had picked up.[83]

Trade in other commodities was affected as well. When comparative trade figures for the first nine months of 1923 and 1924 were released by the United States Consulate-General in Shanghai in October 1924, they showed a 40 percent drop in exports from the city to the United States, or $18,836,808 (gold). Silk shipments had fallen from $24 million (gold) to $16 million (gold). Goat and kid skins, as well as feather exports, accounted for another $1,500,000 (gold) of the drop, and tea was down dramatically, from $1,960,702 (gold) to $1,000,830 (gold). Hair and hairnets were also down from $1,196,411 (gold) to $589,952 (gold). Lace and embroideries were up, from $1,406,589 (gold) to $2,020,843 (gold), while "rather contrary to expectation," shipments of mahjong sets were firm – they were handicraft items made in the city.[84] Commerce in Tianjin was also affected, although it recovered, and by year's end was ahead of pre-war levels.[85]

Cotton was also a problem. No money was available to buy it up-country, which hurt the growers and the traders. Just as important, without cotton, many mills in Shanghai had to stand idle.[86] Textile manufacturing was the city's single biggest industry. When it ran into trouble everyone was hurt, from the owners who had invested in the mills to the workers whose pay fell or who were laid off. The end of the war, however, brought some improvement. A local trading house, Maitland, Fearon and Brand, reported at the end of the third week of October that "the local situation is considerably easier now that the contending belligerent forces are no longer on the boundaries of the settlement, and it is hoped that the piece goods auctions may be started again next week, which should help to inspire confidence."[87]

By the end of the year, the full extent of the damage the war had done to the economy was beginning to become clear. This should not be overstated, but by the same token, it should not be ignored. "The war," wrote the president of the Chinese American Bank of Commerce to an American investor, "has wiped out a good many of the weaker financial institutions in China" (although those that survived, he continued, were

83. "News from Central China," CWR 30.7 (October 18, 1924), 216.
84. "Decreased Silk Shipments Cause Drop of 40% in Shanghai Exports to U.S.A., CWR, October 25, 1924, 236.
85. Rasmussen, 296.
86. "Weekly Cotton Market Report" by A. B. Rosenfeld & Son, CWR, October 25, 1924, 262.
87. "Shanghai Exchange for Week Ending Wednesday, October 22, 1924," CWR, October 25, 1924, 262.

stronger than ever).[88] Particularly in the Shanghai area, few new commercial or industrial enterprises had been begun, either by Chinese or by foreigners. The impossibility of moving commodities meant that existing businesses were brought almost to a standstill: firms previously accustomed to doing $300 in business per day were doing no more than $100 per week. International trade was down; domestic and foreign exchange broke down; government bonds fell to far below par; and some financial houses went bankrupt.[89] Such developments could not but deeply unsettle Chinese society.

88. Xu Enyuan to John Jay Abbot, December 3, 1924, in MacMurray Papers, Princeton University. I am obliged to Professor Noel Pugach for calling this letter to my attention.
89. Intelligence Office, Headquarters U.S. Army Forces in China. "Situation Survey for the Period of October 16th to December 31st 1924" (by Captain Walter C. Phillips), 18 pp, 13, in MIR.

7

The war and society

The financial crisis that spread inland from the coast and north from Shanghai was only one of the developments that disrupted Chinese society in the autumn of 1924. Heavy rainfall produced floods in many areas, from Zhangjiakou in the northwest to the Beijing and Tianjin areas, to Shanghai and its hinterland.[1] The war was not to blame for the rain, which resulted in a considerable quantity of mud – adding to the resemblance between China's modern warfare and the fight in Europe a decade earlier. But many of the other disruptions that affected society through the autumn and winter of 1924 to 1925 were produced by the upheavals of war.

The impact was visible first in Shanghai and its hinterland, Jiangsu and Zhejiang, then as now one of the most prosperous regions of China. From Hangzhou to Suzhou to Wuxi to the Yangzi River, local wealth was abundant. Long established, the towns had grown rich from silk and trade and banking and light industry; from them came the most conspicuously successful members of China's newly affluent middle class.

These people had not been prepared intellectually for what was to come. As the Zhejiang and Jiangsu armies prepared their positions, the Chinese middle classes clung to a variety of hopes. They knew that war within a few miles of Shanghai was probable, but "still it was not believed there was much stomach for fighting and that it would be a listless struggle with considerable looting but little accomplishment by

---

1. During the summer of 1924, floods were reported in Fuzhou (CB, July 5, 5; July 10, 5; August 10, 3); in Jiangxi (CB, July 7, 3; July 11, 3; July 12, 5; July 16, 6; July 22, 6); in Hunan (CB, July 7, 7; July 10, 5, July 11, 5; July 12, 5; July 28, 6); in Hubei (CB, July 16, 3; July 23, 3; August 8, 6); in Zhili, including Tianjin and Beijing (CB, July 16, 7; July 17, 3, 7; July 18, 7, and from then until mid-August); at Zhangjiakou [Kalgan] (CB, July 16, 7; July 17, 3, and then daily until mid-August); in Zhejiang (CB, July 17, 7); in Jiangsu (CB, July 23, 3); in Shandong (CB, August 1, 1; August 9, 3); in Henan (CB, August 5, 3); in Sichuan (CB, August 5, 3); in Suiyuan, or today's Huhehaote in Inner Mongolia (CB, August 8, 3); and Guangdong (CB, August 13, 4).

either party. It was thought most likely that some sort of peace would be arranged."[2] But the authorities meant business. Martial law was proclaimed in Nanjing and all of Jiangsu province, and several hundred policemen were brought in from Tianjin to enforce it.[3]

Meanwhile the Chinese Shanghai General Chamber of Commerce and the American, British, French, Italian, and Japanese governments asked for the establishment of a neutral zone at Shanghai. The Beijing government, however, sensed victory and insisted that any neutrality would have to be real and include prohibition of the use of anything within the zone for naval or military reinforcement, supply of arms, or refuge for defeated troops. It proposed removing the breech locks of the guns at the Wusong forts (held by Zhejiang), disarming General Lu Yongxiang's warships in port, closing the arsenals near Shanghai (Longhua was Lu's headquarters), and expelling General Lu's troops from the proposed zone.[4]

This was a substantial rebuff, but any hope of peace vanished completely when "serious fighting actually began between the two forces on the forenoon of September 3 in the vicinity of Huangdu, 15 miles from Shanghai." People began to realize that the clash there would "probably reach all over China and embroil the country in a general war such as perhaps China has never seen."[5]

Preparations for war had begun disrupting the Shanghai hinterland in mid-August, when Qi Xieyuan mobilized his forces at Nanjing. "Qi's men seized hundreds of junks on the canals between Changzhou and Suzhou, and commandeered all the freight trains at Nanjing."[6] On September 2, 500 junks and as many carts were taken just outside Shanghai, but He Fenglin announced that only those willingly loaned would be used.[7]

Coolies were rounded up and herded into boxcars to be taken to do labor at the front.[8] Impressment of civilians began in Suzhou with "soldiers not only picking up coolies from the streets but going into shops and grabbing the first man at hand. . . . Reports from Changzhou and Wuxi and Nanjing are to the same effect as scenes actually witnessed in Suzhou and Kunshan, and the number of impressed laborers sent down from above Suzhou is ample testimony that impressment must have been carried out wholesale."[9]

A reporter observed that

2. "Fighting Begins between Chekiang and Kiangsu," CWR 30.1 (September 6, 1924), 4.
3. CB, September 10, 1924, 2.
4. NYT, September 26, 1924, 23.
5. CWR, September 6, 1924, 4.
6. Ibid., 6.   7. Ibid., 8.   8. Ibid., 7.   9. Ibid., 8.

the confusion into which the gentry in the threatened war area were thrown was both pitiful and disgusting. In Suzhou, the families of high officers left town before it was generally known that preparations for fighting were being made. Immediately troop movement started, the departure of officials' families [began]; and a general exodus began which lasted until trains stopped running on September 2. The stations along the line seethed with sweaty men and women, tugging their all in clumsy bundles, with crying children tagging on and many nursing babies in arms. There seemed to be no purpose in the flight other than to flee, residents of Wuxi and Nanjing rushing to Suzhou while Suzhou folk entrained for Nanjing or Wuxi. A Suzhou missionary stated that many Suzhou people went to Hangzhou while he had met refugees from Hangzhou in Suzhou. One of his servants moved from one side of Suzhou to the other, and seemed to feel quite satisfied with having escaped from the danger zone.

They feared above all the ruthlessness of the soldiers. Just before leaving, the Suzhou division "had very little money and first went to pawnshops to raise cash on their rather worthless effects. For an article worth possibly a dollar, they would demand $10 and the pawnbrokers pretty generally paid what was asked of them. One who refused had most of his teeth knocked out by a mob of soldiers and was almost beaten to death. The soldiers also went into Suzhou stores and took goods at their own prices." As the soldiers began rounding up shop employees for coolie service, "all stores closed immediately and every one kept indoors, so that Suzhou had the appearance of a deserted village, as compared with its usual bustle far into the night." Elsewhere, "cases of rapine were reported on the evening of August 30 and were probably true as one of the divisions stationed at Kunshan has the reputation of being the best fighters, but the worst vandals, having always been engaged in bandit suppression and therefored enured to wreaking vengeance."[10]

At Yangzhou on September 9, the gentry, intelligentsia, and merchants led a citizens' rally protesting military requisitioning and press-ganging, and demanding the immediate release of all those people who had been impressed. When the police intervened, popular anger increased. The county magistrate tried to coerce people into obeying but was beaten and seriously injured. In the aftermath, all the shops in Yangzhou closed down as a protest.[11]

Meanwhile, in Shanghai's foreign settlements, as we have seen, local defense units were mobilized and marines landed from foreign warships. As refugees began to arrive, especially heavy guards were placed at all approaches, and the Municipal Council ordered the arrest of "all

10. Ibid., 8.   11. CB, September 10, 1924, 2.

suspected dangerous characters" in the settlement.[12] Premiums for war insurance rose sharply in the International Settlement.[13]

As the Jiangsu forces began to close in, foreign worry increased. Further preparations for defense were made during the night of September 19 in the French Concession and the International Settlement. There were signs of alarm in the French Settlement, where most of the shops were closed and shuttered. Existing defense organizations, including the men of the various navies who had landed and the Shanghai Volunteer Corps, were strengthened by the arming of 150 White Russians, who then were stationed at strategic points. All the lesser bridges in the outskirts of the settlement were removed, and strong guards were placed on duty at all concrete structures.[14]

Similar scenes were repeated in the north. Wu Peifu was a Shandong native, and his military recruiters were soon active in the province. The white flags that announced military recruiting seemed to be everywhere, in the streets and even in the small alleys of cities, towns, and remote villages from Jinan, on the railway line, to Caozhou [Heze] in the province's southwest corner. The Shandong people, simple and poor, were ready to enlist, and every day a dozen or more groups of thirty or forty men each could be seen boarding troop trains along the Tianjin–Pukou line which passed through the province. Some were very young, sent by their parents; fifteen-year-olds went to Wu's headquarters at Luoyang, where a special school trained them for a military career.

Materiel was also raised. Around Dezhou in northern Shandong, on the railroad and just south of the front, the government sent orders to county officials to raise a total of more than 4,000 carts, each with a draught horse and a groom, promising to pay 50 yuan for the horse and 100 for the groom if either was killed in battle. These were to be sent directly to Luanzhou, on the railway to the Shanhaiguan front. Two thousand were required immediately.[15] The provincial authorities then ordered each county along the Tianjin–Pukou railway to supply 200 carts, 400 head of cattle (later increased), and 400 cart drivers (later doubled). (A cart was worth between 400 and 1,000 strings of cash; an ox perhaps 300.)[16] The provincial assembly [*sheng yihui*] passed a resolution on September 22 opposing the order.[17] In Feicheng *xian*, a small county southwest of Jinan, the order requisitioning 300 carts arrived at

12. NYT, September 19, 1924, 1.
13. CB, September 10, 1924, 2.
14. NYT, September 19, 1924, 1.
15. CB, September 24, 1924, 5.
16. CB, October 10, 1924, 5.
17. CB, October 13, 1924, 5.

the farmers' busiest season, just as beans were being harvested and wheat planted. The local people telegraphed the provincial governor asking that the requisition be waived. Angered, the governor stated that if the order were not carried out, the county magistrate would be sacked. So the magistrate went to Feicheng and pleaded with the villagers, but the carts were not forthcoming, and he was duly fired. Sometimes carts and men were simply seized at gunpoint. Such incidents were reported at the Dezhou railway station and in the surrounding countryside. At Qihe, on the Yellow River just south of the Tianjin–Pukou railway, soldiers seized forty large wagons and took them with their drivers to the railway line to be sent north. During the night more than thirty people escaped, leaving carts and horses behind. En route to the station three more escaped, and when the seven remaining were placed in one wagon, two more jumped out, one of whom was killed. It was said that these carts would be used to transport ammunition to the front, and then, once the ammunition was unloaded, be filled with straw. A horse would be harnessed to the cart and headed toward areas suspected to have buried mines. The straw would be set on fire, the horse in panic would rush forward, and as it ran onto the suspect ground, it would detonate concealed mines. Such stories only added to the panic among farm people when confronted with military requisitions. Wealthy people were offered the option of paying 300 yuan instead of being drafted, but mechanisms seem to have been capricious enough that few did. Poorer people might flee, and they were sometimes shot down in the roads.[18]

Around October 20, the county magistrate was ordered to produce 500 laborers immediately. Police went into the streets, even into hotels and restaurants, to grab people. For three days all shops closed and the streets were deserted. Then came an order for 200 more people. Police went to the small town of Jiazhuang, where a fair was being held, and rounded up more than fifty. By October 24, more than 200 were sent to the railway station. At the same time, the 26th Division, then at Dezhou, was also press-ganging workers. People were hard to find, however, so the soldiers went to the station, where they confronted the police and took over some of the men the police had just impressed.[19] In all, the Zhili military was estimated to have impressed more than 100,000 men, cattle, and carts. After it was all over in late November, some workers poking around the Tianjin railway yard. found two forgotten railway wagons in which several cattle and sixty-three people had died, unnoticed, many days earlier.[20]

18. "Zhixi junfa madixia de Shandong renmin," *Xiangdao* (1924), no. 88, 732.
19. CB, November 4, 1924, 5.
20. CB, November 24, 1924, 6.

In Mukden, the gathering of soldiers for dispatch to the front also led to trouble. Looting was common, and ordinary citizens were sometimes panic stricken. By September 22, when most of the troops had moved to the front, business picked up a bit. But as in other cities, there were shortages. The Chamber of Commerce was instructed to investigate the grain supplies in the city, and the price of grain rose dramatically, leading to much popular discontent.[21]

Around Shanghai, preparations for war also hit ordinary people hard. In Zhabei, the northern part of the city, martial law had been declared, and the authorities press-ganged citizens to labor on the front. More and more people fled to foreign-controlled areas.[22] Not only people but automobiles as well were requisitioned. Between September 10 and 11, it was reported that about forty, including some owned by foreigners, had been taken over and sent to the front. Residents of the International Settlement were careful to stay within its boundaries, lest their vehicles be confiscated.[23]

In the face of such insecurity and disorder, Chinese who could began to flee to the shelter of foreign guns. A foreign correspondent, on a drive to the lines into the northwest of the city in the second week of September of 1924, observed among the cars and lorries bringing the wounded from the scene of action, "many refugees, most of them people of the well-to-do class who could afford the use of a motor-car for transporting themselves and their more valuable family possessions into the safety of the Settlement."[24] It was a veritable flood, and it was not limited to the gentry alone. "The effect of thousands and thousands of refugees pouring into Shanghai is most noticeable. Probably the majority have little of value excepting their lives and have sought protection with relatives and friends who are equally as poor, and at any rate in poor position to accommodate a number of people, however beloved, indefinitely."[25]

By late August so many Chinese had moved into the International Settlement that rents had doubled, and rooms were still difficult to obtain even at those such prices.[26] By early September it was reported that 200,000 refugees had arrived, and that rents, as well as the prices of grain and daily necessities, had risen greatly as a result.[27] At the end of the first week of September, between 6,000 and 7,000 Chinese refugees a

21. CB, September 26, 1924, 2.
22. CB, September 5, 1924, 2.
23. CB, September 11, 1924, 2.
24. A Correpondent, "Shanghai Battle Sketches," *The Living Age* (1924), pp. 235–6.
25. CWR, September 6, 1924, 8.
26. CB, August 29, 1924, 3.
27. CB, September 9, 1924, 2.

day were arriving in Shanghai, and although food supplies seemed adequate, housing stock was exhausted.[28]

Many of the measures the Municipal Council took to protect the territory were a "direct violation" of Chinese sovereignty: proclaiming a state of emergency, landing naval troops, barricading settlement roads, occupying Chinese territory for military purposes, and forcibly disarming Chinese troops. But Shanghai residents, many of whom had earlier been agitating against foreign administation, dropped their objections "as soon as the first reports of the guns were heard." The Chinese Ratepayers' Association at Shanghai was moved to "express its appreciation of the Council's work for the protection of Chinese property and lives," and did so without mentioning the foreign actions that earlier "could have led to riots and a general strike."[29]

The earliest reports had suggested that Shanghai would remain inviolable. The *New York Times* believed that "ample protection for the safety of foreign residents at Shanghai would seem to be provided by the presence of nearly two dozen warships in the harbor, reinforced by a defense organization of residents." Shanghai itself "would be endangered only through a direct attack by one of the contending Armies. Reprisal, however, would come so surely and speedily that it may be assumed neither of the Chinese leaders will take the risk."[30]

In fact, Shanghai felt the effects of the fighting immediately. The city was entirely cut off on the land side: roads, railways, and canals were all closed, and remained so for the duration of the war. Only traffic to the sea along the Huangpu River could get through.[31] As soon as fighting began, traffic on the Shanghai–Nanjing railway stopped, west of Nanxiang, and telegraph lines were cut as well. Refugees had been pouring into the foreign settlement at the rate of 6,000 per day since late August; until rail service stopped, every train had been full. Foreigners were advised against unnecessary travel, though it was felt that foreign ships and canal boats were probably still safe.[32] On September 29, however, the China Merchants' Steam Navigation Company, the largest Chinese shipping company, stopped all sailings northward from Shanghai, to avoid having its ships seized by General Wu Peifu.[33]

28. CB, September 11, 1924, 2.
29. Anatol M. Kotenev, *Shanghai: Its Municipality and the Chinese* (Shanghai: North-China Daily News & Herald, Ltd., 1927), p. 25.
30. "Full-Sized Civil War in China," *The Literary Digest*, September 20, 1924, 82 (1924), p. 15.
31. "Week of Hard Fighting Gives Little Advantage to Chekiang or Kiangsu," CWR, 30.2 (September 13, 1924), p. 43.
32. Cunningham to Bell, September 3, 1924, SD 893.00/5561.
33. NYT, September 30, 1924, 10.

The effects of war spread upriver to Hankou, where the local police commissioner issued extraordinary orders prohibiting the circulation of newspapers containing rumors about the Jiangsu–Zhejiang War. In Wuchang the authorities established a War Intelligence Bureau to circulate "authentic news" about the fighting. The daily news reports were sent to the papers through the police. Matters were not helped by the "closing up of the Chui Feng Bank, which enjoyed the best of credit during its existence." Some officers absconded with $400,000 (Chinese) in cash, and "the position of native banks in Hankou was much weakened."[34]

A wave of strikes got underway, not all related to the fighting. By far the most serious was by the 10,000 rickshaw pullers, who protested the establishment of a motorbus company on September 15. One bus and the company's offices were damaged, and eight strikers were arrested.[35] In Wuchang, 300 craftsmen who specialized in paste mounting (*biaohujiang*) walked off their jobs, asking for more pay.[36] On October 10, all workers in dyeing plants in Hankou went on strike, demanding higher wages – because of the drop in value of copper coins against silver, mentioned in Chapter 6.[37]

Within the city of Hankou itself, antiforeign agitation had been underway since the summer. Late in October the Foreign Office replied to the Hubei Assembly regarding the expiration of the term of lease of the Hankou British Concession. The Foreign Office had stated that all documentary evidence showed that the term for the British, Japanese, ex-Russian, and ex-German concessions was perpetual. But the Assembly maintained that the lease of the British Concession expired that year, and urged the government to take it back.[38] A special police commission was established to protect the Hanyang arsenal, which was already shipping large quantities of weapons downstream to General Qi's forces, as well as the Hanyang Iron and Steel Works.

By the week ending September 13, Beijing and Tianjin were "in turmoil regarding the war. Victories or defeats have formed the common topic of conversation and pages are daily devoted to news." Troops were starting to move here and there in northern provinces, and Beijing started to censor all telegrams and mail arriving from the south. Methods were "enforced to check rumors and false reports."[39] Censorship

---

34. "News from Central China," CWR, September 27, 1924, 114.
35. CB, September 23, 1924, 5; CB, September 24, 1924, 5.
36. CB, September 25, 1924, 3.
37. CB, October 17, 1924, 5.
38. "News from Central China," CWR, October 25, 1924, 252.
39. "News from North China," CWR, September 13, 1924, 58.

was begun.[40] By late October this policy had been tightened considerably: a new regulation required all Chinese newspapers in Beijing to submit advance copies to the police for approval before publication. This rule also applied to Chinese news agencies, and some suspended publication as a result.[41] In late October the British-controlled *Far Eastern Times* of Beijing was, in effect, suspended from publication by the Beijing police as a consequence of its apparently pro-Mukden policy.[42]

Mobilization in the North also created disruptions similar to what had already been witnessed around Shanghai. In Beijing, "the sudden mobilisation of carts and camels requisitioned for transportation of military stores to some destination unknown was the first sign of what was coming, and the Beijing public thronged the streets to gaze at the endless lines of vehicles, mules, and horses that were being hurried to General Feng Yuxiang's camps at Nanyuan and Tongzhou." Observers admitted that "this requisitioning was handled in an orderly manner as far as one could observe, the police assisting the military by furnishing them with a list of draught animals and carts available, but it remains to be seen whether the owners of these will ever get anything further than the bit of paper acknowledging the seizure of the same."[43]

With special troop trains numbering more than twenty a day, normal operations on the Beijing–Mukden railway were suspended. Ordinary freight cars were withdrawn from service, and express passenger trains were usually three or four hours late. The Beijing–Tianjin section of the luxury Blue Express was suspended on September 25, but air service between the capital and Tianjin was resumed after a summer interval.[44]

As the Zhili military trains moved north through Tianjin, railway lines from the capital to the front were clogged. The residents, many of them foreigners, at the famous resort of Beidaihe, just southwest of Qinhuangdao, were reported to be considerably inconvenienced. So great was the congestion on the single-track line that the trip back to Tianjin was taking forty-eight hours, "which the fugitives are spending in crowded baggage cars without food or water." Eventually a ship was sent to rescue the remaining foreigners in the district.[45]

Nor was confusion limited to the movement of trains carrying vacationers. Zhili's entire logistical system was gravely flawed, from Li Yanqing, the Cao crony in the capital who supervised it and skimmed off

40. CB, September 5, 1924, 6.
41. "News from North China," CWR, October 25, 1924, 251.
42. "News from North China," CWR, 30.9 (November 1, 1924), 286.
43. "Flood, Famine and Civil War in North China," CWR 30.5 (October 4, 1924), 152.
44. "News from North China." CWR, October 4, 1924, 159.
45. NYT, September 22, 1924, 1, 8.

his percentage, right to the front. No military depots or supply centers had been established before the conflict. When they were, they became centers of extortion. Feng Yuxiang, not a neutral source, reports Wu Peifu as dismissing this problem by saying simply "zou dao nali, chi dao nali" ["find food where you are"].[46] On arrival at the front, troops were "being billeted in villages, the inhabitants of which are fleeing in great numbers. As most of the men are being commandeered to build earthworks, women and children are suffering great hardships."[47]

For Southerners, food was the single most important commodity. In the North, however, coal for heating in the winter was just as critical. August and September were traditionally the months when inhabitants of Beijing purchased coal to store for the coming cold. But in the autumn of 1924, both food and fuel were much more expensive in the city than they had been a year before. Flooding had led to a dramatic rise in the prices of both rice and flour in the city from mid-August. The police had tried to control these prices, but without success.[48] Meanwhile, coal was rising in price as well, 24 percent by August 26, from (Chinese) $4.50 to $5.60 per 1,000 *jin*.[49] In the ten days up to September 10, the price tripled. These price rises had several causes. The rising price of grain made it more expensive to employ miners, and flooding had closed some of the mines. But the most important reason was lack of transportation. Even before fighting had broken out in the North, enough railway wagons had been diverted to Jiangsu to limit capacity.[50] The Chamber of Commerce met four times in one day to discuss how to keep order and save the financial situation. In collaboration with the metropolitan defense authorities they undertook an investigation of all granaries and warehouses in the area, and the transport of grain out of the capital was strictly forbidden.[51]

But the price of grain continued to rise.[52] In northwestern Beijing the price of cornmeal rose rapidly, and a limit of two *jin* per person was established.[53] On September 25 the ministry of transportation assigned twenty-five cars for coal on the Beijing–Hankou railway and another ten for grain. As a result the police, the Chamber of Commerce, and the Association of Coal Merchants agreed to lower the price – to $5.60 per 1,000 *jin*.[54] But with the outbreak of serious fighting in the North, the entire Beijing–Hankou railway ceased to function, resuming traffic only

---

46. Feng Yuxiang, *Wo de shenghuo*, vol. 3, p. 499, quoted in Mao Jinling, p. 85, note 112.
47. NYT, September 26, 1924, 23.
48. CB, August 24, 1924, 7.   49. CB, August 27, 1924, 7.
50. CB, September 11, 1924, 6.   51. CB, September 18, 1924, 6.
52. CB, September 23, 1924, 6.   53. CB, September 25, 1924, 6.
54. CB, September 26, 1924, 6.

on November 1.[55] Meanwhile, the foreign residents were becoming concerned. In late September the *corps diplomatique* had contacted the Foreign Ministry to request that some provision be made regarding transport of coal for their use from Tianjin to the capital. The government promised to give some officers exclusive responsibility for supervising coal transport.[56] But clearly this did not work: on October 22 the *corps diplomatique* decided to use foreign troops to protect coal trains on the railway between Kailuan and Tianjin.[57] The Kailan Mining Administration at Qinhuangdao tried to get coal trains through but was hindered in doing so by the movement of troop trains. Efforts were also made to transport coal by boat up the Hai River, but this proved too slow. During the month of November the allied coal trains improved the situation somewhat. But prices per ton of coal were reported by U.S. military intelligence to "have [risen] on an average of two dollars."[58] Transport of grain and coal still had not returned to normal even in mid-November.[59]

No matter how the war went, the people suffered. Sun Chuanfang's Fujian troops brought disorder as they entered Zhejiang. Lu Yongxiang fought brilliantly, but was outnumbered, and as we have seen, eventually withdrew to Shanghai. The Fujian soldiers, proceeding northward in the first days of October, made things worse. The province had been thrown into turmoil by Lu's withdrawal; now Sun's troops did "considerable looting through the country" as they advanced, and Hangzhou itself witnessed minor collisions between the Fujian troops and the police. Civil order in this ordinarily prosperous area was simply breaking down. Ningbo was "in quite open rebellion [against] the present powers in Zhejiang, though unable to present more than passive resistance." Sun Chuanfang's troops headed for Songjiang for a showdown. The result was to throw Songjiang into "an uproar at the prospect of being the center of fighting between Lu's and Sun's forces." Lu conscripted "every coolie for the ranks and for labor." Such residents as could fled to Shanghai, and the city in general was left "in a sorry plight."[60]

Even the end of the Jiangsu–Zhejiang War brought only slight respite. In Shanghai the stunning news had arrived on October 13 that Generals Lu Yongxiang and He Fenglin had fled to Japan. Immediately the whole

55. CB, November 2, 1924, 6.
56. CB, September 25, 1924, 3.
57. CB, October 23, 1924, 6.
58. Intelligence Office, Situation Survey October 16th to December 31, 1924, 13, in MIR.
59. CB, November 12, 1924, 6.
60. "Fengtien Opens Attack on Chihli Forces, "CWR, October 4, 1924, 166.

city panicked about *taobing* (or "taobings" as the foreigners often called them) – defeated and unorganized soldiers who would easily turn to looting, extortion, or banditry. In the city it was feared that "the 30,000 soldiers of Lu" now entrenched in lines around its perimeter "would make a mad rush for Shanghai." But negotiations got underway and by October 14 the Shanghai Chinese Chamber of Commerce had nearly reached agreement with General Yang Huazhao, second in command of the Fujian soldiers who had been fighting for Lu, to pay each man $20 (Chinese) and provide safe transport back to Fuzhou.

The Jiangsu victory seemed to mean that at least the city was no longer a bone of contention between two provinces aligned with two different systems. Furthermore, it brought a renewed connection to what looked to be the victorious side in the north. In the city itself only a few thousand defeated Zhejiang troops remained, armed but under close watch, at the Jiangwan race course, though many more were camped just outside the city, their food paid for by merchants. The Hubei troops were expected to move north to reinforce Wu on the Shanhaiguan front. Wu Peifu had mixed feelings about the future of Shanghai. He agreed in principle that the Longhua Arsenal should be moved to Hanyang, but for the time being he wanted the post of Shanghai defense commissioner to continue to exist and be filled by General Qi Xieyuan, who was represented in Shanghai at this time by General Bai Baoshan. Confidence began to return: as the *China Weekly Review* observed, "All fears of further fighting around Shanghai are evidently dispelled, for practically all of the foreign war vessels have left the Huangpu."[61]

A new civil administration was installed in Shanghai. The *Literary Digest* quoted Associated Press reports to the effect that "the new Chinese administrators are working in conjunction with the foreign authorities, confident that they will be able to avert disturbances incident to the change in local government. But we read further of the Chinese sections of Shanghai being overrun with armed soldiers, causing new concern to the authorities of the foreign settlements, lest some serious disorder occur." Later dispatches told how Marshal Qi Xieyuan had arrived "to arrange for the final rehabilitation of Shanghai district." Among his most pressing tasks would be the demobilization of defeated troops. The plan was to distribute the forces among the armies of the other provinces.[62]

At this point, however, trouble appeared, in the form of General Xu Shuzheng (1880–1925), known as "Little Xu," once military lord of the

61. "China Marks Time Till Wu Succeeds or Fails," CWR, November 1, 1924, 290–91.
62. "New Light on the Civil War in China," *The Literary Digest*, November 1, 1924, 83 (1924), 18.

Anfu group and a close comrade of Duan Qirui, the currently retired Anfu politician who would be Zhang Zuolin's candidate for president of China. His purpose was evidently to try to re-create the second front, in the south, that was so important to Fengtian's overall strategic position. The tide of war in the north looked to be turning against Zhili, a process Xu sought to accelerate. Furthermore, if Xu succeeded in reconstituting the southern front under his own leadership, that would bring his own Anfu group back as major players in Chinese politics and prevent their complete domination by Fengtian. Thus, at the moment of their defeat, Chen Leshan and Yang Huazhao, among other Zhejiang leaders, had sought Xu out to discuss reorganization of resistance. On October 15 Chen and Xu had met to discuss this in the International Settlement in Shanghai. Now Xu offered the defeated Zhejiang soldiers a larger sum than the Chamber of Commerce had, if the men would join him. "Little Xu" soon had some 6,000 soldiers entrenching themselves on the outskirts of Shanghai. The potential strategic importance of this action in the overall Chinese conflict escaped most foreigners; to Shanghai's international community this move "had every semblance of being . . . a threat to squeeze money out of the Shanghai merchants as a guarantee of immunity."[63]

However one read Xu's purpose, though, his actions seemed likely only to push Shanghai deeper than ever into the maelstrom of Chinese civil war. So Xu was arrested by the authorities of the International Settlement and charged with having entered the settlement in violation of an order not to do so made by the Municipal Council on July 5, 1921, when he had sought asylum after the Anfu–Zhili War. This was fair enough, but the timing of the arrest was odd. General Xu had, after all, ignored the order when it was first passed and had lived quietly at 34 Nanyang Road for all of the previous three and one-half years. His attorneys, Messrs. Faison and Heath, immediately appealed to the Mixed Court, which declared the case out of their jurisdiction, and properly belonging to the Court of Consuls. Six days later Xu left for Europe but stopped in Hong Kong, where he was placed under surveillance by the British.[64]

On October 19 a military mutiny occurred when about 1,000 soldiers from the 2nd Battalion of the 38th Regiment of the National 10th Division, ordered to go to Wusong for reorganization, changed their

63. Mao Jinling, 108; "General Lu Flees to Japan – Fate of Army in Balance," CWR, October 18, 1924, 220.
64. Kotenev, *Shanghai: Its Municipality*, 23–4; "Fighting at Shanhaikwan – Shanghai at Peace," CWR, October 25, 1924, 255–6; "China Marks Time Till Wu Succeeds or Fails," CWR, November 1, 1924, 290.

minds and forced their train to return to Shanghai. There they occupied the North Station, and residents of the nearby Zhabei area panicked. Merchants closed their shops, and ordinary people fled to the foreign concessions. At nightfall the soldiers tried to enter the concessions but were resisted by foreign forces. The result was a firefight in which machine guns, artillery, and armored cars were used. In the week after Lu Yongxiang fled, it was reported that his soldiers were roving the streets, looting and setting fires. At Nanxiang fires burned out of control for two days and two nights; most citizens fled to safety, but soldiers roamed the burning landscape, looting. At Wuxiang and Nanxiang the damage was described as greater even than that suffered in the Taiping rebellion. Estimates were that it would take Nanxiang and Liuhe perhaps forty years to recover their prewar levels of prosperity.[65]

In Shanghai proper, it remained for Sun Chuanfang to come to the city and settle the problem of Xu Shuzheng's troops, still entrenched ominously nearby. The defeated soldiers were offered from $20 to $50 (Chinese) plus transportation if they wished to leave the ranks and return home, but most preferred to remain soldiers. They were incorporated into the armies of Jiangsu, Fujian, and Hubei. On October 20 Sun Chuanfang, Qi Xieyuan, and the new defense commissioner of Songjiang and Shanghai, Zhang Yunming, reached arrangement among themselves to keep the peace while dividing the spoils of Shanghai. The newly organized armies of defeated Zhejiang soldiers, under the command of Zhang Yunming, left immediately for the northern front. Sun Chuanfang returned to Hangzhou. Meanwhile, General Qi remained at Changru, a village some five miles from the city. Peace did not return. About 10,000 soldiers of the National 10th Division were at Jiangwan, on the railway between Shanghai and Nanjing. They looted, raped, and even murdered local residents, causing panic in the area, most of whose residents fled to Shanghai.[66]

As the militarists divided up their spheres of influence, there were fears that the latent splits in the Zhili coalition might now come into the open. Many believed that Sun Chuanfang and Qi Xieyuan, who had been allies but were now rivals, would sooner or later clash over possession of the Longhua Arsenal. But there was also hope for demilitarization. A plan was forwarded to move the arsenal and dismantle the forts; the encamped soldiers gradually dispersed. Shanghai breathed a sigh of relief. The restoration of a semblance of authority had "unquestionably saved the Settlements from considerable disorder and looting."[67]

65. CB, October 30, 1924, 3, 5.
66. CB, November 13, 1924, 5.
67. Mao Jinling, 108–9; CWR, October 25, 1924, 256.

The disorder of war had a major impact on workers and students. The disruption of commerce affected employment. In Beijing nearly all rickshaw pullers, whose numbers were estimated as over 100,000, were out of work during the period when transport in and out of the city ceased. Newspapers commented on a visible increase in the number of poor people.[68] The strain caused by the shift in exchange rates between copper and silver also contributed to labor problems in the North. The changing exchange rate caused the real earnings of carpenters to fall, and on September 21 they gathered in Beijing, threatening to strike if their demands were not met.[69] Government employees were not paid. In November five workers in the critically important printing bureau of the Ministry of Finance struck on November 8, refusing to print any more money until money owed them was paid.[70] In Shandong an estimated 100,000 workers were employed in large factories, and the war saw business turn bad. Much production could not be sold and was instead stored in warehouses. Many factories closed. In Qingdao, the Cangkou Huaxin Textile Company dismissed more than 510 workers. With no way to move coal, 100 miners in Baoshan were laid off. It was estimated that a total of between 13,000 and 14,000 workers lost their jobs as a result of the war.[71] In Jinan 1,000 butchers went on strike. With the enforcement of martial law, the police began to collect a new "inspection fee" of five *jiao* per ox and one *jiao* per pig or sheep, to pay for the newly introduced patrol of police on bicycles. The butchers attempted twice to have the fee removed by striking. They did not succeed, however, so they raised the price of meat.[72] In Tangshan, at the workshops of the Beijing–Fengtian Railway, several thousand additional workers were hired when the war began. When it ended, 2,000 were let go, and an estimated 15,000 people whose livelihoods depended indirectly on the workshops were also unemployed. Significantly, these workers blamed "imperialist oppression" for their plight.[73]

In Shanghai many factory workers lost their jobs, at least temporarily. The effects of these economic setbacks would begin to be felt acutely early in 1925: February of that year saw a wave of strikes in Shanghai, with walkouts and lockouts repeatedly affecting the city's extensive textile industry. In the course of one of these a worker named Gu Zhenghong was shot dead by a Japanese guard at the Nagai Wata textile plant,

---

68. CB, November 18, 1924, 7; CB, November 20, 1924, 7.
69. CB, September 22, 1924, 6.
70. CB, November 10, 1924, 6.
71. CB, October 30, 1924, 7.
72. CB, November 25, 1924, 7.
73. CB, November 21, 1924, 3.

an incident whose full consequences will be examined in Chapter 10. The impact of war was also felt immediately in education. The period from the turn of the century to the outbreak of the war had seen rapid growth and extensive innovation in Chinese education. For state-run education it was a sort of golden age, as for example during the chancellorship of Cai Yuanpei (1868–1940) at Beijing University (1916–1919). Private nondenominational institutions also gained great momentum. Between 1904 when Nankai University was established in Tianjin and the end of 1924, twenty-four major colleges had been set up in China, with countless more lesser ones. In Shanghai the three years before October 1924 saw "virtually the simultaneous birth of more than fifteen universities," some of which to be sure were little more than a president's office and a few classrooms, where there had been only six before.[74] Most of the important foreign-sponsored colleges took something like their final form in this period as well: St. John's University in 1905, Ginling University in 1910, Fukien Christian University in 1918, Peking University (after 1928, Yenching) in 1920, Shantung Christian University (after 1931 Cheeloo) in 1924.[75]

In September of 1924 concern was already growing in Beijing that the amount of money being devoted to military expenditures would make it impossible to support schools. All the ministries were putting everything into the war, "and even that was not enough." In Jiangsu the outbreak of war led to school closings in some districts. As of September, twenty-three *xian* reported normal classes, but four, including Yixing, Danyang, and Wujin, were forced to close their schools.[76] By October there were student demonstrations at the First Hubei Normal School in Hankou.[77] In Jinan there were demonstrations at the business, industrial, and agricultural higher schools.[78] In Fujian, the economy was mobilized by a newly established Bureau of Military Supplies, which appropriated all the money that normally would have gone to the provincial ministry of finance. Salaries were not paid, and on October 7 all teachers of middle and high schools in the province went on strike.[79]

74. Anthony C. Li, *The History of Privately Controlled Higher Education in the Republic of China* (Westport, Conn.: Greenwood Press, 1977. Originally published 1954), Table 1, not paginated; C.S. Ho, "Where Education Is Not a 'Noble Business,'" CWR 30.7 (October 18, 1924), 206.
75. See table in Jessie Gregory Lutz, *China and the Christian Colleges 1850–1950* (Ithaca and London: Cornell University Press, 1971), pp. 531–3.
76. *Jiaoyu zazhi* 16.9 (September 1924), 17–18 (Taibei: Taiwan Shangwu yinshuguan ed., n.d.).
77. CB, October 17, 1924, 5.
78. CB, October 1, 1924, 5; CB, October 2, 1924, 5; CB, October 3, 1924, 5; CB, October 4, 1924, 5.
79. CB, October 22, 1924, 5; CB, October 23, 1924, 5; November 4, 1924, 5.

By November educators were reporting that they did not know how they would be able to open schools and had no hope for improvement in the future. In the state schools it was impossible even to maintain the existing previous schedule of classes. Those private colleges that did not qualify for Boxer indemnity funds were being forced to close. The financial panic caused by the war was making it difficult for educators and philanthropists to raise money, while the same financial stringency was leading numbers of fee-paying students to drop out. In Jiangsu an assembly of headmasters decided to open school late, since most of the area was at war, and even without financial difficulties, education would be difficult to carry on. In Zhejiang the provincial Board of Education lacked money, and therefore announced that "owing to the summer heat" it would defer the opening of school by two weeks. But even with the delay, it was able to provide schools only 100 yuan per month, which meant that many of them were placed in impossible situations.[80]

The effects of the war were felt first in the South. Nanjing was repeatedly caught up in the fighting from late August of 1924 until January of 1925. It had been planned to open Ginling Women's College on September 11, but on the advice of the American consul the date was moved to September 20. Despite the uncertainties and difficulty of travel, however, most of the students arrived, though special arrangements had to be made to escort some of them. Students and faculty carried on their work, despite the continuous threat from looting soldiers. The war became heated in the Nanjing area near the end of the first semester, and a dozen students returned home. Therefore when school opened again for the second semester, enrollment had dropped slightly, from 133 to 124, though students still came from the far south and west as well as Manchuria, representing twelve provinces in all.[81] Shanghai was even more directly affected. Many governmental schools had to suspend studies when the war began.[82] St. John's University managed to operate normally through most of the autumn of 1924, despite the Jiangsu–Zhejiang War raging a few miles from its campus. But on two days, when Shanghai itself seemed in danger, panic swept the campus and classes were suspended. The shift of the main theater of the war to the North following the defeat of Jiangsu provided a brief reprieve.

Meanwhile, as the war spread north, education there was hurt as well. By mid-winter the situation in Beijing had worsened dramatically. Since the war had broken out, not a day had passed in which there was not

80. *Jiaoyu zazhi* 16.11 (November 1924), 22–3.
81. Mrs. Lawrence Thurston and Ruth N. Chester, *Ginling College* (New York: United Board for Christian Colleges in China, 1955), pp. 49–50.
82. "Men and Events," CWR 30.4 (September 27, 1924), 112.

panic among educators. Except for a handful of institutions having secure foreign sources of funds, such as Qinghua, or the denominational colleges such as Yenching, or other foreign-supported institutions such as Peking Union Medical College, institutions of higher education, both public and private, were facing great financial difficulty. Thus Jiaotong University, which was directly managed by the Ministry of Communications, had managed to open classes but was perilously short of funds. In the cold weather coal was desperately needed, but the price had risen from 10 or 11 to 17 yuan per ton, and it was not available either in quantity at any price, or on credit. So the students, if they came to class at all, endured the wintry blasts from the Mongolian steppe in entirely unheated buildings. After September the government paid nothing to the schools. It was widely reported that Wang Kemin, the minister of finance and a strong supporter of Wu Peifu, simply took the funds intended for education and turned them over to Wu's war effort.[83] By February it was reported that all the educational institutions in the capital, including primary and middle schools, were in desperate condition, and the teachers were unable to make ends meet.[84]

Such hardships in education could only exacerbate an already existing trend. During the 1920s China's intellectuals and students had been playing an increasingly vocal political role. Beginning with the May Fourth demonstrations of 1919 students in the elite institutions repeatedly took to the streets to air their grievances. Some were parochial grievances over living conditions or school policies, but others had to do with how the country was being run. The incidents recorded in contemporary "tables of school protests" [*xuexiao fengchao biao*] run into the dozens: in 1922, for example, eleven substantial incidents of unrest were reported in universities and technical schools; sixty-six in middle schools, and at least ten in primary schools.[85] Foreign-sponsored institutions were scarcely exempt from this unrest; indeed, if anything they presented a particularly attractive target. In the early 1920s a strong anti-Christian movement developed in China, which profoundly challenged the mission effort and, not least, Christian education.[86] And as the Chinese grew more sensitive about the various privileges and immunities foreigners and foreign institutions had been accumulating since the nineteenth

83. *Jiaoyu zazhi* 17.1 (January 1925), 1.
84. *Jiaoyu zazhi* 18.2 (Feruary 1925), 3–4;
85. "Minguo shiyi niandu xuexiao fengchao biao," *Jiaoyu zazhi* 15 (1922), No. 1, 20920, 20938, 21136, 21140, 21178, 21198, 21280, 21374, 21434, 21580, 21610 (page numbers are for the Taiwan reprint edition of the journal; original pagination not visible. Because the second page of the primary school table is missing, only the first page total is given).
86. Lutz, *Chinese Politics and Christian Missions*, provides a good survey.

century, a movement was launched that specifically targeted foreign-sponsored schools, demanding what was called the "recovery of educational rights."[87] The privations and disruptions of war would only exacerbate these existing grievances.

Not only workers and students suffered. The middle classes, whose support was ultimately essential to any Chinese government, watched its property being gobbled up by taxes and inflation. In the Zhejiang area General Lu ordered a $2 million (Chinese) loan based on rent taxes from the area under his control. Bonds were issued that would be redeemable in ten drawings over five years and that could be presented in lieu of rent. As for General Qi, in all the towns under his control there had been heavy levies. Jiangsu had suffered repeatedly from irregular levies of taxes, and at war's end many localities, through their local representatives and assemblies, had sent telegrams to the central government asking that the 1925 taxes be waived. While the central government was still discussing this request, however, the Jiangsu authorities had already forced the counties in question to pay the taxes, borrowing if necessary to do so.[88]

In Tianjin, the call was made for a loan of $10 million (Chinese).[89] In Xiong *xian* in Zhili, the army established a service bureau to provide military supplies. By January of 1925 they had provided 11,426 yuan of silver, in addition to 4,105 yuan from local treasury funds, all of which greatly burdened the people.[90] In Shandong, taxes for 1925 were collected in October 1924.[91]

Zhang Zuolin felt similar pressure. On October 6 it was reported that Fengtian officials were demanding that people in the suburbs of Mukden pay land taxes [*tianfu*] of some four cents in silver per *mu* (0.1647 acre) to support the military effort. But because the people had suffered greatly from the summer's floods, and because scarcely anything grew on their land in any case, this levy proved impossible to collect.[92]

Finally, there was the direct damage to property caused by the fighting and by soldiers. Around Shanghai nine counties were particularly hard hit by the fighting. Among the towns directly damaged in the war were Songjiang, Qingpu, Jiading, Taicang, Baoshan, Junshan, and Fengxian. These areas, as one news account put it, had once been rich and

87. Alice H. Gregg, *China and Educational Autonomy: The Changing Role of the Protestant Educational Missionary in China, 1807–1937* (Syracuse, N.Y.: Syracuse University Press, 1946).
88. CB, March 31, 1925.
89. CWR, October 4, 1924, 166.
90. Liu Chongben et al., comps., *Xiongxian xinzhi* (1930), ch. 8, 40–1.
91. CB, October 13, 1924, 5.
92. *Shengjing ribao*, October 15, 1924.

prosperous, but the end of the war found their buildings ruined and people scattered. Foreign and Chinese observers estimated the damage in tens of millions of yuan. A French military officer believed that the total damage, including the northern theater, probably amounted to some 500,000,000 yuan.[93] Towns such as Liuhe, Nanxiang, and Songjiang suffered looting and devastating fires immediately after the fighting ceased. The refugees from those sections who fled on the outbreak of war now returned "to what remained of their homes, and faced a hard winter."[94] Relief funds were urgently needed, though no obvious source could be found. Tang Shaoyi (1860–1938) believed that at least 20,000,000 yuan would be needed immediately. In the devastated areas around Shanghai Qi Xieyuan organized local officials and gentry to begin relief work.[95]

The floods of late summer had made the effects of the civil war even worse. As both disasters receded, "an unusually dry cold . . . increased the suffering." The China International Famine Relief Commission estimated that no fewer than 10 million people had been affected, and that something like $230 million (Chinese) would be required to deal with the emergency, but what with an unstable central government, disorganized railway and telegraph facilities, lack of relief funds and exhausted government granaries, as well as banditry and looting "more or less rife in certain provinces," the situation looked grim.[96] The relative peace and prosperity that had characterized these areas until 1924 had vanished, and would not soon return.

93. "Zhanhou de Jiangnan," DZ 21 (1924), no. 23 (December 10), 5–6.
94. CWR, October 25, 1924, 256.
95. "Zhanhou de Jiangnan," 5–6.
96. Intelligence Office, Situation Survey, October 16 to December 31, 1924, 13, in MIR.

8

The war and the Powers

As the fighting got underway, the Powers, and Japan above all, hoped that the war would resolve itself fairly quickly. And the initial feeling was that it would. There was a conviction in the foreign community that Chinese warfare simply could not and must not impinge on its interests, a conviction that led to an initial tendency to focus on trivia – as in the grave complaint, forwarded by Willem Oudendijk, dean of the *corps diplomatique* in Beijing to the Foreign Ministry, that "on account of the large troop movements during the last few weeks it is almost impossible for civilian passengers to obtain places in the ordinary passenger trains for which tickets have been issued them."[1]

As the wars developed, the Powers gradually began to realize just how much was at stake for them in the outcome. At the outbreak of the wars, international relations in East Asia were defined, in theory at least, by the agreements reached at the Washington Conference. The wars, which began approximately two months before the third anniversary of the convening of the conference, brought with them both opportunities for and threats to the Washington System.

The opportunity was for Chinese unity. A victory by Wu Peifu would unify China, a nation whose political disunity had long been the bane of those who sought to put the Washington treaties into effect. How could any agreement with "China" possibly be implemented if that country spoke not with one but with at least three competing voices: those of the administrations at Beijing, Mukden, and Guangzhou? The British above all welcomed the prospect of a single China ruled from Beijing at last. On September 10, 1924, their minister, Sir Ronald Macleay, wired London that the

---

1. Dean's Circular No. 264, Beijing, September 26, 1924. Records Relating to Internal Affairs of China, SD 893.00.5738.

general situation would of course be much improved from our point of view by recovery of central government's control of Manchuria, Zhejiang and Guangdong, whose repudiation of authority and international obligations of Beijing during past two years has produced an impossible situation so far as China's foreign relations are concerned.[2]

Throughout the conflict the British would stick to this point of view, refusing to participate in efforts to mediate and ruling out any military intervention.

Such unity was also a threat to the interests of some Powers, and most notably Japan's. The danger was that Tokyo's carefully nurtured position in Manchuria, which pivoted politically on Zhang Zuolin, might be overturned. That certainly looked like a possibility as the war began. Thus on September 27, 1924, the military governor of Shandong, Zheng Shiqi (b. 1873), had sent a highly optimistic telegram to Cao Kun, the Chinese president. He believed that the army sent by Beijing against Zhang Zuolin in Manchuria, by then numbering perhaps 250,000 men with modern equipment, was strong, and saw a good prospect that "Mukden will be captured in a matter of days."[3]

Welcome to Britain, such a development would be Japan's worst nightmare, for the decisive victory by Zhili that Macleay hoped for, with its "recovery of central government's control of Manchuria," would undo everything Tokyo had striven to establish on the Asian mainland since the late nineteenth century. It would jeopardize, and perhaps eliminate, the "special position" in Manchuria and Mongolia that Japan had established at the cost of much bloodshed in the Russo-Japanese War, and for which it had sought international legal recognition ever since. Japan's role in Manchuria was unlikely to be given up or even modified without a fight by any Japanese government, even one in which foreign affairs were handled by Shidehara Kijūrō, a committed Anglo-American internationalist, present at Washington, whose name is to this day synonymous with liberal foreign policy. Japanese acquiescence, or war in the defense of Japanese interests – these were not attractive choices. Yet the developments in autumn 1924 threatened to pose them in a way that would be very difficult to ignore.

Since before the Washington Conference, friendship with the West had been, for Shidehara at least, Japan's paramount diplomatic goal. Unilateral Japanese action in Manchuria would jeopardize it by destroying the delicately maintained consensus of the Powers concerning China,

---

2. September 10, 1924. FO 371, F 3674.
3. Beiyang Zhengfu da zongtongfu dangan [Archive of the Beiyang Government Presidential Office], 1003.114.

and by placing the United States almost certainly and very likely Britain as well in firm opposition to Japanese actions. For the whole Washington order was based on some careful fudging in regard to the Japanese position in China's Northeast. Unable to agree on exactly what territory constituted China and, because of Chinese objection, prevented from putting into writing any distinction between "China proper" and associated territories such as Mongolia and Manchuria, the conferees at Washington had nevertheless agreed boldly to assert a commitment to respect both China's sovereignty and territorial integrity, both undefined, and made provisions as well to begin the liquidation of foreign privileges there. Japan would never have agreed to the treaty if doing so had seemed to pose even the slightest threat to its "special position" in Manchuria. Japan had been able to sign because it found an implicit guarantee of its position in the American secretary of state's letter of transmittal, which spoke of the Japanese interests as a matter of fact, as well as in the so-called security clause of the Nine Power Treaty, which pledged the signatories not to countenance actions inimical to the interests of friendly powers. As Asada Sadao has demonstrated, the Japanese believed the letter and the clause constituted a recognition and guarantee of their special position in Manchuria.[4] For most of the period since the conference, that compromise had seemed unlikely to be tested in fact: quite the opposite. The complex and seemingly stalemated Chinese political situation looked likely, at least as much as anything Japan or any other Power did, to keep Manchuria safely separate from Beijing. The Japanese depended for their influence there on Zhang Zuolin, and his defeat by Wu Peifu in 1922 had sent him back outside the passes where he seemed both secure and likely to remain dependent on Tokyo. In 1924, however, all of this suddenly began to change. Not only the Washington System, but the peace of Asia itself seemed perhaps to be threatened.

A genuine shift in Japanese policy had taken place as a result of the Washington Conference. At least since the Sino-Japanese War of 1894 to 1895, Tokyo had been convinced that Japan's security could not be guaranteed without a strong presence on the mainland of Asia and an alliance with a major Power. The alliance was concluded with Britain in 1896, and thereafter served as the basis of Japan's international position, accepted "variously as the marrow, the sheet-anchor, the cornerstone, the crux, of the country's diplomacy." In keeping with this alliance

---

4. Asada Sadao, "Japan and the United States, 1921–1925" (Ph.D. dissertation, Yale University, 1963), 287; also "Japan's 'Special Interests' and the Washington Conference, 1921–1922,' *American Historical Review* 56 (1961): 62–70.

Japan had provided naval assistance to Britain in the dark days of World War I when U-boat warfare was threatening to sink all Allied shipping. The price for this support for Britain had been a willingness to help Japan with its first goal, the maintenance of its security position on the Asian continent. Already established in Korea and Manchuria by the early years of the twentieth century, this position was augmented after World War I by succession to the German position in the strategically important Shandong peninsula. At Washington Japan fundamentally modified this conception of security, agreeing both to return Shandong to China and to end the alliance with Great Britain. This it did, with good spirit, although the end of the tie with London left many Japanese feeling "isolated and lonely (*sabishii*)."[5] Tokyo believed, however, that this would be compensated by a full partnership with all the great Powers, as envisaged in the Washington treaties.

The acceptance of Washington and the split with London meant in fact that Japan's two objectives, namely, security in Asia and membership in the club of great Powers, were no longer bound together. They would become at best independent and at worst incompatible goals. They had at a minimum to be secured independently, not an impossible task, at least in Shidehara's eyes. They key to the exercise was to maintain cordial relations, which they expected to be reciprocated, with the other Powers through the Washington System. As Kiyoshi Kawakami (1875–1949) wrote at the time, for Japan the importance of the Washington treaty "lies not so much in what it says as in what it implies . . . that henceforth the four dominant powers are going to act in the spirit of harmony and cooperation."[6] Given such cooperation (and the implicit guarantees made at Washington), Tokyo calculated that the position in Manchuria could be guaranteed as an "informal empire."[7] Direct military force could be deemphasized. Indeed in 1923, General Yamanashi Hanzō (1864–1944), minister of war in the cabinet of Katō Tomosaburō (June 12, 1922–September 2, 1923), had decided to withdraw the four battalions of so-called Independent Railway Guards that were stationed along the South Manchurian Railway (between Changchun and Kaiyuan, Kaiyuan and Mukden, Mukden and Liaoyang, and

---

5. See Ian H. Nish, *Alliance in Decline: A Study in Anglo-Japanese Relations 1908–1923* (London: University of London, 1972), pp. 383, 391.
6. Kiyoshi Kawakami, *Japan's Pacific Policy* (New York, 1929), p. 59, quoted in Ian Nish, *Alliance in Decline*, p. 380. Kawakami was an American-educated journalist, liberal at the time.
7. For "informal empire," see Peter Duus, Ramon H. Myers, and Mark R. Peattie, eds., *The Japanese Informal Empire in China 1895–1937* (Princeton: Princeton University Press, 1989).

Mukden and Andong), though the regular army 6th Division stationed at Liaoyang was not to be touched.[8]

Tokyo hoped that Zhang Zuolin, who controlled Manchuria while enjoying de facto independence from Beijing, would prove cooperative and that his administration would provide a framework in which Japan could enjoy informal empire in the territory without imposing the sort of direct imperial rule excluded by the Washington treaties. The problem with Zhang, however, as Tokyo well understood, was that whereas Japan wanted him to entrench himself at Mukden, his own ambitions (like those of any number of earlier Manchurian overlords) ranged beyond the passes at Shanhaiguan and Gubeikou into China proper. As we have seen, 1922 had found the forces of his Fengtian faction involved near Beijing in heavy fighting with those of the rival Zhili group. But the First Zhili–Fengtian War had ended in a rout which sent him back to Manchuria, a situation that suited Japan just fine. Japan's attitude toward Zhang's subsequent self-strengthening was also ambivalent. To some extent they colluded with him, but they were also aware of the potential divergences of interest that would arise should Zhang become too strong. Until 1924, the complex and seemingly stalemated Chinese political situation looked likely to control that problem and guarantee that Zhang would remain in his northeast kingdom, dependent on Japan. A light military presence, indirect influence through the Old Marshal, the legal strictures of the treaty system, and the consensus of the Powers would, the Japanese hoped, adequately guarantee their position.

These pieces never quite came together. The Japanese military in northeast China leaned informally to Zhang, who in turn showed little sign of abandoning his larger ambitions. At the same time the spirit of harmony and cooperation among the Powers over China, which was so important in particular to Japan, never blossomed, largely as a consequence of the gold franc dispute. The disastrous result was the suspension of implementation of two key provisions of the Washington treaties, and a thorough poisoning of the atmosphere between China and the Powers.[9]

Argument over the gold franc led to repeated postponements of the Special Conference on the Chinese Customs Tariff, scheduled to convene three months after ratification, to begin the process of treaty revision; also deferred was the meeting of the Commission on Extraterritoriality, whose charge was to examine ways to ameliorate and ultimately abolish

8. R. P. Tenney (American consul Mukden) to Edward Bell (Chargé Beijing), September 24, 1924, SD, 893.00/5668.
9. See Wesley R. Fishel, *The End of Extraterritoriality in China* (Berkeley: University of California Press, 1952), pp. 83–5.

that system. Planning, however, did get underway for both. Some in the British government saw the tariff conference as the centerpiece of the whole enterprise, a negotiation that might move far beyond its initial charge, toward a general settlement of China's problems.[10] In 1922 a special commission of the Powers began meeting to discuss the conference, and in September agreed on revision to an effective rate of 5 percent *ad valorem.*[11] In December the British began actively to seek American cooperation in the preparation for the conference, the opening of which was then expected imminently. In January 1923 Victor Wellesley (1876–1949) visited Washington to consult with MacMurray: among his most important points was that the new money China received should be used for constructive purposes and not (as some urged) for further repayments of unsecured debt. Almost simultaneously, Britain began talks with Japan.[12]

Even the unexpected disorders that began to overtake Chinese politics in the years immediately following Washington – the First Zhili–Fengtian War and some so-called bandit outrages – did not initially shake the Powers' determination that the systematic renegotiation of China's international position should go forward. In the Lincheng incident of May 6, 1923, the Blue Express from Pukou to Tianjin was stopped by bandits in Shandong, who killed one foreigner and took more than two dozen captive.[13] This led to calls for international control of China, or at least for creation of an international railway police. The second demand was supported, reluctantly, by the Foreign Office, though opposed by the United States.[14] Even so, plans went forward, but postponements were extended when Cao Kun overthrew President Li Yuanhong in June 1923.[15]

Through the summer before and during the wars of 1924 the British above all were drawing up plans for a further major step along the road mapped at Washington: one proposal was for a second conference, also held at the highest level, to resolve finally the complex questions of Chinese diplomacy and finance. The war's end would provide a need and an opportunity for change.

10. William James Megginson, III, "Britain's Response to Chinese Nationalism, 1925–1927: The Foreign Office Search for a New Policy" (Ph.D. dissertation: George Washington University, 1973), p. 230.
11. FRUS 1922, vol. 1, p. 819; Richard Stremski, "Britain's China Policy 1920–1928" (Ph.D. dissertation: University of Wisconsin, 1968), p. 51.
12. Stremskii, "Britain's China Policy," 52–7.
13. CYB 1924, 818–29.
14. Stremskii, "Britain's China Policy," 57–61.
15. Ibid., 68.

As the tide of battle seemed to flow in Zhili's direction, Japan became more and more concerned. On the day Zhejiang surrendered, the Japanese legation delivered a note to the Chinese foreign ministry in Beijing expressing its concern about their position "in Manchuria and Mongolia." In response Gu Weijun assured them on October 20 that the Chinese government was "resolved to spare no effort in affording . . . due respect" to "security of the lives and property of the nationals of the friendly Powers in China." But as MacMurray noted in Washington, the Chinese answer was drafted in such a way as to avoid "any reference to Manchuria and Mongolia," thus treating Japanese interests there "as though merely an aspect of the question of foreign interests in general."[16]

This can only have seemed ominous to Tokyo, for it threatened to unravel the complex compromise over interests on the Asian continent that had induced the Japanese to sign the Washington treaties in the first place. As we have seen, these treaties seemed simultaneously to assure both Chinese sovereignty and special Japanese rights in Manchuria. To view the pairing of two such contradictory guarantees in a single set of documents as simply cynical would be a mistake. The immediate post–World War I period saw the great powers of Europe just beginning to comprehend that their colonial empires could not survive in their original forms, and therefore starting to undertake not decolonization but, rather, a search – which would lead through self-government to commonwealth status and other such delusive expedients eventually to full independence – for new legal, diplomatic, and institutional forms that could somehow appease the demands of the colonized peoples even while guaranteeing the continued existence of the essentials of the colonizers' interests.

Perhaps no clearer example of this approach could be found than the Japanese informal empire in Manchuria. Treaties spelled out certain privileges there for Japan: economic rights, immunities for citizens, control of railways, the right to station railway guards and certain other troops. Numerous as these treaty provisions were, they did not constitute in themselves an adequate political framework for the rapidly developing Japanese economic position there. That framework Japan sought to provide indirectly, through the patronage and cultivation of Zhang Zuolin.

Initially, in 1924 the process seemed to be working well enough. The China policy that had flowed from the Washington Conference agreements was reaffirmed in May 1924 by the Kiyoura cabinet (January 7, 1924–June 11, 1924). It stressed a desire both for China's independence

16. October 22, 1924, SD 893.00/5670.

and for the maintenance and strengthening of Japan's economic position there. Shidehara had stated the approach strongly in his foreign policy speech to the Diet on July 1 of the same year. He promulgated his axiom of noninterference in China's internal politics [*naisei fukanshō*] while taking care above all to associate Japan's China policy with that of the other Powers and place it within the framework of the Washington treaties.[17]

Steps to scale down Japan's military presence in Manchuria had already been agreed on. These made clear that the Japanese considered that they could adequately guarantee their position by means of a reduced military presence, political influence through the Chinese ruler Zhang Zuolin, and careful coordination of policy with the other Powers: certainly they were not expecting any immediate military threat from a Chinese source.

The developments of late summer and early autumn of 1924 put these calculations to the test. At the outbreak of the Jiangsu–Zhejiang War, Shidehara reiterated the policy of noninterference in a note sent on September 5, 1924, to Debuchi Katsuji (1878–1947), the chief of the Asia Bureau of the Ministry of Foreign Affairs.[18] This approach was in line with that of the other Powers. At the outbreak of hostilities the American secretary of state Charles Evans Hughes wired to Jefferson Caffery (1886–1971), the chargé in Japan, that "The Department's chief concern in the disturbance in China has been to afford adequate protection to American life and property and to maintain an attitude of strict neutrality. There is no thought of any other course of action."[19] In the meantime Shidehara had made the same points to Caffery and to the British minister Sir Charles N. E. Eliot (1862–1931), who made separate calls at the foreign ministry.[20] As the American reported to Hughes:

Foreign Minister Shidehara in the course of a conversation today told me informally that Japan intended to keep neutral with respect to the present struggle in China. . . . He spoke of reports published in newspapers here alleging that Wu Peifu was backed by the United States and Zhang Zuolin by Japan. Both of these reports, he said, were obviously incorrect, and he expressed the hope that they would not gain credence in America.[21]

17. Ikei Masaru, "Dainiji Hōchoku sensō to Nihon," in *Tai-Manmō seisakushi no ichimen: Nichi-Ro sengo yori Taishōki ni itaru*, ed. Kurihara Ken (Tokyo: Hara Shobō, 1966), pp. 197, 193–4.
18. Ikei Masaru, "Dainiji," p. 204; also McCormack, *Chang Tso-lin*, 139–40.
19. The Secretary of State to the Chargé in Japan (Caffery), September 10, 1924, FRUS 1924, vol. 1, p. 372.
20. Ikei Masaru, "Dainiji," p. 206.
21. The Chargé in Japan (Caffrey) to the Secretary of State, September 10, 1924, FRUS 1924, vol. 1, p. 373.

Hope was strong that the war would somehow blow over. But as it grew more severe, it became clear to the Powers that both sides wanted a decision and were willing to fight for it. Whatever that decision proved to be, it would gravely affect the position of the Powers. This in turn meant that the differences papered over at Washington began to come into the open. The Washington Conference had warmly endorsed the idea of Chinese unity. Now Wu Peifu had proclaimed his intention of bringing about such unification by force and looked likely to do so. Some diplomats welcomed this prospect: they believed that if China could be unified and its government thus enabled to speak authoritatively and with one voice, the way would be prepared for fuller implementation of the other Washington Conference agreements. Macleay was of this opinion: as the Jiangsu–Zhejiang conflict took shape in August of 1924 he wired Ramsay MacDonald in London that "if the Zhili faction are able to rid Zhejiang and Shanghai of their opponents and so regain these regions for the Central Government, all Chinese and foreign interests will benefit in the end."[22] And as we have seen, he also welcomed the prospect of Zhili victory in Manchuria.[23] Not all British agreed with Macleay. Until the war Western opinion had been largely sympathetic with Wu Peifu, and distrustful of Zhang Zuolin, who was seen as being too close to Japan. But the war turned the China Association, which represented die-hard treaty-port opinion in Britain, definitely against Wu Peifu, because of the effect the sort of victory he and the Foreign Office were envisioning would have had on British interests in Shanghai. Pressure was such that even the Labour government of Ramsay MacDonald, whose theoretical attitude was one of extreme disinterest toward the British commercial position in China, was forced to meet these concerns by agreeing to the landing of foreign naval contingents to protect the International Settlement and to measures to neutralize the harbor at Shanghai.[24]

The British concerns were as nothing compared with those of the Japanese. How were Prime Minister Katō and Foreign Minister Shidehara to deal with the possible loss of the Manchurian territory for which so much blood had been shed? At a cabinet meeting on September 12 Shidehara confirmed yet again the policy of nonintervention, though with reservations about what would happen if fighting should spread to the Northeast.[25] And on September 21 he responded to increasing criticism by referring to the Washington treaties and in particular to

22. Sir R. Macleay to Mr. MacDonald, August 28, 1924, FO, 371, F 2921/19/10.
23. September 10, 1924, FO, 371, F 3674.
24. Stremski, "Britain's China Policy," 95–6.
25. Ikei Masaru, "Dainiji," p. 206.

their implicit acceptance of the Japanese role in Manchuria. At the conference, Shidehara stated, the importance Japan attached to its position in Manchuria had been clearly established, and note had been taken of it in the writings of the American delegate among others. Although a variety of rationales were being advanced in Japan for leaving the Washington framework, to do so would in fact gravely injure Japan's international standing and trust.[26] As will be seen below, Japan was already beginning to take unilateral actions to frustrate Wu Peifu quite outside the Washington framework.

As the fighting grew worse, and the very sort of decisive victory that some of the British believed to be desirable began to look possible, the fundamental differences between Japan's goals and those of the other Powers became increasingly clear. Shidehara's position regarding Manchuria became more and more difficult to maintain. A decisive victory by either side would undermine his policy, and he tended to avoid considering the possibility. In cabinet, he had already pointed out that the treaties guaranteeing Japanese rights along the Manchurian railway lines would provide sufficient justification for action if Wu should actually enter the territory. And on October 1 he was quoted in the press as "stating that Japan will be obliged to take action in self-preservation, once Manchuria is dragged into the actual war zone."[27]

On October 3 the British ambassador reported to MacDonald that:

it is remarkable how Baron Shidehara clings to the hope that no serious collision between the troops of Zhang Zuolin and Wu Peifu will take place.... [A]t the Ministry for Foreign Affairs the wish is obviously father to the thought.... If Zhang Zuolin were to capture Beijing and set up a new Government there he would probably escape from Japanese tutelage.... On the other hand, if he were defeated and remained in Manchuria, his value to Japan as a friend would greatly decrease, and if he were routed and Wu Peifu's troops occupied Manchuria, the political as well as the military situation might become very awkward. In such a contingency Baron Shidehara admits that the Japanese Government would be obliged to intervene to protect its nationals, but otherwise he assured me that they would adhere to their declared policy of non-intervention.[28]

A series of military setbacks to the Zhili forces on the Shanhaiguan front, notably the Fengtian breakthroughs at Jiumenkou on October 7 and at Shimenzhai on October 14, provided some breathing space for Shidehara. Instead of a rapid Zhili conquest of Mukden, a winter of trench warfare

---

26. Ibid., p. 210.
27. *Manchuria Daily News*, October 1, 1924, enclosed in SD 893.00/5687.
28. Sir C. Eliot to Mr. MacDonald, October 27, 1924, FO, p. 371, F 3582/19/10.

along the Great Wall seemed to be in store. But the prospect that encouraged Tokyo disheartened London. Macleay had written from Beijing in September that "if the present war results in establishing the undoubted supremacy of one of the war lords and the general acceptance of one central authority, it may... 'throw up an opportunity for the Powers to deal in a new and comprehensive way with the Chinese problem as a whole,' but without some process of unification I cannot see how anything of the kind will be possible."[29]

British and Japanese hopes for China were at loggerheads, with each fearing the outcome for which the other hoped. Furthermore, as the fighting unfolded, the pro-Zhang Japanese in Manchuria and Tokyo made their voices heard. In the House of Peers on the very day Shidehara had made his speech announcing nonintervention to the Diet, Debuchi had characterized the policy as in fact little more than following after England and America.[30] And in a note sent on September 5, 1924, to Debuchi, Funatsu Tatsujirō (1873–1947), consul general at Mukden, criticized Shidehara's noninterventionist policy as rather stupid, since a victory by Zhang would provide an opportunity to get Duan Qirui, who was considered more favorable to Japan, back into office. Funatsu did not speak of military intervention, but he believed that Japan should move if Zhang looked about to be defeated, and even if the struggle should end up being arbitrated, intervene in his favor.[31] On October 8 a self-appointed delegation of fourteen members representing the various political groups in the Diet left for China, intending to undertake "with open minds" a first-hand investigation of the situation. This was a sure sign of trouble for Prime Minister Katō even though the members in question were of "very mediocre talents" – "mediocre," according to Debuchi, "even for the average mediocrity in the Diet."[32] And as the situation deteriorated, extremist groups in Japan got into the act. Shidehara was physically attacked, and two unfortunate Japanese aviators, who had enlisted with the Zhili airforce, were assaulted by an ultranationalist named Suzuki.[33]

The result was that even while paying lip service to the long tradition of foreign diplomatic solidarity in Beijing, and the more recent resolutions of the Washington Conference, the Powers began to move decisively

29. Telegram for Sir R. Macleay, September 10, 1924, FO, p. 371, F 3074/19/10.
30. Ikei Masaru, "Dainiji," pp. 210–11.
31. Ibid., p. 204; McCormack, *Chang Tso-lin*, 139–40; Shin'ichi Kitaoka, "China Experts in the Army," in *The Japanese Informal Empire in China*, ed. Peter Duus, Ramon H. Myers, and Mark R. Peattie (Princeton: Princeton University Press, 1989), p. 362.
32. Caffery to Secretary of State, October 8, 1924, SD, 893.00/5711.
33. Ikei Masaru, 211–12; Caffery to Secretary of State, October 6, 1924, SD, 893.00/5727.

toward unilateralism in the autumn of 1924 – and not, as is usually maintained, only after the May 30, 1925, incident (which will be discussed in Chapter 11). The usual argument is that the Powers fell out over what response to make to the resurgent Chinese nationalism enunciated by the Kuomintang. Here we see something rather different: the reemergence of the fundamental conflict between Japan's interests and those of the other Powers (although it is perhaps worth noting that the Zhili goal of a unified China free of subordination to the Powers was essentially identical to that of the nationalist movement of the later 1920s). In any case, the independent actions of the Powers took several directions.

Most British and the Americans believed that the Powers should stand aside and let the Chinese fight it out, even if the result might seem to threaten their interests. The other Powers and the Japanese were more divided in their opinions: most favored mediation, and some called for direct military intervention. The American position of absolute neutrality was spelled out on September 30 in a wire from Secretary of State Hughes to chargé Edward Bell (1882–1924) in Beijing, which stated that although the United States was not "indifferent" to events in China, its policy nevertheless remained one of "aloofness."[34] On October 9 Hughes assured Chinese minister Shi Zhaoji [Alfred Sze] (1877–1958) that the United States was not considering military action, although he knew that Tokyo was under "a good deal of pressure" to do so.[35] British minister Macleay concurred, as we have seen.

But the grand old man of British China policy, Sir John Jordan, strongly recommended mediation in an article in the *Observer* on September 7 which called for the Powers to convene a conference of the two fighting factions.[36] The Japanese minister in Beijing, Yoshizawa Kenkichi, took a similar approach. He urged Shidehara on October 4 to consider the various possibilities raised by the conflict, including victory by Wu and victory by Zhang, and recommended that both sides be severely warned about the danger to Japanese interests. Furthermore, he suggested that money be provided to both in return for their agreement. On October 13 Japanese notes were delivered to Wu Peifu via Gu Weijun in Beijing and to Zhang Zuolin via Funatsu Tatsuijirō, which reiterated Tokyo's concern about the situation and stressed the need, whatever the outcome, to respect and maintain Japan's legal rights. These

34. Hughes to Bell, September 30, 1924, SD, 893.00/5575.
35. "Memorandum of an Interview with the Chinese Minister (Sze)," October 9, 1924, Hughes Papers, Container 174, Folder 62. Cited in Richard Clarke DeAngelis, "Jacob Gould Schurman and American Policy toward China, 1921–1925," p. 310.
36. The *Observer*, September 7, 1924, enclosed in FO 371, F 3057/19/20.

notes fell far short of the active diplomacy Yoshizawa had envisioned. Unable to make up his mind, Shidehara never moved on Yoshizawa's proposal, a fact Yoshizawa would later regret as the forfeit of a favorable chance to establish stability in China.[37]

Representatives of the other Powers were thinking along similar lines. France's minister in Tokyo from 1921 to 1927 (he would subsequently serve in Washington) was the poet Paul Claudel (1868–1955). On October 15 Claudel called on Wang Rongbao (1878–1933), the Chinese minister. The Frenchman spoke of the disasters war had brought to Europe and could bring to China, and then, alluding to the Geneva protocol for the pacific settlement of international disputes which had been concluded a fortnight earlier on October 2, expressed his strong hope that the Chinese might similarly commit themselves to the course of negotiation. Were the Chinese parties to reconcile themselves, he added, the Western powers would be willing to make a range of concessions to Beijing. Even in the vexatious gold franc dispute, Claudel stated, "it would certainly be possible to accommodate the Chinese position."[38]

Claudel saw a role for the Powers in bringing about such an outcome. He had already been in contact with the Japanese authorities and with his British colleague, and a plan was being developed by which the Powers, working through their representatives in Beijing and Mukden, would make strong efforts to persuade the Chinese parties to negotiate. These representations would be oral: no formal notes would be written. The hope was that the Powers, without taking sides, might facilitate a conference at which China's internal conflicts would be settled, and the way thus opened for resolution of pending international questions as well.[39]

After the French ambassador had departed, Wang paid a call on Dr. Wilhelm Solf (1862–1936), the German ambassador. Solf was an Asian linguist who as a young man had studied Sanskrit in Calcutta; he was also a diplomat and had served as foreign minister in the cabinet of Prince Max of Baden that negotiated the armistice ending World War I. But Solf was of little use to Wang: the British minister, Solf told Wang, was not talkative, and with Claudel he was not close; therefore he could not say exactly what the truth of the matter was.[40]

37. Ikei Masaru, "Dainiji," 212–13.
38. Wang Rongbao telegram to Chinese foreign ministry, October 15, 1924, in Shi Aichu, ed. "Wang Rongbao Handian," *Jindaishi ziliao* (Beijing: Zhonghua shuju, 1963), pp. 99–100.
39. Shi, "Wang Rongbao," p. 99.
40. Ibid., pp. 99–100.

Thereupon Ambassador Wang called on Debuchi, who reiterated to him Japan's neutral position. His country would in no way intervene in the present disorder in China. He observed that although it was true that many Japanese favored the Fengtian side, the government would not provide even one penny of financial or one bullet of military assistance. Wang then questioned him about the many military activities being carried out by Japanese in Manchuria on behalf of Zhang Zuolin, but he was told that these Japanese were acting in a purely private capacity; that Japanese were also working privately with Wu Peifu; and that the Tokyo government could not take responsibility for them. As for what would happen if Wu's forces entered the Northeast and required permission to use the railways there to transport troops, Debuchi dismissed this as a hypothetical question that did not then need to be discussed.[41]

On the following day Wang called on Shidehara himself. In order to ascertain the real position of the Japanese government, he first reiterated the Chinese position that in the course of the struggle foreigners and foreign rights would be carefully respected. Shidehara responded by emphasizing two points: first, the Japanese government was determined not to favor either side in the battle; second, Japan would most certainly not take advantage of the disorder for further aggrandizement. The war was a bad thing, not only for China, but equally for Japan. As to some mediating role for the Powers, Shidehara stated that his government had long favored this, but fearing it might be misunderstood within China as interference and lead to a worsening of the situation, he had not actively pursued it. If, however, the Chinese government should be receptive, Japan would be willing to play such a role in connection with the other Powers, rather as the United States had (this was Shidehara's example) at Portsmouth between Russia and Japan. The Powers would urge on both Chinese sides the need for a cease-fire, and then for the selection of delegates, agreement on a place of meeting, and an agenda for discussion. The Powers would serve as honest brokers only and make no attempt to influence the free discussions of the Chinese parties. Regarding this proposal Shidehara urged Wang to secure a reply from his government as soon as possible, so that the process of peacemaking might get underway. Wang wired this information to Beijing, urging that it be brought to President Cao's attention immediately.[42]

Beijing, however, was not receptive. As Wang reported it, although it was true that the Chinese hoped for peace, they also hoped for a

---

41. Ibid., p. 100.
42. Wang Rongbao telegram to Chinese foreign ministry, October 17, 1924, in Shi, "Wang Rongbao," pp. 100–1.

definitive solution to their internal problems, by combat if necessary, and this meant that foreign urgings for yet more compromise would not be welcomed either by the government or by Wu Peifu.[43] Nor did the British support the idea: Macleay wrote of the proposal that although the Powers might offer to mediate with a view of finding some common ground of agreement, "the consensus of the best opinion is that this is impossible." He argued instead that the Powers would do best to wait for China either to unite or to exhaust itself, and that in the meantime, to attempt any bold initiative would be a terrible mistake.[44]

Macleay was also unequivocally opposed to foreign intervention. He wrote:

For the Powers as a whole – let alone any single Power – to saddle themselves with a problem of a magnitude at least 10 times as great as that of Egypt is unthinkable. Our interests in China and those of other Powers, great as they are, would not justify the risk of such an undertaking. The idea can be dismissed without further consideration.[45]

Given the fruitlessness of mediation and the unwillingness of others to cooperate with it, Japan faced in mid-autumn of 1924 the real possibility of a Zhili conquest of Manchuria, acquiesced to by the Powers. Whether it happened or not would depend on the verdict of the battlefield, and it was here that Japan increasingly exercised an indirect influence. The military prospects of both sides had become cloudy by early October. Neither side had succeeded in the sort of lightning war it had planned. Wu's forces reached Shanhaiguan quickly and occupied it before Zhang's army arrived, which was a major strategic setback for Fengtian. Furthermore, Fengtian's ally Lu Yongxiang was defeated at Shanghai in the middle of the month. But as we have seen, by mid-October Fengtian had made two costly breakthroughs on the eastern front. Just as important, on the Rehe front to the west, with Chaoyang as the critical objective, Fengtian had done very well indeed. Zhili sought desperately to reinforce its garrisons there, but problems with transportation frustrated it.

Zhang's gains, however, were not greeted with unmixed pleasure in Tokyo. Like the other Chinese players in the war, Zhang wanted Manchuria united with China: he simply wanted it on his own terms. In

43. Wang Rongbao telegram to foreign ministry, October 21, 1924, in Shi, "Wang Rongbao," p. 101. Some sources say the Japanese initiated the mediation effort and took it up with the French: "Chen Lu guanyu Riben, Faguo dui Zhi-Feng zhanzheng de taidu deng qing dian," September 23, 1924, in Peng Ming, gen. ed., *Zhongguo xiandaishi ziliao xuanji*, vol. 1 *(1924–1927)* (Beijing: Zhongguo renmin daxue chubanshe, 1988), p. 115.
44. Macleay to Foreign Office, September 10, 1924, FO 371, F 3074/19/10.
45. Ibid.

furtherance of this goal he had concluded the Triangular Alliance, a marriage of convenience with Sun Yat-sen at Guangzhou – which meant, ironically enough and to Japan's profound consternation, that radical Kuomintang propaganda may have been more widespread and influential in Manchuria than in the areas of China under Zhili control. To the horror of Japanese in the northeast a pro-Kuomintang newspaper, the *Dong sansheng minbao*, made its appearance in Mukden in November of 1922, and it did much to fan irredentist feelings. By February 1924 there were calls for agreement allowing extradition from Manchuria to China proper (a practical assertion of fundamental Chinese sovereignty) and in May for the recovery of educational rights associated with the South Manchurian Railway.[46]

In response to such developments, Japanese in Manchuria, both officials and private citizens, began to work to make Zhang Zuolin into a pro-Japanese bulwark of Manchurian separatism against increasing trends toward unification of China. Zhang understood their goal, however, and while working with them, he also endeavored to make himself more and more independent. Thus, he refused to honor the monopoly of the South Manchurian Railway, sponsoring the construction of rival lines, and in his choice of weapons and advisers for his arsenals he was eclectic, standardizing his forces to the Arisaka rifle but employing Germans and British at the Mukden munitions works and importing machinery from Europe.

Given Beijing's implacable intention to retake Manchuria, which was indirectly accepted by the Powers, as well as the evident unreliability of Zhang Zuolin himself, Japanese in Manchuria were understandably skeptical of the fundamental premises of Shidehara's diplomacy. Many believed that only an active Japanese role in the territory, including military cooperation, could secure Japan's position there. The general staff of the Kwantung army, for example, prepared a memorandum in October 1923 that argued that international management of the Manchurian problem was not to be depended on.[47] Important Japanese tried to draw close to Zhang Zuolin and influence him. Among his outright supporters were Funatsu Tatsuijirō and General Staff China specialist Honjō Shigeru (1876–1945). Japanese money topped up his coffers, Japanese employees and advisers supervised the manufacture of some of his weapons, the drilling of some of his troops, and even the making of some policy.

As war began, the withdrawal of Japanese railway guards mentioned above was suspended. This was an important indication of Japanese

46. Ikei Masaru, "Dainiji," pp. 198–9.   47. Ibid., p. 199.

official policy, for when pressed in the Diet about what would happen if Wu Peifu should break through Shanhaiguan and move toward Mukden, Shidehara had replied, as we have seen, that existing international agreements would provide sufficient justification for intervention. Such a move by Wu would require him to cross the guaranteed defensive zones of the South Manchurian Railway, for which he would require permission. Japan could deny that permission and use the railway guards against Wu if (as seemed inevitable) he flouted their demands. New Japanese troops were garrisoned in the areas where Wu Peifu seemed likely to attempt his seaborne landings, and in violation of all international agreements (and in the teeth of British protests) the Japanese denied Wu's navy the right to dock at Qinhuangdao. Japanese naval units shadowed Wu's invasion flotilla and contributed much to its failure. While undermining Wu, the Japanese did much to support Zhang. His troops were transported on Japanese railways. When Wu Peifu protested that neutrality should afford him equal access to the Manchurian railways, the Japanese had difficulty in replying. Former Russian soldiers and officers, working as laborers in Japanese enterprises, were "given permission" to leave their jobs and join special all-Russian military detachments in the Fengtian army. A Japanese in Wu Peifu's entourage secretly passed information about Wu's plans and movements to Japanese military intelligence, who in turn passed it on to Zhang Zuolin.[48]

At the same time that the changing military situation posed challenges to the Japanese, it afforded undreamed of opportunities to the Soviet Union. Politically both Mukden and the Beijing governments had always been strongly anti-Communist, and as a result Soviet initiatives in China had been through the marginal instrumentalities of Sun Yat-sen and the infant Chinese Communist party. Sun Yat-sen was marginal because he lacked a strong power base inside China and was therefore forced consistently, whether he liked it or not, to rely on foreign patrons, which in turn made his foreign policy hostage to their interests.[49] Thus at the time of the Twenty-one Demands, when most Chinese were outraged at Japan's attempt to use the war to secure a position of hegemony in China, Sun had written to the Japanese suggesting that if they would back him, he would be willing to make even greater concessions than those Yuan Shikai had approved.[50] As for the Chinese Communist party,

---

48. See Guo Jianlin, "Wu Peifu yu Riben," in *Zhong Ri guanxi yanjiu*, no. 3, ed. Xinan junfashi yanjiuhui (Kunming: Yunnan renmin chubanshe, 1985), pp. 217–34.
49. See the general discussion in C. Martin Wilbur, *Sun Yat-sen: Frustrated Patriot* (New York: Columbia University Press, 1976), pp. 76–111.
50. Marius B. Jansen, *The Japanese and Sun Yat-sen* (Cambridge, Mass.: Harvard University Press, 1954), pp. 192–3, 262, nn. 50, 51.

although it already had a certain intellectual influence, at this time it was organizationally in its infancy. Neither Sun nor the Communists offered Moscow a means for achieving its larger policy objective in China. Moscow was above all worried by being excluded from Europe, and it saw stirring up trouble in Asia as a way of bringing pressure. Breaking out of diplomatic isolation, as much as furthering revolution elsewhere in the world, was the purpose of the Karakhan declaration of 1919, which had renounced extraterritoriality, indemnity payments, the Chinese Eastern Railway, and all territory seized by the tsars. The declaration was attractive to both the Beijing and Guangzhou regimes. But no sooner had it been issued than the Soviets began to backpedal. Furthermore, in keeping with its larger diplomatic strategy, the Beijing government insisted on more or less literal fulfillment of what the declaration promised.

It is sometimes suggested that the USSR pursued a revolutionary policy in Asia, which served as the rationale for its alliance with Sun and the Kuomintang. In fact the Soviets turned to Sun only when initiatives to Beijing were turned down by Gu Weijun. Only after Lev Karakhan had been rebuffed by Gu in Beijing did he make terms with the Kuomintang. Gu had demanded withdrawal of the Soviet Army from Outer Mongolia and the transfer of the Chinese Eastern Railway as conditions for recognition: Sun was willing to be more flexible.[51] Even at the time, in 1922, Soviet Foreign Minister Boris Chicherin (1872–1936) told Sun that the Beijing government was the official government of the Chinese state, "and we are trying to establish normal relations with it."[52] And when an opportunity opened up for Moscow to establish official relations with Beijing, the Soviets brought pressure to bear on Sun to support them. In 1924, after negotiations between Karakhan and Wang Zhengting (1882–1961), the Soviet government was so eager to proceed that it risked undermining its relationship with Dr. Sun and his party in an effort to get them to join in pressure they were orchestrating to make the Beijing foreign minister sign the tentative agreement.[53]

Agreement was finally reached in May of 1924 between Karakhan and Gu. The diplomacy served the interests of both sides. Both China and the USSR had scored a coup: Karakhan, the Soviet representative, was the senior – because he was the only – ambassador to the Chinese government (the rest were ministers), and as such, according to the strict

51. BDRC, vol. 2, p. 256.
52. Wilbur, *Sun Yat-sen*, p. 121.
53. Ibid., pp. 229–42.

rules of protocol, automatically became dean of the *corps diplomatique* in Beijing. Gu had certainly put the cat among the pigeons with that one. Furthermore, the provisions of the agreement between Gu and Karakhan could now serve as a model for other Powers to follow. And there was a threat that did not even need to be uttered: if the other Powers proved too uncooperative with Beijing, closer Sino-Soviet cooperation was always possible. There were some interesting specifics as well. The agreements regarding the Chinese Eastern Railway, in particular, implicitly recognized Beijing's jurisdiction in Manchuria. This would be bad news for Zhang Zuolin, who sought to carry out his own diplomacy and wanted to be sure that if and when the railway was returned, it went to him. It was also rather worrying for Tokyo. Tokyo believed that the Soviet Union was a threat, and Soviet willingness to yield its special position in Manchuria undermined Japan's legal claim, while advancing the interests in Beijing of Tokyo's rival. The agreement was also a body blow to Sun Yat-sen. For both its contents and the pressure put on him to endorse it brought home Moscow's clear calculation that he was not the man of destiny and that in their eyes his government had no future. Moscow's calculations are unexceptionable (although they proved incorrect); the other Powers read the Chinese situation in more or less the same way. Recall that Japan at this time was most worried about a threat to Manchuria from Beijing. Even the Kremlin seemed to have decided to put its bets on the Northern regime.

The war, however, created other options. Moscow can scarcely have enjoyed doing business with the Beijing government: those who believed in revolution (as many Soviets at the time did most sincerely) had little use for the policies or the personality of a Gu Weijun or a Wu Peifu. Realpolitik alone dictated the rapprochement, from both sides. The Beijing government was too powerful to ignore; and opening to Moscow would be too useful to veto on ideological grounds. Why should Beijing help the European imperialists when they were being so unhelpful (the gold franc) to Beijing? But early in the war it became clear that Zhili might not emerge victorious, and Moscow immediately began to explore an approach to China that focused not on the center but, rather, on the periphery: on the emerging opposition to Cao Kun and his colleagues.

It is worth noting that the experience of the Russian civil war in particular provided many parallels for understanding the Chinese internal conflicts of the 1920s, and particularly for the Soviet specialists sent to China. One of the first Comintern representatives to China, V. D. Vilenskii-Sibiriakov, who arrived in 1919, had worked against Aleksandr Kolchak (1874–1920) and the Allied intervention in Siberia, and showed an understandable tendency to see the Chinese situation as paralleling that of the Soviet.[54] Certainly Russia in the civil war had been as divided as was China: at one point in 1918 nineteen self-proclaimed governments had been active on Russian territory, not to mention five "independent" governments under German occupation, as in the Ukraine, and more genuinely independent regimes such as those in Georgia and Finland.[55] Yet the Bolsheviks had ultimately succeeded in imposing unity, not least through skillful recruitment of former tsarist officers and skillful exploitation of divisions among the White generals. Thus Trotsky (Lev Bronstein, 1879–1940) had employed some 50,000 former White officers.[56]

So when the Chinese central government began to weaken, the Soviets were at no loss for stratagems with which to respond. They patched things up with Zhang Zuolin, weakening Beijing by agreeing with him not to take any action against the Chinese Eastern Railway. That meant that Zhang could concentrate his forces on the southern front without worrying that the USSR might move to take advantage of his weakness. It also reassured Japan by suggesting that Soviet and Japanese interests in Manchuria – at least in the short run – might coincide. They clearly diverged in the longer run, because out of weakness Zhang had strengthened his cooperation with Sun Yat-sen. As we have seen, Kuomintang propaganda began to be tolerated in the northeast, and (not for the last time) the vision of a pro-Soviet Manchuria danced in the heads of Soviet China watchers. Finally, the war began to restore Sun's prestige. There were divisions in the Zhili group: some of its members were more sympathetic with Guangzhou than others, and if Zhili could be split, then the possibility emerged of sponsoring a "progressive" militarist in the north.

In autumn of 1924 the Soviets, like the other Powers, had come to believe that the Northern System would survive and that Beijing would probably succeed in its ultimate aim of unifying all of China. The next developments would spoil their calculations as completely as they did those of all the other diplomatic players.

54. V. N. Nikiforov, *Sovetskie Istorikii o Problemakh Kitaia* (Moscow: "Nauka," 1970), pp. 67–8.
55. Adam B. Ulam, *A History of Soviet Russia* (New York: Praeger Publishers, 1976), p. 34.
56. Ibid., 28–30.

9

The turning point

In mid-October of 1924, Wu Peifu looked about to realize his long-term goal of uniting China. All the pieces were falling into place. His lines, according to American military intelligence, were strong. If his troops moved fast enough, the bold pincer movement he was closing around Mukden might defeat Zhang Zuolin or bring him to terms in a matter of weeks. Even a winter stalemate along the northern front would be to his advantage: after the victory on the Shanghai front more men and materiel would be available for the North, and the whole productive capacity of Central China could be harnessed to his war effort. Even foreign reaction to his possible victory looked positive. It was true that the Japanese were deeply worried. But Shidehara was set firmly against intervention, and the British – whom the Japanese would probably follow if the crunch came – were alive to the great advantages of a China that was finally united. But neither the rapid Zhili march into Manchuria nor the stalemate along the frontier came to pass.

Early in the morning of October 23 General Feng Yuxiang, with his 11th Division and the 7th and 8th Mixed Brigades, arrived in Beijing and took possession of the city practically unopposed. The great Ming dynasty gates were closed, the railways were halted, telephone and telegraph communications cut. Feng made his headquarters at a military barracks just west of the Beihai Lake within the old Imperial City wall, which were still commonly called the Zhantansi, after a temple built on the site by Kangxi (r. 1661–1722). The temple, which had been largely destroyed by the Boxers, had been famous for its large Buddha made of sandalwood.[1] From the Zhantansi Feng took control of the forces of order in the capital: Lu Zhonglin (1886–1966) was named commissioner

---

1. See Juliet Bredon, *Peking: A Historical and Intimate Description of Its Chief Places of Interest* (Shanghai: Kelly & Walsh, 1931), p. 228; L. C. Arlington and William Lewisohn, *In Search of Old Peking* (Peking: Henri Vetch, 1935), p. 134. My thanks to Professor Susan Naquin for these references.

of militia and Zhang Bi (b. 1885) placed in charge of the police. Proclamations were issued and pasted up all over the city demanding an immediate cessation of hostilities, the abdication of President Cao Kun, and the arrest and punishment of those responsible for the war. At the Christian General's insistence, and although it had no effect, Cao Kun – now Feng's prisoner – immediately dismissed Wu Peifu from all his offices on October 24 and ordered him exiled to Qinghai. With the Beijing railroad stations and junctions under his control, Feng began moving to secure the area around the capital as well, sending troops as far as Langfang on the line to Tianjin and against forces loyal to Wu Peifu that still remained in the area. A few days later Feng would name a new regency cabinet headed by Huang Fu (1880–1936). His armies and those of his allies were organized with a new title: they became the *Zhonghua Minguo Guominjun*, or National People's Army of the Chinese Republic.[2]

This event, usually called the Beijing coup d'état [*Beijing zhengbian*], is among the few from the period of the Northern System that is still widely known. Because it is usually considered alone, without its military or political context, its significance is not always clearly understood. At first glance, Feng Yuxiang's sudden about-face seems to sum up much about the period of the Northern government: some portray it as a brave and idealistic action by a soldier finally fed up by the corruption around him and determined to open the way for Sun Yat-sen; others dismiss it as little more than a cynical financial transaction in which Feng betrayed Wu in return for a substantial payment from Tokyo. Above all it seems to capture the essence of politics and warfare in the period: admittedly complex and dramatic, but in retrospect without any significance beyond which interchangeable militarist won and which lost. Despite substantial research, the origins of the Beijing coup are not entirely clear even today. What we do know suggests that there was both more, and less, to it than is usually recognized.

There was less to the coup because, contrary to what is commonly thought, it did not by any means doom Wu Peifu. It was a body blow: of that there can be no doubt, but Wu still had military options. In the days immediately following the coup, rumors about Wu's fate flew in the capital: according to some reports he had committed suicide at Qinhuangdao, others stated that he had boarded the *Hai Qi* and was heading for the south, still others that relief forces from his ally Qi Xieyuan would arrive momentarily. All proved wrong. Two days after

---

2. James L. Sheridan, *Chinese Warlord: The Career of Feng Yü-hsiang* (Stanford: Stanford University Press, 1966), pp. 133–6.

Feng's move, at 11:50 A.M. on October 26 General Wu's train arrived at Tianjin East Station. China's outstanding general was not going down without a fight.

Wu's immediate strategy was to hold the Manchurian front and then, when enough reinforcements from the south had arrived in Tianjin, to move down the railway line and drive Feng from the Chinese capital. While awaiting reinforcements, however, Wu moved parts of the 3rd and 14th Divisions to Tianjin, while elements of the 26th Division, already at Machang, were immediately moved up and a "superficial system of trenches" begun west of Yangcun [today's Wuqing, on the railway line just northwest of Tianjin]. At the same time Feng Yuxiang began moving his forces from Beijing along the same railway line toward Tianjin; they dug in near Langfang, the station immediately west of Yangcun.

Militarily the situation was grave but by no means hopeless. Wu faced a two-front war, not for the first time in his career. The key would be to hold Zhang Zuolin on the Manchurian lines while dealing with Feng Yuxiang and Beijing. Since the first was the more important task – what, after all, could Feng Yuxiang accomplish by holding Beijing and nothing else? – Wu's wisest course would probably have been to remain himself in command of the Shanhaiguan front, while detaching small units under trusted subordinates to move south, encircle, and isolate the capital. At a minimum such a strategy could probably have procured a stalemate, which would have been preferable to the decisive defeat that in fact ensued. For once, however, Wu seems to have allowed his temper to override his analytical ability, and he did the opposite. He was outraged by Feng's treachery and wanted to punish it himself. The critical and difficult task of holding the Shanhaiguan front he entrusted to his deputy Zhang Fulai, a man long on bravery but short on military genius, while himself undertaking the much simpler task of investing the capital.[3]

Wu had no reserves in the capital area; as we have seen in Chapter 5, everything had been committed to the front at Shanhaiguan. But he did have twenty transport ships waiting at Qinhuangdao: these he decided to use to carry some troops from the northern front to Tianjin. Wu also expected reinforcements from the south. On October 24 the Zhili generals in control of the Yangzi valley had issued a proclamation stating that Feng's coup had been a breach of moral conduct and pledging their support to Wu.[4]

3. See Guo Jianlin, *Wu Peifu*, vol. 2, p. 593.
4. Odoric Y. K. Wou, *Militarism in Modern China: The Career of Wu P'ei-fu, 1916–1939* (Folkestone, Kent, England: Wm. Dawson & Sons Ltd.; also Canberra: Australia National University Press, 1978), p. 125, note 2, citing *China Illustrated Review*, November 1, 1924, p. 176.

Feng Yuxiang realized that his own position was precarious. Therefore he did not immediately overthrow the Beijing administration as might have been expected: rather, he proceeded cautiously at first, choosing to work through Cao Kun, the president whose corruption Feng had proclaimed as a major reason for his action. Such care indicated that even after the coup, Feng was hedging his bets. He understood that as long as Wu had control of the railways leading to the capital from both north and south it would be only a matter of time before the Zhili commander would concentrate sufficient forces and deal with his rebellious subordinate.

In the end what doomed Wu was not his perhaps temporary loss of control of the Chinese capital but, rather, his inability to secure his hold on the lines of communication, and through them the critical aid of his allies to the south. This fatal development was the result of both Chinese and Japanese actions.

The Chinese players in the military and political game moved to reconsider their positions as soon as Wu's future came into doubt: some of his erstwhile allies resumed neutral and self-defensive postures, preparing for the next realignment of political forces. Because those neutralists controlled key rail links, they were able to prevent those who still wished to aid Wu from doing so. Thus the Henan governor Li Jichen (b. 1881) wanted to send the Jiangxi 3rd Mixed Brigade, the Hubei 2nd Mixed Brigade, and other units, up the railroad from Zhengzhou to help Wu, but Yan Xishan (1883–1960) stopped them 250 miles up the line at Shijiazhuang in Shanxi. From Shanghai Sun Chuanfang dispatched a regiment north, but the railway passed through Shandong, whose military governor, Zheng Shiqi, declared armed neutrality and refused to allow any troops to pass through. Halted south of Jinan, Sun's forces turned back on November 4. Meanwhile in Hubei Xiao Yaonan put Chen Jiamou in charge of forces to relieve Wu, and asked the Hankou General Chamber of Commerce to float a 600,000 yuan loan for him as well. But the provincial assembly called for strict neutrality, and two brigades of troops were stopped by Yan Xishan at Zhengzhou.[5]

The decisive move in this military endgame, however, was made by the Japanese. We have already met Zhang Zongchang, commander of the Fengtian 1st Division, called by his troops the "dogmeat general." With his luxurious private train, harem, and seemingly endless wealth, he was the perfect caricature warlord. But his catchall army, which included large numbers of Russian and Japanese cavalry, was no joke,

---

5. Guo Jianlin, *Wu Peifu*, vol. 2, p. 594; Wou, *Militarism*, p. 125.

and Zhang himself had a sure instinct for the jugular.[6] That much had been clear when he mounted his bold attack on Lengkou in October, which had marked the beginning of the end for Wu Peifu at Shanhaiguan. Now, hearing of Feng's coup, Zhang moved decisively once again.

October 26 found Wu Peifu in his armored train at Tianjin, where the railroad station served as his temporary headquarters. He ordered his troops to entrench themselves at Yangcun, and with Cao Ying's 26th Division at Langfang, and Cao Shijie's 26th Mixed Brigade at Baoding, to coordinate and attack the Guominjun. Expecting aid from the south to arrive in good time, Wu was still in good spirits.[7]

But Zhang Zongchang was closing in on him. The coup had found his troops on the northwest of the Shanhaiguan front. On hearing the news, however, he and Li Jinglin had rushed southward along the Luan River, toward Zhili's main staging point at Luanzhou, on the railway line. On October 27 Zhang Zongchang attacked and broke the Zhili forces covering the line, the 9th and 20th Divisions, and then united with Hu Jingyi's forces to attack and secure Luanzhou the following day. This devastating stroke divided the Zhili forces in two, isolating Wu Peifu at Tianjin while closing the noose around his main forces at Qinhuangdao and Shanhaiguan. These now faced Fengtian armies both to the north and south. The situation became even worse when Li Jinglin widened the breakthrough across Zhili lines of communication by defeating Dong Zhengguo's remaining forces at Tangshan. Then, on October 30, Guo Songling directly attacked Qinhuangdao.[8]

Under these blows, and with their best commander away from the decisive front, the Zhili main forces began to collapse. Zhang Fulai and Jin Yun'e at Qinhuangdao had no alternative but to begin evacuation of their troops there by sea, using naval vessels. Some managed to get back to Tanggu, near Tianjin. But about 20,000 surrendered, with their weapons. Meanwhile Fengtian forces and the Guominjun tightened their encirclement. Zhang Fulai had no option but to order withdrawal on all fronts. This became a rout as Zhang Zuolin and Feng Yuxiang mounted a general attack. At Shanhaiguan and Qinhuangdao Zhili forces lost all ability to resist: about 100,000 surrendered with their weapons, the rest fled.[9]

6. See Anatol Kotenev, *The Chinese Soldier: Basic Principles, Spirit, Science of War, and Heroes of the Chinese Armies* (Shanghai: Kelly & Walsh, 1937), pp. 124–7.
7. Guo Jianlin, *Wu Peifu da Zhuan* (Tianjin: Tianjin daxue chubanshe, 1991), vol. 2, p. 573.
8. Ibid., vol. 2, p. 574; Fu Xingpei, "Di er ci Zhi Feng zhonzheng jishi," *Wenshi ziliao xuanji* (Beijing: Wenshi ziliao chubanshe, 1960), no. 4, 36–7.
9. Guo Jianlin, *Wu Peifu*, vol. 2, p. 573.

Soon the railroad stations at Tianjin were clogged by troop trains attempting to head south. Appalled by the threat of disorder, the Powers refused to allow Wu use of Tianjin proper: five transport ships of wounded and fleeing Zhili troops arrived there, but they were denied permission to land within the twenty-*li* limit established by treaty, and forced to turn back down the Hai River to the sea. On November 1, Wu's western front gave way as well: the thinly held line at Yangcun was broken, and Wu, in his armored headquarters train, returned to the bridgehead just west of the Central Station in Tianjin.

Wu's position was no longer tenable. He was cut off from his main forces near Shanhaiguan, and the authorities to the south were blocking the arrival of reinforcements. Meanwhile Zhang Zuolin was moving in from the northeast, and Feng Yuxiang's forces were only eight miles to the west and advancing. At 3:15 A.M. on November 3, Wu bowed to the inevitable, and with his staff and about 600 loyal troops from the 3rd Division, he left Tianjin for the port at Tanggu. There they boarded one of his transport ships, the *Hongli*, and headed south.[10]

This remarkable denouement was possible only because of Japanese assistance to forces opposing Zhili. Wu Peifu had foreseen the risk of a flank attack along the railway, and to defend against it, he planned to embark troops at Qinhuangdao to reinforce Tianjin and the rail line. But the Japanese had intervened to stop any such move. In clear violation of international law, the commander of the Japanese garrison at Tianjin, Yoshioka Kensaku, ordered that Wu Peifu not be permitted to use Qinhuangdao.[11] The officers of a British submarine stationed at the port further reported that the Japanese added another 500 men to their garrison just in case.[12] Without this Japanese interference, Wu could probably have salvaged at least a stalemate in the north, even after Feng Yuxiang's coup.

As the *Hongli* slipped out of Tanggu harbor, Marshal Wu ordered his men to fire in the air, to show that their spirit was not defeated. Although for the moment he had left the picture in the north, Wu still hoped to rally the Yangzi valley to his cause. In fact, however, the game was up.[13] From *kanglong*, proud dragon, Wu quickly became a figure of

---

10. Pan Chenglu, "Wu Peifu baitui Tianjin suoji," in *Wenshi ziliao xuanji*, no. 41, 158–61 (Beijing: Wenshiziliao chubanshe, 1963); Guo Jianlin, *Wu Peifu*, p. 575. The ship was possibly the *Hung Lee*, a 771-ton steamer belonging to the Ching Kee Steam Navigation Co. CYB 1926, 846.
11. Okano Masujirō, *Go Haifu*, p. 291, cited by Lou Xiangzhe, "Lun di er ci Zhi Feng zhanzheng" (Master's thesis, Nonkai University, 1985), p. 26, note 88.
12. "The Military Situation," July 14, 1925, 3, in MIR.
13. See Ding Wenjiang, ed., *Minguo junshi jinji*, 53–62; "Dongbei zhanzheng de shengfu juedingle," DZ 21 (1924), no. 21, 4–5; Li Jun, "Di er ci ZhiFeng zhanzhengzhong

ridicule. In classic Chinese style, wits soon inverted a few well-known lines from the *Three Hundred Poems of the Tang Dynasty* to sum up his humiliation.[14] Wu's failure doomed as well Zhili's possibility of effectively uniting China. How had it happened?

A major military reason, of course, was Feng Yuxiang's coup. Feng was a stormy petrel in Chinese politics.[15] His death, twenty-four years after the coup, in a fire on the Soviet ship *Pobeda* [Victory] just as it was reaching Odessa from New York, was somehow appropriate. Like almost everything else in his life it was mysterious at the time – and remains so to the present. And in death, as in life, Feng found himself yet again short of his goal. Ever since the revolution of 1911 he had repeatedly made dramatic moves in the game of Chinese politics, but not once did he manage to transform one of these bold moves into something more lasting. The pattern was already clear in 1911 when, as a young Beiyang officer theoretically loyal to the Qing, he planned an uprising in support of the southern revolutionaries at Luanzhou in Zhili, for which he was briefly imprisoned. But he was released and six years later found himself once again in a key position. General Zhang Xun (1854–1923) had led his troops – their hair, worn in queues or pigtails, proclaimed their loyalty – into Beijing to restore the Qing. To crush the rebellion, Duan Qirui summoned the 16th Mixed Brigade, a unit Feng had once commanded but from which he had been removed. When it "became clear that only Feng Yuxiang could order the brigade into action,"[16] however, his command was returned to him and the attempted Qing restoration ended. In 1918 Duan, attempting to unify the country, had Feng move south, but this time Feng had proved unreliable, halting his advance in Hubei and calling for a truce. In 1922, now fighting on the Zhili side, Feng's 11th Division had won the decisive victory at Changxindian that routed Fengtian and settled the First Zhili–Fengtian War. And in 1923,

Zhixi shibai de yuanyin" *Jindaishi yanjiu* (1985), no. 2, 158–70; Wang Weicheng, "Zhi xi de fenlie he er ci zhi feng zhan zhi xi de shibai," in *Beiyang junfa shiliao xuanji*, 2 vols. Ed. Du Chunhe, Lin Binsheng, and Qiu Quanzheng (Beijing: Zhongguo shehui kexue chubanshe, 1981) vol. 2, pp. 92–105.

14. They reversed the order of the two sentences in Wang Changling's "Furonglou song Xin Jian." Since it relies on wordplay involving Wu and Luoyang, the effect cannot be captured in English. However, if one similarly inverted the English translation by Soame Jenyns, it would read, "If my friends in Loyang ask after me/Tell them that my heart is still a slice of ice in a jade bottle./The cold rain was all over the river and night had fallen as I entered Wu/ With to-day's dawn I bid farewell to my friends, for I go to where the mountains of Ch'u stand isolated against the sky." Guo Jianlin, vol. 2, p. 575; *Selections from the Three Hundred Poems of the T'ang Dynasty*, trans. Soame Jenyns (London: John Murray, 1940), p. 85.

15. There is an excellent biography in English: James L. Sheridan, *Chinese Warlord: The Career of Feng Yü-hsiang* (Stanford: Stanford University Press, 1966).

16. BDRC 2.38.

after the bribed presidential election, Feng had supervised the dirty business of forcing Li Yuanhong to vacate the presidential palace.[17]

Feng had supported or betrayed (and often both) all of the men now playing key roles in 1924. The Luanzhou uprising was on behalf of Sun Yat-sen; the crushing of Zhang Xun saved, and the halt in Hubei in 1918 helped to undo, Duan Qirui, and in the aftermath of that last exercise of personal initiative, only Cao Kun had saved Feng from dismissal. So in 1922 Feng had helped Zhili win a critical victory, and in 1923 helped Cao to the presidency. Through all this Feng slowly advanced in power and influence. But although many were willing to make use of his changeability and proclivity for intrigue, those same qualities led few to trust him.

By all accounts, Feng was an impressive man but somehow unstable at the core. Tall and fit, he had been born to a soldier father and himself joined the Beiyang army at the age of fourteen. Always devoted to physical training and martial arts, he promoted an incorrupt style of life among his troops, whom he also indoctrinated through long and passionate lectures, group singing, and endless drill: first with the sort of ascetic Confucianism popular among the *rujiang* [Confucian generals] of the nineteenth century and earlier periods, later with the Methodist Christianity that he embraced at the age of thirty-two. Their Christianity led foreigners to nickname Feng's 11th Division as the "Ironsides," after Cromwell's cavalry. Always Feng struggled for self-improvement: teaching himself to read and write, and as an old man long retired, endlessly practicing the calligraphy which – like the art of Chinese politics – he never quite mastered.[18]

In 1920 Feng had begun to work with the Zhili group. Wu Peifu appointed him to a post in Shaanxi, which soon led both to command of the 11th Division and to the military governorship of the province. His role in the First Zhili–Fengtian War further advanced him to the military governorship of Henan. At this point, however, friction began to develop between him and Wu Peifu. After winning the First Zhili–Fengtian War, Wu had ousted the scholarly Xu Shichang from the presidency and restored Li Yuanhong, whose great prestige, as we have seen, originated with his role as the first military officer to support the revolution of 1911. Li had imposed conditions for accepting the presidency, notably the reduction of military forces and the end of the system of military governorships. This in turn accorded with Wu's desire not to see Feng Yuxiang grow any stronger; in October 1922 President Li was pressured

17. Guo Jianlin, *Wu Peifu*, vol. 2, p. 570.
18. BDRC, vol. 2, pp. 37–43.

to "promote" Feng from the Henan military governorship to the essentially empty post of Inspector General of the Army [*lujun jianyueshi*] in Beijing (Wu's trusted associate Zhang Fulai then received the Henan job). Feng was outraged: "By pushing me around this way," he told a friend, "Jade Marshal Wu [*yushuai*, a common and admiring nickname for Wu Peifu] has gotten me so that I don't know what is the right thing to do, but it looks as if he really wants to take away my gun."[19] This action was controversial even within the Zhili group. Feng's new job offered him no source of revenue. To compensate him, and presumably keep him on the Zhili side, Cao Kun insisted that 200,000 yuan per month be paid to Feng from Henan. Although agreed in principle, this subsidy proved highly unreliable and embittered Feng more than Wu realized.[20]

The growing tension was clear enough to the two men at Luoyang in March 1923, when Marshal Wu celebrated his fiftieth birthday, receiving gifts from guests who came from every corner of China. One presentation made a particular impression: Feng Yuxiang in person presented Wu Peifu with a kettle of plain water, saying "*junzi zhi jiao dan ru shui*" – "your excellency, in his social intercourse, is as clear as water" – literary Chinese that most who witnessed the scene took to be an elegant compliment. But Wu understood he was being mocked and was displeased. [*Dan* also means "insipid" or "weak," and is used to characterize business as "dull"; perhaps Feng was thinking of those payments from Henan that came in so rarely].[21] Disagreement increased a few months later when Cao Kun decided to oust Li Yuanhong and take the presidency for himself – which he did, by harassment, threats, and bribes – supported by Feng Yuxiang and opposed by Wu Peifu.[22]

Given such a background, even before the war began members of the Zhili group would quite naturally be making their own contingency plans, in case things developed in unexpected ways. In Beijing even the foreign community knew that there was disaffection within the group, and in particular that Feng and Wu viewed one another with suspicion. Speculation was rife about how this might affect the war, and Wu Peifu was certainly aware of the problem. Feng meanwhile made plans for himself if the war should go wrong.

In this planning Feng is often depicted as something of an idealist. His Christianity greatly recommended him to the missionary community, and his well-educated second wife, Li Dequan (1896–1972), seems to

19. Guo Jianlin, *Wu Peifu*, vol. 2, p. 569.
20. Ibid., vol. 2, pp. 569–70.
21. Ibid., vol. 2, p. 570.
22. Ibid., vol. 2, pp. 569–70; BDRC, vol. 2, pp. 343–6.

have added to sincere Christianity a set of progressive political inclinations that led both the Chinese and the Russian Communists to take considerable interest in her husband. Li long outlived her husband, serving the People's Republic of China in a number of high, if largely honorific, governmental positions. This fact may go some way toward explaining why today Feng is often portrayed in the People's Republic as the one sincere if slightly naive patriot in the whirlpool of Chinese politics of the 1920s: that, for example, is how he is painted in the 1988 Chinese motion picture *Zhi-Feng Da Zhan* [Clash of the Warlords]. Its Feng is an idealist, disgusted by the machinations of the "warlords," Wu Peifu in particular, and eager above all to be able to bring Sun Yat-sen to Beijing and thus at last resolve China's political problems.[23]

That account has the virtue of clarity. The truth, by contrast, is almost infinitely murky. No one in fact knows just why Feng did what he did. But it should be noted that, Christian or not, the general who supported Cao Kun against Li Yuanhong can claim no particular purity. Likewise, although Feng and Wu may have been rivals, both were patriots, and one can argue that it was particularly odd that someone as anti-Japanese as Feng should have aligned himself with Zhang Zuolin against Wu Peifu. The fact that Sun Yat-sen may have indirectly propositioned Feng is furthermore no proof of patriotism: Sun propositioned everybody. In fact Sun and Feng were rather similar in that respect. Both had a core of conviction and idealism. Yet circumstance and personal ambition repeatedly forced each into ambiguous situations. And in the end, neither succeeded. To understand Feng in 1924 one must keep all these facts in mind, for the accounts of just how Feng came to his decision vary.

Broadly speaking, Feng's coup and the collapse of the North to which it contributed were the result of an improbable but effective alliance among the three groups most threatened by the steady rise of the Zhili faction. These were the old Anfu politicians, whom Fengtian and Zhili had combined to oust in 1920; the Fengtian group, which Zhili had defeated in 1922, and Sun Yat-sen and his Kuomintang in Guangzhou. We have already seen that this implausible compact is usually called the Triangular Alliance [*sanjiao lianmeng*].

The alliance had its origins in the second half of 1919. At that time the Anfu faction led by Duan Qirui was still in power at Beijing, but was already feeling threatened by the growing power of Wu Peifu, both militarily and as an opponent of their pro-Japanese foreign policy. In order to pressure the Anfu faction, Wu Peifu began to make contact with

23. Changchun: Changchun film studio, 1988. 205 minutes.

militarists of the Guangxi group. At the time attacks by these militarists had just forced Sun Yat-sen to abandon his base in Guangzhou for the security of the French Concession in Shanghai.[24] So on the principle that my enemy's enemy is my friend, the leader of the Anfu faction, Duan Qirui, got in touch with Dr. Sun.[25] Duan had his subordinates Wang Yitang (1877–1946), Xu Shuzheng, and Zeng Yujun (1865–1963) visit Sun in Shanghai. Dr. Sun presented them with a copy of one of his books, which was passed on to Duan himself. Duan voiced approval of what he read, or at least claimed to have read, and in return Sun asserted that if Duan would completely accept his ideas, he would consider him a comrade.[26] On November 26, 1919, Sun sent a telegram to Xu Shuzheng, Duan's most important military adviser.[27] Silent cooperation between the two sides gradually developed.[28] This was strengthened in 1920, as Lu Yongxiang, a Duan ally, quietly assisted Chen Jiongming and others in recapturing Guangzhou from the Guangxi generals.[29]

At about the same time, Dr. Sun began making initiatives toward Zhang Zuolin. He sent Ning Wu (1884–1975), who was a native of Manchuria, to see Zhang Zuolin, and in February of 1921, at Ning's urging, Zhang Zuolin sent Brigadier Li Shaobai to meet Sun Yat-sen in Guilin, where the Kuomintang leader was conducting military operations. Sun responded warmly to this initiative, and offered to follow up by sending his deputy foreign minister, Wu Chaoshu [C. C. Wu] (1887–1934), but Zhang Zuolin was less enthusiastic. Zhang was being courted by the Zhili group, which hoped that he would join with them against Anfu. Zhang did, and once Anfu had been overthrown with his help, the Manchurian leader began to have some influence in Beijing, which he welcomed, and consequently he paid less attention to Sun. But as the Zhili group moved to squeeze Fengtian out of any real share of power, Zhang's mind once again turned to Guangdong.[30]

The war of 1920 in which Fengtian had opposed Anfu had naturally sowed discord between the two factions, but they also had a record of cooperation. In 1918 Xu Shuzheng had helped Fengtian to obtain

24. Wilbur, *Sun Yat-sen*, p. 28.
25. See Lou Xiangzhe, "Yue Feng Wan 'sanjiao tongmeng' qianxi," *Tianjin shida xuebao* (1984), no. 2, 39–44.
26. Lou Xiangzhe, "Zhi Feng," p. 17, note 34, citing Luo Jialun, *Guofu pidu moji* (Taibei, 1955), p. 470.
27. Lou, "Zhi Feng," p. 17, note 35, citing *Guofu quanji* (Taibei, 1973) vol. 3, p. 655.
28. Ning Wu, "Sun Zhang lianhe fan Zhi jiyao," in *Wenshi ziliao xuanji*, vol. 41, pp. 115–21.
29. Lou, "Zhi Feng," p. 17; Wilbur, *Sun Yat-sen*, p. 30.
30. Lou, p. 17; Wilbur, 31.

weapons, and after the war both felt that Zhili was becoming too powerful. So in 1922 they began to move to patch things up. Representatives of Duan Qirui and Zhang Zuolin carried out informal consultations about how to oppose Zhili. One was in February at Guangzhou, another in Hong Kong. Each had something to offer the other: Fengtian liked the fact that Duan had influence in the North, and Lu Yongxiang had military forces at Shanghai, while Anfu understood that only Fengtian had the military wherewithal to oppose Zhili.[31]

Using these threads of common interest, Duan Qirui began to organize the Triangular Alliance from his retirement in Tianjin. His goal was to overthrow Zhili. To further it, he sent Xu Shuzheng and Duan Zhigui (1869–1925) to see Zhang Zuolin.[32] In March 1922, Sun Yat-sen sent Wu Chaoshu to Mukden.[33] In Guangdong Li Zonghuang (1887–1978), who had started with the Yunnan army but thrown his lot in with Sun Yat-sen, presented this fact to the Japanese as amounting to effective recognition of Sun by Fengtian, and suggested that the two sides would cooperate to bring about the union of North and South China. Dr. Sun's forces were planning an immediate move to the north from Hunan to take Wuhan.[34] These meetings between Wu Chaoshu and Zhang Zuolin marked the beginning of substantive cooperation between the two sides.

During the First Zhili–Fengtian War, fought in late April and early May of 1922, and after Fengtian's humiliating defeat, Zhang Zuolin expanded this cooperation. On May 1 Zhang had called for unity among all the forces of the southwest and the Yangzi valley opposed to Beijing. When Sun Yat-sen proved unable to help Zhang, he apologized. But it was when Chen Jiongming drove Sun Yat-sen out of Guangzhou on June 15 and 16 that the alliance was sealed. Deeply humiliated, Sun fled to Hong Kong on a British gunboat, and thence on August 9 to Shanghai aboard *The Empress of Russia*.[35]

Sun could not look to Zhang Zuolin for immediate aid: as the loser in the First Zhili–Fengtian War, Zhang had to turn his attention to rebuilding his own power. Meanwhile, with Zhang humiliated and Sun on the run, and much of Central China now under its control, the Zhili group began to speak of using force to unify the country with more confidence than ever before. This concentrated the minds of all Zhili's opponents.

31. Ibid., p. 17.
32. Ibid., p. 18, note 38, citing Beiyang jingji weishu zongsilingbu dangan 1024.153.
33. Ibid., p. 18, note 39, citing Gaimushō, *Nihon gaikō bunsho* (Tokyo: Ministry of Foreign Affairs), Taishō 11, vol. 2, p. 293.
34. Lou, pp. 18–19, citing *Gaikō bunsho*, Taishō 11, vol. 2, p. 293.
35. Wilbur, pp. 31–32.

After the war Sun sent Wang Jingwei (1883–1944) to Mukden twice, once in September and again in December, to strengthen cooperation. At the same time, however, Sun was also negotiating with Wu Peifu, the victor, to see whether he might return to Beijing as president. In 1923 emissaries and telegrams passed back and forth between Sun at Guangzhou, Zhang at Mukden, Duan at Tianjin, and Lu Yongxiang at Hangzhou. Damage to Zhili authority by the fraudulent presidential election of October 1923 provided a further opportunity and stimulus to cooperation, and shortly thereafter Sun told Zhang Zuolin that once Guangdong had been pacified, it would become the base for a northern expedition.[36]

The political goals of the members of the Triangular Alliance were utterly incompatible: Duan was the favorite of the Japanese, Sun was increasingly allied with the USSR, and Zhang Zuolin was firmly anti-Communist. As a result it was not easy for them to come up with concrete plans for cooperation. Close consultation with Fengtian, carried on by Wu Chaoshu, Wang Jingwei, and Ye Gongchuo (1881–1968) for Sun Yat-sen, and Wu Guangxin, Lu Xiaojia, and Deng Hanxiang (1888–1979) for Duan Qirui, however, yielded some plans.[37]

The first clear cooperation came in the Jiangsu–Zhejiang War, in which the alliance supported Lu Yongxiang. Sun Yat-sen repeatedly sent envoys to Lu Yongxiang.[38] On September 4 Lu sent a telegram asking Sun to mobilize troops against Cao and Wu, and on the following day Sun responded, agreeing. At the same time Zhang Zuolin also promised support.[39] On September 18 Sun Yat-sen proclaimed his Northern Expedition, announcing his intention to join with Fengtian in putting down the bandits [*zei*] Wu and Cao.[40] On September 20 the expedition was launched. Two armies advanced into Hunan and Jiangxi, which created headaches for Wu's important ally in the mid-Yangzi area, Xiao Yaonan, and made it difficult for him to provide much aid for the fighting in the north. Subsequently, Sun was kept informed by Lu Yongxiang and Zhang Zuolin of progress on the Chaoyang front, and he expressed his desire that all should advance together.[41] So although Lu Yongxiang lost the Jiangsu–Zhejiang War, cooperation among the three allies meant that Zhili also incurred irremediable losses – in finance, in men, and in equipment.

36. Lou, p. 19, note 43; for negotiations with Wu, see Wilbur, p. 32.
37. Lou, pp. 19–20.
38. Ibid., p. 20, note 44, citing *Jiang Zuobin huiyilu* (Taibei: *Jindai Zhongguo*, no. 35).
39. Ibid., p. 20, note 45, citing *Minguo ribao*, September 3.
40. Sun Zhongshan, "Beifa xuanyan" in *Sun Zhongshan xuanji* xia, 874. See Wilbur, 255–8.
41. *Lu Hai jun Dayuanshuai Dabenying gongbao*, order no. 28, 1924. In *Zhonghua Minguo shiliao congpian*, series 3, no. 1, p. 12.

While the Triangular Alliance coordinated actions against Beijing externally, it also worked to divide the Zhili group from within, and here its greatest accomplishment was persuading Feng Yuxiang to turn against Wu Peifu. The idea that Feng admired and respected Sun Yat-sen should not be discarded out of hand. Feng's personal contacts with Sun Yat-sen dated at least to the autumn of 1920. In 1921 Sun had sent Xu Qian (1871–1940) and Niu Yongjian (1870–1965) to Hankou with a personal letter for Feng, after which Xu Qian became the regular intermediary between Feng and Sun.⁴² The letter stated that the Beijing parliament was entirely illegal, and that Sun hoped Feng would be willing to use revolutionary means [*geming shouduan*] to save the country [*jiu guo*] and join hands with the Kuomintang.⁴³ In the autumn of 1923 Sun also dispatched Kong Xiangxi [H. H. Kung] (1881–1967) with a copy of *Jianguo dagang* [Fundamentals of National Reconstruction] written in his own hand, asking Feng to read it. Feng was apparently impressed.⁴⁴ Before the outbreak of the Second Zhili–Fengtian War, Sun also told Feng that he had already agreed to join with Zhang Zuolin and Lu Yongxiang in opposition to Cao Kun and Wu Peifu. Sun made clear that Feng would be more than welcome in this alliance.⁴⁵

Feng would be joined in his coup by Generals Hu Jingyi and Sun Yue (1878–1928). At this early stage, Sun Yat-sen was also in touch with each of them independently. He sent Yu Youren (1879–1964), Jiao Yitang (1880–1950), Liu Yuncheng, and others to talk to Hu Jingyi. And he dispatched Zhang Ji (1882–1947), Li Shiceng, and Wang Fa to establish relations with Sun Yue.⁴⁶

Cooperation among Feng Yuxiang, Hu Jingyi, and Sun Yue is sometimes dated to September 10, before war in the North had even broken out. On that day Sun Yue visited Feng Yuxiang at Nanyuan, evidently for a service commemorating those of Feng's soldiers who had fallen thirteen years earlier at Luanzhou. James Sheridan recounts how Feng took Sun to an isolated arbor for private discussion.

After some preliminary conversation in which they both agreed that they were little more than "running dogs of the warlords," Feng allegedly remarked to Sun, "Today Wu and Cao are dictating to the government, the nation is in chaos, and the people are troubled. For a long time I have been determined to act on behalf

42. Li Taifen, *Guominjunshi gao*, p. 99; BDRC, vol. 2, p. 119.
43. Lou, p. 21, note 49, citing Yang Xuefeng, "Guo Fu gei Xu Qian ji feng wei jian fa biao de han dian," *Zhuanji wenxue*, 41.5 (1982), 10–13.
44. Zou Lu, *Zhongguo guomindang shigao* (Shanghai: Commercial Press, 1947), p. 1160.
45. Chen Shaoxian, "Xinhai geming hou de Sun Zhongshan zai Guangdong de jiqi jiluo," in *Wenshi ziliao xuanji*, no. 24, 1–16.
46. Lu Zhonglin, "Sun Zhongshan beishang yu Feng Yuxiang," in *Wenshi ziliao xuanji*, no. 89, 150–78.

of the nation to eliminate these evils, but I have not yet dared to move because I am alone." Sun Yue replied that he not only would be willing to cooperate with Feng, but would approach Hu Jingyi, who was also dissatisfied with the present state of affairs, and get his assistance. About a week later a representative came to Feng from Hu Jingyi to discuss plans for revolt.[47]

The exact nature of these plans, however, is not clear. In his autobiography, Feng maintains that his guiding purpose from the start was to help Sun Yat-sen, "China's only revolutionary," whom he planned to invite "to administer everything" once he was master of the situation. Although Feng's behavior after the coup provides no evidence to confirm this account – neither before nor after did Feng speak of Sun Yat-sen – neither does it disprove it. Feng certainly had plenty of communication with the Kuomintang; furthermore, the short-lived cabinet named by Feng had strong Kuomintang sympathies, and Sun Yat-sen did come north after Wu's defeat. Nevertheless, scholars have viewed Feng's account with justified skepticism, as written long after the events, at a time when Sun had become the symbol of revolution, in order to bolster Feng's reputation.[48]

More credence has been attached to the idea that Feng was bribed to turn against Wu. Some reject this idea out of hand. Li Sihao (1882–1968), who served as minister of finance in the Duan Qirui government, argues strongly that Feng never received money. He asserts first that if Feng had, he, Li, would have heard of it. Second, Li maintains that neither Duan nor Zhang was likely to have done such a thing: Duan was not the sort of person who paid bribes, and Zhang, according to Li, was so fond of money that he would not lightly have disbursed several millions. Third, Li notes, as soon as Zhang entered Beijing, he quarreled with Feng, which would have been unlikely if he had just bought him. To this may be added one more fact: Feng himself, although devious, was arguably not up for sale, and it would seem genuinely out of character for him to accept a straightforward bribe.[49] At least one author, however, believes that Li is simply not telling the truth.[50]

The evidence that Feng received money in connection with the Beijing coup is overwhelming and confirmed by a variety of independent sources.

47. Sheridan, *Chinese Warlord*, p. 133.
48. Ibid., pp. 137–8. Sheridan cites *Wo de shenghuo*, pp. 492, 493, 502–5; *Guominjun geming shi*, ch. 8, 1–4, which "emphasizes that Feng was caught up in a new wave of revolution and that his connections with the [Guomindang] were very close." B. Lennox Simpson [Putnam Weale], *The Vanished Empire* (London: Macmillan, 1926), p. 207, makes Feng a dangerous radical.
49. Xu Shoucheng, "Li Sihao xiansheng shengqian tan cong zheng shimo," in *Shanghai wenshi ziliao xuanji*, vol. 51, cited by Lou, p. 22, note 53.
50. Lou, p. 22.

Yu Liyan, a follower of Duan, testifies that he met with Zhang Zuolin and repeatedly accepted amounts of money, including from 800,000 to 900,000 in silver dollars [*da yang*] as well as 2 million Japanese yen from the Fengtian Specie Bank [Shōkin Ginkō]. When Yu gave the money to Duan, Duan told him, "This is for Feng Yuxiang to cover three months' military supplies."[51] Zhang Zuolin's subordinate Ma Bingnan describes the same operation.[52] Guo Yingzhou went to Luanping to see Feng, and gave him a check for 1 million yuan.[53] Zhang also delivered 500,000 yuan to Duan through the Huifeng bank, for the purpose of wooing Feng.[54] These actions are further confirmed by Zhang Zuolin's close associate Fu Xingpei and Duan's follower Deng Hanxiang.[55] An investigation carried out after the fact by Zhili also concluded that the reason Feng turned was that he had been bribed with 12 million Fengtian dollars.[56] According to this account, Feng had sent his secret representative to Duan stating that he was willing to lead three armies against Wu, but he would need money.[57]

These accounts are confirmed by Japanese records. On October 12, 1924, Zhang Zuolin received 1 million yen to give Feng, and on October 13 Zhang told the consul general in Mukden, Funatsu Tatsuijirō, that he would deliver 1.5 million yen to procure Feng's cooperation.[58] Kenkichi Yoshizawa also recalls that Zhang Zuolin delivered 1 million yen to Feng, working through Duan Qirui and members of the Anfu clique. When Zhang Zuolin met Feng in Tianjin, Feng told him that the million was for Hu Jingyi and Sun Yue.[59] One of Zhang Zuolin's Japanese advisers also admits to having taken part in this activity.[60]

In the aftermath of the coup Zhang Zuolin himself spoke more or less openly of the bribing of Feng. At a dinner in Tianjin, given by Duan Qirui, at which Feng Yuxiang, Deng Hanxiang, Zeng Yujun, and others were present, an angry Zhang Zuolin stormed out after he indirectly

---

51. Yu Liyan "Zhang Zuolin tongguo Duan Qirui wajie Zhixi de neimu," in *Wenshi ziliao xuanji*, no. 51, 49–52.
52. Ma Bingnan, "Er ci Zhi-Feng zhanqian Zhang Zuolin yu Feng Yuxiang de lalong," in *Wenshi ziliao xuanji*, vol. 4, 54–57.
53. Wang Tan, "Cao Kun luxuan zongtong shimo," in *Wenshi ziliao xuanji*, no. 35, 21–33.
54. Zheng Xi, "Zhixi de fenhua ji shibai," in *Tianjin wenshi ziliao xuanji*, no. 23, cited by Lou, p. 22, note 57.
55. Fu Xingpei, "Zhi Feng"; also Deng Hanxiang, "Wo suo liaojie de Duan Qirui," in *Beiyang junfashi shiliao xuanji*, xia, 287–301.
56. Beiyang Zhengfu lingsui junshi dangan huiji. 1026.106, cited in Lou, p. 22, note 59.
57. Beiyang zhengfu da zongtongfu dangan 1003.98, cited in Lou, p. 22, note 60.
58. Gaimushō, *Nihon gaikō bunsho*, Taishō 13, vol. 2, p. 397, cited by Lou, p. 22, notes 61 and 62.
59. Tōa dōbunkai, *Zoku taishi kaikoroku* (Tokyo, 1941; reprinted Hara Shobō, 1973), vol. 2, p. 976, cited in Lou, p. 23, note 63.
60. *Zoku taishi kaikoroku*, vol. 2, pp. 900–1, cited in Lou, p. 23, note 64.

attacked Feng, saying that "protecting the country is the soldier's job. But in this connection we cannot speak in the same breath of those who have rallied to the virtuous cause, and those whom we have simply bought." Feng appeared distinctly uncomfortable, and afterward Duan assured him of safe passage back to Beijing.[61] Others testify that at the same dinner Zhang asked whether Feng had received the money that was sent, and Feng said that he had.[62] Once talking to Cao Kun's follower Wang Tan (b. 1886), Zhang Zuolin said "as for having Feng Yuxiang fight for us, that was a matter of buying him for 1,200,000 Japanese yen [*xiao yang*], and he cannot be allowed to discuss matters of state [*Guo shi*]."[63] Zhang also stated that Funatsu had given Duan Qirui 500,000 yen to suborn members of the Zhili group.[64] The evidence is overwhelming that lots of money changed hands, but just how the bribing was done remains cloudy.

According to some accounts, the Japanese-educated Huang Fu was the chosen intermediary. In one version the initial contact was probably made "several months before the coup occurred" and thus well before Feng made arrangements with Sun Yue and Hu Jingyi. To convince him to participate, Huang Fu was authorized to offer Feng 1.5 million yen, and perhaps more to be paid after Wu had been defeated.[65] Whatever these earlier arrangements may have been, as soon as the war broke out, a new Japanese effort was undertaken to secure Feng's role in Wu's downfall. On hearing of the war's outbreak, according to Gavan McCormack, Teranishi Hidetake, a reserve army colonel and retainer of Sumitomo Joint Stock Company, immediately cabled Duan Qirui urging him to join in the anti-Zhili war. Teranishi then traveled to Mukden, where he met Zhang Zuolin, and then to Tianjin. At about the same time, one of Zhang's Japanese advisers, Machino Takema, was sent to Tianjin to represent him in negotiations there; another, Matsui Nanao, worked in Mukden. While Teranishi and Machino established communications with Duan, Duan in turn negotiated with Feng, employing as principal go-between Huang Fu. The "clinching argument" in all of this, according to McCormack, was a cash payment.[66] Certainly Feng met repeatedly with Japanese officers, and on the march back from

61. Deng Hanxiang, "Jiangzhe zhanzheng de qianyin houguo," in *Wenshi ziliao xuanji*, no. 35, 34–40; also Zeng Yujuan, "Wo bei Guominjun daibu he tuozou de jingguo," in *Wenshi ziliao xuanji*, no. 51, cited by Lou, p. 23, note 65.
62. Liu Huanwen, "Zhang Zuolin lalong Feng Yuxiang dao Zhi de jingguo," forthcoming, in *Tianjin wenshi ziliao*, cited by Lou, p. 23, note 66.
63. See Wang Tan, "Cao Kun luxuan zongtong shimou."
64. *Nihon gaikō bunsho*, Taishō 13, vol. 2, pp. 361–2, cited in Lou, p. 23, note 68.
65. Sheridan, *Chinese Warlord*, p. 142.
66. McCormack, *Chang Tso-lin*, pp. 131–2.

Gubeikou was accompanied by Matsumoro Takayoshi, a young Japanese officer with whom he was familiar, who had been sent from Beijing by the Japanese legation.[67] Such facts suggest that from an early date, Feng was turning to the Japanese and accommodating himself to what, according to Sheridan, would have been an ideal arrangement for Japan: namely, "an alliance between the pro-Japanese [Anfu] politicians, led by Duan Qirui, and Feng's army."[68]

Two points in this account, however, are troubling. First, it is difficult to explain why Feng agreed to play the Japanese game; second, it is not clear why, if he did, Wu (who was no fool and had plenty of warning) should have let him. Feng Yuxiang had a certain integrity and was not known for his pro-Japanese sympathies. In his meeting with Sun Yue he deplored warlordism and spoke of the need to save the country, one suspects not without sincerity. Why, then, would he subsequently sell himself to the Japanese? As for Wu Peifu, he was well aware of the intrigues surrounding the war and could have forestalled Feng at the outset by adopting a basically defensive strategy of holding the passes, where he had quickly taken command of the high ground. Yet he did not: instead he adopted a high-risk approach which envisioned total defeat of Zhang Zuolin through amphibious operations of a sort never before attempted in Chinese warfare. Furthermore, not only did he adopt such a strategy, but *he assigned a key role in it to Feng*, even giving him the best of the Zhili artillery.

Why? Remember that the war in the North caught Zhili unprepared and forced Wu to make the best of a bad situation. Feng controlled major forces and could not be left out of a war with Fengtian. So perhaps the best guess about Wu's calculation is that he counted on the momentum of victory to keep Feng in line. The road from Beijing to Chengde and beyond is a difficult one. Feng's forces were supposed to leave Beijing through the Dongzhimen gate, then go to Shunyi and Miyun and then via Niulangshan on to Gubeikou, a pass 690 feet above sea level and 70 miles from Beijing, where the Ming had constructed extensive fortifications. The path was not easy: it ordinarily required, according to weather conditions, "about a week when riding good ponies."[69] To take men and artillery along this road would be no mean feat. From Gubeikou, Feng was supposed to advance toward the old Qing summer capital at Rehe and then turn toward Mukden. It is sometimes suggested that Wu Peifu purposely assigned Feng the difficult

---

67. Sheridan, *Chinese Warlord*, pp. 144–5; McCormack, *Chang-Tso-lin*, p. 134.
68. Sheridan, *Chinese Warlord*, p. 141.
69. E. S. Fischer, *Guide to Peking and Its Environs Near and Far*, rev. ed. (Tientsin and Peking: The Tientsin Press, 1924), pp. 148–9.

route of attack because he wanted him to fail, and that he purposely denied him weapons and ammunition to ensure this. Such analysis seems completely misguided. In fact, Wu Peifu assigned this crucial role to Feng because, in the absence of actual money, sweat equity earned by winning the victory was Wu's best way of keeping Feng on the Zhili side.

The approach to the capital through Chengde has repeatedly proved important in battle. For that reason the Ming built some of its strongest fortifications there. In March 1933 Chiang Kai-shek would confess to Hu Shi that the unexpectedly rapid Japanese advance from that direction was one of the factors that had led him to adopt his policy of yielding to Tokyo over the short run.[70] As we have seen, the Chengde front had figured repeatedly in Zhili military calculations in the months before the war. Beginning in 1923 a new thirty-foot-wide military transport road nearly 300 miles long had been constructed from Chengde to Luanzhou on the Beijing–Mukden railway line.[71] The northeastern or Rehe front was decisive in Wu's strategy: for him to have undercut Feng there would have been to undermine his own strategy. So the choice of Feng for this difficult task was, if anything, a tribute to Wu's estimation of Feng's troops (the 11th Division was one of Zhili's two best) and his generalship. Feng's success was essential if Wu's larger strategy of encirclement was to work.

The problem for Wu was – as we have seen in Chapter 6 – that Zhili was nearly bankrupt as the war began. And almost none of what funds they did have were assigned to Feng. At the outbreak of hostilities, payments from the central treasury to support Feng's 11th Division were in arrears of between six and eleven months. Cao Kun repeatedly ordered payments to Feng, but these were delayed and misappropriated by Wang Kemin, the minister of finance, and Cao Kun's favorite Li Yanqing (also called Li Liu), chief of the office of revenues and expenditures. Feng found he actually had to bribe Li to obtain any payment: this frustration embittered him, turning him against even Cao Kun. After the coup Feng would detain Cao, but he would kill Li outright.[72]

Nor were the effects of this financial problem limited to Feng alone. Wang Chengbin had suffered humiliation when forced – in the presence of others – to beg Wu Peifu for money, and Hu Jingyi was also frustrated by the inability of the Zhili government to keep his army supplied. Money was at the root of the whole problem. If Wu Peifu had been able

---

70. Hu Shi diary, in the collection of Columbia University Library, entry for March 13, 1933.
71. Fischer, *Guide*, p. 147.
72. Guo Jianlin, *Wu Peifu*, vol. 2, p. 584.

to pay his subordinates even a bit more, the mutiny would likely never have occurred.[73]

Wu simply lacked the immediate resources to do that, and had therefore to secure loyalty by offering responsibility in, and therefore large shares of the reward for, the victory to come. When associates reminded Wu of Feng's notorious unreliability, he would agree. "I know he is unreliable. But I have awarded him the Lengkou front and the road from Rehe into Fengtian. Given that, I don't think he will mutiny."[74] And indeed it would scarcely make sense for Feng, out of pique (or even in consideration of a bribe) to toss aside what the American military attaché described as the possibility of "a victorious advance into Manchuria."[75] When the war began it looked likely that Feng would be able to sweep with little resistance into the strategically crucial area to the northwest of Mukden and then, commanding the Fengtian flank and rear, join with Wu Peifu in closing the encirclement around Zhang. As joint author of such a decisive victory, Feng would be greatly strengthened and able to insist on real rewards in the settlement that would follow. Conceivably Feng and Wu might themselves have drawn more closely together in the aftermath, and Cao Kun, an unpopular figure with whom Wu had serious disagreements, have found himself odd man out. Despite their disagreements, Feng understood that possibility of a shared victory must ally him to Wu. Any doubts would have been quelled by consideration of what would happen if Wu should win alone. The possibility existed: he might draw the Fengtian main force to Shanhaiguan, pin it there, and then quickly land troops behind it. Such a victory would marginalize Feng, most likely for good.

The outcome on the battlefield, then, was what decided Feng. The plot with Sun Yue and Hu Jingyi was for all three men a fall-back position, prudently prepared in advance. If the war went Wu's way, Feng intended to do what was necessary to earn a place at the victors' table. But if it went badly, he was prepared as well. His arrangements with Sun Yue and Hu Jingyi ensured that the three of them would not throw their own forces away in a costly war of attrition with Fengtian. This logic is confirmed by the way events unfolded.

Feng insisted that at least some arrears be made up before he would even leave Beijing. Even after his *chufafei* ["setting out payment"] of 150,000 yuan had been delivered, however, he showed no great enthusiasm for advancing. By the time he reached Gubeikou, toward the

73. Ibid., vol. 2, p. 584.
74. Ibid., vol. 2, p. 592.
75. Report. Situation Survey for the period of October 16th to December 31st 1924, 1–2, in MIR.

end of September, strong Fengtian forces were already astride the route he had hoped to follow to Mukden. Not surprisingly, then, Feng delayed, realizing that the war now would be decided on the Shanhaiguan front. If Wu succeeded there, then Feng should be prepared to push forward as planned. But stalemate or defeat at the main battlefield would present Feng with the moment to strike. From his position at the front Feng Yuxiang secretly negotiated both with other disaffected Zhili commanders and with the Fengtian adversary.

The goal, as Feng Yuxiang enunciated it to the other dissatisfied Zhili commanders – Wang Chengbin, Sun Yue, Hu Jingyi, and Wang Huaiqing – was to unite with the Fengtian, Anfu, and Guangdong forces in order to oust Wu Peifu and Cao Kun, "put Sun Yat-sen in charge of politics and Duan Qirui in charge of the military, while Zhang Zuolin agreed to remain outside the passes [i.e., in Manchuria]." This was an unrealistic assessment of what was possible, but the will to believe was strong, and Zhang Zuolin furthermore spread misinformation about his own real ambitions. To help the plan along, Duan transferred money to Feng at Gubeikou, while Zhang Zuolin's personal envoy, Ma Bingnan, assured Feng Yuxiang and his Zhili associates that the Old Marshal had no territorial ambitions in China proper: "It is only necessary that Cao Kun and Wu Peifu be overthrown and Fengtian's purpose will have been achieved. Zhang Zuolin will never again send his armies inside the passes."[76]

Although Wu Peifu knew something of the brewing conspiracy from his secret police, he was not aware how many of his subordinates shared Feng Yuxiang's grievances and were therefore willing to join him. On October 3, realizing that Feng was making a very halfhearted advance along one of the key routes of the campaign, Wu ordered Wang Chengbin to go to Gubeikou to "supervise" him – unaware that Wang was similarly disaffected and already part of the conspiracy.[77]

As the situation on the Shanhaiguan front deteriorated, Feng began to think that the time had come for the mutiny, and met at Luanping, near Chengde, with representatives from the other conspirators. The capital, after all, had been left all but undefended by Wu Peifu's original dispositions, with only the presidential guard and a few other small units. But unexpectedly, on October 12, Zhang Fulai arrived from Henan with three divisions and a brigade, originally intended for Shanhaiguan, but which Wu now ordered to garrison the city of Beijing, the key railroad junctions at Fengtai and Changxindian, and other important points. Wu

76. Guo Jianlin, *Wu Peifu*, vol. 2, p. 561.
77. Ibid., vol. 2, p. 562.

Peifu had just arrived at the Shanhaiguan front: he was confident that he could save the situation there without any new troops, and by ordering Zhang to garrison the capital, he signaled his suspicions to Feng Yuxiang, who had to abandon his plan.[78]

The situation did not develop as Wu had hoped. Even with him in personal charge at the Shanhaiguan front, the battle went badly. Still trusting Wang Chengbin to watch Feng Yuxiang, Wu decided to call up Zhang Fulai's forces from Beijing. By October 17, the capital was once again undefended. Feng reckoned the moment had finally arrived for the mutiny. He summoned a secret meeting, once again at Luanping, at which the die was cast: Feng Yuxiang, Hu Jingyi, and Sun Yue would launch the coup.

As units commanded by the conspirators moved away from the front toward the capital, some cutting the railway links, others occupying nearby strategic points, still others moving to secure the city of Beijing itself, Fengtian mounted a coordinated attack on Wu Peifu's forces at Anminzhai, on his flank at Shanhaiguan, hoping to cut his rail line of communication with Qinhuangdao. On October 21 the political dimension of the plan began to be manifested. Duan Qirui called a press conference in Tianjin, at which he announced that the battle at Shanhaiguan was in effect already over and that Zhili would be con-clusively defeated in a matter of days. It was time, therefore, for all Chinese to cease fighting and look to the future. Duan called for the summoning of a representative assembly to settle national affairs and suggested that he would be willing to serve should his country need him. Feng Yuxiang arrived at the capital on October 23.[79]

So although much still remains unclear about the coup, it is clear that Feng Yuxiang's decision to move came late in the day and was affected above all by consideration of the developing situation on the battlefields. Had Wu Peifu been doing well at Shanhaiguan, Feng would probably eventually have joined in the fighting, if only in order to share the victory. But the days immediately before the decision to mutiny had seen some severe setbacks on that front. At a minimum, the stalemate at the Great Wall and the Fengtian victories to the northeast eliminated any possibility of an easy triumph for Feng. Those developments, and not some much earlier conspiracy, were almost certainly what made the difference. James Sheridan stresses this contingent and improvised character of the whole undertaking, even suggesting "that Feng's sudden return to the capital was his own idea, and that the original plan called for him to hurry his forces from Rehe to Luanzhou and attack the rear of

---

78. Ibid., vol. 2, p. 564.   79. Ibid., vol. 2, pp. 566–7.

Wu's army in cooperation with Hu Jingyi. This is a persuasive possibility, for neither the Japanese, Zhang Zuolin, nor Duan Qirui were eager to see Beijing occupied by Feng's troops."[80]

Certainly Feng had very little idea of what to do with Beijing once he had taken it. Perhaps by appearing to deliver victory to Zhang Zuolin at a time when it was in fact his already, Feng sought to guarantee a place for himself in the councils of the Old Marshal as well. As for the bribes, they were not critical. Who could assure that Feng would stay bought? The money would be welcome no matter who won, and although Tokyo was its ultimate source, cash in hand did as much to free Feng from dependence on foreigners as to tie him to Japan.

After the fact, however, the Japanese privately took much of the credit for Feng's action. General Ugaki Kazushige (1868–1956), minister of the army, confided to his diary that:

before the balance between the two sides should be completely broken, [we] mobilized politicians, businessmen, political parties, etc., with the idea that we would have to afford considerable support to the present power holder, Zhang, through both visible and invisible channels, in order to make Japan's position in Manchuria much stronger (the feeling at the time when the confrontation of the two armies at Shanhaiguan began); and just on the eve of the decisive battle, the subsequent situation developed as a result of our secretly providing considerable support.[81]

And according to the biography of Field Marshal Uehara Yūsaku, the army chief of staff, it was "in no small measure due to the Field Marshal's stratagems behind the scenes that Zhang Zuolin was barely able to maintain his position, and that Wu Peifu, who boasted of his ever-victorious army, met with overwhelming defeat."[82] Uehara had appointed Hayashi Yasakichi as military attaché in Beijing. Hayashi in turn sent Matsumoro Takayoshi to Feng Yuxiang's camp to plan military operations, and according to the biography of Uehara, Matsumoro played a key role in bringing Feng and Zhang Zuolin together.[83]

Certainly Japanese money played a role in promoting Feng Yuxiang's plot; given the stereotype of the venal warlord, moreover, that money has tended to attract the most scholarly attention. It is probable that far

---

80. Sheridan, *Chinese Warlord*, vol. 2, p. 144.
81. Ugaki Kazushige, *Ugaki nikki* (Tokyo, 1954), p. 42, quoted in McCormack, *Chang Tso-lin*, p. 133.
82. Gensui Uehara Yūsaku denki hensan iinkai, *Gensui Uehara Yūsaku-den*; cited in Ikei Masaru, "Dainiji Hochoku senso to Nihon." In *Tai-Manmo seisakushi no ichimen: Nichi-Ro sengo yori Taishoki ni itaru*, pp. 193–225. Ed. Ken Kurihara (Tokyo: Hora Shobo, 1966), p. 228; cited in McCormack, *Chang Tso-lin*, p. 133, note 86.
83. Sheridan, *Chinese Warlords*, p. 144; Uehara biography, cited in Ikei, "Dai Niji," p. 220; both cited by McCormack, *Chang Tso-lin*, p. 134, notes 87 and 88.

more important than the money was the covert role that Japan played militarily in the conflict, a role that helped to create a military situation in which it made sense for Feng to turn his back on his Zhili allies. We have already seen how extensive were Japanese military supplies to Mukden. Zhang Zuolin summed up this relationship with Tokyo by saying, "If we are fighting Wu Peifu, then when we want an airplane, we get an airplane; when we want an artillery piece, we get an artillery piece; whatever we ask for, we get."[84]

Such an attitude was clear in the autumn of 1924. In September the Japanese military, citing the special conditions then existing, discarded its previous policy of supporting Zhang Zuolin only through ostensibly civilian means, and openly moved large amounts of equipment belonging to the Sanxingtun 6th Brigade, including rifles, machine guns, mortars, and horses, from Changchun to Fengtian to strengthen the Fengtian 6th Division.[85]

At the same time the Japanese consul general urged the foreign ministry unconditionally to supply weapons to Fengtian.[86] Japanese supplies played a decisive role for Fengtian. At one key moment they rushed 40 million rounds of rifle ammunition and 100,000 artillery shells to Zhang Zuolin's forces. Zhang Xueliang remarked, "If we had not received this ammunition, we would have had no choice but to go to Mongolia and become bandits."[87]

Japan also provided intelligence and advice to Zhang. Gavan McCormack lists fourteen Japanese officers ranking from major to major general who worked closely with Zhang Zuolin, and the actual number may have been as high as fifty – or more.[88] Chinese accounts state that perhaps as many as one-quarter of all lower-level Fengtian officers had Japanese advisers.[89] Other Japanese provided intelligence. Some sixty Japanese soldiers at Luanxian railway station continuously wired information about the front-line conditions to Fengtian.[90] Japanese signals intentionally interfered with Wu's radio communications.[91] When Zhili

84. Zhou Dai, "Di er ci Zhi Feng zhan shi Yan Xishan yu Zhi Wan Feng de guoxi doujiao," in *Wenshi ziliao xuanji*, no. 41, 129.
85. *Nihon gaikō bunsho*, Taishō 13, vol. 2, 344–5, cited in Lou, "Zhi Feng zhonzheng", p. 25, note 76.
86. *Nihon gaikō bunsho*, Taishō 13, vol. 2, 350–1, cited in Lou, p. 25, note 77.
87. Wei Yisan, "Di er ci Zhi-Feng zhanzheng Zhang Zuolin gojie riben de liang jian shi," in *Jindaishi ziliao* 2 (1978), 178–9.
88. McCormack, *Chang Tso-lin*, pp. 120–1.
89. Gu Tiaosun. *Jiazi neiluan shimou jishi*. Shanghai: Zhonghua shuju, 1924. In JDBH, vol. 5, pp. 191–361, at p. 196.
90. Beiyang zhengfu da zongtongfu dangan, Wang Zhaolong zhi Zhang Kunshan jiangjun baogao, 1025.323; cited by Lou, 25 note 83.
91. See Impey, *The Chinese Army*, caption of illustration facing page 28.

assembled its fleet at Yantai with the intention of landing at Yingkòu or Huludao, the Fengtian forces learned of the plan from the Japanese.[92] Most devastating of all, Wu's trusted Japanese adviser Okano Matsujirō was in fact a spy, specially assigned by Uehara, who informed the Japanese legation in Beijing of Wu's every move.[93]

The Japanese further damaged Wu by broadcasting false information, which helped convince Zhili militarists in the Yangzi area not to come to Wu's aid. According to Impey, it was a false report that Wu had been defeated at Qinhuangdao that persuaded Feng Yuxiang to move.[94] Japanese agents interfered with great effect in Wu's financial operations.[95] Colonel Matsui Nanao coordinated direct Japanese involvement on Zhang's side. He assigned Japanese officers to various sectors of the Fengtian army while himself working in Zhang's staff headquarters, bringing pilots from Japan and helping to prepare the Fengtian air force.[96] Some of these Japanese officers were very good: Wu Junsheng (1863–1928), who commanded the Fengtian Fifth Army, was "simply astounded" by the battlefield ability of Colonel Korenaga Shigeo.[97] When necessary, the Japanese intervened directly in the fighting. Japanese units were sent from northern Manchuria south to the Great Wall line as the fighting broke out. The Japanese navy fired on Wu Peifu's squadron as it sailed from Qinhuangdao to reconnoiter the Manchurian coast.[98] In all, Japanese aid made a critical difference: Wu Junsheng later remarked to Funatsu, "In this war it was entirely with the help of the Japanese government and people that the present result has come about."[99]

Given all of this, questions arise about Japan's official diplomacy.[100] How much did Shidehara know, and when did he know it? We have already argued that Shidehara was a convinced opponent of intervention, willing even to resign rather than agree to direct Japanese military action in Manchuria. Yet for all this, Shidehara seems to have been

---

92. Ding Wenjiang, *Minguo junshi jishi*, shang, 60.
93. *Nihon gaikō bunsho*, Taishō 13, vol. 2, pp. 371–2; Tianjinshi zhengxie bianyizu, ed. *Tu Fei Yuan [Doihara] milu*, p. 7; cited by Lou, p. 28, notes 104 and 105.
94. Sheridan, *Chinese Warlord*, pp. 143–4; cited in McCormack, *Chang Tso-lin*, p. 132, note 89; Impey, "Chinese Progress," p. 104.
95. Tu Fei Yuan milu [Doihara diary], p. 8; cited in Lou, p. 26, note 90.
96. McCormack, *Chang Tso-lin*, p. 134.
97. Conversation of Funatsu and Wu on December 9, reported in Funatsu's dispatch of December 10, 1924; Japanese Foreign Ministry Archives 1614 6, 9562, cited by McCormack, *Chang Tso-lin*, p. 143, note 92.
98. Hu Wenrong, "Cong hufa jiandui dao Bohai jiandui de jingguo," in *Shandong wenshi ziliao*, vol. 1.
99. McCormack, *Chang Tso-lin*, p. 143, note 92.
100. These are well discussed by McCormack, *Chang Tso-lin*, pp. 139–43.

aware of the secret machinations being undertaken by Japan, in complete violation of international agreements, to bring down Wu Peifu. On October 12 Funatsu sent a telegram to Shidehara reporting that Zhang and Feng might be brought together; much the same message was conveyed to him on October 15 by Yoshizawa.[101] On October 16 Yoshioka Kensaku, the Japanese commander in Tianjin, wired Shidehara that Zhang Zuolin had passed a substantial bribe through Duan Qirui to persuade Feng Yuxiang to lay down his arms.[102] On October 20 Yoshizawa sent a telegram to Shidehara informing him in detail of the plans: Feng Yuxiang's forces were to begin to return to Beijing on October 18, while Hu Jingyi would go to Fengrun and Kaiping from Zunhua and Sun Yue would keep order in the capital.[103] Clearly Shidehara knew what the other Japanese were up to.

While thus exposing Shidehara's diplomacy as disingenuous, the fact that he knew so much about these secret operations also makes his diplomacy somewhat easier to understand. Once the Japanese were confident that they had managed to avert the real threat of Zhili conquest of Manchuria, the danger of a split with the other Powers receded, and diplomatic dealings became more relaxed. The other signatories to the Washington treaties would have been outraged by direct Japanese military intervention of the sort that the Japanese had been contemplating and might have taken if Wu Peifu had been successful. Furthermore, the possibility remained that at some future time conflict over Manchuria might divide Tokyo from its erstwhile diplomatic colleagues – and indeed that time came soon enough, just seven years after the threatened crisis of 1924. But for the moment the danger had been averted, appearances had been preserved, and it was possible to return to business as usual.

By indirectly helping to divide the Zhili forces, providing military assistance to Zhang Zuolin, and directly intervening against Wu Peifu at sea and at Qingdao to prevent him from stopping Zhang Zongchang's drive against the railway after the coup, Japan almost certainly tipped the military balance, which had originally inclined toward Zhili, in favor of Fengtian. Tokyo did not bother to conceal its satisfaction at Wu's collapse and what it hoped would be Duan Qirui's reemergence as China's chief executive. The Japanese success was not the result of a single bold stroke – Feng Yuxiang's coup – but, rather, of a whole

---

101. *Nihon gaikō bunsho*, Taishō 13, vol. 2, pp. 402–3, cited in Lou, p. 28, note 98.
102. *Nihon gaikō bunsho*, p. 406, cited in Lou, p. 28, note 99.
103. *Nihon gaikō bunsho*, p. 407, cited in Lou, p. 28, note 100.

pattern of intervention. Furthermore, Feng moved only after Fengtian had scored the impressive victories that closed off his road to Manchuria.

That the coup was in effect forced on Feng Yuxiang rather than chosen is confirmed by its results, which, as he could have anticipated, served Feng badly. If Feng found Wu difficult to work with and lacking in Feng's kind of revolutionary zeal, he must surely have realized that the old bandit Zhang Zuolin would be a hundred times worse. For Feng Yuxiang, being master of Beijing for a few weeks was preferable to suffering the total defeat Wu Peifu did. But the end result was much the same for him. Zhang Zuolin neither wanted nor needed Feng in his new administration. Zhang felt no need either for the radical constituency represented by Feng's short-lived cabinet or for Feng's military assistance, and in short order he swept both away. The cabinet was dissolved, and Feng himself retired to a temple in the Western Hills. Surely he had considered these possibilities before acting. His coup was an act of desperation, designed, as the ancient Chinese strategist Sun Zi put it, to keep his own forces intact at a time when his alliances and hopes of victory were already perishing on the battlefield.

Although Feng's action may have been forced on him, Japan's was the product of deliberation and strategy. Having a strong nationalistic government in Beijing had always been intolerable for Tokyo, and whenever one threatened to appear, the Japanese government did what it could to bring it down. This was what it had done earlier to Yuan Shikai, had just finished doing to Wu Peifu, and would do once again to Chiang Kai-shek. What Tokyo hoped for was a Chinese government at once strong enough to keep order, abide by the treaties, and unify the country, yet weak enough as to have no choice but conform to Japanese wishes. This was an impossible goal, as Japan repeatedly discovered but never seemed to learn. The internal contradictions of the policy became absolutely clear as the war ended. Zhili defeat was followed by a total collapse of order in China, worse than anything since 1912, and the rise of a radical antiforeign political movement, all quite frightening to Japan. Yet the defeat and its consequences had been produced, above all, by Japan's assiduous and coordinated efforts.

General Feng Yuxiang. (From Impey, *The Chinese Army*, frontispiece.)

After the Beijing *coup d'état* Feng Yuxiang's men searched automobiles entering the Legation Quarter and prevented any from passing out and into the northern section of Beijing. (*Illustrated London News*, November 29, 1924, p. 1033; courtesy of *Illustrated London News* Picture Library.)

The Tianjin Conference, November 1924. *Standing*, Wu
Guangxin, minister of War; *seated, left to right*, Feng Yuxiang,
Zhang Zuolin, Duan Qirui, Lu Yongxiang. (From O. D.
Rasmussen, *Tientsin: An Illustrated Outline History*. Tientsin:
Tientsin Press, 1925, facing p. 272.)

Sun Yat-sen, photographed shortly after his arrival in Tianjin, December 1924. (From Rasmussen, *Tientsin*, facing p. 273.)

10
The collapse of the North

On November 5, 1924, the new cabinet sponsored by Feng Yuxiang undertook an action of great symbolic importance. It revised the *youdai Qingshi tiaojian* or "articles of favorable treatment for the Qing house," the solemn abdication agreement concluded twelve years earlier with the Qing dynasty by the new Republican government, thereby removing the right of the former rulers to continue to live in the Forbidden City. The very same day, Feng's commissioner of militia, Lu Zhonglin, and chief of police, Zhang Bi, set out to announce the order. They did not have to go far. The Zhantansi was almost within sight of the Forbidden City. Upon hearing the order, Puyi convened the last imperial audience of the Qing dynasty. After making gifts to the more than 470 eunuchs and 100 palace ladies still working in the Forbidden City, he dismissed them. In the afternoon five cars sent by Lu Zhonglin carried Puyi and his ladies to the former palace of his grandfather, Prince Chun. Although Foreign Minister Wang Zhengting explained that this move was prompted by "public opinion," it was in fact opposed by most politicians, including Duan Qirui. Only Sun Yat-sen spoke out in favor of it.[1]

From a practical point of view, ousting Puyi made little difference. Nevertheless the departure of the last emperor from the Forbidden City was an appropriate symbol for the basic change caused by the wars of 1924: namely, the end of the Northern System. It would be profoundly misleading to speak of the China that existed when the wars began as an "old regime." The monarchy had gone twelve years earlier, and the new rulers were of a different race and had their roots, not in anything old or traditional but, rather, in the late Qing modernization, particularly military modernization. They were largely new men, the products of military academies established after the turn of the century and of the

1. Tao Juyin, *Beiyang junfa tongzhi shiqi shihua*, rev. ed., 3 vols. (Beijing: Sanlian, 1983), vol. 3, p. 1358. Tao was a journalist who lived through the events, of which his account is the most detailed and complete, if not always the most reliable.

new opportunities for advancement provided by China's expanding and modernizing armed forces. Few of them had family landholdings; such wealth as they had (and not all did), even if sometimes obtained politically, was drawn ultimately from the modern commercial life of the treaty ports, the factories, and the railroads. Their education was as likely to be nonexistent or narrowly professional as it was to be classical and Confucian.

Nevertheless, in their political position within China and the predicament in which they found themselves facing the foreign powers, as well as in less tangible ways, these rulers – the men fighting the wars of 1924 – had a profound continuity with the late Qing. Many of them had begun as soldiers of the Qing and joined the Republic only as grown men. They retained a considerable respect for the Qing ruling house. Their lives and their political attitudes bore the stamp of a Northern approach to the administration of China and to its foreign relations that may be traced back to the Yuan (1279–1368). If not an "old regime," theirs was at least a stable-seeming system of rule that drew on a long tradition of culture, politics, and way of life, and one that – suitably modified to meet the needs of the twentieth century – was almost universally considered by Chinese and foreigners alike to represent the future as well. Indeed, the war between Zhang Zuolin and Wu Peifu was understood as a struggle for that future. So certain did that future seem and so worth commanding that both men poured their resources – military, financial, political, and personal – into the battle with an abandon rarely seen before.

But the wars undermined that future. They destroyed the entire way of life described in Chapter 1. They exploded both the political unity and the military capacity of the Beijing government; among the Chinese population they disrupted in particular the lives of urban merchants, students, and workers; they impressed intellectuals firsthand with the perils of militarism, and they deeply shook the confidence of the foreign community. Above all they helped to create the conditions – military, political, and even intellectual – in which the revolutionary movement that began on May 30, 1925, was able, within a few years, to succeed. Indeed, Feng Yuxiang's summary treatment of Puyi was perhaps the first major example in political action (there had been plenty of talk and writing about it) of what would now become a dominant pattern of action in China's twentieth century: namely, the pitiless attack on the past.

The combatants in the wars of 1924, and Wu Peifu in particular, had staked nearly everything on the military outcome. Like not a few such men and regimes both before and after, neither Wu nor his adversary

Zhang Zuolin enjoyed victory. Rather, they destroyed themselves in wars of their own making, pulled down their regime around them, and opened the way for the enemies they feared most.

The chaotic conclusion of the wars set in train a series of events that shifted the whole pattern and direction of political contention in China. They had gravely undermined the structures that had held China together since 1912, and in their aftermath those structures simply collapsed. Even the shadow of effective political power at the center disappeared. Wu was unable to recoup his position, and neither Feng nor Zhang proved able to fill it. Personal relations among the Northerners became so embittered that it was difficult for them to trust one another or work together again. Their military wherewithal was reduced and their prestige diminished. The most important Zhili military units were either disbanded or reorganized. The security of the Chinese middle class and of the foreign presence was thrown into question. The country, which had seemed to be knitting together, began to divide into contending regions. A power vacuum was created. China gradually slid into what its own historians call the period of *hunzhan* – confused or chaotic fighting.[2]

Wu had come very close to bringing off a dramatic triumph for the North. Using a combination of military force and personal diplomacy, he had built a power base slowly, gradually bringing more and more provinces under his influence, at the same time strengthening the connections among them, and their relationship to the central government. In a series of small but skillfully fought wars he had greatly simplified the military map until but one serious rival, Zhang Zuolin, remained. As we have seen, Wu would not have chosen to fight Zhang in 1924. But when war was initiated despite his counsels, he had no choice but to treat it as the final contest for which he had been preparing and to stake everything on the elimination of that rival. Wu's hope was that victory would compensate for all the hardships. The damage that military mobilization would inflict on the economy, the exhaustion of government resources and credit; the grumbling of his allies and subordinates; and the personal unpopularity war would naturally cause – all would be more than recompensed by military and political triumph. What was more, victory might come sooner than expected: as the Chinese at last saw a winner emerging from the prolonged struggle, they would begin to submerge their differences and join him, while foreigners, seeing an

---

2. See, e.g., Zhang Tongxin, *Guomindang xin junfa junzhan shilue* (Ha-er-bin: Heilongjiang renmin chubanshe, 1982). The aftermath of the war receives little scholarly attention. Much information may be found in Ding Wenjiang, *Minguo junshi jinji*, 63–160.

effective government at last taking shape, would respond with support and conciliation.

Such a strategy was based on a clear understanding of the interaction of war and politics in China. The country had always been too big to unite by force, but over and over again in the past a dramatic victory by one military contender had led others to join him. Such a military victory, furthermore, had repeatedly opened the way for the reconstruction of civil government. Of all the Chinese generals of the time, Wu seemed most likely to achieve such a feat. He was the one who moved most boldly, willingly fighting on more than one front, always searching for the means to outflank or encircle. His conviction was that such military boldness would breed success, and in doing so, cement the loyalty of doubtful colleagues like Feng Yuxiang while winning new recruits to his side. Wu was looking, in other words, for the "bandwagoning" that we have discussed in Chapter 2. As mentioned, however, a single setback could upset the bandwagon and turn participants to self-preservation, or "balancing." This was what happened now, at a time of unprecedented institutional weakness.

The institution most dramatically weakened by the war was the army. The ground on which the Beijing government had stood for a dozen years was the relatively stable existence of its military. The national army had been the basis of political authority and the ultimate guarantor of domestic order since the late Qing. While never entirely unified or unquestioningly obedient, it nevertheless had maintained a certain cohesion. When that military disappeared or fell into chaos, the government was not slow to follow.

Before the wars of 1924, China's army consisted of thirty-five national divisions and twenty-eight national mixed brigades. Of these, twenty-two divisions and a comparable number of mixed brigades were controlled by Zhili. As a result of the war, eleven of these divisions and seven mixed brigades were abolished or disbanded. After 1924 the 3rd, 6th, 9th, 13th, 14th, 15th, 19th, 20th, 23rd, 24th, and 26th Divisions and the 1st, 4th, 6th, 12th, 14th, 16th, and 26th National Mixed Brigades ceased to exist.[3] This disbandment spelled the effective end of Zhili military power. Only nine Zhili divisions continued to exist after the war: these were the 1st (Cai Chengxun), the 2nd (Sun Chuanfang), the 5th (Sun Zhongxian), the 8th (Wang Ruqin), the 11th (Feng Yuxiang), the 12th (Zhou Yinren), the 16th (Wang Tingzhen), the 18th (Lu Jinshan), and the 25th (Xiao Yaonan), plus two Shaanxi divisions not included in the original count. Of these, the strongest, that of Feng

3. CYB 1925, 1160.

Yuxiang, was now in opposition; most of the rest belonged to the Zhili remnant in Central China and the Southeast.[4]

The elimination of Zhili hegemony within the army accelerated the trend toward division. Although Feng Yuxiang's Guominjun picked up some of the disbanded troops, the real immediate beneficiary of Wu's defeat was Zhang Zuolin. At the beginning of the war, Zhang's forces had numbered perhaps 170,000 men. By the early months of 1925, they had increased to perhaps 250,000.[5]

It is difficult to overstate the key importance of this remaking of military organization. As the wars of 1924 began, Wu Peifu's coalition had included a preponderance of the best trained and most experienced units. But most of these military forces were consumed in the course of the wars; what remained disappeared in the disbandments that followed. Units were divided up, officers reshuffled, long-established personal bonds sundered. Those who destroyed what had been the Beiyang military system did so in the hope of reconstructing something like it under their own auspices. But that proved impossible.

At the same time, the victors proved unable to work together, and the uneasy defensive coalition of the losers broke apart. On every level, from the military to the institutional to the political, the Northern System, precarious enough at the outset, began to collapse. And as it did so, not only its present but also its future came into question. We shall soon see how the newly divided military system continued to make war on itself after 1924, creating ever-increasing disorder in both the military and political realms. Chaos loomed both internally and externally.

On October 30, a disheartened Macleay told London that "it must be admitted that the present crisis has left the general outlook more confused and uncertain than any of its frequent predecessors since the revolution of 1911."[6] Events would prove him right.

The defeated Marshal Wu Peifu had departed by sea from Tianjin a few hours before dawn on November 3. Without his authority, the city became uneasy. Thousands of Wu's troops remained crowded into its railway yards and stations, heavily armed even if leaderless and defeated. Foreign troops were on station and alert, but it was the Chinese police who immediately began disarming Wu's men. The job was well along when Feng Yuxiang's first units arrived at 2:00 P.M. on the same day. Feng's troops took over, and the disarming of Wu's forces was completed by the morning of November 4.

4. Odoric Wou, *Militarism*, p. 266, Appendix 1.
5. CYB 1925, 1145.
6. Macleay to MacDonald, October 30, 1924, FO 371, F 4082/19/10 No. 74.

Feng was not long the unchallenged master of Tianjin. First, General Wang Chengbin moved to secure a position for himself. Wang had originally been sent by Wu to Feng's camp to observe him, and his willingness to go along with the plan for the coup had been important to its success. Naturally he expected to share the spoils. He immediately took back command of the former 23rd Division, which had been his before the coup. Then, on November 3, he installed himself in the governmental office in Tianjin as the new governor of Zhili, and, since his own forces were weak by comparison with those of his allies, he began recruiting among Wu's former followers.[7]

Wang was only one general, and he possessed only one division. Rather more ominous for Feng Yuxiang was the arrival at Tianjin East Station, at 6:30 P.M. on November 5, of the first of Zhang Zuolin's forces – according to U.S. military intelligence "all Russians and Japanese in Chinese uniform."[8] They moved first against Wang Chengbin. Li Jinglin sent forces to remove him from the government office, and Wang fled into the Japanese Concession, from which he dared not emerge; his 1,200 newly recruited troops were disarmed. The Fengtian forces then proceeded to divide up the Zhili remnants among themselves. Zhang Zongchang, a Shandong native like their former commander Wu Peifu, was able to appeal to many of Wu's troops, who were from the same province. In the end, Li Jinglin and Zhang Zongchang each got about four mixed brigades of former Zhili forces.[9] None of this augured well for Feng Yuxiang, most of whose soldiers were based at the Central Station, along with Hu Jingyi and his Shaanxi forces. What would happen when Zhang Zuolin's soldiers began arriving there as well? Would the victors cooperate, or would they quarrel over the division of the spoils?

The answer was not slow in appearing. The first Fengtian troop trains pulled into Tianjin Central Station early in the morning of the sixth of November and then moved south during the day toward Machang. By the seventh, Zhang's forces formed the majority in Tianjin, and Feng Yuxiang's units began to withdraw. His 7th and 8th Mixed Brigades began returning to Beijing. Hu Jingyi's forces left the railroad station for the so-called Chinese city, the part of Tianjin not under foreign administration, and then withdrew. On the tenth, the protagonists themselves arrived: Feng Yuxiang from Beijing with his staff and a small bodyguard, and Zhang Zuolin from Mukden amid great hoopla. The Chinese city, where Zhang made his headquarters, was decked out with flags and

7. Tao Juyin, *Beiyang junfa*, vol. 3, p. 1359.
8. "The Military Situation," July 14, 1925, 3–4, in MIR.
9. Tao Juyin, *Beiyang junfa*, vol. 3, p. 1359.

other decorations in his honor. Five Fengtian aircraft flew in to a temporary airfield near the city, and troop trains from Mukden continued to arrive steadily.[10] It looked as if Zhang had his eye on the Chinese capital and maybe territories beyond.

Feng Yuxiang had hoped that, after defeating Wu, Zhang Zuolin would return to Manchuria. He had been promised as much by Zhang's envoy, Ma Bingnan, as the coup was being prepared. But the Old Marshal's ambitions were for more than overlordship in the northeast. His real goal was to extend his influence to the most important parts of China proper, from Tianjin to Beijing and Shanghai. So having arrived in Tianjin, the Fengtian forces did not stop but instead immediately moved west from Tianjin up to Langfang on the Tianjin–Beijing line. Ultimately their goal would be to move as far as Shanghai, where they would reverse the verdict of the Jiangsu–Zhejiang War by helping Lu Yongxiang to oust Qi Xieyuan. But to begin with, Zhang Zuolin decided to put Zhang Zongchang in charge of Shandong while moving the incumbent, Zheng Shiqi, to Anhui. Following this plan, he sent Zhang Zongchang down the Tianjin–Pukou railroad as far as Dezhou, just on the Shandong side of the border with Hebei.

Zheng Shiqi was not pleased. He declared the province neutral, refused to permit the Fengtian forces to enter, and began to rip up the railway line and prepare for resistance. On November 16, therefore, Zhang Zongchang withdrew to Cangzhou, about halfway back to Tianjin. At the same time Zhang Zuolin steadily tightened his grip on Tianjin. On November 14 he abandoned his original airfield, south of the city, and established a new one to the northwest near the old French arsenal, where he placed fifteen aircraft, including thirteen new Spads. These developments worried Feng Yuxiang. To counter the southward Fengtian thrust along the Tianjin–Pukou line, he deployed his own troops between Changxindian and Shijiazhuang, along the Beijing–Hankou line which ran parallel, farther inland.[11]

Militarily, war between Zhang and Feng looked like only a matter of time. All the victors realized that the only way to avoid another ruinous conflict would be to create a civilian administration capable of restoring some equilibrium. And for leader of that administration, their minds converged on the figure of Duan Qirui. Once a top military aide to Yuan Shikai, long-time leader of the Anfu clique, and several times premier in the late 1910s, he had retired from politics after his defeat in the Zhili–Anfu War of 1920 and was living quietly in Tianjin, where he devoted

---

10. "The Military Situation," July 14, 1925, in MIR.
11. Tao Juyin, *Beiyang junfa*, vol. 3, p. 1379.

himself, so he let it be known, to the study of Buddhism. Zhang Zuolin had fixed on Duan much earlier as his nominee for chief executive in Beijing, and on October 26 Feng Yuxiang had offered him the post of marshal (*dayuanshuai*) of the newly formed Guominjun. Four days later, many generals, responding to Feng, called for Duan to be made commander of all the united armed forces. Duan was also backed by the Japanese: on October 29 Lu Yongxiang returned to Mukden from Beppu, a hot springs resort in the southernmost Japanese island of Kyushu. Zhang Zuolin asked him to reassume his post as military commander of the Jiangsu–Shanghai area (*JiangHu lianjun zongsiling*); the following day, Zhang and Lu together issued a wire jointly supporting Duan for the top military post.[12]

Duan, however, understood the situation and played his hand with care. He seemed to be the indispensable man; clearly both Feng and Zhang were eager that he should front for them. His own goal, however, was real power. Since he no longer controlled any military forces, he could obtain that only by maneuvering between his would-be patrons and avoiding capture. His plan as it seems to have taken shape was to secure backing from both Feng Yuxiang and Zhang Zuolin, and then to reach out to moderate Zhili elements as well – a move that would isolate Wu Peifu while, by giving him three rather than two factional bases, provide Duan even greater room for maneuver. He would then attempt to reconstruct China's civil order by convening a grand national assembly which would address the whole range of institutional and policy problems facing the country while at the same time providing a legitimate civilian basis for his own assumption of paramount authority.

This plan would not be easy to realize, for the new situation in Beijing was anomalous and unprecedented. The coup had created a de facto government while leaving the previous constitutional structure intact. For this reason, Feng Yuxiang urged the formation of a political committee (*zhengwu weiyuanhui*) as the highest organ of government, and he also attempted to form a cabinet. But Feng had only a limited ability to attract followers – what political scientists call alignment potential[13] – and his attempts to create an administration for himself were ignored by those he most hoped would join. Duan objected to his proposals, as did Zhang Zuolin, whose ally Wang Yongjiang declined to come to Beijing to take up the office Feng offered him. Duan, likewise, held aloof from Feng's orchestration of a new government, nor was the new cabinet

12. Tao Juyin, *Beiyang junfa*, vol. 3, p. 1357.
13. For more on this phenomenon, and faction formation in general, see Andrew J. Nathan, *Peking politics 1918–1923: Factionalism and the Failure of Constitutionalism* (Berkeley: University of California Press, 1976), pp. 27–58.

recognized by the Powers. On November 14, the acting prime minister, Huang Fu, organized a dinner to introduce the new cabinet, but the *corps diplomatique* collectively declined to attend, and the occasion had to be postponed.[14]

Meanwhile, military tension between Fengtian forces and the Guominjun grew, and with it the need to resolve the impasse over civilian administration. After repeated urging, Duan managed to get both Feng and Zhang to meet at his home in the Japanese Concession in Tianjin, the first time on November 10. In a series of meetings that came to be known as the *Tianjin huiyi* [Tianjin conference], the three leaders attempted to hammer out their differences on both military and civil questions.

On military strategy, their differences were clear. Zhang's approach was like Wu Peifu's, except that the direction in which he wanted to move was reversed. Zhang wanted to continue a rapid advance southward to mop up completely the remnants of the Zhili forces and to resolve the confused situation between Jiangsu and Zhejiang in Shanghai. Duan, however, did not like the idea of more fighting and called instead for an appropriate pause and the use of political means to resolve problems. In front of Duan, his senior and superior, Zhang could not very well insist on his point of view. As for Feng Yuxiang, he was the weakest of the three, unwilling to oppose Duan, and particularly concerned to avoid the head-on confrontation with Fengtian forces that seemed to be brewing in the capital region.

Duan's first major achievement was to defuse the potentially explosive military rivalry between Feng Yuxiang and Zhang Zuolin. He brought about an agreement on four points, which effectively assigned separate spheres of influence to the competing Guominjun and Fengtian forces. The commanders agreed that Fengtian forces would go no farther than Dezhou on the Tianjin–Pukou line; that no force would be used in the southeast; that Wu Peifu would not be arrested; and that an "Aftermath Conference" (*shanhou huiyi*) would be convened to discuss the organization of a government and all related questions.

This approach, however, did not meet with universal approval. Although repeatedly split or dismissed, the parliament elected in 1913 still existed, and some of its members saw the time as ripe for a return to the constitutional ideals proclaimed in the early Republic. Members concerned with the continuity of legal institutions and untainted by bribery in 1923 thought the best idea would be to summon an extraordinary session of the parliament to deal with the new situation.

14. Tao Juyin, *Beiyang junfa*, vol. 3, pp. 1358–9.

They argued that the *Zhonghua minguo xianfa* of October 10, 1923, the constitution that Cao Kun had promulgated, was invalid, and called for adoption of the *Zhonghua minguo linshi yuefa*, or provisional constitution of the Republic of China, of March 11, 1912, as the basis for a transitional government to serve until the parliament could choose a temporary president and begin drafting a constitution. The legal complexities of such a course were formidable. Few parliamentarians were entirely untouched by the corruption of the years immediately preceding, and the irregular ways in which their terms had been extended and their numbers supplemented created many difficulties. Perhaps decisive was the fact that although such a course made much sense in the abstract, none of the powerful constituencies of the time really wanted a return to constitutional rule. The military was opposed to it, and as for the Kuomintang, which in the past had called for just this approach, its policy had changed to a demand for revolution. The parliamentarians thus lacked any power base, and their movement came to nothing.[15] Political uncertainty in Beijing looked set to last a long time. Pressure from the South, however, forced the Northerners to act.

After Wu Peifu left Tianjin, Feng Yuxiang announced a reward of 50,000 yuan for him dead and twice that amount alive. Duan Qirui, the elder statesman trying to broker a nationwide political solution from his residence in Tianjin, sent telegrams to all the coastal provinces warning them not to permit Wu to land. But Wu proved difficult to control. On November 7 he reached Yantai, on the northern coast of Shandong, where the Zhifou Defense Commissioner [*zhenshoushi*] Zhang Huaibin resupplied him with food and fuel. On November 12 he reached Wusong, just north of Shanghai, where he transferred to a ship sent by Xiao Yaonan, and sailed up the Yangzi, arriving in Nanjing on the fifteenth of November.[16] Feng, victorious, could win scarcely anyone to his side; Wu, humiliated, looked as if he might rally Central China to his cause and yet return. His alignment potential was still real.

In Nanjing Wu found the representatives of the Zhili group from South and Central China already assembled. When it became clear shortly after Feng's coup that Wu would not be able to recover immediately, the Zhili forces elsewhere began to consider how to respond. Qi Xieyuan convened representatives of ten provinces (Jiangsu, Anhui, Jiangxi, Zhejiang, Fujian, Shaanxi, Henan, Sichuan, Hunan, and Hubei) to form an alliance with headquarters in Nanjing that would organize and coordinate mutual defense.

15. Ibid., p. 1365.   16. Ibid., p. 1362.

Their position was not an easy one. For the moment, these provinces were threatened militarily from the north.[17] But they were also potentially powers in their own right. They had substantial resources, and although at present defeated and disorganized, they could realistically look forward to recovery and even victory. But war would not be a wise choice for them in the weeks immediately following Wu Peifu's debacle. Far better would be for them to work to divide Zhang Zuolin and Feng Yuxiang. This was exactly what Duan Qirui was hoping to do for his own purposes – to play off Feng against Zhang – and this provided a common interest between the defeated Zhili group in Nanjing and Duan in Tianjin. Duan wanted to bring moderate Zhili forces in to offset his two principal military backers; Zhili was also eager to do just this, for it would help to divide the opposition. An opportunity existed for Qi and his followers to gain a breathing space even while using Duan's prestige to bring their more immediate enemies, Feng Yuxiang and Zhang Zuolin, under control.

So in the first week of November the Zhili forces, both as individuals and in the names of a province or provinces, sent numerous messages to Duan urging him to come out of retirement and assume control of the political situation. They praised Duan and spoke of the possibility of Duan and Wu cooperating. They strengthened Duan's hand further on November 12 when, meeting in Nanjing, they resolved that until a formal government was established, they would ignore orders coming from Beijing.[18]

This strategy was not entirely to Wu Peifu's liking. In a speech to the assembly of the ten provinces in Nanjing, he expressed his approval of the organization they had formed but questioned their tactics. Wu believed that the best strategy for Zhili would be to stress the illegality of the Beijing regime, and make themselves the guardians of constitutionality and legal continuity (*fatong*). To further this aim, he had drawn up during his journey from Tianjin a plan for a "Constitutional Protection Government." Rather than temporize with the new Beijing authority, Wu was ready to pick another fight. He saw that as the only chance. The representatives of the provinces were worried by this. Aware of how divided they were internally and how unprepared militarily, they refused to endorse Wu's proposal until it was agreed that the break with Beijing would be announced only after military and other arrangements had been completed.[19]

17. Lai et al., *Beiyang junfa shigao*, p. 308.
18. Tao Juyin, *Beijang junfa*, vol. 3, 1360–1.
19. Ibid., 1362.

On November 16 Wu sailed from Nanjing. At Jiujiang he met the Jiangxi *duli*, Cai Chengxun. On November 17 he arrived at Hankou where he handed over to Xiao Yaonan for distribution the telegram announcing the "Military Government to Protect the Constitution" [*huxian junzhengfu*], signed by twenty-one prominent figures representing ten provinces. The new government would be headquartered in Wuchang and modeled on the pattern already used in Guangdong and Hunan.[20]

Because this telegram was at odds with the internal policy of the Zhili provinces, which was to support Duan in order to protect themselves, it led to confusion in the Zhili ranks. The upshot was that by November 19 the Zhili representatives were once more stating qualified support for Duan. Wu, however, was trying to reconcile opposites. He maintained that supporting the constitution and keeping peace were not contradictory goals; he even agreed that Duan could be supported, provided that he left Beijing and came to the southern capital.[21]

These actions brought the quarreling factions in Beijing up sharply. They understood that unless they pulled together, a reconstituted Zhili force might well threaten them from the south. Duan in particular realized that his initial strategy of coopting Zhili would never work as long as Wu's position was hostile. So he began to readjust his strategy to one of maneuvering between Zhang Zuolin and Feng Yuxiang. The risk, of course, was that he would be left without the support of either.

On November 15, 1924, Duan Qirui was nominated as provisional chief executive [*Zhonghua minguo linshi zhizheng*] by Zhang Zuolin, Lu Yongxiang, Feng Yuxiang, Hu Jingyi, and Sun Yue. Duan agreed to emerge from retirement only after a considerable amount of inviting, not only by the generals in Tianjin but also by the Zhili militarists other than Wu Peifu, as well as by powerful figures of the Southwestern "lianzhipai," including Tang Jiyao (1883–1927), Zhao Hengti (1880–1971), Xiong Kewu (1885–1970), and Chen Jiongming. As their name suggested, however, this last group wanted Duan to form a federal [*liansheng zizhi*] government.[22]

Because of Wu Peifu's actions in Wuhan, Duan was urged by Feng Yuxiang, Zhang Zuolin, and the others to establish a new government as

---

20. Signatories included Qi Xieyuan, Sun Chuanfang, Xiao Yaonan, Liu Zhenhua, Wu Xintian, Wu Pifu, Du Xigui, Ma Lianjia, Cai Chengxun, Zhou Yinren, Sa Zhenbing, Zhang Fulai, Li Jichen, Liu Cunhou, Liu Xiang, Yang Sen, Yuan Zuming, Huang Yucheng, Jin Handing, Lin Hu, and Hong Zhaolin, representing Jiangsu, Zhejiang, Hubei, Shaanxi, Anhui, Jiangxi, Fujian, Henan, Sichuan and Guangdong (Hunan not included). Tao Juyin, *Beijang junfa*, vol. 3, p. 1363.
21. Ibid., p. 1364.
22. Ibid., p. 1365.

quickly as possible. Duan accordingly traveled to Beijing on November 22, and on November 24 he took the oath of office at the Ministry of the Army.[23] He could scarcely take up residence in the old government compound, where Cao Kun was still under house arrest, so he established his provisional executive offices at No. 1 Iron Lion Lane [*Tie shizi hutong*: today No. 3 Zhang Zizhong lu]. And he faced another problem as well – the city of Beijing was still under the control of Feng Yuxiang's forces.

Zhang Zuolin and Feng Yuxiang had arrived from Tianjin just as Duan was being inaugurated. To the mystification of some observers, both were giving every sign of suddenly wishing to leave politics. Feng submitted his resignation from all offices (which Duan refused to accept) and announced his intention to travel abroad. He had brought the country to conditions in which peace could be restored. Now he urged the new government to carry on further radical reforms: most importantly, the demobilization of troops and the abolition of military governorships throughout the country. All of Feng's officers indicated their willingness to advance or withdraw with their leader. Feng even dropped hints about a possible beautiful friendship, suggesting that Wu Peifu join him on a trip to Europe and America. Now that both men were out of politics, there was no reason they should not work together to save China. Feng also called personally on Zhang Zuolin to explain his determination to resign; after listening politely, Zhang urged him to give up the idea so that the two of them could share the heavy responsibilities of governing. In fact Feng was under pressure from both Duan and Zhang Zuolin. To free the capital from Feng's military control, Duan ordered Wu Guangxin and Liang Hongzhi (1883–1946) to go to the Zhantansi on November 26 to detain Feng. But when they arrived the courtyard was already empty. Feng and his forces had gone to the Western Hills to "rest."[24]

Shortly thereafter, on December 2, Zhang too departed Beijing, for Tianjin. Except for the Fengtian forces that he left in charge of certain administrative buildings, he withdrew all his men. He even announced that all Fengtian forces were to be moved back beyond the passes and made it clear that he had cut his ties with the government. There was not a single Fengtian official in the cabinet, he said, and not one Fengtian soldier working in a ministry. His troops would be withdrawn from the railway lines. And on December 5, he announced that he was giving up the military offices he held in the Northeast.

To the uninitiated, this behavior by Zhang Zuolin and Feng Yuxiang seemed bizarre. In fact both men were trying to force Duan to choose

---

23. Ibid., p. 1366.   24. Ibid., p. 1380.

sides. They were trying to "advance by withdrawing" [*yi tui wei jin*], which would make Duan aware of how little real power he possessed, and thus turn decisively to one or the other of them. Zhang Zuolin was frustrated because even before he had arrived in Beijing, he had already proposed to Duan that his close associate Li Jinglin should replace Lu Zhonglin as the commander of metropolitan defense forces, thus giving effective military control of the city to Zhang. But Duan would not accept that, just as he would not agree with Zhang's plan to advance on Shanghai. By abruptly leaving the capital, Zhang forced Duan's hand; the provisional chief executive immediately sent an emissary to Tianjin.[25]

Zhang never had any intention of withdrawing his forces beyond the passes. And he was planning finally to finish off Qi Xieyuan in the Yangzi valley regardless of what Duan said. In Tianjin, Zhang had already met with his military colleagues and explained his plan to help his friend Lu Yongxiang in Shanghai. On December 7, Duan's special emissary Liang Hongzhi returned to Beijing and reported all this. Duan understood that if Zhang were seen to be doing as he liked without regard to the Beijing executive, that would hurt his prestige. So he moved to mandate himself the things that Zhang wanted in any case. On December 11, Duan issued an order removing Qi Xieyuan from office, and naming close associates of Zhang instead. Han Guojun (1857–1942) would be the transitional Jiangsu governor [*duban*]; Li Jinglin would take the same office in the Zhili; and Lu Yongxiang would assume the post permanently in Jiangsu. Zhang thus took control of the Zhili base in the Yangzi area through direct and official means.[26]

Even while making such concessions, however, Duan was moving to secure a foundation for his own power that would be as independent as possible of his two military patrons. He signaled this intention on December 13 when he swept away China's much-abused but technically still extant constitutional structure, abolishing, with the concurrence of his cabinet, the provisional constitution of 1912 and the constitution of 1923, and dissolving parliament – and this time both actions proved final.[27]

At the same time Duan began a subtle courtship of Zhili. Cao Kun at this time was still under house arrest in the Yanqing lou in Zhongnanhai, awaiting rescue by the Jade Marshal. Duan issued an ugly-sounding bill of indictment against Cao and sent his own men to take him into custody. Although on the surface this appeared ominous for Cao Kun, in fact it helped the ousted president by removing him and his associates from the real threat posed by Feng Yuxiang and his men. And Duan

25. Ibid., p. 1381.   26. Ibid., pp. 1381–2.   27. Tung, *Political Institutions*, p. 79.

Qirui made clear his disapproval of Feng's treatment of Puyi. On his very first day in office he issued an order lifting the surveillance on the former Qing emperor. On November 29 Puyi managed to flee from Prince Chun's mansion to the Japanese legation, where Yoshizawa treated him with great solicitude, arranging for formal Qing-style New Year's greetings in early February 1925 and subsequently guiding him to the haven of the Japanese Concession in Tianjin.[28] These were bad omens for Feng Yuxiang. Then the third player in the Triangular Alliance, Sun Yat-sen, got into the act, further complicating matters.

In the years since his month as provisional president in 1912, the star of the onetime father of the Chinese revolution had been fading. Asked in September 1924 about a possible threat from Sun Yat-sen's Guangzhou-based army, Wu Peifu had been dismissive: He "said that the difficulty there was practically solved and that the Beijing Government expects to see its authority restored soon."[29] It was a reasonable forecast. Sun's political authority had long been confined to a toehold in Guangzhou which over the preceding two years had become increasingly precarious. Only Soviet military and technical aid, which he had been receiving since early 1923, had enabled him to crush the Guangzhou Merchants' Corps in August 1924 – an incident that revealed just how unpopular he had become with some. The reliability of Sun's Soviet support, however, had been put in doubt by the establishment in May 1924 of diplomatic relations between Moscow and Beijing. Sun's place in the Triangular Alliance discussed in Chapter 2 was also precarious: Zhang Zuolin despised Sun's revolutionary principles and supported him only for reasons of realpolitik. Now, apparently the winner, Zhang would feel free to end the marriage of convenience. Nevertheless, the autumn of 1924 found Sun himself making an impressive reentry onto the Chinese political scene, while his Kuomintang gradually expanded to fill the political vacuum created by the collapse of the Northern System. Less than a month after the wars of 1924 ended, Sun Yat-sen was on a ship bound north.

Sun, who had celebrated his fifty-eighth birthday on November 12 amid great rejoicing, left Guangzhou for Hong Kong on the following day aboard the gunboat *Yongfeng*, which was accompanied by the Soviet sloop *Vorovskii*. On November 14 he embarked from the British colony for Shanghai, accompanied by his young wife, Song Qingling, and a suite of eighteen persons. Arriving three days later in Shanghai, he spent

28. Tao Juyin, *Beijang junfa*, vol. 3, p. 1370. It is perhaps worth noting that by detaching Puyi from the palace and the Chinese political system, Feng Yuxiang made him – a player still having a certain value – available to the Japanese.
29. NYT, September 21, 1924, 25.

four days at his home in the French Concession considering what moves to make in the complex yet opportunity-filled situation that the civil war within the Northern group had created. He met Kuomintang colleagues and, true to form, blasted British imperialism in a letter to the Shanghai-based *North China Daily News*, which had editorialized that he (like "Little Xu" and various other Chinese political figures) should be kept out of the International Settlement lest the city's neutrality be compromised. Also true to form, Sun made political overtures to both sides in the civil conflict. He met with representatives of Duan Qirui, Feng Yuxiang, and Hu Jingyi, the victors ensconced in the North; he also approached the Zhili forces regrouped in the Yangzi valley under the leadership of Qi Xieyuan.[30]

From Shanghai Sun sailed for Kobe, enroute to Tianjin. The Japanese government refused to meet him. Prime Minister Katō and Foreign Minister Shidehara received instead two representatives sent by Duan Qirui. Minister of Communications Inukai Tsuyoshi (1855–1932), a former friend (and minister Yoshizawa's father-in-law), did not meet him either, sending a vice-minister in his place. But Sun did meet parliamentarians; the head of the Kawasaki Shipbuilding Company; and Toyama Mitsuru (1855–1944), "the power behind the Black Dragon (or Amur River) Society" [Kokuryūkai, an ultranationalist group devoted to revolution in China and a strong position for Japan in Manchuria]; as well as officers from the ministry of war and general staff. Sun was apparently seeking political and financial support for himself and for his foreign policies, but according to C. Martin Wilbur "he was asking too much; nor would he, as a quid pro quo, confirm in perpetuity Japan's rights and interests in Manchuria."[31]

Sun finally arrived in Tianjin on December 4, 1924, where a crowd of some 10,000 people representing fifty different groups had been turned out by the local Kuomintang to greet him at the dock. Two weeks later, the Nationalists and Communists combined forces to organize a huge assembly to welcome him.[32] From Tianjin, Sun traveled by rail to

---

30. C. Martin Wilbur, *Sun Yat-sen: Frustrated Patriot* (New York: Columbia University Press, 1976), pp. 270–1. Jerome Ch'en, "Dr. Sun Yat-sen's Trip to Peking, 1924–1925," in *Readings on Asian Topics*, Scandinavian Institute of Asian Studies, Monograph Series, no. 1 (1970), pp. 75–99. For the debate over Sun's admission to the International Settlement, see *North China Daily Herald*, November 8, 1924, p. 224; November 22, p. 303. See also Saggitarius [H. G. W. Woodhead], *The Strange Apotheosis of Sun Yatsen* (London: Heath, Cranton, 1939).

31. Wilbur, *Sun Yat-sen*, pp. 272–3.

32. Zhonggong Tianjin shiwei dangshi ziliao zhengji weiyuanhui, Tianjin shi zonggonghui gongyunshi yanjiushi, Tianjinshi lishi bowuguan, eds, *Wusa yundong zai Tianjin* (Beijing: Zhonggong dangshi ziliao chubanshe, 1987), pp. 2–3.

Beijing. The Duan administration wanted to play down his arrival and circulated reports and leaflets condemning him for the suppression of the Guangzhou merchants' militia. The mechanics of his arrival were handled not officially but by Cai Yuanpei (1868–1940), president of Beijing University and a longtime friend of Sun's. Cai sent a detachment of the student cadet corps to the station, where they eased the official guards away from the platform, and then themselves, bayonets fixed, provided security for Sun's arriving train. As Sun stepped from the railroad carriage, they shouted slogans against the unequal treaties, while in response to questions, he stated that he had come to help "resolve the questions confronting the nation." Then the students escorted Sun, in Cai's own car, to the Hôtel de Pékin.[33]

Sun's national prestige mounted during this northward progress, which would turn out to be his last trip (he would die of cancer in Beijing on March 12, 1925). The crushing by his troops of the Merchants' Corps in Guangzhou in mid-October, an action that left much of Guangzhou's commercial district in smoking ruins, had badly damaged his reputation. But in the atmosphere of disillusionment and expectancy that accompanied the end of the wars in the North, both Sun's person and ideas once again exerted a powerful appeal. There were rumors that the Northerners might name Sun president, a move that could potentially unite the warring factions while restoring the prestige of the generals. As we have seen, Feng Yuxiang would insist years later that such had always been his plan.[34] Now it was essential that Zhang Zuolin and Duan somehow forestall a direct linkup between Feng Yuxiang and Sun Yat-sen's Kuomintang in the conflict – which now dominated the North – between Zhang and the Guominjun of Feng Yuxiang.

From Beijing Dr. Sun traveled to Tianjin to meet the men attempting to map out a future for the country. On arriving he went almost immediately to the Cao Family Garden, Zhang Zuolin's mansion, to pay a courtesy call. The following day the Marshal reciprocated, arriving at the Zhang Family Garden [*Zhangjia huayuan*] while Sun Yat-sen was still asleep. Zhang was not put off, and stated that he could simply talk, and Sun, if he chose, need not respond. So he entered Sun's chamber, where the two men talked secretly. According to subsequent accounts, Zhang urged Sun to abandon his pro-Soviet policies, which he felt were arousing much unnecessary foreign opposition, and proposed himself as an

33. Cheng Houzhi, "Huiyi wo zai BeiDa de yiduan xuesheng shenghuo, *Wenshi ziliao xuanji*, no. 43 (Beijing: Wenshiziliao chubanshe, 1964, reprinted 1980, pp. 196–209); Wilbur, *Sun Yat-sen*, p. 273.
34. Wilbur, *Sun Yat-sen*, pp. 271, 275–6.

intermediary should Sun wish to communicate with the foreign Powers. When Duan Qirui heard that Sun was in Tianjin, he sent Xu Shiying (1873–1964) with warm greetings.[35]

Duan had no real intention of deferring to Sun. Rather, he was already moving to lessen both Zhang Zuolin's and Feng Yuxiang's leverage over himself, and Sun was far less threatening than they were. Duan's plan was first to divide the contending forces of Feng and Zhang by giving them each secure territorial bases, and thus to prevent a destabilizing competition between them. This he began to do on December 10. He reorganized command in the Northeast, making Zhang Zuolin *duban* in Fengtian as well as *duban* of Northeast border defense, Zhang Zuoxiang *duban* in Jilin, and Wu Junsheng *duban* in Heilongjiang. Zhang Zuolin would remain in overall charge as the regional *zhihui*. Parallel arrangements were made for Feng Yuxiang less than a month later. On January 3, 1925, Duan named Feng Yuxiang the northwest border defense *duban*; sent Li Mingzhong to Suiyuan; and put Song Zheyuan (1885–1949) in charge of the core 11th Division. Zhang Zhijiang was already *duban* in Chahar. Feng now had a substantive position in the Northwest that was similar to what Zhang had in the Northeast, though not as powerful. The railways were also divided: Tianjin–Pukou went to Fengtian, Beijing–Hankou to Feng Yuxiang. The two men had been placed on the same level and their power divided into areas of influence. They swore brotherhood; the tensions between their forces were relaxed; and the Duan government rested more securely on this new foundation.[36] As for Sun Yat-sen, he might be accommodated and neutralized by means of a political spectacle.

By December 1924, Duan's political strategy was moving beyond military questions to acquire a broader shape. Feeling was strong in China that some sort of great national deliberative assembly might offer peacefully the route to unification that had so far proved militarily elusive. Sun Yat-sen had been advocating a People's Assembly [*guomin huiyi*] for such a purpose, and what Duan proposed now, an Aftermath Conference [*shanhou huiyi*], had a similar purpose. Shortly after taking office, Duan had ordered Yao Zhencao to draw up an agenda for such a meeting. This was passed by the cabinet on December 20 and announced on December 24, with February 1 to be the opening day.[37] The groups to be invited included (1) outstanding national leaders, that is, Sun Yat-sen

---

35. Tao Juyin, *Beiyang junfa*, vol. 3, pp. 1374–6; Lai et al., *Beiyang junfa shigao*, p. 311.
36. Tao Juyin, *Beiyang junfa*, vol. 3, pp. 1382–3.
37. Fei Baoyan, *Shanhou huiyi shi* (Beijing: Huanyu, 1925); Lai et al., *Beiyang junfa shigao*, p. 311.

and Li Yuanhong; (2) meritorious military leaders; (3) representatives of all the provinces, as well as Mongolia, Tibet, and Qinghai; and (4) persons of outstanding achievement. An initial planning session would involve about thirty, with individuals taking part in person or through their representatives. The Aftermath Conference itself would have several tasks. The most important would be to plan the organization of a national assembly. It would also provide proposals for reorganizing the military system and finances, and recommend a structure for the transitional government that would hold authority while the new constitution and administration were being prepared.[38]

The plan offered the sliver of a possibility that civilian government might be restored. As the plan was being worked out, the foreign Powers were reassessing their attitude toward Duan and moving toward him cautiously, with abundant encouragement from the Japanese. In his inaugural address, Duan had spoken broadly of strengthening the Republic, reforming the internal situation, and maintaining China's credit abroad – *wai chong guo xin*. This last phrase was taken as an indication of willingness to honor the existing treaties and foreign debts, and it led the *corps diplomatique* to take the first step toward establishing relations with the new regime. The capital diplomats decided to recognize Duan's regime as the de facto government of China, while expressing the hope that it would not take up arms against Wu Peifu. The Japanese in particular looked with favor on the new government and were most solicitous about its interests; Yoshizawa was very active in introducing its members to the representatives of the foreign Powers. He even proposed that Japan lend Duan money, secured by the tobacco and alcohol tax revenues; but when the idea leaked out both the other foreign Powers and many in China expressed enough opposition to halt the idea.[39]

On December 9 the *corps diplomatique* decided to have the dean of the corps, Oudendijk, go to the Chinese Foreign Ministry to say that the Powers were willing to cooperate with the provisional government in the solution of difficult problems, and to express their relief that the new administration had declared its intention to honor the treaties. In consequence, the Powers hoped it would prove possible in the immediate future to begin the meetings envisioned by the Washington Conference. On December 20 the foreign ministry replied, reiterating the intention to honor existing commitments and welcoming the start of the meetings planned at Washington. Strong incentives existed for the Chinese side to move. One of the first results was the settlement, essentially on French terms, of the gold franc dispute. On February 19, the foreign ministry

38. *Beiyang junfa*, vol. 3, pp. 1372–3.   39. Ibid., pp. 1366–7.

and the finance ministry approached de Martel, suggesting that both sides work on the problem in a spirit of compromise. A settlement was finally reached in early spring, and ratified in December of 1925.[40]

By late winter of 1924 to 1925 it looked, superficially at least, as if the complex equilibrium of Chinese military and political factions and foreign interests might be reestablished, as had been done so many times earlier. The Aftermath Conference met in Beijing from February 1 to April 21 of 1925. As winter turned to spring, however, it became clear that its complex proceedings would have little or no effect on China's future. Instead, the verdict of the battlefield would continue to dominate, and an unpleasant verdict it was. Low-level hostility erupted wherever the forces of the victors of 1924 encountered one another or when local commanders still resisted them. Although it was costly and disruptive, the fighting of winter and spring of 1924 to 1925 offered less and less prospect of decision. The logic of the battles was local, not national. Their purpose was to conserve power, not to extend it. The prospects were for increasing fragmentation: for an expansion of military activity over more territory, even as it lost both its own logic of victory and any link whatsoever with civilian politics.

Minister Macleay had been correct. Nineteen twenty-four brought the worst crisis for the Beijing-based political system since the abdication of the Qing. The superficial calm that at first returned to the capital and its immediate environs at war's end concealed acute and ultimately insoluble problems beneath. Duan's ingenious attempts to transform a power vacuum into authority for himself failed, and as the spring of 1925 arrived, it was clear that China confronted anarchy.

The problem was that the contenders for power were too evenly balanced. So, as in a parliament without a strong majority the small parties can exert disproportionate influence, so in China at this time the personal calculations and stratagems of ambitious individuals became very important. Fighting shifted mode in consequence, from the strategically conceived war of decision, which Wu Peifu had just attempted unsuccessfully, to war of political maneuver. It was a war of political maneuver, furthermore, in which none of the contenders had an entirely clear policy or strategy.

Neither Feng Yuxiang nor Zhang Zuolin had military strength comparable to Wu Peifu's Zhili coalition, just shattered. So for either to think of simply imposing his authority over China by force was completely unrealistic. Success for either would depend on political acumen

40. Ibid., pp. 1367–9.

and most importantly on the ability to find allies enough to tip the political and military balance in his direction.

The most obvious ally for both was the remnant Anfu faction, driven from national power in 1920 but still influential. Wu Peifu had long understood its potential importance. His strategy had always been to deal with the Anfu remnant in Shanghai by bringing them into Cao Kun's government – he had proposed Lu Yongxiang as vice-president – thus eliminating the danger of a two-front war, and permitting himself to concentrate on his primary adversary, Zhang Zuolin. Now both Feng Yuxiang and Zhang Zuolin attempted to give the Anfu group a parallel role.

Feng Yuxiang hoped that Duan would control Zhang Zuolin, thus facilitating a division of authority whereby Feng would become arbiter of power in China proper – within the passes – while Zhang would be undisturbed in his possession of Manchuria. Since Feng did not remotely possess military forces capable of securing Shanghai, to permit Anfu to resume its position there would be a concession that would cost him nothing.

Zhang Zuolin, by contrast, was more ambitious militarily. His intention was to secure Shanghai for himself, initially by using Lu Yongxiang and the Anfu faction, but to discard them in favor of his own men as soon as the situation permitted. Zhang, however, overreached in a way that doomed his ultimate goal. Wu Peifu, recall, had wanted to avoid fighting in Shanghai but had been forced into it by Qi Xieyuan. Zhang Zuolin, by contrast, actively sought engagement in the Yangzi region. It would turn out, however, that Feng Yuxiang was a stronger threat in the North than he had expected. Zhang would therefore be forced to withdraw from Shanghai in order to confront Feng in a destructive war that could have been avoided if Zhang had been willing to bring the Anfu group in as his allies.

These weaknesses in the victors' camp quickly became apparent, even as Duan tried to reconcile the interests of Zhang, Feng, and the Zhili remnants. As has been mentioned, jostling between Guominjun and Fengtian forces was underway in Henan within days of the Beijing coup's success. The hostility gradually spread into Central China, where the momentary factional unity that had been created on the eve of the war disintegrated completely, and major fighting extended to Zhengzhou and Kaifeng. As for Duan's attempt to divide Feng and Zhang by assigning each an area of influence, it simply led to more war as each tried to occupy his assigned territory and ran quite naturally into the resistance of those already established there. Finally, neither side was really willing to stick to the area assigned, and by January and February of 1925 the struggles in Central China were drawing Feng and Zhang toward military confrontation.

The most serious instability was at Shanghai. The coup in Beijing plunged the city into a new period of uncertainty. Upon hearing of the coup, the just-victorious General Qi left for his secure base at Nanjing. Responding to Wu Peifu's call for reinforcement, he had prepared detachments of Hubei troops to be moved north by rail. The expectation was that from Pukou they would head for Tianjin to join Wu Peifu in his march against Feng Yuxiang in the capital. As we have seen, however, the proclamation of neutrality in Shandong by Zheng Shiqi – an Anfu general – prevented any reinforcements from reaching Wu from the South.

Instead, the coup proved the signal for an immediate Fengtian thrust toward the lower Yangzi region.[41] Even before the Duan government had been installed, Zhang Zongchang had begun moving down the Tianjin–Pukou railway toward Jiangsu and eventually Shanghai. Again Zheng Shiqi declared Shandong neutral and refused to permit Zhang Zongchang's forces to pass. They were forced to return to Cangzhou. But at the beginning of December Duan agreed to permit Fengtian forces to occupy Jiangsu while guaranteeing Zheng's position in Shandong. As Anfu faction members, both Lu Yongxiang and Zheng Shiqi were suspicious of Fengtian intentions, but the guarantee plus the Duan government's backing for the move against Shanghai altered Zheng's calculations, and he now permitted the passage of Fengtian troops through his territory. On December 10 he announced the abandonment of his neutrality; on December 11 the Duan government stripped Qi Xieyuan of his post as military governor of Jiangsu.[42]

When this order was announced, Qi decided to declare independence from the central government. He changed his title and moved the 6th Division, which he personally controlled, into the area of Zhenjiang and Wuxi. This would be the first line of defense against the Fengtian forces and, if necessary, they would be able to fall back on Nanjing. Duan, however, had no desire to see warfare break out in the area. He invited Qi to come north to take up another position of responsibility, and named Gong Bangduo the commander of the 6th Division in succession to Qi, making He Fenglin the commander of the 19th Division in place of Gong. But Qi was unwilling to give up the 6th Division, and Gong, unable to take it over, was therefore unwilling to give up his 19th

41. Ding Wenjiang, ed., *Minguo junshi jinji*, 165–91.
42. Tao Juyin, *Beiyang junfa*, vol. 3, p. 1388; "The Military Situation," July 14, 1925, 6–7, in MIR. Colin Mackerras, *Modern China: A Chronology from 1842 to the Present* (San Francisco: W. H. Freeman, 1982), says Qi was removed on December 12.

Division. Qi in any case moved the 19th Division from Shanghai to Nanjing; Gong declared himself ill and thus avoided getting involved.[43]

Qi's position, however, was not strong. Without Wu Peifu, the Zhili alliance of ten provinces [*shisheng tongmeng*] was disintegrating. Among the Jiangsu forces not a single general supported Qi's declaration of independence. So on December 14 Qi turned over his seals of military command and authority to the provincial governor, a civilian, Han Guojun. He remained, however, in Nanjing. And on the same day the Jiangsu army commanders made clear their unwillingness to submit to control from the North by means of a joint telegram which expressed their support of Han Guojun and opposed the dispatch of a high military official from any other faction to take control of military authority, an act that would change the status quo. The highest-ranking Jiangsu general, Chen Diaoyuan, had himself sent a telegram on December 13 in which he opposed Lu Yongxiang's southern expedition. The Jiangsu commanders wanted to keep things as they were. One way to do this would be to abolish the supreme military post of Jiangsu *duban* and demilitarize Shanghai. Such a price was worth paying to keep Lu Yongxiang from returning.[44] The Zhili forces in the Yangzi valley were now in a position not unlike that of the Anfu forces before the wars: too weak to win themselves but quite able to play the role of dog in the manger when threatened by ambitious outsiders.

Caught in the wash of these larger machinations, the situation in Shanghai became ever more chaotic. As had already happened in the cities of Tianjin and Beijing after the coup, representatives of the warring factions, as well as the occasional free-lance militarist, were carving out areas of control in and around Shanghai. Gong Bangduo, whom Duan was attempting to elevate, had established himself in Zhabei. At the other end of town – at Longhua – Zhang Yunming, who was aligned with the local forces, was also laying claim to official control of the city. The *corps diplomatique* in Beijing worried that the contest for control of Shanghai might burst out into full-scale war, so on December 8 it sent the Dutch minister to the foreign ministry in Beijing to urge the necessity of demilitarizing Shanghai and abolishing the military posts there. Further complicating all this were the activities of Lu Yongxiang, who was on his way South, and who had already sent both He Fenglin and Chen Leshan to Shanghai to resume the offices from which they had been removed at the time of the Jiangsu victory a few months earlier.[45]

43. Tao Juyin, *Beiyang junfa*, vol. 3, p. 1388.
44. Ibid., 1388–9.
45. Ibid., 1388.

In all of this, Qi Xieyuan was still a force to be reckoned with. It was true that he had given up some of his formal roles, but he had not given up his military power. Furthermore, the larger situation gave him room for maneuver. The cracks were increasingly obvious within the group holding Beijing, between Feng Yuxiang's forces and those of Zhang Zuolin. While not supporting Qi fully, the Jiangsu commanders nevertheless expressed deep hatred for Lu Yongxiang. And in and around Shanghai, civilians, merchants, and others were frantically searching for some means of demilitarization in order to avoid the catastrophe of another war. All of these developments helped Qi.

Qi ran into difficulties as well. When he ordered Wu Hengzan's 2nd Division to move to Nanjing, the 3rd Brigade of that division refused to accept the assignment. On December 24, a mutiny broke out in Suzhou, in which the brigade commanders all fled, two regiment commanders were detained, and the soldiers elevated the artillery and battalion commander Qin Guang to command. These forces then declared their independence from Qi. As long as they held control of Suzhou, the rail connection between Shanghai and Nanjing was broken, and Qi's armies in Shanghai and Ningbo were isolated. This greatly weakend his position against the Fengtian forces.[46]

Other forces opposed to Zhang Zuolin were fighting among themselves as well. Twelve days after the mutiny, conflict broke out between Sun Chuanfang, who was an ally of Marshal Qi's, and the 4th Division of the former Zhejiang army, the one whose wavering had led to the decision to surrender. General Sun had taken this unit over at the end of the Jiangsu–Zhejiang War, and it had seemed loyal until its former commander, Chen Leshan, reappeared and resumed command. Under the changed circumstances, it might make sense to leave the pro-Qi alliance and link up once again with the winners. Fighting between Sun Chuanfang and Chen continued into January, when Sun captured Songjiang. Chen and his forces then began falling back into the immediate Shanghai area. Four thousand of his troops reached the boundaries on January 4, and established themselves in two villages, one about a mile northwest of the Roman Catholic cathedral at Xujiahui, the other on Hongrao Road near the airport.[47]

Now a series of dramatic developments occurred that looked set to deliver the Southeast into the hands of the Northerners. On December

---

46. Ibid., 1389.
47. Anatol M. Kotenev, *Shanghai: Its Municipality and the Chinese* (Shanghai: North-China Daily News & Herald, Ltd., 1927), p. 116, citing Police Commissioner's Report, December 1924, and "Municipal Gazette," January 15, 1925; also Municipal Council's Report, 1925, p. 59.

23, Zheng Shiqi sent a telegram to Chen Diaoyuan proposing secret discussions on the question of how to resist the imminent Fengtian attack. At the time, Chen's defense line at Xuzhou was the most forward position on the route that the Fengtian forces would follow south. But if Zheng were to join the southern Zhili remnant and thus bring in Shandong, the whole situation would change. Chen saw an opportunity here, but he also feared a double cross, so before leaving for the North he instructed his forces that if by December 25 he had not returned, they should assume he was being held hostage in Jinan and should immediately put into effect their original plan to resist Fengtian.

Chen then went by rail to Jinan, where he was met at the platform by his two enemies, Wu Guangxin and Zhang Zongchang. After some discussion the three generals got back on the train and went to Tianjin, arriving on December 24, and going immediately to see Zhang Zuolin. The Old Marshal was in an expansive and accommodating mood. He assured his visitors that he had no ambitions with regard to Jiangsu but that he did insist that Lu Yongxiang and Qi Xieyuan should cease their quarrel and reach a settlement in which one of them stepped down and allowed the other to take over. Zhang suggested that Chen Diaoyuan change sides and called on him to sign two telegrams: one expressing support for Duan's central government and for Lu's southern expedition, the other calling upon Qi to give up his military power and leave Nanjing. Chen agreed.[48]

The next day, December 25, Chen went with Wu Guangxin and Zhang Zongchang to Beijing, where he met Duan Qirui himself. In return for his cooperation, Duan offered Chen the office of Jiangsu Military Coordinator [*junwu huiban*]. In return Chen agreed to send his family to Beijing as hostages to guarantee his loyalty. On December 26, Chen returned to Tianjin for a conference with Zhang Zuolin and Lu Yongxiang. It was decided that Chen would first go to Xuzhou, where he would begin making arrangements. Next, the Fengtian forces would move as far south as Hanzhuang. Only then would Lu Yongxiang himself head south.

What had started as a plan to win Shandong over to the Southern side had ended up turning Chen Diaoyuan to the Northern side and delivering the key railway junction at Xuzhou – the gateway to Jiangsu, Nanjing, and Shanghai – to Fengtian. By means of this complicated plan, which at once worked within the structure of the new central government, while also gravely weakening the Southern position by opening the road to Nanjing, it was hoped gradually to deprive Qi of his

48. Tao Juyin, *Beiyang junfa*, vol. 3, p. 1389.

authority without stirring up the Jiangsu generals. With all arrangements made, Chen headed south, only to discover when he got to Tai'an that his forces had followed his original instructions and had destroyed a section of track at Liguoyi in order to prepare to stop the Fengtian forces. Chen, however, told them to repair the track, which they did. On December 28, Fengtian forces took over Xuzhou, and one regiment continued to Bengbu in Anhui.[49]

Nanjing was now impossible to hold. Qi departed on December 28 by boat to Shanghai (rail travel was ruled out because Suzhou was still under the control of the mutineers). There he took personal command of his own troops and began mopping up Chen Leshan's forces.[50] On December 31, Fengtian forces headed south from Bengbu, but the Jiangsu forces destroyed the railroad from Huaqiying to Dongge, thus forcing them to stop at Chuzhou. It was beginning to look as if the pattern of the Jiangsu–Zhejiang War might be followed, with Shanghai held this time by Qi and his Zhili forces, while Fengtian and its new Anfu allies besieged it from Jiangsu.

Two days later Zhang Zongchang turned up to straighten things out. Zhang arrived at Pukou, just across the river from Nanjing, with a terrifying force of White Russians. The introduction of these troops into Chinese warfare was an innovation. Despite the "unfavorable impression" they made "because of their filthy condition and the fact that even some of the officers were seen lying drunk on the streets before some of the lower class Chinese brothels," they proved to be effective fighters, helping the Fengtian forces "to advance to Shanghai almost as quickly as the means of transport would permit."[51] On January 6, Zhang crossed to Nanjing and called on Han Guojun. On January 10, Lu Yongxiang made his way from Xuzhou to Nanjing. The Fengtian forces were now in place for a decisive push down the railroad to Shanghai.[52]

Qi Xieyuan and his associates did not give up. They formed and re-formed alliances, but Duan Qirui showed great resourcefulness in gradually dividing them. Eventually Qi was forced to take refuge in the Shanghai concessions, where his military activities clearly violated the city's avowed neutrality. The Duan government therefore asked the *corps diplomatique* to deny Qi access to the concessions, as they had done earlier in the case of Xu Shuzheng. But the *corps* put the question aside and did

49. Ibid., p. 1390.
50. Kotenev, *Shanghai: Its Municipality*, p. 117.
51. John K. Davis (U.S. Consul, Nanjing) to Department of State, January 31, 1925, 54, 47. SD 893.00/6104.
52. Tao Juyin, *Beiyang junfa*, vol. 3, p. 1390.

not act. In any case, Qi was meeting with little success, and his alliance with Sun Chuanfang was looking ever more precarious.[53]

Meanwhile, the military position of the Fengtian forces was growing stronger by the day. On January 13, they had crossed the river from Pukou to Nanjing. By January 17, they were directly engaged with Qi's forces. On January 18, they had occupied Zhenjiang and Danyang, and on January 19, they took Changzhou. Zhang Zongchang used his White Russian forces, who so unnerved Qi's men that they melted back to Wuxi. (At this point rail communications between Shanghai and Wuxi had been restored by a second mutiny which had begun on January 11 and succeeded by January 14.) With the battle becoming critical, Qi came in person to Wuxi on January 19, setting up his headquarters at the Gaoqiao railway station. The Fengtian forces did not want to attack immediately, so beginning on the following day, they simply consolidated their positions. At the same time, Qi lacked the strength to attack them. There was a brief pause in the struggle.

Now it was the turn of Sun Chuanfang, who had been allied with Qi, to show his hand. Initially, he had sent forces to join Qi at Wuxi. But on January 22, he suddenly withdrew these and sent a telegram to Duan Qirui suggesting that if Beijing would stop Lu Yongxiang's advance and order foreign troops out of Jiangsu, he would deliver Jiangsu, Anhui, Jiangxi, and Fujian to the center. At the time Sun made this proposal, Chen Diaoyuan, now allied with Fengtian, was advancing on Yixing, and Sun's forces, under Lu Xiangting, were engaged against them at Changxing.[54]

Abandoned by Sun, Qi was now left to defend Wuxi and Shanghai by himself. A Fengtian division and General Nechaev and his White Russians were moving in on him. On January 26, a detachment of the Wuxi merchants' militia was patrolling near the Gaoqiao railway station. The story has it that Qi Xieyuan mistook these forces for a vanguard of the Fengtian army. Terrified, he attempted to board his train for Shanghai, but panic spread so rapidly among his forces that he was unable to find his way through the crush. So he set out on foot along the railroad line. Luckily, he found a handcar which eventually got him to Suzhou. Qi's forces had an unsavory reputation, however, and merchants in Suzhou were deeply worried and immediately sent a representative to the station to plead with Qi not to fight in Suzhou. They found the general ravenous, sweat-soaked, and filthy, and after a quick breakfast at the station, he got on the train for Shanghai.[55]

On January 28, in Shanghai, Qi announced his retirement, turned

---

53. Ibid., p. 1391.　54. Ibid., p. 1392.　55. Ibid., p. 1393.

over all his forces to Sun Chuanfang, and embarked for Japan. The Fengtian forces had occupied Wuxi the day before, and on this very day their vanguard, fifty Russians and three Chinese, pulled into Shanghai's North Station in an armored train. On January 29, Zhang Zongchang arrived and took charge. Lu Yongxiang named Gong Bangduo to take over the two defeated divisions, the 6th and the 19th. But, except for those troops that had fled, the losers were already under Sun Chuanfang's control. Shortly thereafter, 10,000 Fengtian troops under General Zhang Zongchang occupied the city and took control of the Chinese districts. General Sun Chuanfang, however, continued to occupy the Jiangnan arsenal, which, on January 15, Duan Qirui had ordered should be used only for commercial and industrial purposes. The Duan Qirui government sent Marshal Wu Guangxin, minister of war, to negotiate a settlement between the Fengtian forces and Sun Chuanfang.[56]

It was the story of Beijing in October and November 1924 all over again. Sun Chuanfang – the local defector who had helped to deliver the territory to Fengtian, as Feng Yuxiang had delivered Beijing – now became an obstacle to unified control. And the arrival of Fengtian forces in Shanghai did not lead to a resolution of the confrontation any more than they had in Beijing. Rather, with the intermediation of Shanghai civil organizations, Sun Chuanfang and the Fengtian army divided the city into areas of influence, within which each would gather disbanded soldiers. As for the arsenal, it was agreed that the Shanghai General Chamber of Commerce should take it over, and once order was restored, the two armies would withdraw their troops from the city. Lu Yongxiang and Zhang Zongchang sent representatives to Hangzhou to discuss the issue with Sun Chuanfang. Between January 28 and January 31, Lu Yongxiang, Sun Chuanfang, and Zhang Zuolin all announced by means of telegrams that they would not invade the city. On January 31, Wu Guangxin went to Shanghai, where he carried on discussions with Wang Jinyu (1884–1951), the representative of Zhang Zongchang and Sun Chuanfang. It was agreed that Sun Chuanfang would withdraw to Songjiang and the Fengtian forces would move to Kunshan. A new peace treaty between Zhejiang and Jiangsu was signed on February 3, with Sun himself going to Shanghai to sign, then immediately returning to Hangzhou. On February 4, the arsenal was taken over by the merchants, and on February 5, Sun's army withdrew completely from the city.[57]

After Sun withdrew, the Fengtian forces remained in Shanghai in violation of the agreement. Sun Chuanfang sent a telegram to Duan

56. Ibid., Kotenev, p. 118.   57. Ibid., p. 1393.

urging compliance. At this time Zhang Zuolin was promoting local autonomy under the slogan "Suren zhi Su" [Let Jiangsu people control Jiangsu] and had installed his secretary Zheng Qian (1870–1929), a Jiangsu native, as the provincial governor. His purpose was to force Lu Yongxiang to step down, then to put Zhang Zongchang in as the Jiangsu *duban*. By such steps, Zhang Zuolin planned to incorporate Shanghai, with its unmatched wealth and resources, into his personal area of control. The treaty had simply been a ruse.[58]

Sun Chuanfang now embraced the principle of provincial autonomy as well and asked the Duan government to name Wu Guangxin (also a Jiangsu native) as *duban* in place of Lu Yongxiang. Zhang Zuolin would never accept such a move, and Duan also had no reason to be attracted to it. So Sun adopted a fallback position. He would agree that Zhang Zongchang could be *duban* but wanted Wu to be provincial governor. This would satisfy Zhang Zongchang and thus encourage him to implement the peace treaty, place Wu in an important position, and allow Sun a respite from the struggle with the Fengtian forces.[59]

The confused situation in Shanghai was drawing in more and more Fengtian resources, without a solution. In the meantime, Feng Yuxiang remained undefeated in the North in a position that potentially threatened the precarious line of communication between Mukden and Shanghai. Zhang Zuolin and his allies had to ask themselves what their chief objective was. Was control of Shanghai the key to their ambitions? Or might it be more important to deal first with the troublesome problem of Feng Yuxiang, closer to home? On February 8, Zhang Zuolin's son, Zhang Xueliang, and Han Linchun came to Shanghai to inspect, and on February 14 they returned to Mukden with Zhang Zongchang. There Zhang Zuolin called a military meeting to discuss the situation. Some favored a bold military stroke in Shanghai, putting Lu Yongxiang in charge of Zhejiang and Fujian and pressuring the Duan government to remove Sun Chuanfang from office. But the majority at the meeting felt that the primary enemy of the Fengtian group at this point was Feng Yuxiang. At this time, the Guominjun was running into local resistance in Henan, and the majority of conferees felt that Fengtian should take advantage of the opportunities presented there, leaving the issues of Jiangsu and Zhejiang to be resolved later. Zhang Zongchang was therefore transferred from Shanghai and made "bandit extermination" [*jiaofei*] commander in Jiangsu, Anhui, and Shandong. His headquarters were moved to Xuzhou, whence it would be easy to advance into Henan. Shanghai would not be entirely abandoned, but no further advances

58. Tao Juyin, *Beiyang junfa*, vol. 3, pp. 1392–4.   59. Ibid., p. 1394.

would be attempted there. So on February 27, Zhang Zongchang announced his support for Lu Yongxiang and denied any interest in becoming the *duban* of Jiangsu. This did not, however, solve Lu's problems. He was still directly opposed by the local authorities and tolerated by the Fengtian generals only until they could take control completely. So instead of taking the office, he urged that it be abolished.[60]

Leaving Shanghai, the Fengtian main forces now concentrated on Henan, where the fighting between a resourceful local militarist, Han Yukun (1888–1925), and the Guominjun was becoming increasingly heated. After some initial Guominjun victories, Han's subordinate Zhang Zhigong mounted a fierce attack in cooperation with the secret society called the Red Spears [*hongqianghui*] that began on March 9 and succeeded in capturing the railway stations at Longmen and Luoyang.[61] Luoyang was thrown into complete confusion, and it looked for a moment as if the Guominjun victory in the city that had once been Wu Peifu's headquarters might be reversed. The Guominjun Third Army was thrown into the battle; Sun Yue, Yue Weijun (1883–1932), and Fan Zhongxiu (1888–1930) all took charge at the front lines. Han's forces were gradually defeated. Without ammunition or the possibility of reinforcement or counterattack, Han Yukun retired to Songxian, where on April 2 he took poison and killed himself.[62]

As agreed at their Mukden meeting, the Fengtian forces of Zhang Zongchang had attempted to take advantage of the opportunities afforded by the Guominjun's difficulties. After his arrival in Xuzhou, Zhang Zongchang had sent a telegram on March 6, offering "assistance" to Hu Jingyi. Hu was so terrified by the possibility of Zhang's "aid" that after he had taken Luoyang he hurried back to Kaifeng on March 10 to prepare defenses against the Fengtian forces, while politely declining Zhang's generous offer. Fortunately for Feng Yuxiang, the situation in West Henan resolved itself as we have seen, with the defeat of Han Yukun. This meant that the Second and Third Guominjun Armies could regroup to deal with Zhang Zuolin.[63]

Out of all this campaigning Fengtian had not secured any decisive victory. Politically, the Beijing government was only partially under their control. Militarily, they had not prevailed completely anywhere, not against the Zhili remnants in the Shanghai area or against Feng

---

60. Ibid.
61. For the Red Spears, see Elizabeth J. Perry, *Rebels and Revolutionaries in North China, 1845–1945* (Stanford: Stanford University Press, 1980).
62. Tao Juyin, *Beiyang junfa*, vol. 3, p. 1397.
63. Ibid., pp. 1397–8.

Yuxiang's forces in Henan. They had done some hard fighting, but their struggles had not clarified the military situation; rather, they had rendered it more complex.

Less than a year earlier, on the eve of the wars of 1924, a rather precarious order had existed in China. Dominating everything was the possibility of a victory at the national level by either Wu Peifu or Zhang Zuolin. This potential – and once the war began, the momentum of battle – had the effect of forcing local militarists and fence-sitters to choose sides. But once the possibility of victory at the national level had disappeared, the logic of military action went into reverse. Instead of seeking to join the winning coalition, local authorities tried to conserve what was theirs, or even increase it, but without any immediate thought of the national situation. With national unity seemingly out of the question, the issue became how to arrange the division of China. This was a process that drew local militarists inward. No longer did they look for alliances with larger coalitions. Instead, they operated increasingly as independent actors, seeking to establish their own secure kingdoms. In the broad picture of Chinese politics and war, a logic of division had replaced the drive for unification.

The fighting of 1924 and 1925 had profoundly altered nearly every factor in the equations of politics and power in China in ways that the participants themselves understood only dimly. Effective authority had been undermined in the center and disrupted or even destroyed elsewhere; at the same time, local militarization had increased as each contender in the political struggle sought to secure his own base area. The physical and psychological immunity of the great treaty-port economic centers to Chinese politics and war had come to an end. The sense, shared at home and abroad, that the Northern government would eventually unify China began to weaken.

Neither Chinese nor foreigners knew even how to begin to deal with the situation. Former senses of possibility and probability, of what was secure and what was dangerous – indeed, a whole sense of China – were gone. The war had created vacuums – of national authority, of military power, of political imagination. Soon new ideas, new social groups, new politics, and ultimately new authorities would begin to try to fill them.

239

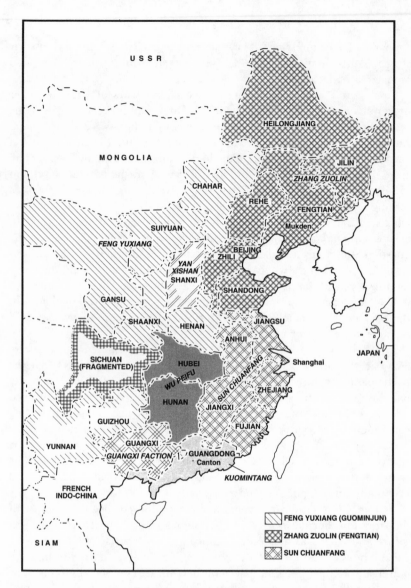

Distribution of Power, 1926

11

1925: Politics in a new key?

The new politics made a dramatic debut in Shanghai in late May. On Saturday, May 30, 1925, Kenneth John McEuen (b. 1879), commissioner of police for the Shanghai Municipal Council, left work early. Some protests were planned for that day, but Shanghai was always bubbling and the commissioner, a true old China hand, was not concerned. Born in Hong Kong, the son of a Royal Navy captain, educated in England and in a training course with the Royal Irish Constabulary in Dublin, McEuen had returned to China in 1900 and remained ever since, working his way up in the Shanghai municipal service.[1] This particular Saturday would see the annual spring meet at the racecourse, an event McEuen did not want to miss. He was a keen horseman – as a young man he had played polo in the interport league of teams from China's foreign settlements – and so at 12:15 P.M. he left his office in the municipal building and headed first to the Bund for lunch at the Shanghai Club and then out Bubbling Well Road (as the extension of Nanjing Road was then known) to the racetrack.[2] While Commissioner McEuen was watching the horses, modern Chinese nationalism began.

Nanjing Road, Shanghai's main thoroughfare, is always crowded, especially on Saturday, but this day people were particularly numerous. A demonstration had been called to protest the killing on May 15 of a Chinese worker named Gu Zhenghong by a Japanese textile factory guard whom he had been menacing. The crowd that turned out was both large and, as the day wore on, increasingly angry. Order in this part of Shanghai was the responsibility of the Louza [*laozha*] police

---

1. Carroll Lunt, ed., *The China Who's Who 1926 (Foreign)* (Shanghai: Kelly & Walsh, 1926), p. 177; Zhongguo shehui kexue yuan jindaishi yanjiusuo fanyishi, comp., *Jindai laihua waiguo renming cidian* (Beijing: Shehui kexue chubanshe, 1981), p. 301, which gives McEuen's date of birth as 1878.
2. See Japan, Department of Railways, *Guide to China*, 2nd rev. ed. (Tokyo: Japanese Government Railways, 1924), pp. 285, 288.

station, just off the Nanjing Road, under the command of Inspector Everson.

Shortly before 2:00 P.M. Everson arrested five students who had been causing trouble and took them in for questioning. Other students followed them back to the station and a crowd gradually gathered outside. By 3:00 P.M. perhaps 2,000 protesters filled the street in front. McEuen passed by at about this time on his way to the racecourse, but he saw no cause for concern. The police in the station, however, only 100 strong, began to feel a certain alarm. This increased when seventy protesters broke into the charging room to demand the release of the students. The protesters were driven back after a scuffle, but the police grew more alarmed when members of the crowd outside, according to some witnesses, began to shout, "Kill the foreigners!"

Everson feared that the station might be stormed, and at 3:37 P.M. he shouted a warning in both English and Chinese that the crowd must stop or he would shoot. Ten seconds later he ordered his men – a detachment of Sikh and Chinese constables – to fire. Forty-four shots rang out, and within a few minutes four people lay dead, seven more were dying, and some twenty were wounded. Then abruptly came silence as the crowd, stunned by what had happened, broke and fled for shelter. Police patrols moved out of the station into the streets. Minutes later, ambulances came for the dead and wounded.[3] Nothing was ever the same again.

Shanghai was no stranger to violence. The very Louza police station in front of which the May 30 shootings took place had been attacked by a mob in 1905. The crowd had driven "the Foreign and Sikh Police" into the station "amidst a hail of bricks and stones," then "forced an entry into the station, turned out the fires in the grates of the various rooms on the ground floor, and thus set fire to the station in three or four places." Meanwhile the town hall had also been under attack and "the Police there fired on the mob, killing three men and two other innocent shop assistants sitting behind closed shutters on the opposite side of the road." Only "the arrival of a landing party from the British warships in port" finally ended the rioting.[4] And May 4, 1919, had also been violent in Shanghai. Yet in the end these earlier incidents had led to very little.

---

3. Description quoted, with minor changes, from Nicholas R. Clifford, *Shanghai, 1925: Urban Nationalism and the Defense of Foreign Privilege* (Ann Arbor: Michigan Papers in Chinese Studies, no. 36, 1979), p. 16; see also Richard W. Rigby, *The May 30th Movement: Events and Themes* (Canberra: Australian National University Press, 1980), pp. 34–6.
4. Anatol M. Kotenev, *Shanghai: Its Municipality and the Chinese* (Shanghai: North-China Daily News & Herald, Ltd., 1927), p. 132.

As a result, Shanghailanders had long since learned to take disorder in their stride. According to Kotenev:

Residents and authorities of all classes in Shanghai, both foreign and Chinese, were accustomed to the constant fermentation among the Chinese extremists, students and laborers, which, as a rule, in spite of a threatening appearance, ended without much complication at the first sign of firmness displayed either by the foreign or the Chinese authorities.[5]

The same had been true in the other treaty-port centers of industry and commerce. But the wars of 1924 had weakened the forces of order: Chinese civil authority in Shanghai had changed as many as four times, depending upon how one counted, and was by no means settled; the Chinese armies that a year earlier would quickly have brought any real disturbance under control were scattered and disorganized. At the same time, the wars had increased the urban population's sense of grievance and insecurity. Fighting had raged in the city's immediate suburbs. More than 200,000 refugees had fled into the shelter of the foreign concessions. The Yangzi trade and commerce with North China had both been adversely affected. The city administration was still in chaos. Similar patterns of events had affected Beijing, Tianjin, and Hankou, as well as a host of medium- and smaller-size cities and towns around them. In all these places there was a certain amount of tinder for unrest even in the best of times. Shanghai, because of its concentration of industry and population, was perhaps the most volatile. On May 30, 1925, the spark was struck and a conflagration erupted, not just in Shanghai, but across China.

A year earlier, the May 30 incident would almost certainly have been localized and brought under control fairly easily. But in 1925, within a few days of the shootings all of China began to be swept up in a tide of protest that brought riots, demonstrations, strikes, and boycotts, which were quickly named collectively the May Thirtieth Movement. In Shanghai, large disorders broke out immediately after the protesters had been killed; foreign troops began patrolling the streets, and several more Chinese died in clashes with them. In Beijing on June 3 at least 30,000 students struck and demonstrated. In Hankou, up the Yangzi from Shanghai, eight Chinese demonstrators were killed by British machine-gun fire on June 11 and violent protest began. In Hong Kong, a general strike directed against the British got underway on June 19 and spread quickly to Guangzhou. That city in turn became very tense, and on July 23 an incident occurred that was even bloodier than that of May 30 in

5. Ibid., 129.

Shanghai. Sixty thousand demonstrators, including armed cadets from the Kuomintang's Huangpu [Whampoa] Military Academy, attempted to force the bridge that led from Guangzhou proper across the Shaji ["Shakee"] creek – really little more than a ditch – into the foreign settlement on Shamian Island. Someone started to shoot (it was never agreed who), and perhaps fifty-two Chinese were killed as British troops and Chinese demonstrators exchanged fire.[6] On June 25, a national general strike was called and in Beijing 100,000 people demonstrated, demanding that troops be sent to drive the British out of China.[7]

As this movement spread, it acquired the full panoply of organizational and material accompaniments now regularly associated with such incidents in China, ranging from organizing committees, memorial services, and special editions of journals, to some Western-looking monuments, rings, handkerchiefs, and a specially struck memorial medal.[8] It also acquired a clear set of demands. Demonstrators wanted an immediate end to extraterritoriality and everything that went with it; they demanded abolition of the treaty system. And to the distress of foreign residents of China, not only radicals, but "even those Chinese who had always been regarded as 'reasonable' and 'responsible' lent their voices to the demand for a more or less complete overhaul of China's relations with the major powers."[9]

Almost from the moment the shots were fired in Shanghai, May 30, 1925, was recognized as a date marking a major transition. Like the Tiananmen massacre sixty-four years later, it precipitated what can without exaggeration be called a shift in consciousness. The sight of blood on Nanjing Road in Shanghai, as on Changanjie in Beijing, changed everyone's mind. Here is how Ba Jin [Li Feigan, b. 1904], a radical novelist of the time, described one student's reaction:

At the entrance to Yunnan Road [he] saw the child who had been killed a short while before. He thought: about half an hour ago the crowd was marching peacefully toward the police station to ask the police to set free the students who had been unjustly arrested. They thought the police were human beings endowed with reason and human sympathy, that human blood flowed in their veins. They thought that uniforms and weapons could not have destroyed their human nature. But reality proved that they were bloodthirsty beasts. On the most

---

6. Donald A. Jordan, *The Northern Expedition: China's Revolution of 1926–1928* (Honolulu: The University Press of Hawaii, 1976), pp. 8–9.
7. Colin Mackerras, *Modern China: A Chronology from 1842 to the Present* (San Francisco: Freeman, 1982), p. 302.
8. See the illustrations at the front of Shanghai shehui kexue yuan lishi yanjiusuo, ed. *Wusa yundong shiliao* (Shanghai: Shanghai renmin chubanshe, 1981), n.p.
9. Richard W. Rigby, *The May 30 Movement: Events and Themes* (Canberra: Australian National University Press, 1980), p. vii.

crowded street of the city they deliberately slaughtered unarmed people. For this there was no precedent in Chinese history. The imperialist oppression that had endured for so many years ached like a deep wound in [his] heart. He struggled inwardly. He felt the time for patience was over. He felt he wanted to spill his blood, to sacrifice his young life that he might show that not all among this people were lambs that allowed themselves to be led without resistance to slaughter. He looked again at the corpse of the murdered child. His eyes shone with fire, his whole body began to burn as though on fire, his heart beat violently.[10]

Ba Jin's words reflect what a modern Chinese account calls the "change in political atmosphere" that had been developing since even before the first shots were fired at Huangdu.[11] I have already recounted some of the objective changes that brought this about: the utter breakdown of loyalties within the previously dominant Zhili group, the disbandment or reorganization of long-established military units, the financial panics and commercial crises, the increasing volatility and disorder of society. But the whole of these changes was more than the sum of their parts. The war had an indirect impact that is at least as important as the direct impact, if much harder to assess. In Europe it is standard to point to World War I as marking a clear line of transition in culture and the imagination.[12] Something similar happened in China. Warfare there was on a much smaller scale than in Europe, but it nevertheless shocked and destabilized society. Minds were opened to new ideas; reality seemed to confirm new analyses; the breakdown of the old order made action and expression easier.

The European experience of World War I had produced a body of literature ranging from theories of militarism to artistic expressionism. Like the World War I weapons that had been used to fight it, this new European consciousness began to flood into China as the Chinese attempted to understand the meaning of their war and the resultant collapse of the Northern System that had come in its wake. As in Europe, a whole set of previously marginal political approaches and vocabularies began to move toward the center.

These, above all, came from the Left. Concepts such as militarism,

10. Ba Jin, *Siqu de taiyang* [The Setting Sun] (Shanghai: Kaiming, 1949), pp. 8–9, trans. in Olga Lang, *Pa Chin and His Writings: Chinese Youth Between the Two Revolutions* (Cambridge, Mass.: Harvard University Press, 1967), pp. 89–90, to which reference is made in Nicholas R. Clifford, *Shanghai, 1925: Urban Nationalism and the Defense of Foreign Privilege*, Michigan Papers in Chinese Studies, no. 36 (Ann Arbor: University of Michigan, 1979), p. 16, note 35.
11. Lai Xinxia, Guo Jianlin, and Jiao Jingyi, *Beiyang junfa shigao* (Hubei renmin chubanshe, 1983), p. 310.
12. The classic work is Paul Fussell, *The Great War and Modern Memory* (New York: Oxford University Press, 1975).

imperialism, and revolution began to enter debate and, indeed, to define it as never before. It is worth examining just how this process took place. Arif Dirlik has pointed out that because the arrival of revolutionary ideas and organizations has been so taken for granted in China, scholars consequently have often failed to examine closely enough the precise instrumentalities and social context that give revolution "its meanings and its possibilities."[13] Dirlik's work casts much light on these issues for the May Fourth period, and his approach is suggestive for the post–Zhili–Fengtian War period as well. The changes brought by war did not create new ideas or directly make revolutionaries, but they did create a physical and intellectual environment in which it was possible for new concepts to enter and ultimately to dominate the broader debate.

A good example is the concept of militarism – the source of the familiar idea of the *junfa* [warlord] that still figures so importantly in analyses of this period, even today. Contrary to what is widely believed, "warlord" is neither a Chinese word nor a Chinese concept. Rather, like militarism, it is a European import that first began to be used in China just before the period with which we are concerned. The introduction of the two concepts is probably owed to Chen Duxiu (1879–1942), founder of the Chinese Communist party. Initially, however, they showed little sign of catching on. In one of his essays, Chen tells how the end of World War I was greeted rather differently in China and Japan although both countries had been involved against Germany. When word of victory reached Tianjin, the Chinese students there had taken to the streets in celebration. Chen recounts how they constructed a "national spirit boat" [*guohunzhou*][14] in which two students sat, one made up as Guan Yu (d. A.D. 219), the famous general who came in the Qing dynasty to be venerated as the Chinese god of war, and the other as Yue Fei (1103–1142), the patriotic hero of the Southern Song. Chen was struck and a bit discouraged by just how traditional the Tianjin victory celebration was. It drew upon a traditional Chinese vocabulary of martiality: like patriots in Europe who expressed their understanding of the Great War (World War I) by referring to the age of chivalry and knighthood, the Chinese students of Tianjin looked to the past. Evidently they saw nothing inherently wrong with warfare or the military; they were only concerned that their cause and their nation should be victorious.

13. Arif Dirlik, *The Origins of Chinese Communism* (New York: Oxford University Press, 1989), 257–8.
14. The idea of *guohun* or "national spirit" [or "soul"] was an important feature of the new Chinese patriotism that was developed under the Qing in the late nineteenth and early twentieth centuries. See Laurence A. Schneider, "National Essence and the New Intelligentsia," in *The Limits of Change: Essays on Conservative Alternatives in Republican China*, ed. Charlotte Furth (Cambridge, Mass.: Harvard University Press, 1976), p. 59.

Chen found the activities of the Tianjin students deeply disheartening, and he contrasted them with those of their Japanese counterparts. In Tokyo 5,000 students from Keiō University had marched through the streets to celebrate the victory. But they had borne no images of Japanese heroes of the past. Rather, they carried lanterns and a huge banner on which were written the three character: *tō gunbatsu* ["Down with warlords"]. On the surface the "warlords" that the Japanese students were criticizing were those of Germany, just defeated. But as Chen and everyone else understood, in fact the real targets were not German but Japanese "militarists." In the course of the Taishō period (1912–26), the influence of military figures in Japanese politics had come under increasing attack. Chen Duxiu mentioned two in particular, Nogi Maresuke (1849–1912), who had commanded the siege of Port Arthur, and Tōgō Heihachirō (1848–1934), the victor of Tsushima.[15] Not only were the Japanese students not celebrating past Japanese heroes: they were taking the opportunity presented by the defeat of Germany to attack genuine Japanese military heroes of the present. Chen could not help but be troubled by the contrast between the two groups of students. The Chinese were still "worshipping" Guan Yu and Yue Fei, "the Chinese equivalents of Nogi and Tōgō," whereas the Japanese, by contrast, understood that they were all "militarists" and therefore enemies of the people.[16]

The short article in which Chen contrasted these two vignettes probably represents the first use in modern Chinese of the term *junfa* and an important step in the introduction into China of the understanding of militarism that provides its meaning. From its European origins in the works of Rosa Luxemburg (1870–1919) and others, the Marxist theory of militarism made its way to China by at least two routes: one through Japan, where the words *gunbatsu* [the same characters as the Chinese *junfa* but better translated as "military clique"] and *gunkokushugi* [militarism] had made their appearance in the Taishō era; the other through the Soviet Union, whence rhetoric and images developed fighting the White forces in the civil war were introduced by the Soviet advisers who helped the Kuomintang develop its propaganda effort.[17]

15. Nogi, called the "last samurai," was subsequently military councillor, and from 1907 head of the Peers' School. Tōgō served as chief of the naval general staff (1905–9), supreme military councillor, admiral of the fleet (1913) and supervisor of the Crown Prince's studies. See the entries in Janet E. Hunter, comp., *Concise Dictionary of Modern Japanese History* (Berkeley: University of California Press, 1984), pp. 150, 227.
16. Chen Duxiu, "Dao Junfa" (December 29, 1918), in *Chen Duxiu wenzhang xuanbian* (Beijing: Shenghuo, Dushu, Xinzhi sanlian shudian, 1984), vol. 1, p. 312.
17. For militarism, see Volker R. Berghahn, *Militarism: The History of an International Debate 1861–1979* (New York: St. Martin's, 1982); for the Japanese and Chinese usages see

Although this vocabulary and these images were available in left-wing circles, they did not begin to dominate discussion in China until the period we are discussing. Only in 1924 and 1925 did the word *junfa* or "warlord" begin fully to displace other terms, signaling an important shift in the way the Chinese understood their society and politics and the pathologies thereof. It makes sense that the wars of 1924 seemed to confirm the reality of the "warlord" for the Chinese just as World War I had for the Europeans.[18]

The related concept of imperialism had also been available in China since the 1910s but, like militarism, gained persuasive power in the aftermath of the war.[19] Its spread owed much to the influence of Sun Yat-sen. Since 1923, when he had reorganized his Kuomintang party along Soviet lines, Sun's political rhetoric had steadily moved Left. Sun's new political emphasis was very much in evidence during his trip north. Following the guidelines of the Communist International, the Second Congress of the Chinese Communist party in July 1922 had passed a resolution pointing out an intensification of imperialism as capitalists turned to the non-European world to recover their war losses. In this process Chinese capital was allying with foreign interests against the interests of the Chinese nation:

As Chinese capitalism has slowly developed, Chinese capitalists are now making an alliance with the feudal warlords in China for the protection of their special interests. For the same reason, the foreign imperialists, whose stake in China is even greater than that of the native capitalists, are also supporting the feudal warlords.

The resolution called on the Chinese people to "overthrow the feudal warlords" and "stop civil wars, so that internal peace can be established within China."[20] In February 1924 the first National Congress of the

Yoshio Matsushita, *Meiji no guntai* (Tokyo: Shubundo, 1963), pp. 183–4; Tadao Kabashima, *Meiji Taishō shingo zokugo jiten* (Tokyo: Tokyōdō, 1985), p. 109; Gao Mingkai and Liu Zhengtan, eds. *Xiandai Hanyu Wailaizi Yanjiu* (Beijing: Wenzi gaige chubanshe, 1958), p. 90; on broader intellectual background see Germaine A. Hoston, *Marxism and the Crisis of Development in Prewar Japan* (Princeton: Princeton University Press, 1986); Arif Dirlik, *Revolution and History: The Origins of Marxist Historiography in China, 1919–1937* (Berkeley: University of California Press, 1978), esp. pp. 21–53; Lee Feigon, *Chen Duxiu: Founder of the Chinese Communist Party* (Princeton: Princeton University Press, 1983); for a general review see Arthur Waldron, "The Warlord: Twentieth Century Chinese Understandings of Violence, Militarism, and Imperialism." *American Historical Review*, 96.4 (October 1991), 1073–1100.

18. On this development, see Waldron, "The Warlord."
19. See Cai Zhongxing, *Diguo zhuyi lilun fazhan shi* (Shanghai: Shanghai renmin chubanshe, 1987).
20. Second Congress, held in Shanghai between July 16 and 23, 1922. Wang Jianmin, *Zhongguo Gongchandang Shigao* (Taibei: n.p., n.d.), vol I, 58–9; trans. in Dun J. Li, *Modern China: From Mandarin to Commissar* (New York: Scribner's, 1978), pp. 197–8.

Kuomintang had approved a united front with the Communist party, under anti-imperialist and antimilitarist slogans. These were repeated in Sun's proclamation of the Northern Expedition of 1924, which, he explained, was "not only against Cao Kun and Wu Peifu, but against all warlords and against the imperialism which supported them. Once imperialism had been overthrown, China would escape its position as a semicolony and create a free and independent state."[21] In the course of his northward progress, Sun would reiterate these themes and repeat his concrete demands. Of these, the most important was for the immediate and unilateral repudiation of the so-called unequal treaties.

In substance this differed little from the policy the Northern government had been following. Until 1925 the Beijing government could and did speak for Chinese nationalism. We have seen in Chapter 1 how its highly professional diplomatic corps had steadily recovered foreign concessions and begun an attempt (greatly boosted by the Washington Conference) to unravel the entire fabric of the treaty system by negotiation and litigation. On March 10, 1923, little more than a year before the outbreak of the Zhili–Fengtian War, the Beijing government had demanded the return by Japan of Lüshun and Dalian and the abrogation of the agreements connected with the Twenty-one Demands of 1915. When this was refused, a demonstration in support of the Chinese demands took place in Shanghai.[22] On the eve of the war Gu Weijun was locked in stubborn combat with the French over the gold franc issue. During the war he showed a stony determination in the face of Japanese demands for reassurances about Manchuria. His implacable nationalism won Gu Weijun considerable prestige at home and abroad. For instance, when his wife, Huang Huilan, daughter of the celebrated overseas Chinese "sugar king" of what is today Indonesia, traveled across the USSR in the winter of 1927, thousands of Chinese laborers waited through snowy nights at Siberian railroad stations to greet her.[23] Recent attention to Gu in the People's Republic of China, culminating with the publication of his memoirs, reflects recognition of just how much he and his government spoke for Chinese nationalism.[24] In the early and middle 1920s Chinese public opinion still looked to the Northern government to take the lead on nationalistic issues. One can

21. Wilbur, *Sun Yat-sen*, pp. 34–5, 257–8. The proclamation of the Northern Expedition of 1924 is found in *Geming wenxian* 10, 1489–1491, and in Milton J. Hsieh, *The Kuomintang: Selected Historical Documents 1894–1969* (New York: St. John's University Press, 1970), pp. 87–90.
22. Mackerras, *Modern China*, p. 290.
23. Madame Wellington Koo with Isabel Taves, *No Feast Lasts Forever* (New York: Quadrangle, 1975), p. 177.
24. *Gu Weijun huiyilu* (Beijing: Zhonghua shuju, 1983).

speculate that had Zhili proved successful in its confrontation with Fengtian, its nationalistic approach would have grown even stronger. But war removed that possibility.

Military defeat undermined the nationalistic credibility of the Northern government. Wu Peifu was eliminated; of the contenders for power, he was the one least involved with foreign interests. His place was taken by Zhang Zuolin, who was rightly perceived as cooperating, if only for tactical reasons, with Japan, and Feng Yuxiang, who drew increasingly close to the Soviet Union. Gu Weijun was replaced as foreign minister first by Wang Zhengting; then the post, although offered to Tang Shaoyi, was vacant until 1925. Wang Zhengting, who was pro-Kuomintang, proved in rhetoric if not in substance to be as strong a Nationalist as Gu had been. But because his government lacked both a firm internal foundation and international recognition, he could not in fact pursue a strong nationalistic agenda.

After the wars of 1924, the Northern government began to forfeit its status as spokesman for Chinese interests, first because its personnel became more inclined to cooperate with foreign powers than their predecessors had been, and second because without a strong base inside China, it was forced to look to one or another Power for support. The immediate post-coup diplomacy, first of the Huang Fu cabinet and then of the Duan administration, was concerned with getting diplomatic recognition back. To do that, however, as the representative in fact of only one military faction in an increasingly divided China, would require making concessions. Sensing that China was weak, the Powers sought reconfirmation of their privileges while dragging their feet over matters already agreed, such as the convening of the Tariff Conference and the Commission on Extraterritoriality. The weak Beijing government had little choice but to acquiesce, and it is not surprising that previously intractable issues, such as the gold franc dispute, were solved by Chinese concessions under the Duan administration.

Duan Qirui's statement that he would increase China's credit abroad was designed to secure the support of the Powers, which was crucial to his plans for reconstructing the Northern government. But it opened him to radical criticisms whose credibility had been greatly increased by the chaos of the war. The Northern leaders, whose attempt to unify China by force had just come crashing down around them, were increasingly unable to provide any convincing justification for their activities beyond personal self-interest.

Sun Yat-sen, by contrast, offered a coherent (if arguably inaccurate) account of why China was in chaos and how it had to change. China was the victim of imperialism, a force whose machinations sustained the activities of the generals who had just laid waste to important sections of the country. Instead of temporizing with the foreign powers, it was time for China to stand up and simply end the imperialist presence.

As Sun Yat-sen traveled north, he proclaimed the need to repudiate all the "unequal treaties." Welcoming crowds greeted Sun wherever he went. They were organized by party workers who had been sent to the major industrial centers after the Kuomintang national congress of February 1924, when the united front with the Communists had been approved. As Sun made his demands they received organized echoes: the slogans "fandi feiyue" ["oppose imperialism, abolish the treaties"] and "zhichi Sun Zhongshan zhaokai guomin huiyi" ["Support Dr. Sun in calling a National People's Assembly"] were widely disseminated. In Beijing, Tianjin, and Shanghai there appeared groups belonging to the "fan diguo zhuyi da tongmeng" ["great anti-imperialist alliance"].[25] Telegrams began to arrive in favor of Sun's National People's Assembly: by November 1924 groups in Shanghai, Nanjing, Guangzhou, Xuzhou, Anhui, Hunan, Hubei, Zhejiang, Beijing, Tianjin, Baoding, Jinan, Qingdao, Shijiazhuang, and Zhangjiakou had all made their sentiments heard.[26]

Sun Yat-sen's new rhetoric of anti-imperialism and antimilitarism filled the conceptual vacuum in China after the Zhili–Fengtian War just as its antecedents in Europe had filled a similar vacuum immediately after World War I. This development was part of a general shift to the Left in Chinese political debate during this period, easy to understand if one considers what had been happening in China. It permitted the Kuomintang (and to a lesser extent, the Communists) to capture the flag and become recognized as the "authentic" voice of the Chinese nation.

This patriotic movement in turn invigorated left-wing politics. The Kuomintang congress of February 1924 had sent activists to major cities to undertake textbook-style organizing activities, but these had scarcely set China aflame. Thus:

[I]n Tianjin, activists founded a Local Executive Committee of the Socialist Youth League and a Local Executive Committee of the CCP. The former concentrated on student work, while the party's Executive Committee assigned cadres, usually from an intellectual background, to organize railroad workers, printers, dockworkers, and mill operatives. Again, initial contact was made with mill workers by founding two common schools (*pingmin xuexiao*).[27]

---

25. Lai et al., *Beiyang junfa shigao*, p. 310.
26. Ibid., p. 314.
27. Gail Hershatter, *The Workers of Tianjin, 1900–1949* (Stanford: Stanford University Press, 1986), p. 212.

Until the war, there was little real progress. Then the May Thirtieth Movement swept up society. In the Northeast the movement rippled through the territories where Japanese influence was strongest. As the nature of the opportunity became clear, the Kuomintang began to send organizers north from Shanghai, Beijing, and Tianjin. In Shenyang, on June 5, Chinese workers at the British–American Tobacco Company went on strike. On the same day students at a British-run medical college convened a meeting at which it was decided to demonstrate in front of the government headquarters. On June 10, a large and initially peaceful protest began, which the authorities had considerable difficulty in dispersing. Eventually police and soldiers were used to break it up. And the movement spread to other places in Manchuria by June 15. By June 21 the authorities were consulting with the Japanese consul in Changchun about how to deal with the trouble. In faraway Qiqihar the students were sent home early for summer vacation.[28]

On June 1, 1925, the Tianjin students went on strike and distributed leaflets describing the Shanghai events to city dwellers. The various political organizations founded by the insurgent parties in the previous year, such as the Anti-Imperialist Alliance (*fan diguozhuyi da tongmeng*) and the People's Assembly (*guomin huiyi*), began to sponsor emergency meetings. The *National Salvation Daily* (*Jiuguo ribao*) began to be published. On June 5 10,000 people protested in Tianjin, and on June 11 a Japanese-run paper, the *Tianjin Daily News*, was struck. Thus, two weeks after May 30, substantial protest was already under way. It increased in scale dramatically. On June 14, perhaps 200,000 demonstrators marched through the city, and six days later the first strikes at textile and printing plants got under way. All classes in Chinese society were outraged by the May 30 incident, but as the Kuomintang and the Communist party increasingly attempted to mobilize patriotic feeling for their internal political goals, some Chinese became alarmed. When a great demonstration was announced for the one-month anniversary of the incident on June 30, the Tianjin General Chamber of Commerce (*zongshanghui*) prohibited shop workers from participating, but to no effect, and the largest demonstration yet was successfully carried off.[29]

The Kuomintang and radical organizers who had come to Tianjin in 1924 had accomplished very little initially. But now, with the demonstrations, came increasing success in organizing labor and other sectors of society against both foreigners and the government. On July 8, with strikes spreading, a Tianjin general labor union (*zonggonghui*) was

28. Zeng Fanxiu and Liu Xiaohui, "Wusa yundong zai Dongbei" *Dongbei shida xuebao* 3 (1981), 96–101.
29. Nan Shi, "Tianjin de Wusa fandi yundong," *Lishi jiaoxue* 1965, no. 5, 37–8.

founded. Later in the same month Chinese seamen employed on British and Japanese vessels began jumping ship, and a mariners' union was established. On August 10, more than 2,000 dock workers struck shipping lines serving Dalian and Osaka.[30]

Missions and foreign-run education were deeply affected by the May Thirtieth Movement. At St. John's University a series of clashes between F. L. Hawks Pott (1864–1947), the president and a man by no means unsympathetic to China (as a young Anglican priest he had braved opinion and married a respectable Chinese woman), and students over participation in the Shanghai student strike and the flying of the Chinese flag at half staff, among other issues, led many Chinese students and faculty to resign and found a new institution, Guanghua University. In Guangzhou the vice-president of Lingnan University, Alexander Baxter, initially opposed student participation in a protest parade. Eventually he was forced to resign. As Jessie Lutz notes, in both cases the initial incidents "were minor and might have been settled peaceably in other years," but in 1925, neither the popular mood nor the structure of authority made that likely.[31]

Some students were so dissatisfied that they withdrew and transferred to state institutions, leading in the fall of 1925 to a noticeable decline in enrollment. In June and July the Seventh Congress of the Student Union of China, meeting in Shanghai, called for new attacks on Christianity. In August the Anti-Christian Federation renewed its campaign against Christianity and mission schools. These were natural developments, for as targets neither Britain nor Japan was entirely satisfactory. The Christian colleges, by contrast, were concrete presences that could be attacked.[32]

The most important development of 1925, however, was the emergence of a new style of politics. Students of nationalism have long been aware of how politicians seeking to harness patriotic sentiment will each try to adopt stronger demands than the other, leading to an escalation that can polarize internal politics while making any genuine diplomacy virtually impossible.[33] Just this happened in the post-1924 period, as the political division of China among contending military groups was redefined by

30. Ibid., pp. 38–9.
31. Jessie Gregory Lutz, *China and the Christian Colleges, 1850–1950* (Ithaca, N.Y.: Cornell University Press, 1971), pp. 248–9.
32. Ibid., pp. 250–1. For enrollment figures, see Earl H. Cressy, *Christian Higher Education: A Study for the Year 1925–1926*, China Christian Education Association Bulletin no. 20. Shanghai, 1928, p. 27.
33. See R. S. Milne, *Politics in Ethnically Bipolar States: Guyana, Malaysia, Fiji* (Vancouver and London: University of British Columbia Press, 1981), esp. pp. 184–9 where he discusses the concept of "outbidding."

the suddenly galvanized rhetoric of nationalism to produce a complex patriotic bidding war. The May Thirtieth Movement offered new hope in particular to Feng Yuxiang, the man who, as we have seen, the others were trying to force out. In 1925, with Duan and Zhang Zuolin looking for foreign respectability and support, Feng Yuxiang and the Southern insurgents had the opportunity to capture the ground of more radical nationalism.

By May 30, 1925, Feng had been almost completely marginalized in Chinese politics. His rivals had forced him from Beijing, and early in 1925 he had moved his headquarters to Kalgan [Zhangjiakou], where the old caravan route to Mongolia crossed the Ming Great Wall defense line. In Kalgan, Feng was far from Chinese centers of intrigue but just across the border from areas of Soviet interest and control. The chaos in China had presented the USSR and the Kuomintang with new opportunities, so that both made overtures to Feng, intermediated by one of his advisers, Xu Qian, who was a longtime supporter of the Kuomintang. In April 1925 Feng accepted Kuomintang political workers in his army in return for Soviet military instructors and desperately needed aid.[34]

The patriotic wave brought opportunities to Feng. When word of the May 30th incident reached his headquarters at Kalgan, he pulled out all the patriotic stops. All troops were ordered to wear black bands of mourning on their left arms, to be removed only when the situation was completely resolved. A map of "national humiliation" was drawn, in which Hong Kong, Taiwan, and other areas under "imperialist occupation" were colored red with blood. All soldiers were to look at it every day. The regular singing of a song lamenting national humiliation was ordered, 10,000 pictures of the martyrs of Nanjing were printed and distributed, and the opera *Shanghai de beiju* [The Tragedy of Shanghai] was produced. On June 6 Feng and other commanders sent a telegram to the Duan Qirui government urging it to do what was necessary and offering their military assistance. Feng further suggested that the coffins containing the martyrs should be sent around the country and halt for a time in various cities to build up the anti-imperialist feelings of the people. On June 8 and 12 Feng sent telegrams to the various student assemblies, as well as to the merchant associations, suggesting his willingness to serve. And on June 12 he addressed the Zhangjiakou students. When he spoke of the horrible killings by the imperialists, they burst into tears. The actions Feng called for paralleled those the students advocated.

34. BDRC, vol. 2, 40.

Shall we shut the doors and scold the enemy? Shall we run out into the street, grab a foreigner and beat him up? Crying...has no use. We need to break economic relations, strike in industry, strike against schools, close the markets, in order to force imperialism to accept the conditions the people have established.[35]

It made political sense for Feng Yuxiang to take up the more extreme May Thirtieth Movement position. After long and difficult negotiations, Britain and the Northern government were moving toward a resolution of sorts in connection with the incident; popular passions gradually cooled, and as for the various radical organizations the movement had left in its wake, many were systematically eliminated by Zhang Zuolin as he attempted to consolidate Fengtian control in North and Central China. By winter 1925, Feng's Guominjun was locked in a war for survival against Zhang Zuolin's superior Fengtian forces. So Feng Yuxiang sought to unleash again against Zhang the passions of the summer. Thus when the Guominjun entered Tianjin on December 24, the new authorities released political prisoners, legalized banned organizations, and turned over to the unions property belonging to the Fengtian group.[36] Even after the Guominjun had been driven out again, Feng Yuxiang continued to use patriotic strategies.

The same political pressures began to affect foreigners. It was a trying time for missionaries. An examination of the mission yearbooks and annual reports for the years from 1924 to 1926 reveals a sudden preoccupation with an unexpectedly explosive nationalism. As one missionary wrote in 1926:

The situation was much more strained than any account will enable the people at home to understand. There have been anti-foreign and anti-Christian outbursts in China before but none where the Chinese Christians were so swept by the general agitation that they separated even from their oldest missionary friends.[37]

Quite understandably, many missionaries began to join with the Chinese in demanding an end to foreign privilege. Objectively, the new Chinese nationalism had been made possible by the split in the Beijing government and by the destruction and chaos of war. Subjectively it had also been stimulated by a redefinition of China's own social pathology, one that, as we have seen, drew on a foreign vocabulary. Not surprisingly, it

---

35. Li Guangyi and Ji Xinbao, "Wusa yundong zhong de Feng Yuxiang," *Henan Daxue Xuebao*, 1985, no. 4, pp. 123–6.
36. Nan Shi, "Tianjin de Wusa fandi yundong," pp. 37–9.
37. The Presbyterian Church in the U.S.A. Board of Foreign Missions, *Report on China and Japan, 1926* (New York: The Board of Foreign Missions of the Presbyterian Church in the U.S.A., 1927), p. 78.

struck a responsive chord among foreigners, both those who lived in China – mostly missionaries – and the diplomats who dealt with China, as well as in public opinion overseas. All began to shift their own assessments of China and its future, and as had been true at the time of the Washington Conference, these shifts in foreign expectations had an impact on the ways in which the Chinese defined their own political strategies. After May 30th more and more members of the foreign community, including some of the diplomats, were convinced "that it was no longer feasible or even desirable to maintain the position which they had enjoyed in China up to the time of the movement."[38]

Most diplomats were bewildered. John Van Antwerp MacMurray had just been named minister to China, the post he had craved throughout his career, and was still at sea when the May 30 incident occurred. Neither his new job nor China turned out to be what he had expected. MacMurray was not, as he is sometimes portrayed, a man fundamentally unsympathetic to Chinese aspirations. But he was someone who, ever since the Washington Conference, had envisioned an orderly and legal process to meet those aspirations – not an unrealistic hope, for it had been spelled out in the treaties and the Beijing government shared it. But the collapse of the North and the rise of radical politics in the chaotic aftermath of war made its realization impossible. So from the moment of his arrival MacMurray found himself dealing with a situation unlike anything for which his previous experience had prepared him. He recognized this fact: After a few months in his new post he wrote to Assistant Secretary of State Nelson T. Johnson (1887–1954) that he had "deceived himself [while in Washington], going on thinking under the illusion that China was the same last May as it was in 1918," and confessed that he had spent his first seven months as minister "unlearning whatever ideas I had formed as counselor in days gone by." Later he would tell his mother that the situation was going "beyond Alice-in-Wonderland in sheer insanity.... What is going to come of all of it, I can't guess. I do not pretend to see as much as forty-eight hours into the future."[39]

For a dozen years the Powers had framed their ideas about China's future in terms of the Washington System and worked together to minimize their differences in the interest of maintaining a unified China

38. Rigby, *The May 30th Movment*, p. vii.
39. MacMurray to Johnson, November 13, 1925; MacMurray to his mother, February 21, 1926, and April 11, 1926; MacMurray Papers. Quoted in Thomas Buckley, "John Van Antwerp MacMurray: The Diplomacy of an American Mandarin," in *Diplomats in Crisis: United States–Chinese–Japanese Relations, 1919–1941*, ed. Richard Dean Burns and Edward M. Bennett (Santa Barbara: Clio Books, 1974), p. 36.

that would be able to fill the place defined for it by the Washington treaties. For China to do that, however, demanded that it have a generally acknowledged central government. This it did until the period with which we are concerned. Indeed, the Powers tended to take that government absolutely for granted: alternately pressuring it, lecturing it, denying it money and weapons, while blithely assuming that such actions could have no consequences for the general political stability of China. Now all that had changed. With stability breaking down, the Powers began to rethink their positions – and to embrace, albeit unenthusiastically, the new definitions that had become dominant since the war.

The change even extended to literature and the arts. I have already quoted Ba Jin's description of the May 30 incident itself. In its wake, authors began increasingly to apply radical analyses to the reality around them. A good example is the work of Mao Dun (Shen Yanbing, 1896–1981). His account, in *Midnight* (1933), which is set in 1930, of how the Shanghai bond markets rose and fell as warlord troops advanced and withdrew is unforgettable and could well describe the financial panic of 1924 narrated in Chapter 6.[40] The hero is Wu Sunfu, a patriotic industrialist who is attempting to develop his enterprises free of foreign capital, on a purely Chinese base. He is also a financial speculator, and with his brother-in-law, a banker, he shorts the bond market as a civil war rages:

Even if we had covered yesterday, we should still have made a loss. The situation's quite clear: what with the Hankou area being threatened, and the fighting along the Longhai line dragging on, prices are bound to drop sooner or later. If only we can stop the rise and keep the price down, we've got nothing to lose.[41]

But interventions by bankers and speculators keep prices high. At the book's climax even his banker brother-in-law abandons him, and the patriot Wu Sunfu, who is striving to build Chinese industry free of foreign capital, is ruined.

"What!" he gasped. "Up again? . . . Somebody buying in while we're holding the price down? . . . Who? . . . What! My brother-in-law? . . . Well, I'll be damned! . . . We're sunk, then! Finished."[42]

Midnight is a novel on a grand scale: a panorama of Shanghai at a certain moment in its history, and critics quite understandably have focused their attention on Mao Dun's craft and art. As Prusek points out,

40. See, for example, Mao Tun, *Midnight* (Hong Kong: C & W Publishing, 1976), pp. 322–3.
41. Mao Tun, *Midnight*, p. 268.
42. Ibid., p. 522.

however, Mao Dun does not simply depict; he analyzes. His work is animated by a "striving to identify ever more precisely the forces at work in society," a striving that "determines to a great extent the way in which he organizes his materials."[43] Several authors have explored this aspect of his work.[44] In *Midnight*, the fundamental structure appears to draw on the theories of Rudolf Hilferding (1877–1941). Indeed, in its implicit economic and social theories, the book appears to be virtually a *roman à clef* of Hilferding's contention that industrial capital (Wu Sunfu) and financial capital (Wu's brother-in-law) are ultimately antagonistic. The book's message is that what ultimately dooms Wu's industrial enterprises is not warfare or illiquidity but economic conflict.[45] While Mao Dun's thought and art have many sources, it is hard not to suspect that financial crises caused by war spurred him on the search for inclusive understanding that made him a pioneer of left-wing writing in China.

Parallel changes occurred in the visual arts – for example, in the ways cartooning presented soldiers and war. By the 1910s humorous sketches of Chinese soldiers were appearing in magazines like *Shanghai Puck*, founded by the pioneering cartoonist Shen Bochen (1889–1920), which sold about 10,000 copies per issue in Shanghai and the Yangzi valley.[46] Shen's early sketches of soldiers were clearly influenced by Western models. "The Struggle Between South and North" [*NanBei zhi zheng*] published in 1918 is a good example. It shows two soldiers in Western uniform confronting each other with sword and bayonet while standing on a prostrate figure in more traditional garb, labeled "China."[47] Although the cartoon makes a political statement, it still has a certain whimsy; it remains a cartoon. In this – as in its style – it is reminiscent of the work of William C. Morris (1874–1940), a frequent contributor to the New York *Puck* during those years. He was known for his "easy cartoony style that was pleasing to the eye" and which "by virtue of its lightness generally precluded any fierce partisanship."[48] The other great

43. Jaroslav Prusek, *Three Sketches of Chinese Literature* (Prague: Oriental Institute in Academia, 1969), p. 34.
44. For example, V. F. Sorokin, *Tvorcheskii Put' Mao Duna* (Moscow: Izdatel'stvo Vostochnoi Literarury, 1962); V. Rudman, ed. and trans.; *Pered Rassvetom*, by Shen Yanbing (Moscow: Gosudarstvennoe Izdatel'stvo Khudozhestvennoi Literatury, 1952), pp. 3–14.
45. Hilferding published *Finance Capital* in 1910. See Tom Bottomore, "Hilferding, Rudolf" in *A Dictionary of Marxist Thought*, p. 203.
46. See Bi Keguan and Huang Yuanlin, *Zhongguo manhuashi* (Beijing: Wenhua yishu chubanshe, 1986), pp. 47–56.
47. Ibid., plate 68.
48. Maurice Horn, ed., *The World Encyclopedia of Cartoons* (London and New York: Gale Research Company in association with Chelsea House, 1980), vol. 1, pp. 400–1.

political cartoonist of the time, Dan Duyu (1896–1972), portrayed soldiers more critically than did Shen. His visual vocabulary was borrowed not from the Left but probably from Louis Raemakers (1869–1956), who chronicled World War I as a procession of barbaric Germans, plucky Dutch lads in wooden shoes, and undraped ladies representing democracy. Dan's lady with the lamp on the cover of his "Album depicting national humiliation" [*Guochi huapu*, 1919] is reminiscent of Raemaekers, as is his use of the skeleton in "Welcoming the specter" ["Yin gui ru men"] (1919).[49] *Shanghai Puck* closed in 1918, and Chinese cartooning slumped. Recovery in the mid-1920s brought a new approach and a new set of visual images.

With the May Thirtieth Movement came new and often bluntly didactic cartoons. They were visual equivalents of *Midnight*, inhabited by the same archetypical characters – workers, warlords, imperialists, capitalists – all borrowed ultimately from Europe but applied to local subjects. In 1925 revolutionary artists turned out a broadsheet (*huabao*) showing General Wu Peifu as a small dog held on a short leash by a dominating figure of Uncle Sam. Lest anyone miss the point, this was labeled "The truth about imperialism and warlords." Among the most striking examples of the new sensibilities are the works of Huang Wennong (d. 1934). Huang was a master of attacks on imperialism, and it would be no surprise to find his work in publications of the Left. In 1925 he was invited to contribute to the long-established and popular *Dongfang zazhi* [*Eastern Miscellany*]. He even designed the cover for the special edition devoted exclusively to May 30th. So virulent was his anti-British and anti-American cartooning that it led to a lawsuit in Shanghai.[50] Much careful investigation will be required before all of the routes by which Western political categories and artistic images reached China. But there can be no doubt that, particularly following the wars of 1924, the climate there was increasingly receptive to them.

With this pervasive change in the way China was conceived and portrayed, a whole genre of foreign writing moved toward its terminal point as well. The essentially prewar sensibility was finished. It had been full of romance and condescension and claimed to cherish the arts and culture of old China even though it refused, in the classic fashion of colonial writing, to take seriously the politics or aspirations of the place it described. It was replaced by a new revolutionary realism, just as romantic and distorted, but in new ways. The novella of the season in

49. Bi and Huang, plates 73, 75. Compare J. Murray Allison, comp., *Raemaekers' Cartoon History of the War* (New York: Century, 1918), vol. II, pp. 146, 194; vol. III, p. 206.
50. Bi and Huang, *Manhua shi*, plate 80; ibid., 76–8.

Peking in 1924 was "La Chine en Folie" by Albert Londres (d. 1932), an exoticizing account of the country and its people – of Zhang Zuolin ["Fantastique histoire"], Beijing ["la ville chimérique de l'anarchie totale"], Shanghai ["Un monstre"], and finally China itself ["En vérité, je vous dis qu'elle est folle"] – that captures perfectly the peculiarly detached, almost dissociated, sense of China cultivated by some foreigners of the time who were resolutely unaware of the deadly seriousness of Chinese politics and war.[51] Appropriately, Londres's work in turn provides the vacation reading matter for a character in Ann Bridge's *Peking Picnic* (1932), another masterpiece of the old genre set in the late 1920s. In *Peking Picnic*, the characters still use the old vocabulary of *dujun* warfare: thus Miss Hubbard, the infinitely resourceful lady's maid at the British legation, correctly predicts war, because "the boys were saying at the 'Y' this afternoon that one of these Doojoons, as they call them, was setting out to attack Peking."[52] But the genre passed away abruptly as the political events of the late 1920s caught up with the arts in the 1930s. A year after *Peking Picnic*, the defining work of the new genre of romantic realism was published: *Man's Fate* (1933) by André Malraux (1901–76).

Meanwhile, as the diplomats scratched their heads and the Kuomintang moved to take advantage of the situation, the divided Northerners were caught wrong-footed and responded ineffectively. The Powers were deeply worried by the wave of unrest and seem to have expected the Chinese to step in and put it down. But no Chinese government, least of all Duan's at Beijing, could take the side of the foreign Powers against the patriotic outrage of the Chinese people. On the other hand, that patriotic outrage was feeding the Northerners' political enemies, so they did not want to encourage it too much either. The result was a confused policy in which halfhearted efforts were made to suppress the disorder, while a hard-line foreign policy was adopted in dealings with the Powers.

Thus, on June 13 Zhang Xueliang led 2,000 of his troops into Shanghai to restore order there. In Tianjin, with the movement showing no sign of abating, precautions began to be taken. The British sent 400 troops from Shanhaiguan and Qinhuangdao to Tianjin, and secretly hired some White Russians who were trained to operate machine guns. The British and Japanese consuls got in touch with Zhang Zuolin and Li Jinglin, hoping that they would move to restore order. The consuls feared that if Settlement or foreign forces used firearms to put down the

51. Albert Londres, "La Chine en Folie," in *Les oeuvres libres*, no. 30 (December 1923), pp. 231–85.
52. Ann Bridge [pseudonym of (Lady) Mary O'Malley], *Peking Picnic* (Boston: Little, Brown, 1932), p. 33.

trouble it would only exacerbate the situation. The Fengtian generals seem to have shared the foreign view. In August some 8,000 Fengtian troops swept the city, killing dozens of workers and making about 500 arrests. The various unions of students and workers were all prohibited; and with the restoration of firm military control, the revolutionary movement in Tianjin came to an end for the moment.[53] But without its institutional foundation, the Northern System could not be put back together again. Even when military action was taken in some cities, the movement did not come to an end elsewhere. Power had become divided, and although Zhang might lock the radicals up, Feng could be counted on to set them free. It was an entirely new game.

From the beginning, the May Thirtieth Movement has been thought of above all as a psychological event that set in train a whole series of consequences. Chinese scholars call its force "world shaking"; it had "the power to topple mountains and turn over seas."[54] The new consciousness, furthermore, is often portrayed as having galvanized the hitherto inert Chinese masses into action. Wen-Han Kiang, the longtime executive secretary of the Chinese YMCA's student division, calls May Thirtieth "an outburst of the accumulated resentment against the irrationality and injustice of the 'unequal treaties' which the imperialist powers imposed on China."[55] MacMurray describes it as ushering in "a type of nationalism, in which the immemorial Chinese dislike of foreigners and the consciousness of grievance were directed by Communist advisers into a frenzied impulse of defiance and self-assertion."[56] The spark of May Thirtieth is thought of as having set China "aflame with the fever of nationalism."[57] In the mass movement that it sent surging over China, Harold Isaacs saw "a weapon of immense power," one that would sweep a new government to power in less than two years.[58] It confronted the Powers with new and unanticipated demands. "The question was no longer what the Western nations and Japan would

53. Nan Shi, "Tianjin de Wusa," p. 39.
54. Zeng Fanxiu and Liu Xiaohui, "Wusa yundong zai Dongbei" *Dongbei shida xuebao*, 1981, no. 3, p. 96; Zhonggong Tianjin shiwei dangshi ziliao zhengji weiyuanhui et al., eds., *Wusa yundong zai Tianjin*, p. 1.
55. Wen-Han Kiang, *The Chinese Student Movement* (Morningside Heights, N.Y.: King's Crown Press, 1948), p. 84.
56. Arthur Waldron, ed., *How the Peace Was Lost: The 1935 Memorandum "Developments Affecting American Policy in the Far East," Prepared for the State Department by Ambassador John Van Antwerp MacMurray* (Hoover Archival Documentaries. Stanford: Hoover Institution Press, 1992), p. 60.
57. Warren I. Cohen, *America's Response to China: An Interpretative History of Sino-American Relations*, 2nd ed. (New York: Knopf, 1980), p. 111.
58. Harold R. Isaacs, *The Tragedy of the Chinese Revolution*, 2nd ed., rev. (Stanford: Stanford University Press, 1961), p. 73.

demand of China, but what an intensely vocal and nationalistic China would demand of them."[59] A new concept had been born: for 1924 the *Readers' Guide to Periodical Literature* lacks even a heading under China for "Nationalist movement"; for 1925 it lists 155 items under that classification.

Nineteen twenty-five saw a fundamental shift not only in the objective facts of Chinese politics but also in the ways that politics were understood. The change was identified then, as it is now, as the rise of nationalism. In the sense in which students of nationalism now examine the phenomenon, May 30, 1925, is a classic example of the "national moment" – the instant when a whole series of quantitative changes, long accumulating, are transmuted into a qualitative shift in consciousness, a shift so deep that in retrospect it becomes almost impossible to recover the sense of identity that was superseded. Precisely because it is such a good and well-documented example, 1925 also provides a good perspective from which to reconsider the concept.

59. Dorothy Borg, *American Policy and the Chinese Revolution, 1925–1928* (New York: The American Institute of Pacific Relations, 1947; reprint ed. with new introduction by the author, New York: Octagon Books, 1968), p. 1.

The War as seen by the *New York American*. (From *China Weekly Review* 30.9, November 1, 1924, p. 268.)

Warlord fighting puppets and foreign puppeteers: cartoon from *Kladderadatsch* reproduced in *Dongfang zazhi* (Eastern Miscellany), 32 (1925), 13.

Soviet-influenced cartoon, prepared by Kuomintang First Army political department, 1926. The club is labeled "power of the masses"; the two figures being clubbed are "Imperialism" and "Warlord". (From Bi Keguan and Huang Yuanlin, *Zhongguo manhuashi*. Beijing: Wenhua yishu chubanshe, 1986, plate 95.)

(*Below*) The May Thirtieth Movement: communist leader Li Lisan (1899–1967) addresses a crowd in Shanghai. (From *Wusa yundong shiliao*, ed. Shanghai Shehui Kexue Yuan, lishi yanjiuso. Shanghai: Shanghai renminchubanshe, 1986, vol. 2.)

Conclusion

The transformation that seemed to have begun in 1925 moved steadily toward completion. The unrest that had begun with the May 30 demonstration in Shanghai was never contained, and it prompted the proclamation two days later by the Kuomintang of a new National government of the Republic of China in Guangzhou. A year to the day after that, as the Northern military factions were slipping into an exhausting war among themselves, Chiang Kai-shek ordered the beginning of the Northern Expedition, and 100,000 Kuomintang troops set out from Guangzhou. Two years earlier such a move would have been suicidal: Chiang's troops never could have matched the army, for example, that Wu Peifu mobilized against Zhang Zuolin. But the wars of 1924 had so disrupted and weakened the North that – as Chiang Kai-shek understood – his forces now had a good chance even though they were outnumbered, on paper at least, by those of the Northern government. Fighting would be bitter and close in places during the great civil war that followed, but Chiang's assessment was ultimately vindicated. The correlation of forces in China had changed, to the grave disadvantage of the Northern government. By April 1927 Chiang Kai-shek had captured Nanjing and established his new National government there; in the spring of 1928 his triumph was complete in the capital region as well. On June 3 a defeated Zhang Zuolin boarded a special for Mukden; three days later Beijing fell to the army of Yan Xishan, a general who had begun to join Wu Peifu four years earlier when his success looked likely, and who now threw in his lot with the new victors. In short order followed a series of symbolic changes in geographical names that would endure until 1949. The northern city that had been China's political center since the Yongle period of the Ming, Beijing [northern capital], became Beiping [northern peace], Zhili became Hebei, and the seat of political authority shifted south to Nanjing [southern capital] in the Yangzi valley.

263

These were momentous and inspiring events that demand interpretation. So far our chronicle has provided such interpretation indirectly by looking not so much at the climactic events themselves as at the neglected and complex developments that we have argued made them possible. In conclusion, it is perhaps worth looking more directly at the implications of our story.

On a factual level, we have sought to paint a new picture of the years from 1916 to 1928. Chinese society during this period was not in quite the pathological state sometimes portrayed. There was substantial economic growth, more freedom of the press and of expression than in any subsequent period until very recently, and a flowering of culture – for example, in the private educational and related institutions across the spectrum from Christian denominational colleges to the workers' schools of the Left. Nor was the central government of the time the nullity it is sometimes assumed to have been. This was a period of professedly parliamentary rule, a rarity in Chinese history, and though its accomplishments were few and real power was usually elsewhere, the fact that the parliament remained a focus of legitimacy almost to the end of the period should not be ignored. Cabinet members of the time were among the most personally impressive of any period in twentieth-century Chinese history. And although the reach of the central government was limited, it was not nonexistent. The military, as we have seen, was far better organized and equipped than is often assumed. This was not a time of independent warlords charging around without reference to one another; if anything the fighting we have examined has been striking for the degree of strategic coordination it demonstrated. In any case, the stereotype of the warlord became popular only toward the end of the time we have discussed. As for the wars themselves, they were caused in China during this period – as in Europe and elsewhere – as much by complex institutional and political failure as by individual personal ambitions. So, broadly stated, we have argued that it is profoundly misleading to understand the period from 1916 to 1928 as a chaotic interlude, a sort of confused interregnum, between the traditional order of the Qing and the definitive modern order of either the Kuomintang or the Communists. As is now becoming clearer and clearer, the appearance of unity and order created by those two parties was superficial and short-lived. In fact, that illusory order is the anomaly in modern Chinese history. Normality is closer to what we call "chaos" in the period this book has treated – the perennial and inconclusive quests for power, the alliances and clashes of groups, the flourishing of every kind of diversity, all within governmental structures whose control is only partial.

More specifically, our story has been about power – about the collapse in 1924 of the power of the Chinese central government, then under the control of the Zhili group, and the ensuing consequences. This power was to a very large degree military. It rested on a superior military establishment, with the ability, demonstrated clearly over the previous four years, to humble its military adversaries. And it vanished when that military superiority collapsed. It was thus power of a fairly straightforward and empirically measurable kind: soldiers, guns, warships, aircraft. It was ability, in this case ability to coerce, close to the root meaning of the word *power* itself, from *pouvoir*, and ultimately the Latin *posse*, meaning "to be able."

It is clear that military coercive ability was only one dimension of power during this period. Just as important was the political. China, as we have stated repeatedly, has always been too large to be ruled by force alone. Force is therefore useful not only when it coerces but also when it translates into political persuasion – when it wins over people who could oppose or resist but choose to align with someone they believe will prove to be a winner. This is the political defined in a straightforward way, referring to institutions and individuals, meetings and votes, alliances, defections, and so forth: political in its root sense, having to do with the activities of citizens and the state.

Furthermore, as we have analyzed them, both the military and the political dimensions of power during this period were realms of voluntary action and contingency. Thus, the wars we have described could well have ended differently than they did. In the Jiangsu–Zhejiang conflict, for example, Qi Xieyuan's forces almost scored a decisive breakthrough at Liuhezhen on September 4. They were turned back only when reinforcements arrived in the nick of time, reinforcements from the Fujian forces of Yang Huazhao, whose improbable journey to Shanghai we have traced. Such a breakthrough would have ended the war less than a week after it started, brought Shanghai into the Zhili camp at very little cost, and stopped the Zhili–Fengtian War before it had started. All of this is entirely conceivable militarily. But its consequences would have extended far beyond military operations or their absence. A strengthened central government, under almost unchallenged Zhili control, would have been the probable result. Similar contingencies can be envisioned for Zhang Zuolin and the other players. The same is true for political action. Cao Kun's decision to seek the presidency was one of the fundamental factors that weakened the Zhili group during this period. If Cao had left Li Yuanhong undisturbed – he certainly could have done – history would have been different. Specific and contingent actions and events in both the military and political realms had major, even decisive significance to general outcomes – including the beginning of the Chinese National Revolution in 1925. For had the wars of 1924 consolidated Beijing's strength – as they could have – instead of weakening it, the Northern Expedition would never have taken place, and the whole shape of East Asian history in the late 1920s and early 1930s would probably have been very different.

Such possibilities, however interesting and even informative it may be to consider them, belong to the realm of speculation. In analyzing what did take place during this period, my basic approach has been to move the study of war higher up on the interpretative agenda. I have suggested that warfare can provide a framework in which social, economic, and even intellectual change become intelligible. More specifically, I have maintained that the destruction and disruption caused by the wars of 1924 were indispensable preconditions for the success of the May Thirtieth Movement and the Nationalist Revolution that followed. I have, in other words, tried to provide hitherto missing social, institutional, and military context.

Yet, with few exceptions, this is not how the history of the period has been written up to now. We do not possess a comprehensive political and military narrative for it in Chinese or any other language. Specific events, as well as the names of political and military (as opposed to cultural) figures, are largely unknown. Conventionally, the aspects of power that have been documented and analyzed are more likely to be exclusively cultural or linguistic rather than political or military. And instead of approaching the period as a sequence of events and contingencies, historians have focused on other themes. Sometimes this has simply meant other subject matter: thus, we have some excellent economic, social, intellectual, and cultural history for the period. But sometimes the inattention to events and contingencies reflects something more: the conviction that general mechanisms can be identified and that their impetus in this period is so decisive as to make political and military events almost ephemeral by comparison. Two sorts of mechanisms are regularly proposed: class differentiation, and development of national consciousness.

We have seen, in the "Introduction" and in Chapter 11, that these interpretations were being applied to the events of the 1920s even as they were still unfolding. On class, some Chinese increasingly adopted an understanding of the structure of their society that had its origins in the West and that was intimately tied up with the revolutionary hopes and disappointments of Europe and the USSR. Likewise, particularly among Western observers, there was a tendency to see the events in China as the product of a rising nationalism similar to the one they believed was emerging in Europe and all over the world in the post–World War I period.

Both were reasonable approaches. To contemplate the lot of, say, Shanghai factory workers, was almost immediately to think of Engels or Marx, or at least Charles Dickens. Likewise, the patriotism of the early Chinese Republic and its desire to wipe away national humiliations would seem familiar to anyone who knew the stories of European nationalism. Since the culminating event in our narrative, the May Thirtieth Movement, is generally interpreted in this way, let us now examine more carefully what the concept of nationalism can and cannot tell us about it.

In the period following World War I, the nationalist interpretation of history in general was expounded in an enormous literature, which ranged from Carlton Hayes's (1882–1964) scholarly *Historical Evolution of Modern Nationalism* to George Antonius's (1892–1942) popular *Arab Awakening* to Arnold Toynbee's (1889–1975) *Study of History*, all of which took nationalism as a fundamental explanatory concept.[1] It was easy to see events in China as part of the same pattern. Toynbee, who wrote the analyses of China for this period in the highly influential *Survey of International Affairs*, certainly thought they were; so too did Harley Farnsworth MacNair, long a faculty member at St. John's University in Shanghai, who published a book called *China's New Nationalism* in 1926.[2]

The writing of Chinese history has changed remarkably little since. To read almost any book on China's history after the end of the Qing is to be confronted repeatedly with the idea of nationalism as an animating and directing power. By the late nineteenth century, Paul Cohen tells us, "Nationalism was rapidly becoming the chief stimulus behind Chinese reform thought," and he finds a specific example in Wang Tao's (1828–97) "incipient nationalism."[3] Much the same claim is made for the period immediately before the end of the Qing regime: As Joseph Esherick puts it, "The decade preceding the 1911 Revolution had been one of rising nationalism."[4] Ernest P. Young has written of Yuan Shikai's

1. Carlton Hayes, *The Historical Evolution of Modern Nationalism* (New York: Macmillan, 1931); George Antonius, *The Arab Awakening: The Story of the Arab National Movement* (Philadelphia: Lippincott, 1939). On Toynbee see Elie Kedourie, *The Chatham House Version and other Middle-Eastern Studies* (London: Wiedenfeld and Nicolson, 1970).
2. *Survey of International Affairs* (London: Royal Institute for International Affairs, various years); Harley Farnsworth MacNair, *China's New Nationalism and Other Essays* (Shanghai: Commercial Press, 1926); see also his *China in Revolution: An Analysis of Politics and Militarism under the Republic* (Chicago: University of Chicago Press, 1931).
3. Paul A. Cohen, *Discovering History in China: American Historical Writing on the Recent Chinese Past* (New York: Columbia University Press, 1984), p. 31; "Wang T'ao and Incipient Chinese Nationalism," *Journal of Asian Studies*, 26.4 (August 1967): 559–74.
4. Joseph W. Esherick, *Reform and Revolution in China: The 1911 Revolution in Hunan and Hubei* (Berkeley: University of California Press, 1976), p. 216.

failure to "seize the high ground of nationalism" at the time of the Twenty-one Demands.[5] According to Immanuel Hsü, the emergence of "Nationalism" as a "new force" was marked by the demonstrations of May 4, 1919.[6]

As Chinese politics become more radical, the importance retrospectively imputed to nationalism correspondingly increases. Not only is the success of the Kuomintang explained through it; so also is that of the Communists. In 1968 Mary Wright argued that nationalism was the "moving force" of the whole Chinese revolution of the twentieth century.[7] And as Maurice Meisner points out, there is "a strong tendency to interpret Chinese Communism as a species of nationalism."[8] The classic example is perhaps Chalmers Johnson, who invokes nationalism to explain the military success of the Communists in the civil war, distinguishing between the "elite nationalism" of the Kuomintang and a new "peasant nationalism" whose emergence he dates to no earlier than 1937.[9] Even those who criticize Johnson do not discard nationalism as an explanatory concept. Rather, their concern in most cases is to stress the Communist role in creating and propagating it, arguing, as Meisner does, that "the Communists brought nationalism to the countryside; they did not simply reflect it."[10] James Thomson speaks of a shift to "national communism" after China left its Soviet alliance in the 1960s.[11] And in a book whose influence on informed American opinion would be difficult to overestimate, John Fairbank argues that "the principal fact confronting us is the nature and reality of Chinese nationalism."[12]

Even within this nationalism-laden historiography, however, the events of the mid-1920s have a special place. The change of regime in 1911 and 1912 had blended national grievances with a variety of local aspirations and military subversion; the Communist victory of 1949 had strong class and international components as well as undoubted national feeling. The

5. Ernest P. Young, *The Presidency of Yuan Shih-k'ai: Liberalism and Dictatorship in Early Republican China* (Ann Arbor: University of Michigan Press, 1977), p. 186.
6. Immanuel C. Y. Hsü, *The Rise of Modern China*, 2d ed. (New York: Oxford University Press, 1975), p. 605.
7. Mary Clabaugh Wright, "The Rising Tide of Change," in *China in Revolution: The First Phase, 1900–1913*, ed. Mary Clabaugh Wright (New Haven: Yale University Press, 1968), p. 3.
8. Maurice Meisner, *Mao's China: A History of the People's Republic* (New York: Free Press, 1977), p. 39.
9. Chalmers Johnson, *Peasant Nationalism and Communist Power: The Emergence of Revolutionary China, 1937–1945* (Stanford: Stanford University Press, 1962), pp. 23–5.
10. Meisner, *Mao's China*, p. 39.
11. James C. Thomson, Jr., *While China Faced West* (Cambridge, Mass.: Harvard University Press, 1969), p. xi.
12. John King Fairbank, *The United States and China*, 4th ed., enl. (Cambridge, Mass.: Harvard University Press, 1983), pp. 460–1.

"great revolution" [*da geming*] of the 1920s, however, looked like a triumph of something close to unalloyed nationalism. Our problem arises when we try to understand just what that means. What is nationalism? How does it work? Is it right to envision it as propelling a revolution?

Here it is important to remember exactly what the word *nationalism* denotes. It does not mean simply strong patriotic emotions, pride in country, willingness to die for it – although it is sometimes used in that way. Nationalism means specifically an intention, if necessary, to redraw the political map. As Elie Kedourie puts it, nationalism teaches "that humanity is naturally divided into nations, that nations are known by certain characteristics which can be ascertained, and that the only legitimate type of government is national self-government."[13] Where political power does not equal national power – as in pre–nineteenth-century Europe, where kings and emperors controlled multinational domains, or a colonial world where foreigners dominated indigenous nations – nationalism demands change.

A remarkable process of such change took place in Europe, beginning in the nineteenth century and gaining momentum after World War I. Elites and populations seem to have embraced the doctrines of nationalism and created new political entities in accord with them. Old structures – such as the Holy Roman Empire or the Habsburg monarchy – disappeared. In their place arose the new nation-states: Italy, Germany, Hungary, Yugoslavia, and Czechoslovakia among others. Why people should have wanted this and, even more puzzling, why national differentiation and reconstruction should have succeeded and, indeed, still be under way are questions that have engaged students of society since the nineteenth century. For they are unexpected developments. As Ernest Gellner has pointed out, neither Marxism nor classical liberalism predicts or explains this strictly defined nationalism. In 1848 *The Communist Manifesto* observed that "national differences and antagonisms between peoples are daily more and more vanishing" – and for good liberal reasons – "owing to the development of the bourgeoisie, to freedom of commerce, to the world market, to uniformity in the mode of production and in the conditions of life corresponding thereto."[14] Faced with the continuing vigor of nationalism, historians who share this rather

---

13. Elie Kedourie, *Nationalism*, 3d rev. ed. with Afterword. (London: Hutchinson, 1985), p. 9.
14. Karl Marx and Friedrich Engels, "Manifesto of the Communist Party," in *Basic Writings on Politics and Philosophy: Karl Marx and Friedrich Engels*, ed. Lewis S. Feuer (Garden City, N.Y.: Anchor Books, 1959), p. 26; Ernest Gellner, *Thought and Change* (first pub. 1965; reprint ed., Chicago: University of Chicago Press, 1978), pp. 147, 148.

reasonable assessment are forced to confront what Gellner calls the problem of the "Wrong Address": that somehow "the spirit of history or the human consciousness" had "by some terrible postal error" delivered the "awakening message . . . intended for *classes*" to nations instead.[15] Much modern writing about nationalism is essentially an attempt to deal with this problem. E. J. Hobsbawm's work is one example. It still tries to link nation and class and wonders whether nationalism may not have been the program of " 'middle peasants,' the rural stratum most firmly rooted in traditional agrarian society, fighting to maintain or reestablish the customary way of life."[16] Another example is the work of Benedict Anderson, whose beautifully titled *Imagined Communities* provides a refined (but ultimately unsatisfactory) account of how material developments lead to national consciousness.[17]

For Europe, the problem is not yet solved. The most promising approaches, however, may focus on language, as in the works of Karl Deutsch and Miroslav Hroch (as well as Ernst Gellner, already mentioned), which draw ultimately on intellectual traditions that took shape in the late years of the multinational Habsburg Empire.[18]

To state the essence of the problem: the doctrine of nationalism was developed in Europe in the early modern period; the puzzles of nationalism are puzzles of European history. Clearly there are parts of the world outside of Europe where the European historiography has some real relevance – Latin America, certainly. But is it wise to universalize it uncritically? Do we not run the risk of obscuring indigenous patterns and structures?[19] And in particular – does the European concept of nationalism really speak to the issues of modern Chinese history?

China, after all, seems in relatively little need of the nationalist's prescriptions. For most of its history it has been, *par excellence*, a society in which culture and politics overlap. Even allowing (if only for the sake of

15. Ernest Gellner, *Nations and Nationalism* (Ithaca, N.Y. and London: Cornell University Press, 1983), p. 129.
16. Eric Hobsbawm, "Some Reflections on Nationalism," in T. J. Nossiter, A. H. Hanson, and Stein Rokkan, eds., *Imagination and Precision in the Social Sciences, Essays in Memory of Peter Nettl* (London: Faber & Faber, 1972), p. 400; *Nations and Nationalism since 1780: Programme, Myth, Reality* (Cambridge: Cambridge University Press, 1990).
17. Benedict Anderson, *Imagined Communities: Reflections on the Origin and Spread of Nationalism* (London: Verso, 1983; 2d ed., 1991).
18. Karl Deutsch, *Nationalism and Social Communication* (Cambridge, Mass.: M.I.T. Press, 1953); Miroslav Hroch, *Social Preconditions of National Revival in Europe: A Comparative Analysis of the Social Composition of Patriotic Groups among the Smaller European Nations* (Cambridge, England: Cambridge University Press, 1985). For the Austrian background, see John Schwarzmantel, *Socialism and the Idea of the Nation* (London: Harvester Wheatsheaf, 1991).
19. On this, see Partha Chatterjee, *Nationalist Thought in the Colonial World: A Derivative Discourse?* (London: Zed Books for the United Nations University, 1986).

argument) that the Qing was a "foreign" dynasty and that portions of the Qing empire were culturally non-Chinese, the fact remains that China did not face anything like the problems that nationalism usually addresses. There was no need to carve a "China" out of some larger polity or to assemble it, à la Cavour or Bismarck, out of a lot of small pieces. The map as already drawn would do: a republican regime could succeed an imperial house relatively easily, in the same capital, and rule the same provinces, through many of the same people. Likewise, the problem of citizenship was far simpler for China than for European states. A large literature has shown how modern European national identities were forged relatively recently out of precursors that were quite different.[20] Once again, even if we allow for the sake of argument the importance of the creation of a national language in the form of *baihua*, the fact remains that identification with China as what psychologists call a social reality was strong long before the modern period.[21] So strong was this identification that advocates of wholesale Westernization, such as Hu Shi (1891–1962) could argue quite convincingly that no conceivable amount of change would undermine it: "No matter how radically the material existence has changed, how much intellectual systems have altered, and how much political systems have been transformed, the Japanese are still the Japanese and the Chinese are still the Chinese. . . . Those of us who are forward looking should humbly accept the scientific and technical world culture and the spiritual civilization behind it. . . . There is no doubt that in the future the crystallization of this great change will, of course, be a culture on a Chinese basis."[22] In the study of the West, much attention has recently been focused on the invention or construction of identity – via monuments, rituals, and the systematic inculcation of memory.[23] This, too, seems perhaps less important for China than for European countries, despite the effort put into the elaboration of monuments and national symbolism, for example, in the design of the tomb and the arrangement of the funeral of Dr. Sun Yat-

---

20. A good example is Eugen Weber, *Peasants into Frenchmen: The Modernization of Rural France, 1879–1914* (Stanford: Stanford University Press, 1976).
21. For social reality, see L. Festinger, "Informal Social Communication," *Psychological Review* **57** (1950): 271–82.
22. Hu Shih, "Criticism of the 'Declaration for Cultural Construction on a Chinese Basis'." (1935), in Wm. Theodore de Bary, ed., *Sources of Chinese Tradition* (New York: Columbia University Press, 1960), 856–7.
23. Influential examples are George L. Mosse, *The Nationalization of the Masses: Political Symbolism and Mass Movements in Germany from the Napoleonic Wars Through the Third Reich* (New York: Howard Fertig, 1975); Maurice Agulhon, *Marianne au combat: l'imagerie et la symbolique républicaines de 1789 à 1880* (Paris: Flammarion, 1979), and E. J. Hobsbawm and Terence Ranger, eds., *The Invention of Tradition* (Cambridge, England: Cambridge University Press, 1983).

sen.[24] The reason yet again is that the sense of Chinese community, its functional equivalent, is far better established than the European sense of national community. For this reason, the Western concentration on the problematical quality of Chinese identity in the modern period – so thoroughly explored by Joseph Levenson – is perhaps misplaced.[25] As is increasingly being recognized, in China the social and cultural community has been both prior to and stronger than the state in a way that is rather different from the European cases usually taken as the norm.[26]

I do not mean by this argument to suggest that the concept of nationalism should not be applied to China at all. Clearly, the way that Chinese people think of their relationship to one another and to the state has changed over the last century. Indeed, this change is one of the great themes of modern Chinese history. But compared to Europe, it has been a change emanating from different conditions and different structures, and thus one whose course cannot easily be interpreted through European models. If I were to sum up the differences, I would argue that personal and group identity were better established in China before the change began, but that institutional structures were less prepared for the modern world. Hence, twentieth-century Chinese history has focused not so much on the question of who is or is not Chinese, or where the community ends (although such questions certainly exist), as on questions of appropriate institutions and political structure.

With these points in mind, let us now consider the events of the May Thirtieth Movement and the Nationalist Revolution. To begin with, do the facts fit the Nationalist account? Did a dramatic and highly consequential shift in the way the Chinese thought of themselves occur during the 1920s? This is an important question, because it is the sudden appearance and apparently great potency of a new nationalism that historians have difficulty accounting for. The evidence is mixed. On one hand we have accounts from the time, both Chinese and Western – many of which have already been cited – clearly indicating a sudden and palpable change in the political climate. We have shifts in political styles, demands, and rhetoric. Yet there is dissenting testimony as well. Important recent work on the Nationalist Revolution suggests that, far from being swept along on a wave of popular fervor, the Kuomintang

24. See Xu Youchun and Wu Zhiming, eds., *Sun Zhongshan Fengan Dadian* (Beijing: Huawen chubanshe, 1989).
25. Joseph R. Levenson, *Confucian China and Its Modern Fate: A Trilogy* (Berkeley: University of California Press, 1968).
26. See the special issue of *Daedalus* 120.2 (Spring 1991), "The Living Tree: The Changing Meaning of Being Chinese Today" for articles touching on this question.

had considerable difficulty in mobilizing mass support and devoted much effort to expounding its revolutionary messages to a largely indifferent populace.[27]

Was there a basic difference between nationalism as understood by the Kuomintang and as understood by the Beijing government? Perhaps. But it is important to be aware of just how tendentious much historical writing on this topic is. Most accounts of the 1925–28 revolution have been written by sympathizers of either the Kuomintang or the Communists – parties that, although disagreeing profoundly about more recent history, are in accord about the meaning of the events of the mid-1920s and quarrel only about which of them is the legitimate heir of the revolution. To strengthen their nationalistic credentials, historians writing in both camps systematically denigrate or even ignore the achievements of the Northern government and suggest in particular that a nationalistic foreign policy agenda was adopted by China only after the revolution. But in fact there is considerable policy continuity between the Northern government's foreign ministry and that of the Kuomintang (once the extreme antiforeignism of the early Northern Expedition had cooled).

The policy continuity suggests a substantial continuity of sentiment and understanding as well. The goals, the means, and even the personnel of Chinese foreign policy changed relatively little as a result of the 1925–28 revolution. Both the initiatives taken by the new Nanjing government and the reactions of the Powers to them had their roots in the diplomacy of the earlier 1920s and even of the 1910s. This would appear to be true even of the developing confrontation between China and Japan.

These facts lead to the general question of continuity versus change in this period. Can one recognize the foreign policy continuity between the Beijing and Nanjing governments (even ignoring the evidence of the articles cited above that trace nationalist feeling in China at least to the nineteenth century) while believing that 1925 marked something dramatically new? It is not easy. And even if one accepts that 1925 did mark something new, how is its appearance to be explained? To return to the question posed in the "Introduction," why did the May Thirtieth Movement start in 1925, and not 1924, or even 1919?

An answer to these questions must begin by putting the "new" nationalism of the 1920s into context. The standard account tells us little more

27. See in particular John Fitzgerald, "The Irony of the Chinese Revolution," in *The Nationalists and Chinese Society 1923–1937: A Symposium*, ed. John Fitzgerald (Melbourne: History Department, University of Melbourne, 1989), pp. 13–43.

than that on May 30, 1925, Chinese tolerance of foreign privilege ended in an explosion of protest. Except for a few stereotyped allusions to "militarism" or "warlords," this standard version leaves out entirely any reference to the developments we have examined in the preceding chapters. It treats the upsurge of nationalism primarily as an intellectual event, the manifestation of a change in consciousness. It says nothing about the shifting fortunes and credibility of the central government, the gradual destruction of its coercive capabilities, and the wartime disruption of the hitherto relatively stable commercial life of the treaty ports. This is history written in a vacuum, and as explanation it is unsatisfactory. Sometimes it comes close to saying in effect that May 30, 1925, was the day the Chinese finally said, "We're mad as hell, and we're not going to take it any more."[28]

Shifts in consciousness may be real, but they are scarcely ever as sudden or spontaneous as they may seem at the time; nor are they often as powerful to affect the objective structures of society as is regularly asserted. Nationalistic feelings, after all, were certainly in evidence much earlier. The Chinese did not suddenly become exasperated by foreign privilege in the late spring of 1925. They were already exasperated at the Washington Conference, and at Versailles, and when the Twenty-one Demands were presented, and when the Boxer Protocol was imposed, and even when the treaty of Nanjing was signed at the end of the Opium War. Why did they explode into passionate and successful action in 1925? The answer, as suggested in the "Introduction," is because of war. Once the wars of 1924 and their consequences are supplied as background and context, the emergence of the May Thirtieth Movement becomes intelligible. It may well be true that the ways nationalism was thought of before and after May Thirtieth are significantly different. But it is our contention that the most important change in 1925 was not so much in consciousness as in the institutional framework within which consciousness was articulated.

When objectively stated, the narrative of the period from 1924 to 1925 reveals not so much the rise of nationalism as the breakdown of the Beijing government and the Northern System associated with it. This breakdown was caused by a war that had nothing to do with nationalism. It was the collapse of that system's objective ability to coerce – and concurrently of its morale, cohesion, and prestige – that provided the opening for social and intellectual forces that had hitherto been kept in check or expressed in other ways.

28. Cf. Paddy Chayevsky (1923–81) *Network* (screenplay, 1976); John Bartlett, *Familiar Quotations* (15th ed., 1980), p. 901.

The victory of the Kuomintang in the Northern Expedition is usually attributed to the party's identification with nationalism and social revolution and to its effective use of nationalist propaganda. Undoubtedly there is truth to those points. But as Dirlik points out regarding the events of May 4, 1919, radical consciousness alone is a fragile quantity, easily dissipated; to succeed, it must acquire intellectual and organizational structure – a difficult process that may ultimately subvert the original impulse. The Communist party offered such structures after May 4. So did the Kuomintang–Communist alliance in the period during and after the wars of 1924. Military Attaché John Magruder observed after a trip to Hankou in the spring of 1927 that the basic character of the Chinese in the Kuomintang army there differed not at all from what he had known since his first service in China in 1920. What prevented the Kuomintang army from splitting into factions as he would have expected was a structure. An organization borrowed from the Soviet Union had been "superimposed upon the Chinese organization" of the Kuomintang army.[29]

The collapse of the Beijing government's military power presented an opportunity to Chiang Kai-shek and his well-trained Soviet-style forces in Guangdong. It also provided opportunities nearer to home. In the key cities of Central and North China – Hankou, Shanghai, Tianjin, Beijing, and Mukden, for example – social radicalism finally had its opportunity. Radical organizers were no longer automatically arrested. Furthermore, the suffering and disorder caused by the war provided constituencies for the Left, which had hitherto had considerable difficulty recruiting converts outside the intelligentsia. Transport ceased for much of the war: sailors, railway workers, and others found themselves out of work. Factories closed for lack of raw materials and markets, so unemployment grew. Food supplies to some cities were low; prices rose; fuel was short in winter. Such conditions were favorable for forays into organizing the working class.

Workers were not the only or even the most severe sufferers from the war. I have traced in some detail the effects of the war on the groups in Chinese society whom one would expect to have formed the backbone of support for the Beijing government – namely, middle-class urban dwellers, merchants, bankers, traders, money-shop proprietors. To my knowledge no one, Chinese or Western, has previously pointed out the full extent of the financial crisis that the war precipitated. Bankers and investors were hard hit by the rising price of silver and the collapse of

29. Military Attaché to Army Chief of Staff, Washington, April 1, 1927, 3 pp., MIR, VII, 0102–4.

275

the government bond market. Bankruptcies of traditional banks rippled from the major centers of Shanghai, Hankou, and Tianjin into smaller cities. The ensuing liquidity crisis, along with the almost complete cessation of transportation of commercial goods along key trade routes – most notably those connecting Shanghai to its hinterland – caused severe problems for China's mercantile classes. Inflation ravaged the Northeast. Credit was often unavailable to finance transactions, or transactions could not be completed. Defaults and bankruptcies mounted, and serious debate developed concerning the exact meaning of the standard *force majeure* clause contained in commercial contracts. Who *was* responsible for nonfulfillment of an agreement because of war?

The situation was reminiscent in certain ways of that in 1911 when (for different reasons) the capital of Chinese railway investors was threatened. The still-nascent middle classes, who might have been expected to support the Qing, turned against it. Certainly by 1925 there can have been no love lost between the bankrupt traders of the treaty-port cities and the government that had helped to create their predicament. Furthermore, the foreign role is worth noting. Chinese merchants, depending on their own political authorities for security and on their own vulnerable financial institutions for support, were disproportionately hurt in the financial crisis of 1924. Foreign traders could, to some extent, stand above the fray. They were unlikely to see their assets confiscated and, since they alone did not fear to keep money outside of Shanghai, they had an advantage in completing transactions. Some of the anti-foreignism of the middle classes must have reflected the degree to which they were hurt by this unfair economic competition of the 1924–25 period.

More broadly, the war had the effect of discrediting the claims of the Beijing government to the mantle of nationalism. We have already seen how strongly the Beijing foreign ministry under Gu Weijun had pursued treaty revision, the end of extraterritoriality, and related policies. Gu's policies can only be described as nationalistic – indeed, extremely so. But they were not repudiationist, like the Kuomintang's. Gu believed that he could work through international law and diplomacy to untie the knots that kept China bound in an unequal international status. In this respect, his policy showed great success. But, after the breakdown of the Beijing government and Gu's replacement as foreign minister, the situation changed. The Beijing government now required foreign support, and it was willing to seek it at the expense of its nationalistic credentials, as when it settled the gold franc dispute essentially on France's terms. Because it had become a weak player, Beijing had to forfeit the high ground of nationalism and look for foreign support, just as Zhang Zuolin and Sun Yat-sen had long done.

This was not all. The economic logic of the war made the repudiationist approach to China's foreign loans and treaties – rejected by both Gu Weijun and Duan Qirui – extremely attractive, even logical. As long as the Washington treaties had some likelihood of coming into force, a resolution of China's financial problems through higher tariffs and greater access to customs revenues was an appealing option. The war, however, increased the already crushing burden of Chinese internal debt. The reason Beijing could not pay its many bondholders was that customs and salt revenues were largely hypothecated by treaty for the service of foreign debts and indemnities. The war had complicated this problem by increasing the amount of debt and destroying the value of outstanding bond issues because of default. Had the Washington System come into effect, or had the often-mooted "Dawes plan" for China been created, it might have been possible to reconcile the claims on government revenues of foreigners and Chinese.[30]

The foreign powers increasingly shied away from any such collective action. The tensions among them were growing. The veto exercised by France and other countries who saw the postwar settlement as little more than an opportunity to secure the agreement by a weakened Chinese government for the payment even of doubtful claims was too powerful. The prospect, even for an internationalist diplomat and skilled lawyer like Gu, was for a China locked in ever more tightly to an onerous and unrealistic schedule of foreign debt repayments – repayments that would be implemented at the cost of not honoring internal debt. From the countries it had fought in World War I, Germany received a loan of 800 million gold marks. China, by contrast, got nothing from the Powers that professed to be its friends. Under such circumstances, it is scarcely surprising that radical policies of straightforward treaty repudiation should have come to appeal, not simply to nationalistic firebrands but also to men (at least formerly) of property. The Soviet Union had already shown the way toward repudiation of treaties and debts, and it is not puzzling that the Chinese were willing to follow.

Most scholars have argued that the end of the Washington System began in 1925 with the advent of the new nationalism. MacMurray certainly believed that, as does Dorothy Borg, who would disagree with

---

30. "A 'Dawes' Financial Plan for China!" *China Weekly Review* (December 6, 1924), p. 1. The reference is to the plan developed by a committee chaired by General Charles G. Dawes (1865–1951) and accepted in April of 1924 to deal with Germany's crushing war reparations by means of a large loan against scheduled repayments.

him about nearly everything else: Her classic, *American Policy and the Chinese Revolution,* begins with May 30, 1925.[31] The same is true for Akira Iriye. In *After Imperialism* it is the nationalism of the May Thirtieth Movement that undermines the Washington System and makes war with Japan the "cost of sovereignty" for China.[32] But, as we have seen, the Washington System had already been torn to shreds by the autumn of 1924. The gold franc controversy had starved the Beijing government of resources to which it was entitled and which it needed desperately. The international response when Wu's forces menaced the Japanese special position in Manchuria made it clear that, when it came to the crunch, the Anglo-American powers would not be willing to stand with Japan against a strong China (and there was no clear reason why they should). Thus, Japanese unilateralism became simply a matter of time. The success of the new politics of 1925 reflected this breakdown.

The protests and violence of the May Thirtieth Movement arose and spread not only because grievances were greater and consciousness was changing but also most importantly because previously existing authority and legitimacy had collapsed, destroying itself unintentionally in civil war. With the uncontrolled mass movement there came, true enough, increasing union and party memberships and rising prestige of the Kuomintang and the Communist parties. But these were not causes of the May Thirtieth Movement. They were its consequences. It was the virulence of the protest that propelled the newly allied Nationalists and the Communists forward, not the other way around. As one Communist party member would later remark, "We did not make May Thirtieth; it was made for us."[33]

Even that, however, was not the last word. Although May Thirtieth may have been made for the Communists, it did not, much to their disappointment, lead to their triumph. Instead, Chiang Kai-shek was able to ride the radical tiger and dismount successfully. Why? Because he did not need the radicals' constituency. The effect of the war had been utterly to discredit those politicians to whom the middle and commercial classes would traditionally have looked, to cut those classes loose and, as we have seen, make them receptive to appeals for imme-

31. See Arthur Waldron, ed., *The 1935 Memorandum "Developments Affecting American Policy in the Far East," Prepared for the State Department by Ambassador John Van Antwerp MacMurray* (Hoover Archival Documentaries. Stanford: Hoover Institution Press, 1992), pp. 61, 69–72, and introduction; Dorothy Borg, *American Policy and the Chinese Revolution.*
32. Akira Iriye, *After Imperialism: The Search for a New Order in the Far East 1921–1931* (New York: Atheneum, 1969), pp. 254–77.
33. George Sokolsky, *The Tinder Box of Asia* (New York: Doubleday, Doran, 1932), p. 36. Quoted in Richard W. Rigby, *The May 30 Movement: Events and Themes* (Canberra: Australian National University Press, 1980), p. 252.

diate repudiation of the "unequal treaties" and similar policies. The Beijing government had in effect disappeared, leaving the center without a claimant. Chiang Kai-shek, previously marginal, was able to move to that center and leave his erstwhile Communist allies isolated on the margin.

All of which may prompt some reflections about the phenomenon of nationalism in general, viewed from the perspective of China. Why, over the long term, affiliation to nations has superseded or preempted affiliation to dynasties or economic classes remains a subject of contention among social theorists, one this study cannot resolve. But several points are worth noting. The first is that, at least for China in the 1920s, the sentiment of nationalism turns out to be a far less powerful or important explanatory concept than has previously been recognized. Far from being a driving force, it is almost a fifth wheel. Nationalism, irredentism, anti-Japanese and antiforeign feelings – all were present among the elite and other sections of the population as the decade began. The changes that occurred in mid-decade were not so much in the content of consciousness (in any case, a notoriously difficult subject to study) as in the political and institutional environment of China. Institutions that had oriented people broke down. And disoriented people were then thrown back for a sense of security and identity on social, communal, and other noninstitutional affiliations.

Few terms used by analysts of nationalism stir more argument than does "primordial," with its suggestion that who one is or what country one belongs to is to some extent objective: a "given." This is an idea highly uncongenial to those interpreters who see nationalism as something new, contingent, and constructed.[34] Yet, while admitting that much about national identification is the product of state action and cultural manipulation, surely any understanding of the power of nationalist ideas must take into account the way that they tap deeply felt sentiments and attachments – to home, to family, to mother tongue.

This point should be borne in mind when we consider May Thirtieth. Our narrative has demonstrated that the massive outpouring of national sentiment at the time of May Thirtieth was more a consequence than a cause of events. China in 1924 was reasonably calm and stable. Politics were understood in terms of institutions, groups, and personalities – parliament versus the president, Zhili versus Fengtian, Sun Yat-sen versus Zhang Zuolin. Issues of nationalism, strictly understood, were

---

34. Much of the argument about the "primordial" goes back to a single article by Clifford Geertz, "The Integrative Revolution: Primordial Sentiments and Civil Politics in the New States," pp. 105–57, in *Old Societies and New States*, ed. Clifford Geertz (New York: Free Press, 1963).

largely confined to foreign policy, and there the Beijing government was doing an effective job of promoting a strong agenda. Radical politics, contrary to both Kuomintang and Communist accounts after the fact, were in fact making little progress. Most Chinese were getting on with making money and acquiring education in the time-honored way. There was little sign that national consciousness and the latent sense of outrage at foreign privileges were changing or rising dramatically, that sooner or later they would erupt into violence.

What made May Thirtieth work was not, initially, a change in the way people thought. Rather, shifts in the institutions in which they lived created an unexpected and rather frightening sense of uncertainty, a political and emotional vacuum which led them to fall back on those affiliations sometimes called "primordial." These, however, while animating mobs and inspiring slogans, were not the stuff of which to build a new regime. As analysts have long recognized, the deep emotional affiliations that can galvanize a crowd or a national population when touched – as in Shanghai on May 30, 1925, or in India after the Amritsar Massacre of April 13, 1919, or in countless other cases – may be powerful, but in general they are too multifarious and mutually incompatible to be accommodated easily by any single institutional structure. They do not lead to the state. Rather, if anything, they supply potential for fission, and thus must be held in check by more objective rational and unifying institutions.

Certainly this seems to be the case for China. Powerful as the traditional Chinese sense of identity may be, it is nevertheless not uniform, and it accommodates local, ethnic, linguistic, and familial factors in a diverse and often tension-ridden whole. A shared outrage at foreigners, without either police to contain it or diplomats to harness it, briefly filled the institutional vacuum of the mid-1920s. But the real Nationalist revolution was not the May Thirtieth Movement: It was the assumption of control by the Kuomintang with its new and stable political and military institutions; it was, as always in China (and often, one suspects, elsewhere), not the releasing of a nation; it was the building of a state.

Bibliography

Archival sources

I. Chinese materials

At the National Second Historical Archives of China [Zhongguo di er Lishi danganguan] in Nanjing, the following files were consulted:

Bei 26. Beiyang zhengfu lujunbu dangan [Archive of the Beiyang Government Department of the Army]

1001. Beiyang Zhengfu neiwubu dangan [Archive of the Beiyang Government Ministry of the Interior]

1002. Beiyang Zhengfu dangan [Archive of the Beiyang Government]

1003. Beiyang Zhengfu da zongtongfu dangan [Archive of the Beiyang Government Presidential Office]

1004. Beiyang zhengfu linshi zhizhengfu junwuting dangan [Archive of the Military Affairs Office of the Provisional Chief Executive Office of the Beiyang Government]

1014. Beiyang Zhengfu canlu banshichu dangan [Archive of the Beiyang Government Army General Staff Department]

1023. Beiyang Zhengfu bujun zongsiling yamen [Archives of the Commander of Gendarmes of the Beiyang Government]

1024. Beiyang Zhengfu Jingji weishu zongsilingbu dangan [Archive of the Beiyang Government Commander of Metropolitan Defense Forces]

1025. Beiyang Zhengfu ReChaSui xuanyueshishu dangan [Archive of the Beiyang Government Inspector General of Rehe Chahar and Suiyuan]

1026. Beiyang Zhengfu lingsan junshi dangan [Miscellaneous Military Archives of the Beiyang Government]

1027. Beiyang Zhengfu caizhengbu dangan [Archive of the Beiyang Government Ministry of Finance]

(Note: in the archives themselves the abbreviation Bei ["north"] is often used instead of the 100 prefix.)

Particular use was made of the following subfiles:

281

1003.105. Zhi Lu Yu xuanyuefushi Wang Chengbin zai Miyun, Gubeikou, Chengde, deng di baogao bushu dui Feng zuozhan qingkuang laidian [Telegrams from the Zhili vice-inspector of Shandong and Henan Wang Chengbin at Miyun, Gubeikou, Chengde and other places concerning military operations of troops deployed against Fengtian, October 4–18, 1924]

1003.106. Gefang tanbao Fengfang junshi huodong qingkuang youguan wendian [Intelligence reports concerning Fengtian military activities, February–October 1924]

1003.108. Zhijun zai Shanhaiguan, Gubeikou, Luanzhou deng didai ge jiangling guanyu cuibo dui Feng zuozhan junshi jiedan laidian [Telegrams from Zhili military commanders at Shanhaiguan, Gubeikou, Luanzhou, and other regions concerning the need to accelerate preparations for war against Fengtian, July–October 1924]

1003.109. Zhijun zongsiling Wu Peifu deng guanyu chaban zai Qinhuangdao dui Feng zuozhan junjie shixiang laiwang wendian [Correspondence with Zhili commander in chief Wu Peifu and others concerning military supplies for battle with Fengtian forces at Qinhuangdao, September 16–October 22, 1924]

1003.113. Hu Jingyi baogao jiu "tao ni jun" yuanjun di er lu siling zhi bing qingyuan Pingquan weiji laidian [Hu Jingyi telegram reporting assumption of office of commander in chief of the second support brigade of the "anti-rebel army" and urgent request for relief of Pingquan, September–October 1924]

1003.174. Suiyuan dutong Ma Fuxiang baogao huihe ReCha liang qu lianfang dongyu ji youguan junwu shixiang laidian [Telegrams from the Suiyuan supervisor Ma Fuxiang concerning the combining of Rehe and Chahar to create a united defense in the East, January–September 1924]

1003.296. Junshichu banli lingbo jiaotong dianxun jungong deng qicai shixiang youguan hanjian [Dispatches from the Junshichu concerning the arrangement of transportation, communication, and construction equipment, January–October 1924]

1003(2).37. Zhijun zongsiling Wu Peifu deng jiangling zai Qinhuangdao zhihui dui Feng zuozhan qingkuang ji youguan junwu laiwang wendian [Communications to and from the Zhili commander in chief Wu Peifu and others commanding Qinhuangdao concerning the battle with Fengtian and related military matters, October 11–23, 1924]

1003(2).43. Gefang tanbao Su-Zhe zhanzheng ge qingkuang hanjian [Intelligence reports concerning the Jiangsu–Zhejiang War, September 1924]

1003(2).49. Su-Zhe-Wan xunshi Qi Xieyuan baogao dui Zhe zuozhan ji Lu (Yongxiang) He (Fenglin) qiantao bushu shanhou qingkuang laiwang dian [Telegrams to and from the xunshi of Jiangsu Zhejiang and Anhui Qi Xieyuan reporting the battle with Zhejiang and plans for dealing with the possible escape of Lu Yongxiang and He Fenglin, September–October 1924]

1024.87. Chakou zi Tianjin jifa guanyu jielu Zhixi neimu zhi youyin xinwengao [collected news dispatches from Tianjin dealing with internal affairs of Zhili group September–November 1923]

1024.88.2. Chakou kanzai buli Zhixi xiaoxi, Shanghai faxing zhi Minguo ribao deng baokan [Collected news stories unfavorable to Zhili group published in the *Shanghai Minguo ribao*, January–July 1924]

1024.93. Chakou Hangzhou Fengtian faxing guanyu kanzai Jiang-Zhe zhanzheng xiaoxi zhi ge baokan [Collected news items from the pro–Fengtian Hangzhou press dealing with the Jiangsu–Zhejiang War, February–September 1924]

1024(2).80. Zhenchachu Wang Guangyu deng guanyu er ci Zhi-Feng zhanzheng qingxing baogao [Intelligence reports from Wang Guangyu and others concerning the Zhili–Fengtian War, September–October 1924]

1025.26. Beijing ge tongxunshe xinwengao [Draft news dispatches from various Beijing agencies, August–September 1924]

1025.135. Youguan er ci Zhi Feng zhanzhengzhong baogao junqing deng gexiang wendian [Dispatches and telegrams concerning military conditions during the Zhili–Fengtian War, September 1924]

1025.136. Youguan baogao Jiang-Zhe zhanzheng qingkuang ji jie Zhe Lu gexiang wendian [Dispatches and telegrams concerning the Jiangsu–Zhejiang War and exposing the activities of Lu Yongxiang of Zhejiang, January–November 1924]

1026.136. Guanyu Beiyang junshi jigou xiuzao he lingfa jiedan gexiang wenjian (3 files) [Concerning the manufacture and distribution of weaponry and ammunition by Beiyang military organizations, n.d.]

II. Western materials

Records of the Department of State Relating to Political Relations of the United States With China, 1910–1929. National Archives Microfilm Publications Microcopy No. 339.

Records of the Department of State Relating to Political Relations Between China and Other States, 1910–1929 National Archives Microfilm Publications Microcopy No. 341.

U.S. Military Intelligence Reports, China 1911–1941. Edited by Paul Kesaris. Guide prepared by Robert Lester. Microfilm. Frederick, Md.: University Publications of America, 1983.

National Archives, Washington. International Affairs: China. Record Group 59, 893 Series.

Public Record Office, London. Foreign Office General Correspondence, Far Eastern Department, FO 371 Series.

Houghton Library, Harvard University: Joseph G. Grew Papers; Jay Pierrepont Moffat Papers; William Phillips Papers.

The Hoover Institution, Stanford University: Julean H. Arnold Papers; André Chauvain Papers; Stanley K. Hornbeck Papers; Nicholas A. Zebrak Papers.

Seeley Mudd Library, Princeton University: George F. Kennan Papers; John Van Antwerp MacMurray Papers.

Bibliography

Western sources

Periodicals

The American Review of Reviews: An International Magazine
National Economic Bulletin. New York: The China National Economic Bureau.
The China Weekly Review
The China Year Book (annual). Edited by H. G. W. Woodhead. Peking and Tientsin: The Tientsin Press.
The Chinese Economic Bulletin HC426.C43
The Chinese Economic Monthly
Foreign Relations of the United States
The Literary Digest
The New York Times
The North China Herald

Film

"Modern Warfare in China in 1924–25: Struggle Between Mukden (Fengtien) and Peking (Chihli)." [Russian title: "Sovremmenia Voina v Kitae"]. Imperial War Museum (London), Film 2424.

Books and Articles

Abend, Hallett. *My Life in China, 1926–1941.* New York: Harcourt, Brace, 1943.
Académie Diplomatique Internationale. *Dictionnaire Diplomatique comprenant les Biographies des Diplomates du Moyen Age à nos jours, constituant un traité d'Histoire Diplomatique sur six siècles.* Publié sous la direction de M. A.-F. Frangulis. Paris and Geneva: Académie Diplomatique Internationale, n.d.
Agulhon, Maurice. *Marianne au combat: l'imagerie et la symbolique républicaines de 1789 á 1880.* Paris: Flammarion, 1979. English edition, trans. Janet Lloyd. Cambridge, England: Cambridge University Press, 1981.
Agulhon, Maurice. *Marianne au combat.* Paris: Flammarion, 1979.
Allison, J. Murray, comp. *Raemaekers' Cartoon History of the War.* New York: Century, 1918.
American Law Institute. *Restatement of the Foreign Relations Law of the United States.* St. Paul, Minn.: American Law Institute, 1987.
Anderson, Benedict. *Imagined Communities: Reflections on the Origin and Spread of Nationalism.* London: Verso, 1983.
Andersson, J. Gunnar. *China Fights for the World.* London: Kegan Paul, Trench, Trubner, 1938.
Antonius, George. *The Arab Awakening: The Story of the Arab National Movement.* Philadelphia: Lippincott, 1939.
Arlington, L. C., and Lewisohn, William. *In Search of Old Peking: City of Palaces and Temples.* Peking: Henri Vetch, 1935.

Bibliography

Arnold, Julean. *China: A Commercial and Industrial Handbook.* Department of Commerce Bureau of Foreign and Domestic Commerce, Trade Promotion Series, No. 38. Washington, D.C.: U.S. Government Printing Office, 1926.

———. *Some Bigger Issues in China's Problems.* Shanghai: Commercial Press, 1928.

Asada, Sadao. "Japan's 'Special Interests' and the Washington conference, 1921–1922." *American Historical Review* **56** (1961): 62–70.

———. "Japan and the United States, 1915–1925." Ph.D. dissertation, Yale University, 1963.

———. *Japan and the World, 1853–1952: A Bibliographic Guide to Japanese Scholarship in Foreign Relations.* New York: Columbia University Press, 1989.

Auden, W. H., and Isherwood, Christopher. *Journey to a War.* London: Faber & Faber, 1939.

Baker, J. E. "Chinese Military Rail Transport." *China Weekly Review*, December, 20, 1924, pp. 73, 78.

Bamba, Nobuya. *Japanese Diplomacy in a Dilemma: New Light on Japan's China Policy, 1924–1929.* Kyoto: Minerva Press, 1977.

Barnett, Robert W. *Economic Shanghai: Hostage to Politics, 1937–1941.* New York: Institute of Pacific Relations, 1942.

Bau, Mingchien Joshua [Bao Mingqian]. *Modern Democracy In China.* Shanghai: Commercial Press, 1923. Reprint ed., Washington, D.C.: University Publications of America, 1977.

Beal, Edwin George. *The Origin of Likin (1853–1864).* Cambridge, Mass.: Chinese Economic and Political Studies, Harvard University, 1958.

Beasley, William G. *Japanese Imperialism, 1894–1945.* Oxford, England: Clarendon Press, 1987.

Bederman, David J. "The 1871 London Declaration, Rebus Sic Stantibus and a Primitivist View of the Law of Nations." *American Journal of International Law* **82** (1988): 1–40.

Bedeski, Robert Edward. "The Politics of National Unification: China, 1928–1936." Ph.D. dissertation, University of California, Berkeley, 1969.

Bergère, Marie-Claire. *L'âge d'Or de la Bourgeoisie Chinoise 1911–1937.* Paris: Flammarion, 1986.

Berghahn, Volker R. *Militarism: The History of an International Debate 1861–1979.* New York: St. Martin's, 1982.

Binns, Christopher C. "John Van Antwerp MacMurray: An Old China Hand in the New China – 1925–1928." BA thesis, Princeton University, 1969.

Bland, J. O. P. *China: The Pity of It,* 2d ed. London: Heinemann, 1932.

Blanning, T. C. W. *The Origins of the French Revolutionary Wars.* London and White Plains, N.Y.: Longman, 1986.

Boorman, Howard L., ed. *Biographical Dictionary of Republican China.* New York: Columbia University Press, 1967.

Borg, Dorothy. *American Policy and the Chinese Revolution, 1925–1928.* New York: The American Institute of Pacific Relations, 1947; reprint ed., with new introduction by the author, New York: Octagon Books, 1968.

————, and Okamoto, Shumpei, eds. *Pearl Harbor as History: Japanese-American Relations 1931–1941*. New York: Columbia University Press, 1973.

Bose, Nemai Sadhan. *American Attitude and Policy in the Nationalist Movement in China (1911–1921)*. Bombay: Orient Longman, 1970.

Bouissou, Jean-Maire, *Seigneurs de guerre et officiers rouges (Warlords and Red Officers)*. Tours: Maison Maries, 1974.

Boulter, V. M., comp. *Survey of International Affairs 1925 Supplement Chronology of International Events and Treaties 1st January, 1920–31st December, 1925*. London: Oxford University Press, 1928.

Bredon, Juliet. *Peking: A Historical and Intimate Description of its Chief Places of Interest*. Shanghai: Kelly & Walsh, 1931.

Bridge, Ann. *See* O'Malley, Mary Dolling Sanders.

Brooks, Barbara J. "China Experts in the Gaimushō, 1895–1937," in *The Japanese Informal Empire in China 1895–1937*, pp. 369–94. Ed. Peter Duus, Ramon H. Myers, and Mark R. Peattie. Princeton: Princeton University Press, 1989.

Buckley, Thomas H. "John Van Antwerp MacMurray: The Diplomacy of an American Mandarin." In *Diplomats in Crisis: United States–Chinese–Japanese Relations, 1919–1941*, pp. 27–48. Ed. Richard Dean Burns and Edward M. Bennett. Santa Barbara: Clio Books, 1974.

————. *The United States and the Washington Conference, 1921–1922*. Knoxville: University of Tennessee Press, 1970.

Buhite, Russell T. *Nelson T. Johnson and American Policy Toward China, 1925–1941*. East Lansing: Michigan State University Press, 1968.

Bullington, John P. "International Treaties and the Clause 'Rebus Sic Stantibus'." *University of Pennsylvania Law Review* 76 (1927): 153–77.

Burns, Elinor. *British Imperialism in China*. London: The Labour Research Department, 1926.

Burns, Richard Dean, and Bennett, Edward M., eds. *Diplomats in Crisis*.

Bush, Richard Clarence III. "Industry and Politics in Kuomintang China: The Nationalist Regime and Lower Yangtze Chinese Cotton Mill Owners 1927–1937." Ph.D. dissertation, Columbia University, 1978.

Carr, E. H. *Nationalism and After*. New York: Macmillan, 1945.

Challener, Richard, ed. *United States Military Intelligence 1917–1927*. New York and London: Garland Publishing, 1978.

Chan, Anthony B. *Arming the Chinese: The Western Armaments Trade in Warlord China, 1920–1928*. Vancouver: University of British Columbia Press, 1982.

Chan, F. Gilbert, and Etzold, Thomas H., eds. *China in the 1920s: Nationalism and Revolution*. New York: New Viewpoints, 1976.

Chan, K. C. "The Abrogation of British Extraterritoriality in China 1942–43: A Study of Anglo-American–Chinese Relations." *Modern Asian Studies* 11 (1977): 257–91.

Chao, Kang. *The Economic Development of Manchuria*. Michigan Papers in Chinese Studies, no. 43. Ann Arbor: Center for Chinese Studies, University of Michigan, 1983.

Chatterjee, Partha. *Nationalist Thought and the Colonial World – A Derivative Discourse?* London: Zed Books for the United Nations University, 1986.

Ch'en, Jerome. "Dr. Sun Yat-sen's Trip to Peking, 1924–1925." In *Readings on Asian Topics.* Scandinavian Institute of Asian Studies, Monograph Series, no. 1. Lund: Student litteratur, 1970.

———. *The Military–Gentry Coalition: China Under the Warlords.* University of Toronto–York University Joint Centre on Modern East Asia Publications Series, vol. 1, no. 4. Toronto: University of Toronto–York University Joint Centre on Modern East Asia, 1979.

———. "Local Government Finances in Republican China." *Republican China* 10 (April 1985): 42–54.

Cheng, Yu-Kwei. *Foreign Trade and Industrial Development of China: An Historical and Integrated Analysis Through 1948.* Published under the auspices of The American University and The China International Foundation. Washington, D.C.: University Press of America, 1956.

Chesneaux, Jean. *The Chinese Labor Movement 1919–1927.* Translated from the French by H. M. Wright. Stanford: Stanford University Press, 1968.

Chi, Madeleine. *China Diplomacy, 1914–1918.* Harvard East Asian Monographs, no. 31. Cambridge, Mass.: East Asian Research Center, Harvard University, 1970.

———. "China and the Unequal Treaties at the Paris Peace Conference of 1919." *Asian Profile* 1 (1973): 49–61.

Ch'i, Hsi-sheng. *Warlord Politics in China 1916–1928.* Stanford: Stanford University Press, 1976.

Chiang, Monlin [Jiang Menglin]. *Tides From the West.* New Haven: Yale University Press, 1947; reprint ed., Taibei: China Academy, 1974.

Ch'ien, Tuan-sheng. *The Government and Politics of China.* Cambridge, Mass.: Harvard University Press, 1950.

China. Bureau of Foreign Trade. *China Industrial Handbooks: Kiangsu. First Series of the Reports by the National Industrial Investigation.* Shanghai: Bureau of Foreign Trade, Ministry of Industry, 1933.

China. Imperial Maritime Customs, *Treaties, Conventions, etc. Between China and Foreign States.* Shanghai: Inspectorate General of Customs, 1908.

China. Maritime Customs. *Annual Reports and Returns of Trade.* Shanghai, 1864–1948.

China, Maritime Customs. *Decennial Reports on the Trade and Development of Ports Open to Foreign Trade,* Statistical Series no. 6; 1922–1931 (1932).

China, Whangpoo Conservancy Board. *The Port of Shanghai.* General Series, no. 8. Shanghai: A.B.C. Press, 1928.

The China Year Book (annual). Edited by H. G. W. Woodhead. Peking and Tientsin: Tientsin Press.

"China on the Rocks of Revolution." *Current Opinion* 77 (December 1924): 693–4.

Chirol, Sir Valentine, Tsurumi, Yusuke, and Salter, Sir James Arthur. *The Reawakening of the Orient.* New Haven: Yale University Press, 1925.

Chow Liang-yen, "Wu Peifu and Great Britain, 1917–1927," paper presented at the Twenty-second Annual Meeting of the Association for Asian Studies, 3–5 April, 1970.

Chow, Tse-tsung. *The May Fourth Movement.* Stanford: Stanford University Press, 1960.

Christian Education in China. A Study made by an Educational Commission Representing the Mission Boards and Societies Conducting Work in China. New York: Committee of Reference and Counsel of the Foreign Missions Conference of North America, 1922.

Christie, Clive John. "The Problem of China in British Foreign Policy, 1917–1921." Ph.D. dissertation, Cambridge University, 1971.

Chu, Chin. "The Tariff Problem in China." *Studies in History, Economics and Public Law edited by the Faculty of Political Science of Columbia University,* vol. 72, no. 2. New York: Longmans, Green for Columbia University, 1916.

Chu, Don-chean. *Patterns of Education for the Developing Nations: Tao's Work in China 1917–1946.* Tainan, Taiwan: Kuo-chang Printing Co., 1966.

Chu, Pao-chin. *V. K. Wellington Koo: A Case Study of China's Diplomat and Diplomacy of Nationalism, 1912–1966.* Hong Kong: Chinese University Press, 1981.

Chu, Pao-chin. "V. K. Wellington Koo: The Diplomacy of Nationalism," in *Diplomats in Crisis,* pp. 125–52.

Clark, Peter G. "Britain and the Chinese Revolution, 1925–1927." Ph.D. dissertation, University of California, Berkeley, 1973.

Clausewitz, Carl von. *On War.* Edited and translated by Michael Howard and Peter Paret. Princeton: Princeton University Press, 1984.

Clayton, E. H. *Heaven Below.* New York: Prentice-Hall, 1944.

Clifford, Nicholas R. *Shanghai, 1925: Urban Nationalism and the Defense of Foreign Privilege.* Michigan Papers in Chinese Studies, no. 36. Ann Arbor: University of Michigan, 1979.

——. *Spoiled Children of Empire: Westerners in Shanghai and the Chinese Revolution of the 1920s.* Hanover, N.H.: Middlebury College Press, 1991.

Close, Upton. *See* Hall, Josef Washington.

Clyde, Paul Hibbert. *United States Policy Toward China: Diplomatic and Public Documents 1839–1939.* Durham, N.C.: Duke University Press, 1940.

Coates, P. D. *The China Consuls.* Hong Kong: Oxford University Press, 1988.

Cohen, Paul A. "Wang T'ao and Incipient Chinese Nationalism." *Journal of Asian Studies* 26 (August 1967): 559–74.

——. *Discovering History in China: American Historical Writing on the Recent Chinese Past.* New York: Columbia University Press, 1984.

Cohen, Warren I. "America and the May Fourth Movement: The Response to Chinese Nationalism, 1917–1921," *Pacific Historical Review* 35 (1966): 83–100.

——. *The Chinese Connection.* New York: Columbia University Press, 1978.

——. *America's Response to China: An Interpretative History of Sino-American Relations,* 2d ed. New York: Knopf, 1980.

Bibliography

————. ed. *New Frontiers in American–East Asian Relations: Essays Presented to Dorothy Borg.* New York: Columbia University Press, 1983.

Cole, Bernard David. "The United States Navy in China, 1925–1928." Ph.D. dissertation, Auburn University, 1978.

Collester, Janet Sue. "J. V. A. MacMurray, American Minister to China, 1925–1929: The Failure of a Mission." Ph.D. dissertation, Indiana University, 1977.

Collins, Larry, and Lapierre, Dominique. *Freedom at Midnight.* New York: Avon Books, 1976.

Conference on the Limitation of Armament, Washington, November 12, 1921–February 6, 1922. Washington, D.C.: U.S. Government Printing Office, 1922.

Conference on the Limitation of Armament, Washington, November 12, 1921–February 6, 1922, Subcommittees. Washington, D.C.: U.S. Government Printing Office, 1922.

Conway's All the World's Fighting Ships 1922–1946. Annapolis, Md.: Naval Institute Press, n.d.

Coons, Arthur Gardiner. *The Foreign Public Debt of China.* Philadelphia: University of Pennsylvania Press, 1930.

Coox, Alvin D., and Conroy, Hilary, eds. *China and Japan: Search for Balance Since World War I.* Santa Barbara: ABC–Clio, 1978.

Corbett, Charles Hodge. *Lingnan University: A Short History Based Primarily on the Records of the University's American Trustees.* New York: The Trustees of Lingnan University, 1963.

A Correspondent. "Shanghai Battle Sketches," *The Living Age* (1924): 235–9.

Craighill, Marian G. *The Craighills of China.* Ambler, Penn.: Trinity Press, 1972.

Creamer, Thomas A. "Hsüeh-yün: Shanghai's Students and the May Thirtieth Movement." Master's thesis, University of Virginia, 1975.

Cressy, Earl H. *Christian Higher Education: A Study for the Year 1925–1926.* China Christian Education Association Bulletin, no. 20. Shanghai, 1928.

Crow, Carl. *Handbook for China (Including Hongoing),* 4th ed. Shanghai: Carl Crow, n.d. (preface 1925).

Crowley, James B., ed. *Modern East Asia: Essays in Interpretation.* New York: Harcourt, Brace & World, 1970.

Darwent, C. E. *Shanghai: A Handbook for Travellers and Residents.* Shanghai: Kelly & Walsh, 1920.

Dayer, Roberta Allbert. "The British War Debts to the United States and the Anglo-Japanese Alliance, 1920–1923." *Pacific Historical Review* **45** (1976): 569–95.

————. *Bankers and Diplomats in China 1917–1925: The Anglo-American Relationship.* London: Frank Cass, 1981.

DeAngelis, Richard Clarke. "Jacob Gould Schurman and American Policy toward China, 1921–1925. Ph.D. dissertation, St. John's Unviersity, 1975.

de Bary, Wm. Theodore, ed. *Sources of Chinese Tradition.* New York: Columbia University Press, 1960.

De Martel, D., and De Hoyer, L. Translated by D. De Warzee. *Silhouettes of Peking.* Peking: China Booksellers, 1926.

De Ruffé, R. D'Auxion. *Is China Mad?* Translated from the French by R. T. Peyton Griffin. Shanghai: Kelly & Walsh, 1928.

Dirlik, Arif. "Culture, Society and Revolution: A Critical Discussion of American Studies of Modern Chinese Thought." *Republican China* 10 (1985): 22–33.

———. *The Origins of Chinese Communism.* New York and Oxford: Oxford University Press, 1989.

Dittmer, Lowell. *China's Continuous Revolution: The Post-Liberation Epoch, 1949–1981.* Berkeley: University of California Press, 1987.

Doenecke, Justus D., comp. *The Dipomacy of Frustration: The Manchurian Crisis of 1931–1933 as Revealed in the Papers of Stanley K. Hornbeck.* Stanford: Hoover Institution Press, 1981.

Dolsen, James H. *The Awakening of China.* Chicago: The Daily Worker, 1926.

Dooly, William G., Jr. *Great Weapons of World War I.* New York: Walker, 1969.

Drage, Charles. *General of Fortune: The Story of One-Armed Sutton.* London: Heinemann, 1963.

Dupuy, R. Ernest, and Dupuy, Trevor N. *The Encyclopedia of Military History from 3500 B.C. to the Present.* New York: Harper & Row, 1970.

Duus, Peter. *Party Rivalry and Political Change in Taishō Japan.* Cambridge, Mass.: Harvard University Press, 1968.

———, Myers, Ramon H., and Peattie, Mark R., eds. *The Japanese Informal Empire in China 1895–1937.* Princeton: Princeton University Press, 1989.

Edgerton, Robert B. *Like Lions They Fought: The Zulu War and the Last Black Empire in South Africa.* New York: Ballantine Books, 1988.

Eley, Geoff. "Remapping the Nation: War, Revolutionary Upheaval, and State Formation in Eastern Europe, 1914–1923." Paper presented at the McMaster Conference on "Jewish-Ukrainian Relations in Historical Perspective," October 19, 1983.

Ellis, L. Ethan. *Frank B. Kellogg and American Foreign Relations 1925–1929.* New Brunswick: Rutgers University Press, 1961.

Ellison, Duane C. "The United States and China, 1913–1921: A Study of the Strategy and Tactics of The Open Door Policy." Ph.D. dissertation, George Washington University, 1974.

Embree, Ainslie T., ed. *Encyclopedia of Asian History.* 4 vols. New York: Scribner's, 1988.

Esherick, Joseph W. *Reform and Revolution in China: The 1911 Revolution in Hunan and Hubei.* Berkeley, Los Angeles, and London: University of California Press, 1976.

Esthus, Raymond A. "The Changing Concept of the Open Door, 1899–1910." *Mississipi Valley Historical Review* 46 (1959): 435–54.

Etō, Shinkichi. "The Policy Making Process of the Proposed Interception of the Peking–Mukden Railway – Tanaka Diplomacy and Its Background." *Acta Asiatica*, no. 14 (March 1968): 21–71.

———. "China's International Relations, 1911–1931." In *The Cambridge History of China*, vol. 13, *Republican China, 1912–1949, Part II*, pp. 74–116. Ed. John K. Fairbank. Cambridge, England, Cambridge University Press, 1986.

Etzold, Thomas H. "In Search of Sovereignty: The Unequal Treaties in Sino-American Relations, 1925–1930." In *China in the 1920s*, eds. F. Gilbert Chan and Thomas H. Etzold, pp. 176–96.

Fairbank, John K., Reischauer, Edwin O., and Craig, Albert M. *East Asia: The Modern Transformation*. Boston: Houghton Mifflin, 1965.

———. *Chinabound: A Fifty-Year Memoir*. New York: Harper & Row, 1982.

———. *The United States and China*, 4th ed., enl. Cambridge, Mass.: Harvard University Press, 1983.

———, ed. *The Cambridge History of China*, vol. 12, *Republican China 1912–1949, Part I*. Cambridge, England: Cambridge University Press, 1983.

Falls, Cyril. *The Art of War from the Age of Napoleon to the Present Day*. New York: Oxford University Press, 1961.

Farwell, Byron. *The Great War in Africa, 1914–1918*. New York and London: Norton, 1986.

Fedorenko, N., trans. and ed. *Izbrannoe*, by Shen Yanping. Moscow: Gosudarstevennoe Izdatel'stvo Khudozhestvennoi Literatury, 1955.

Feetham, R. C. *Report to the Shanghai Municipal Council*, 3 vols. Shanghai, 1931.

Feigon, Lee. *Chen Duxiu: Founder of the Chinese Communist Party*. Princeton: Princeton University Press, 1983.

Festinger, L. "Informal Social Communication," *Psychological Review* **57** (1950): 271–82.

Fenn, William Purviance. *Christian Higher Education in Changing China*. Grand Rapids, Mich.: Eerdmans, 1976.

Feuer, Lewis S. *Basic Writings on Politics and Philosophy: Karl Marx and Friedrich Engels*. Garden City, N.Y.: Anchor Books, 1959.

Field, Frederick V. *American Participation in the China Consortiums*. New York: Institute of Pacific Relations, 1931.

Fifield, Russell H. *Woodrow Wilson and the Far East: The Diplomacy of the Shantung Question*. New York: Crowell, 1952.

Fincher, John H. *Chinese Democracy: The Self-government Movement in Local, Provincial and National Politics, 1905–1914*. New York: St. Martin's, 1981.

Fischer, E. S. *Guide to Peking and Its Environs Near and Far*. Fully revised edition. Tientsin and Peking: Tientsin Press, 1924.

Fishel, Wesley R. *The End of Extraterritoriality in China*. Berkeley: University of California Press, 1952.

Fitzgerald, John, ed. *The Nationalists and Chinese Society 1923–1937: A Symposium*. Melbourne: History Department, University of Melbourne, 1989.

———. "The Irony of the Chinese Revolution." In *The Nationalists and Chinese Society*, pp. 13–43. Ed. John Fitzgerald.

Fogel, Joshua, ed. and trans. *Life Along the South Manchurian Railway: The Memoirs of Itō Takeo*. Armonk, N.Y.: Sharpe, 1988.

Foreign Relations of the United States (annual). Washington, D.C.: U.S. Government Printing Office.

The Foreigner in China. Shanghai: North China Daily News & Herald, 1927.

Freyn, Hubert. *Chinese Education in the War*. Shanghai: Kelly & Walsh, 1940.

Fung, Edmund S. K. "Anti-Imperialism and the Left Guomindang." *Modern China* **11** (1985): 39–76.

———. *The Diplomacy of Imperial Retreat: Britain's South China Policy, 1924–1931.* Hong Kong: Oxford University Press, 1991.

Furth, Charlotte, ed. *The Limits of Change: Essays on Conservative Alternatives in Republican China.* Cambridge, Mass.: Harvard University Press, 1976.

Fussell, Paul. *The Great War and Modern Memory.* New York: Oxford University Press, 1975.

Gaing, Ohn. "American Policy in China 1922–1927." Ph.D. dissertation, Georgetown University, 1953.

Gale, Esson M. *Salt for the Dragon: A Personal History of China, 1908–1945.* East Lansing: Michigan State College Press, 1953.

Gálik, Marián. *Mao Tun and Modern Chinese Literary Criticism.* Wiesbaden: Franz Steiner Verlag, 1969.

Garner, James W. "Revision of Treaties and the Doctrine of *Rebus Sic Stantibus.*" *Iowa Law Review* **19** (1934): 312–29.

Garushiants, Iu. *Dvizhenie 4 Maia 1919 g. v Kitae.* Moscow: "Nauka," 1959.

Gellner, Ernest. *Thought and Change.* (1965) Reprint ed., Chicago: University of Chicago Press, 1978.

———. *Nations and Nationalism.* Ithaca, N.Y., and London: Cornell University Press, 1983.

"General Feng's Coup and What It Has Produced." *China Weekly Review* **30** (November 1, 1924): 267–9.

George, Brian T. "The State Department and Sun Yat-sen: American Policy and the Revolutionary Disintegration of China, 1920–1924." *Pacific Historical Review* **46** (1977): 387–408.

Geertz, Clifford. "The Integrative Revolution: Primordial Sentiments and Civil Politics in the New States." In *Old Societies and New States,* pp. 105–57. Ed. Clifford Geertz. New York: Free Press, 1963.

Gilbert, Rodney. *What's Wrong With China?* London: Murray, 1926.

Gillin, Donald G. *Warlord: Yen Hsi-shan in Shansi Province 1911–1949.* Princeton: Princeton University Press, 1967.

———, and Myers, Ramon H., eds. *Last Chance in Manchuria: The Diary of Chang Kia-Ngau.* Stanford: Hoover Institution Press, 1989.

Gladeck, Frederick Robert. "The Peking Government and the Chinese Eastern Railway Question, 1917–1919." Ph.D. dissertation, University of Pennsylvania, 1972.

Glaim, Lorne Eugene. "Sino-German Relations, 1919–1925: German Diplomatic, Economic and Cultural Re-entry into China after World War I." Ph.D. dissertation, Washington State University, 1973.

Goldstein, Avery. *From Bandwagon to Balance-of-Power Politics: Structural Constraints and Politics in China, 1949–1978.* Stanford: Stanford University Press, 1991.

Goodnow, Frank J. *China: An Analysis.* Baltimore: Johns Hopkins University Press, 1926.

Granat, Stanley J. "Chinese Participation at the Washington Conference, 1921–1922." Ph.D. dissertation, Indiana University, 1969.

Gregg, Alice H. *China and Educational Autonomy: The Changing Role of the Protestant Educational Missionary in China, 1807–1937.* Syracuse, N.Y.: Syracuse University Press, 1946.

Guide to China, 2d ed. Tokyo: Japanese Government Railways, 1924.

Guide to Tientsin, presented by the Astor House Hotel, Ltd. N.p., n.d. In collection of Brown University Library.

Hagerman, Edward. *The American Civil War and the Origins of Modern Warfare: Ideas, Organization, and Field Command.* Bloomington and Indianapolis: Indiana University Press, 1988.

Hall, Josef Washington. [Upton Close] *In the Land of the Laughing Buddha.* New York: Putnam, 1924.

Hao, Yen-p'ing, "Treaty Ports," In *The Encyclopedia of Asian History,* vol. 4, pp. 131–3. Ed. Ainslie T. Embree. New York: Scribner's, 1988.

Hayes, Carlton. *The Historical Evolution of Modern Nationalism.* New York: Macmillan, 1931.

Heinrichs, Waldo. *American Ambassador: Joseph C. Grew and the Development of the United States Diplomatic Tradition.* Boston: Little, Brown, 1966.

———. "The Middle Years, 1900–1945, and the Question of a Large U.S. Policy for East Asia," in *New Frontiers in American–East Asian Relations,* pp. 77–106. Ed. Warren I. Cohen. New York: Columbia University Press, 1983.

Hershatter, Gail. *The Workers of Tianjin, 1900–1949.* Stanford: Stanford University Press, 1986.

Hewlett, Sir Meyrick. *Forty Years in China.* London: Macmillan, 1943.

Ho, C. S. "Where Education Is not a 'Noble Business.'" *The China Weekly Review* **30** (October 18, 1924): 206.

Hobsbawm, Eric. "Some Reflections on Nationalism." In *Imagination and Precision in the Social Sciences, Essays in Memory of Peter Nettl,* pp. 385–406. Ed. T. J. Nossiter, A. H. Hanson, and Stein Rokkan. London: Faber & Faber, 1972.

———. *Nations and Nationalism since 1780: Programme, myth, reality.* Cambridge, England: Cambridge University Press, 1990.

———, and Terence Ranger, eds. *The Invention of Tradition.* Cambridge, England: Cambridge University Press, 1983.

Hogg, Ian. *Grenades and Mortars.* New York: Ballantine Books, 1974.

Holubnychy, Lydia. *Michael Borodin and the Chinese Revolution, 1923–1925.* University Microfilms for East Asian Institute: Columbia University, 1979.

Horn, Maurice, ed. *The World Encyclopedia of Cartoons.* 2 vols. London and New York: Gale Research Company in association with Chelsea House Publishers, 1980.

Hornbeck, Stanley K. *The Situation in China.* New York: The China Society of America, 1927.

———. *The United States and the Far East: Certain Fundamentals of Policy.* Boston: World Peace Foundation, 1942.

Bibliography

Bibliography

Bibliography

Horne, Alistair. *The Fall of Paris: The Siege and the Commune, 1870–1871.* Harmondsworth, England: Penguin, 1981.

———. *The Price of Glory: Verdun 1916.* Harmondsworth, U.K.: Penguin, 1964.

Hosoya, Chihiro. "Britain and the United States in Japan's View of the International System, 1919–1937." In *Anglo Japanese Alienation 1919–1952,* pp. 3–26. Ed. Ian Nish. Cambridge, England: Cambridge University Press, 1982.

Hoston, Germaine A. *Marxism and the Crisis of Development in Prewar Japan.* Princeton: Princeton University Press, 1986.

Houn, Franklin W. *Central Government of China 1912–1928: An Institutional Study.* Madison: University of Wisconsin Press, 1957.

Howard, Michael. *The Franco-Prussian War: The German Invasion of France, 1870–1871.* First published 1961. London and New York: Methuen, 1981.

Hoyt, Frederick B. "Americans in China and the Formation of American China Policy, 1925–1937. Ph.D. dissertation, University of Wisconsin, 1971.

———. "The Open Door Viewed as a Chinese Dynasty." *Australian Journal of Politics and History* 22 (1976): 21–35.

Hroch, Miroslav. *Social Conditions of National Revival in Europe: A Comparative Analysis of the Social Composition of Patriotic Groups among the Smaller European Nations.* Cambridge, England: Cambridge University Press, 1985.

Hsieh, Milton J. *The Kuomintang: Selected Historical Documents 1894–1969.* New York: St. John's University Press, 1970.

Hsieh, Winston. "The Ideas and Ideals of a Warlord: Ch'en Chiung-ming (1873–1933)," *Papers on China,* vol. 16, Harvard University, Cambridge, Mass. 1962.

Hsü, Immanuel C. Y, *China's Entrance into the Family of Nations: The Diplomatic Phase 1858–1880.* Cambridge, Mass.: Harvard University Press, 1960.

———. *The Rise of Modern China,* 2d ed. New York: Oxford University Press, 1975.

Huang, Chinliang Lawrence. "Japan's China Policy Under Premier Tanaka, 1927–1929." Ph.D. dissertation, New York University, 1968.

Huang, Philip C. C. *The Peasant Economy and Social Change in North China.* Stanford: Stanford University Press, 1985.

Huang, T. Young. *The Doctrine of Rebus Sic Stantibus in International Law.* Foreword by V. K. Wellington Koo. Shanghai: Comacrib Press, 1935.

Hunt, Michael H. "Americans and the China Market: Economic Opportunities and Economic Nationalism, 1890–1931." *Business History Review* 51 (1977): 276–307.

———. *The Making of a Special Relationship: The United States and China to 1914.* New York: Columbia University Press, 1983.

———. *Ideology and U.S. Foreign Policy.* New Haven: Yale University Press, 1987.

Hunter, Janet E., comp. *Concise Dictionary of Japanese History.* Berkeley: University of California Press, 1984.

Hyde, Charles Cheney. "The Relinquishment of Extraterritorial Jurisdiction in Siam." *American Journal of International Law* 15 (1921): 428–30.

The I Ching or Book of Changes. The Richard Wilhelm Translation Rendered into English, trans. Cary F. Baynes. Foreword by C. G. Jung. New York: Pantheon Books, 1950.

294

Ikei, Masaru. "Ugaki Kazushige's View of China and His China Policy, 1915–1930." In *The Chinese and the Japanese*, pp. 199–219. Ed. Akira Iriye. Princeton: Princeton University Press, 1980.

Impey, Lawrence. "Flood, Famine, and Civil War." *North China Herald*, October 11, 1924, p. 49.

————. "Chinese Progress in the Art of War." *China Weekly Review*, December 27, 1924, pp. 101–4.

Impey, Lawrence. *The Chinese Army as a Military Force*, 2d and enl. ed. Tientsin: Tientsin Press, 1926.

Institute of Politics, Williams College. *Report of the Round Tables and General Conferences at the Sixth Session*. Ed. Henry M. Wriston. Mimeograph: Williamstown, Mass., Institute of Politics, 1926.

The Institute of Politics at Williamstown, Massachusetts: Its First Decade. Williamstown, Mass.: Institute of Politics, 1931.

Iriye, Akira. *After Imperialism: The Search for a New Order in the Far East 1921–1931*. Cambridge, Mass.: Harvard University Press, 1965.

————. *Across the Pacific: An Inner History of American–East Asian Relations*. New York: Harcourt Brace Jovanovich, 1967.

————. "The Failure of Military Expansionsim." In *Dilemmas of Growth in Prewar Japan*, pp. 107–39. Ed. James Morley. Princeton: Princeton University Press, 1971.

————. "The Failure of Economic Expansionism: 1918–1931." In *Japan in Crisis: Essays on Taishō Democracy*, pp. 237–69. Ed. Bernard S. Silberman and H. D. Harootunian. Princeton: Princeton University Press, 1974.

Isaacs, Harold R. *The Tragedy of the Chinese Revolution*, 2d rev. ed. Stanford: Stanford University Press, 1961.

Israel, John. *The Chinese Student Movement, 1927–1937. A Bibliographical Essay Based on the Resources of the Hoover Institution*. Stanford: Calif.: Hoover Institution, 1959.

————. *Student Nationalism in China, 1927–1937*. Stanford: Calif.: Stanford University Press for The Hoover Institution, 1966.

————, and Klein, Donald W. *Rebels and Bureaucrats: China's December 9ers*. Berkeley, Los Angeles, London: University of California Press, 1976.

Jacobs, Dan N. *Borodin: Stalin's Man in China*. Cambridge, Mass.: Harvard University Press, 1981.

Jansen, Marius B. *The Japanese and Sun Yat-sen*. Cambridge, Mass.: Harvard University Press, 1954.

The Japan Biographical Encyclopedia and Who's Who. Tokyo: Rengo Press, 1958.

Japan. Department of Railways. *Guide to China with Land and Sea Routes Between the American and European Continents*. 2d rev. ed. Tokyo: Japanese Government Railways. 1924.

Jeanneney, Jean-Nöel. "L'affaire de la Banque industrielle de la Chine (1921–1923)." *Revue Historique* **514** (1975): 377–416.

Jenyns, Soame, trans. *Selections from the Three Hundred Poems of the T'ang Dynasty*. London: John Murray, 1940.

Jiang, Arnold Xiangze. *The United States and China.* Chicago: University of Chicago Press, 1988.

Johnson, Chalmers. *Peasant Nationalism and Communist Power: The Emergence of Revolutionary China, 1937–1945.* Stanford: Stanford University Press, 1962.

Johnson, George B., and Lockhoven, Hans Bert. *International Armament With History, Data, Technical Information and Photographs of over 400 Weapons.* Cologne, Germany: International Small Arms Publishers, 1965.

Johnston, R. F. *Twilight in the Forbidden City.* London: Gollancz, 1934.

Jones, Francis Clifford. *Extraterritoriality in Japan and the Diplomatic Relations Resulting in Its Abolition, 1853–1895.* New Haven: Yale University Press, 1931.

———. *Shanghai and Tientsin with Special Reference to Foreign Interests.* With an Introduction by Harold M. Vinacke. San Francisco: American Council Institute of Pacific Relations, 1940.

Jordan, Donald A. *The Northern Expedition: China's National Revolution of 1926–1928.* Honolulu: University Press of Hawaii, 1976.

Josephson, Harold. "Outlawing War: Internationalism and the Pact of Paris." *Diplomatic History* 3 (1979): 377–90.

Kane, Harold Edwin. "Sir Miles Lampson at the Peking Legation, 1926–1933." Ph.D. dissertation, University of London, 1975.

Kapp, Robert A. *Szechwan and the Chinese Republic: Provincial Militarism and Central Power, 1911–1938.* New Haven: Yale University Press, 1973.

Kartunova. A. I. *V. K. Bliukher v Kitae, 1924–1927 gg.: dokumentirovannye ocherk.* Moscow: "Nauka," 1970.

Kedourie, Elie. *The Chatham House Version and other Middle-Eastern Studies.* London: Wiedenfeld and Nicolson, 1970.

———. *Nationalism,* 2d ed. London: Hutchinson University Library, 1985.

Keenlyside, William M. "British Policy in China 1925–1928." Ph.D. dissertation, Clark University, 1938.

Keeton, George W. "The Revision Clause in Certain Chinese Treaties." In *The British Year Book of International Affairs, 1929,* pp. 111–36. London: Humphrey Milford; Oxford University Press, 1929.

Keltie, John Scott, and Epstein, M., eds. *The Statesman's Year-book.* London: Macmillan, 1925.

Kennan, George F. *American Diplomacy 1900–1950.* Chicago: University of Chicago Press, 1951.

———. *Memoirs, 1925–1950.* Boston: Little, Brown, 1972.

Kennedy, Thomas L. *The Arms of Kiangnan: Modernization in the Chinese Ordnance Industry, 1860–1895.* Boulder, Colo.: Westview Press, 1978.

Kiang, Wen-Han. *The Chinese Student Movement.* Morningside Heights, N.Y.: King's Crown Press, 1948.

Kiernan, V. G. "Nationalism." In *A Dictionary of Marxist Thought,* pp. 346–9. Ed. Tom Bottomore. Cambridge, Mass.: Harvard University Press, 1983.

Kindermann, Gottfried-Karl. "The Sino-Soviet Entente Policy of Sun Yat-sen 1923–1925." Ph.D. dissertation, University of Chicago, 1959.

King, Wunsz. *China at the Washington Conference 1921–1922.* New York: St. John's University Press, 1963.

Kirkpatrick, Jeanne J., ed. *The Strategy of Deception: A Study in World-wide Communist Tactics.* New York: Farrar, Straus, 1963.

Kirwin, Harry W. "The Federal Telegraph Company: A Testing of the Open Door," *Pacific Historical Review* **22** (1953): 271–86.

Kitaoka, Shin'ichi. "China Experts in the Army." In *The Japanese Informal Empire in China 1895–1937,* ed. Duus, Myers, and Peattie, pp. 330–68.

Klein, Ira. "Whitehall, Washington, and the Anglo-Japanese Alliance, 1919–1921." *Pacific Historical Review* **41** (1972): 460–83.

Koo, Hui-lan Koo (Madame Wellington Koo). *An Autobiography as Told to Mary Van Rensselaer Thayer.* New York: Dial Press, 1943.

Koo, Wellington [Gu Weijun]. *Memoirs,* microfilm of typescript available in rare books and manuscripts room, Columbia University Library.

———. *The Status of Aliens in China.* Studies in History, Economics and Public Law. Ed. the Faculty of Political Science of Columbia University, vol. 50, no. 2. New York: Columbia University Press, 1912.

Kotenev, Anatol M. *Shanghai: Its Mixed Court and Council.* Shanghai: North-China Daily News & Herald, 1925.

———. *Shanghai: Its Municipality and the Chinese.* Shanghai: North-China Daily News & Herald, 1927.

———. *The Chinese Soldier: Basic Principles, Spirit, Science of War, and Heroes of the Chinese Armies.* Shanghai: Kelly & Walsh, 1937.

Ku, Hung-Ting. "The U.S.A. versus China: The Nanking Incident in 1927." *Tunghai Journal* **25** (1984): 95–110.

Kuhn, Philip A. *Rebellion and Its Enemies in Late Imperial China: Militarization and Social Structure, 1796–1964.* Cambridge, Mass.: Harvard University Press, 1970.

Kuznets, Simon, Moore, Wilbert E., and Spengler, Joseph J., eds. *Economic Growth: Brazil, India, Japan.* Durham, N.C.: Duke University Press, 1955.

Kwang, Eu-yang. *The Political Reconstruction of China.* St. John's University Studies, no. 1. Shanghai: St. John's University, 1922.

Lane, Ortha May. *Under Marching Orders in North China.* Tyler, Tex.: Story-Wright, 1971.

Lang, Olga. *Pa Chin and His Writings.* Cambridge, Mass.: Harvard University Press, 1967.

Lary, Diana. *Region and Nation: The Kwangsi Clique in Chinese Politics 1925–1937.* Cambridge, England: Cambridge University Press, 1975.

———. "Warlord Studies." *Modern China* **6** (October 1980): 439–70.

———. *Warlord Soldiers: Chinese Common Soldiers, 1911–1937.* Cambridge, England: Cambridge University Press, 1985.

———. "Violence, Fear and Insecurity: The Mood of Republican China." *Republican China* **10** (April 1985): 55–63.

Lattimore, Owen. *The Desert Road to Turkestan.* Boston: Little, Brown, 1930.

Lau, Kit-Ching. "Sir John Jordan and the Affairs of China, 1906–1916, with

Special Reference to the 1911 Revolution and Yüan Shih-k'ai." Ph.D. dissertation, University of London, 1968.

Lautenschlager, Roy S. *On the Dragon Hills.* Philadelphia: Westminster Press, 1970.

Lazo, Dmitri Daniel. "An Enduring Encounter: E. T. Williams, China, and the United States." Ph.D. dissertation, University of Illinois at Urbana–Champaign, 1977.

Leary, William M. *The Dragon's Wings: The China National Aviation Corporation and the Development of Commercial Aviation in China.* Athens: University of Georgia Press, 1976.

Lee, Sophia. "Yanjing University, 1937–1941: Autonomy or Compromise?" *Sino-Japanese Studies* 2 (December 1989): 42–68.

Lensen, George Alexander. *The Damned Inheritance: The Soviet Union and the Manchurian Crises 1924–1935.* Tallahassee: Diplomatic Press, 1974.

Leong, Sow-theng. *Sino-Soviet Diplomatic Relations, 1917–1926.* Honolulu: University of Hawaii Press, 1976.

Leys, Simon. *See* Ryckmans, Pierre.

Li, Anthony C. *The History of Privately Controlled Higher Education in the Republic of China.* Washington, D.C.: Catholic University of America Press, 1954. Reprint, Westport, Conn.: Greenwood Press, 1977.

Li Chien-nung. *The Political History of China, 1840–1928.* Trans. Teng Ssu-yu and Jeremy Ingalls. Stanford: Stanford University Press, 1967 (first published 1956).

Li, Dun J. *Modern China: From Mandarin to Commissar.* New York: Scribner's, 1978.

Liddell Hart, B. H. *The Future of Infantry.* London: Faber & Faber, 1933.

Lieu, D. K. *See* Liu, Ta-chün.

Lin, Ch'i-hung. *Political Parties in China.* With a Foreword by Dr. J. C. Ferguson. Peking: Henri Vetch at the French Bookstore, 1930.

Lin, Yü-tang. *With Love and Irony.* New York: John Day, 1940.

———. "In Memoriam of the Dog-Meat General." In *With Love and Irony,* 195–8.

Liu, Kwang-Ching, ed. *American Missionaries in China: Papers from Harvard Seminars.* Cambridge, Mass.: East Asian Research Center, 1966.

Liu, Kwang-Ching and Richard J. Smith. "The Military Challenge: The North-West and the Coast." In *The Cambridge History of China,* vol. 11, *Late Ch'ing, 1800–1911, Part 2,* pp. 202–73. Ed. John K. Fairbank and Kwang-Ching Liu. Cambridge, England: Cambridge University Press, 1980.

Liu, Ta-chün. *China's Industries and Finance.* Peking: Chinese Government Bureau of Economic Information, 1927.

———. *The Growth and Industrialization of Shanghai.* Shanghai: China Institute of Pacific Relations, 1936.

Liu, Ta Jen. *A History of Sino-American Diplomatic Relations 1840–1974.* Taipei: China Academy, 1978.

Lo, Hui-min. *Foreign Office Confidential Papers Relating to China and Her Neighbouring Countries 1840–1914.* Paris: Mouton, 1969.

Loh, Pinchon P. Y. "The Popular Upsurge in China: Nationalism and Westernization, 1919–1927." Ph.D. dissertation, University of Chicago, 1955.

Londres, Albert. "La Chine en Folie." In *Les Oeuvres Libres*, **30** (December 1923): 231–85.

Louis, William Roger. *British Strategy in the Far East 1919–1939*. Oxford: Clarendon Press, 1971.

Lovett, Robert Morse. "Siamese Precedent for China: Extraterritoriality and Tariff Autonomy." *New Republic* **46** (March 31, 1926): 167–9.

Lowe, Donald M. *The Function of "China" in Marx, Lenin, and Mao*. Berkeley: University of California Press, 1966.

Lunt, Carroll, ed. *The China Who's Who 1926 (Foreign): A Biographical Dictionary*. Shanghai: Kelly & Walsh, 1926.

Lutz, Jessie Gregory. *China and the Christian Colleges 1850–1950*. Ithaca and London: Cornell University Press, 1971.

———. *Chinese Politics and Christian Missions: The Anti-Christian Movements of 1920–28*. Notre Dame, Ind.: Cross Cultural Books, 1988.

Lynn, Jermyn Chi-Hung. *See* Lin, Ch'i-hung.

Macartney, C. A. *Survey of International Affairs 1925*; vol. II. London: Oxford University Press, 1928.

McCord, Edward Allen. "The Emergence of Modern Chinese Warlordism: Military Power and Politics in Hunan and Hubei." Ph.D. dissertation, University of Michigan, 1985.

———. "Recent Progress in Warlord Studies in the People's Republic of China." *Republican China* **9** (February 1984): 40–7.

McCormack, Gavan. *Chang Tso-lin in Northeast China, 1911–1928: China, Japan, and the Manchurian Ideal*. Folkestone, Kent, England: Dawson & Sons, 1977.

Mackenzie-Grieve, Averil. *A Race of Green Ginger*. London: Putnam, 1959.

Mackerras, Colin. *Modern China: A Chronology from 1842 to the Present*. With the assistance of Robert Chan. San Francisco: Freeman, 1982.

MacKinnon, Stephen R. *Power and Politics in Late Imperial China: Yuan Shi-kai in Beijing and Tianjin, 1901–1908*. Berkeley, Los Angeles, and London: University of California Press, 1980.

McLean, Donald B., comp. and ed. *Japanese Artillery: Weapons and Tactics*. Wickenburg, Ariz.: Normount Technical Publications, 1973.

MacMurray, John Van Antwerp. *Treaties and Agreements with and Concerning China*, 2 vols. New York: Carnegie Endowment, 1921.

MacNair, Harley Farnsworth. *China's New Nationalism and Other Essays*. Shanghai: Commercial Press, 1926.

———. *Modern Chinese History: Selected Readings*. Shanghai: Commercial Press, 1927.

———. *China in Revolution: An Analysis of Politics and Militarism under the Republic*. Chicago: University of Chicago Press, 1931.

McNeill, William H. *The Pursuit of Power: Technology, Armed Force, and Society since A.D. 1000*. Chicago: University of Chicago Press, 1982.

Mao Tun. *See* Shen, Yanping.

March, Andrew L. *The Idea of China: Myth and Theory in Geographic Thought.* New York: Praeger, 1974.

de Martel, D., and de Hoyer, L. *Silhouettes of Peking.* Trans. D. de Warzee. Peking: China Booksellers, 1926.

Martin, John Patrick. "Politics of Delay: Belgium's Treaty Negotiations with China, 1926–1929." Ph.D. dissertation, St. John's University, 1980.

Marwick, Arthur. *War and Social Change in the Twentieth Century: A Comparative Study of Britain, France, Germany, Russia and the United States.* London: Macmillan, 1974.

Marx, Karl, and Engels, Friedrich. "Manifesto of the Communist Party. In *Basic Writings on Politics and Philosophy: Karl Marx and Friedrich Engels,* pp. 1–41. Ed. Lewis S. Feuer. Garden City, N.Y.: Anchor Books, 1959.

Matsuda, Takeshi. "Woodrow Wilson's Dollar Diplomacy in the Far East: The New Chinese Consortium, 1917–1921." Ph.D. dissertation, University of Wisconsin – Madison, 1979.

May, Ernest R., and Thomson, James C., Jr., eds. *American East Asian Relations: A Survey.* Cambridge, Mass.: Harvard University Press, 1972.

Meisner, Maurice. *Mao's China: A History of the People's Republic.* New York: Free Press, 1977.

Megginson, William James, III. "Britain's Response to Chinese Nationalism, 1925–1927: The Foreign Office Search for a New Policy." Ph.D. dissertation, George Washington University, 1973.

Miliband, S. D. *Bibliograficheskii Slovar' Sovetskikh Vostokovedov.* Moscow: Glavnaia Redaksiia Vostochnoi Literatury, 1975.

Millard, Thomas. *The End of Extraterritoriality in China.* Shanghai: ABC Press, 1931.

Milne, R. S. *Politics in Ethnically Bipolar States: Guyana, Malaysia, Fiji.* Vancouver: University of British Columbia Press, 1981.

Moore, John Allphin, Jr. *The Chinese Consortiums and American China Policy: 1909–1917.* Ph.D. dissertation, Claremont (California) Graduate School, 1972.

Morley, James, ed. *Dilemmas of Growth in Prewar Japan.* Princeton: Princeton University Press, 1971.

———, ed. *Japan's Foreign Policy 1868–1941: A Research Guide.* New York: Columbia University Press, 1974.

———, ed. *Japan Erupts: The London Naval Conference and the Manchurian Incident, 1928–1932: Selected Translations from Taiheiyō Sensō e no michi: kaisen gaikō shi.* New York: Columbia University Press, 1984.

Morrison, G. E. *The Correspondence of G. E. Morrison.* 2 vols. Ed. Lo Hui-min. Cambridge, England: Cambridge University Press, 1976–8.

Morse, Hosea Ballou, and MacNair, Harley Farnsworth. *Far Eastern International Relations.* Cambridge, Mass.: Houghton Mifflin, 1931.

Morton, William Fitch. *Tanaka Giichi and Japan's China Policy.* Folkestone, England: Dawson & Sons, 1980.

Mosse, George L. *The Nationalization of the Masses: Political Symbolism and Mass*

Movements in Germany from the Napoleonic Wars Through the Third Reich. New York: Howard Fertig, 1975.

Murphey, Rhoads. *Shanghai: Key to Modern China.* Cambridge, Mass.: Harvard University Press, 1953.

Murphy, Ethel Andrews. "Celestial Opera Bouffe." *Travel Magazine.* Floral Park, N.Y., **40** (April 1923): 15.

Myers, Ramon H., ed. *Economic Trends and Problems in the Early Republican Period.* New York: Garland Publishing, 1980.

————, and Peattie, Mark, eds. *The Japanese Colonial Experience, 1895–1945.* Princeton: Princeton University Press, 1984.

Nathan, Andrew J. *Modern China, 1840–1972: An Introduction to Sources and Research Aids.* Ann Arbor: University of Michigan, 1971.

————. *Peking Politics 1918–1923: Factionalism and the Failure of Constitutionalism.* Berkeley: University of California Press, 1976.

————. "A Constitutional Republic: The Peking Government, 1916–28. In *The Cambridge History of China,* vol. 12, *Republican China 1912–1949, Part 1,* pp. 259–83. Ed. John K. Fairbank. Cambridge, England: Cambridge University Press, 1983.

The National Sun Yatsen University: A Short History. Canton, China: Sun Yat-sen University, 1934.

Nearing, Scott. *Whither China? An Economic Interpretation of Recent Events in the Far East.* New York: International Publishers, 1927.

"The New Political Lineup and Its International Significance." *China Weekly Review* **30** (November 15, 1924): 329–31.

Nikiforov, V. N. *Sovetskie Istorikii of Problemakh Kitaia.* Moscow: "Nauka," 1970.

Nish, Ian H. *The Anglo-Japanese Alliance: The Diplomacy of Two Island Empires, 1894–1907.* Westport, Conn.: Greenwood Press, 1966.

————. *Alliance in Decline: A Study in Anglo Japanese Relations 1908–1923.* London: University of London, 1972.

————. *Japanese Foreign Policy 1869–1942.* London: Routledge and Kegan Paul, 1977.

————. ed. *Anglo-Japanese Alienation 1919–1952.* Cambridge, England: Cambridge University Press, 1982.

Nossiter, T. J., Hanson, A. H., and Rokkan, Stein, eds. *Imagination and Precision in the Social Sciences, Essays in Memory of Peter Nettl.* London: Faber & Faber, 1972.

Oblas, Peter B. "Treaty Revision and the Role of the American Foreign Affairs Adviser, 1909–1925." *Journal of the Siam Society* **60** (1972): 171–86.

O'Malley, Mary Dolling Sanders [Ann Bridge]. *Peking Picnic.* Boston: Little, Brown, 1932.

————. *The Ginger Griffin.* Boston: Little, Brown, 1934.

————. *A Family of Two Worlds: A Portrait of Her Mother.* New York: Macmillan, 1955.

————. *Facts and Fictions: Some Literary Recollections.* New York: McGraw-Hill, 1968.

O'Malley, Owen St. Clair. *Phantom Caravan.* London: J. Murray, 1954.

Oudendijk, Willem-Jacob. *See* Oudendyk, William J.

Oudendyk, William J. *Ways and By-Ways in Diplomacy.* London: Peter Davies, 1939.

Outerbridge, Leonard M. *The Lost Churches of China.* Philadelphia: Westminster Press, 1952.

Pan Wei-tung [Pan Weidong]. *The Chinese Constitution: A Study of Forty Years of Constitution Making in China.* Washington, D.C.: Institute of Chinese Culture, 1946.

Papageorge, Linda Madson. "The United States Diplomats' Response to Rising Chinese Nationalism, 1900–1912." Ph.D. dissertation, Michigan State University, 1973.

Parker, Geoffrey. *The Military Revolution: Military Innovation and the Rise of the West, 1500–1800.* Cambridge, England: Cambridge University Press, 1988.

Peking, Metropolitan Police. *Soviet Plot in China.* Peking: Metropolitan Police Headquarters, 1927.

Peking, Special Conference on the Chinese Customs Tariff, October 1925–April 1926. Peking: n.p., 1928.

Pelcovits, Nathan A. *Old China Hands and the Foreign Office.* New York: King's Crown Press, 1948.

Perry, Elizabeth J. *Rebels and Revolutionaries in North China, 1845–1945.* Stanford: Stanford University Press, 1980.

Pillsbury, Michael Paul. "Environment and Power: Warlord Strategic Behavior in Szechwan, Manchuria and the Yangtze Delta." Ph.D. dissertation, Columbia University, 1977.

Poe, Dison Hsueh-feng, "Political Reconstruction, 1927–1937." In *The Strenuous Decade: China's Nation-Building Efforts, 1927–1937,* pp. 33–79. Ed. Paul K. T. Sih. New York: St. John's University Press, 1970.

Pollard, Robert T. *China's Foreign Relations, 1917–1931.* New York: Macmillan, 1933.

Pong, David. "The Ministry of Foreign Affairs during the Republican Period, 1912–1920." In *The Times Survey of Foreign Ministries of the World,* pp. 135–53. Ed. Zara Steiner. London: Times Books, 1982.

Pott, F. L. Hawks. *A Short History of Shanghai, Being an Account of the Growth and Development of the International Settlement.* Shanghai: Kelly & Walsh, 1928.

Powell, M. C., ed. *Who's Who in China,* 3d ed. Shanghai: The China Weekly Review, 1925.

Powell, Ralph. *The Rise of Chinese Military Power, 1895–1912.* Princeton: Princeton University Press, 1955.

Power, Brian. *The Ford of Heaven.* London: Peter Owen, 1984.

The Presbyterian Church in the U.S.A. Board of Foreign Missions, *Report on China and Japan, 1926.* New York: The Board of Foreign Missions of the Presbyterian Church in the U.S.A., 1927.

Presseisen, Ernst L. *Before Aggression: Europeans Prepare the Japanese Army.* Tucson: Published for the Association for Asian Studies by the University of Arizona Press, 1965.

Prusek, Jaroslav. *Three Sketches of Chinese Literature.* Prague: The Oriental Institute in Academia, 1969.

Pugach, Noel H. "Progress, Prosperity and the Open Door: The Ideas and Career of Paul S. Reinsch." Ph.D. dissertation, University of Wisconsin, 1967.

———. "Embarrassed Monarchist: Frank J. Goodnow, and Constitutional Development in China, 1913–1915," *Pacific Historical Review* 42 (1973): 499–517.

———. "American Friendship for China and the Shantung Question at the Washington Conference," *Journal of American History* 44 (1977): 67–86.

———. "Anglo-American Aircraft Competition and the China Arms Embargo, 1919–1921." *Diplomatic History* 2 (1978): 351–71.

———. *Paul S. Reinsch: Open Door Diplomat in Action.* Millwood, N.J.: KTO, 1979.

Pye, Lucien W. *Warlord Politics: Conflict and Coalition in the Modernization of Republican China.* New York: Praeger, 1971.

———. *The Spirit of Chinese Politics: A Psychocultural Study of the Authority Crisis in Political Development.* Cambridge, Mass.: The M.I.T. Press, 1968.

Quigley, H. S. "Constitutional and political development in China Under the Republic." *Annals of the American Academy of Political and Social Science,* November 1925, pp. 8–14.

Quint, Howard H., and Ferrell, Robert H., eds. *The Talkative President: Calvin Coolidge.* Amherst, Mass.: University of Massachusetts Press, 1964.

Ramsdell, Daniel Bailey. "Japan's China Policy, 1929–1931 – A Fateful Failure." Ph.D. dissertation, University of Wisconsin, 1961.

Ramsey, Alex., ed. *The Peking Who's Who.* Peking: Tientsin Press, 1922.

Ramsey, S. Robert. *The Languages of China.* Princeton: Princeton University Press, 1987.

Rasmussen, O. D. *Tientsin: An Illustrated Outline History.* Tientsin: Tientsin Press, 1925.

Rawski, Thomas G. *Economic Growth in Prewar China.* Berkeley: University of California Press, 1989.

Rawlinson, John L. *China's Struggle for Naval Development, 1839–1895.* Cambridge, Mass.: Harvard University Press, 1967.

Reeves, William, Jr. "Sino-American Cooperation in Medicine: The Origins of Hsiang-Ya (1902–1914)." In *American Missionaries in China: Papers from Harvard Seminars,* pp. 129–81. Ed. Kwang-Ching Liu. Cambridge, Mass.: East Asian Research Center, 1966.

Reid, Brian Holden. *J. F. C. Fuller: Military Thinker.* New York: St. Martin's, 1987.

Reinsch, Paul S. *Intellectual and Political Currents in the Far East.* Boston: Houghton Mifflin, 1911.

Reinsch, Paul S. *An American Diplomat in China.* New York: Doubleday, 1922.

Remer, C. F. *The Foreign Trade of China.* Shanghai: Commercial Press, 1926.

———. *Foreign Investments in China.* New York: Macmillan, 1933.

Report of the Commission of Extraterritoriality in China. Washington, D.C.: U.S. Government Printing Office, 1926.

Rhoads, Edward J. M. "Lingnan's Response to the Rise of Chinese Nationalism: The Shakee Incident (1925)." In *American Missionaries in China: Papers from*

Harvard Seminars, pp. 183–213. Ed. Kwang-Ching Liu. Cambridge, Mass.: East Asian Research Center, 1966.

Rigby, Richard W. *The May 30 Movement: Events and Themes.* Canberra: Australian National University Press, 1980.

———. "The May Thirtieth Movement: An Outline." Ph.D. dissertation, Australian National University at Canberra, 1975.

Rockhill, William Woodville. *Treaties and Conventions with or concerning China and Korea, 1894–1904, together with various state papers and documents affecting foreign interests.* Washington, D.C.: U.S. Department of State, 1904.

Rosinger, Lawrence K. *China's Wartime Politics 1937–1944.* Princeton: Princeton University Press, 1945.

Rozanski, Mordechai. *A Descriptive Guide and Subject Index to Microcopy, No. 329.* Philadelphia: University of Pennsylvania Press, 1971.

———. "The Role of American Journalists in Chinese–American Relations, 1900–1925." Ph.D. dissertation, University of Pennsylvania, 1974.

Rudman, V., ed. and trans. *Pered Rassvetom,* by Shen Yanping. Moscow: Gosudarstvennoe Izdatel'stvo Khudozhestvennoi Literatury, 1952.

Ryckmans, Pierre [Simon Leys]. *Chinese Shadows.* New York: Viking Press, 1977.

Saggitarius. *See* H. G. W. Woodhead.

Sapozhnikov, V. G. *Pervaia grazhdanskaia revoliutsionnaia Voina v Kitae, 1924–1927 gg. Voenno istoricheskii ocherk.* Moscow: Gosprolitizdat, 1954.

Sayre, Francis Bowes. "The Passing of Extraterritoriality in Siam." *American Journal of International Law* 22 (1928): 70–88.

Scanlan, Patrick John. "No Longer a Treaty Port: Paul S. Reinsch and China, 1913–1919." Ph.D. dissertation, University of Wisconsin, 1973.

Schiffrin, Harold Z. "Military and Politics in China: Is the Warlord Model Pertinent?" *Asia Quarterly: A Journal From Europe* 3 (1975): 195.

Schneider, Laurence A. "National Essence and the New Intelligentsia." In *The Limits of Change: Essays on Conservative Alternatives in Republican China,* pp. 57–89. Ed. Charlotte Furth. Cambridge, Mass.: Harvard University Press, 1976.

Seton-Watson, Hugh. *Nations and States: An Enquiry into the Origins of Nations and the Politics of Nationalism.* Boulder, Colo.: Westview, 1977.

Sforza, Carlo. *Makers of Modern Europe: Portraits and Personal Impressions and Recollections.* London: Elkin Mathews & Marrot, 1930.

Shanghai of To-day: A Souvenir Album of Fifty Vandyck Prints of "The Model Settlement." Introduction by O. M. Green. 2d ed. enl. Shanghai: Kelly & Walsh, 1928.

Shao, Hsi-ping. "Tuan Ch'i-Jui, 1912–1918: A Case Study of the Military Influence on The Chinese Political Development." Ph.D. dissertation, University of Pennsylvania, 1976.

Shen Yanping [Mao Dun]. *Midnight.* Hong Kong: C & W Publishing, 1976.

Sheridan, James L. *Chinese Warlord: The Career of Feng Yü-hsiang.* Stanford: Stanford University Press, 1966.

———. *China in Disintegration: The Republican Era in Chinese History, 1912–1949.* New York: Free Press, 1975.

304

————. "Chinese Warlords: Tigers or Pussycats?" *Republican China* 10 (April 1985): 35–41.

Sih, Paul K. T., ed. *The Strenuous Decade: China's Nation-Building Efforts, 1927–1937.* New York: St. John's University Press, 1970.

Silberman, Bernard S., and Harootunian, H. D., eds. *Japan in Crisis: Essays on Taishō Democracy.* Princeton: Princeton University Press, 1974.

Simpson, B. Lennox [Putnam Weale]. *Why China Sees Red.* New York: Dodd, Mead, 1925.

————. *The Vanished Empire.* London: Macmillan, 1926.

Snow, Edgar. *People on Our Side.* New York: Random House, 1944.

Snow, Helen F. [Nym Wales]. "Notes on the Chinese Student Movement, 1935–1936." Guidance Notes Prepared for the Nym Wales Collection of the Far East in The Hoover Institution on War, Revolution, and Peace, at Stanford University, Stanford, California. Mimeograph, 1959.

Sokolsky, George. *The Tinder Box of Asia.* New York: Doubleday, Doran, 1932.

Solecki, J. J., trans. "Blucher's 'Grand Plan' of 1926." *China Quarterly* 35 (1968): 18–39.

Sorokin, V. F. *Tvorcheskii Put' Mao Duna.* Moscow: Izdatel'stvo Vostochnoi Literarury, 1962.

Soosa. N. M. "The Legal Interpretation of the Abrogation of the Turkish Capitulations." *Dakota Law Review* 3 (1931): 335–64.

Soyeshima, Michimasa, and Kuo, P. W. *Oriental Interpretations of the Far Eastern Problem [Lectures of the Harris Foundation 1925].* Chicago: University of Chicago Press, 1925.

The Special Conference on the Chinese Customs Tariff. Peking: n.p, 1928.

Spector, Stanley. *Li Hung-chang and the Huai Army: A Study in Nineteenth-Century Chinese Regionalism.* Seattle: University of Washington Press, 1964.

Speer, Robert E., and Kerr, Hugh T., presenters. *Report on Japan and China of the Deputation sent by the Board of Foreign Missions of the Presbyterian Church in the U.S.A. to visit these fields and to attend a series of Evaluation Conferences in China in 1926.* New York: The Board of Foreign Missions of the Presbyterian Church in the U.S.A., 1927.

Starr, Daniel P. "Nelson Trusler Johnson: The United States and the Rise of Nationalist China, 1925–1937." Ph.D. dissertation, Rutgers University, 1967.

Strand, David. *Rickshaw Beijing: City People and Politics in the 1920s.* Berkeley: University of California Press, 1989.

Stremski, Richard. "Britain's China Policy 1920–1928." Ph.D. dissertation, University of Wisconsin, 1968.

————. "Britain and Warlordism in China: Relations with Feng Yü-hsiang, 1921–1928." *Journal of Oriental Studies* 11 (January 1973): 91–106.

Strong, Anna Louise. "Chang and Feng and Wu: A Simplification of the Chinese Political Puzzle into Its Elementary Terms." *Asia* 26 (July 1926): 596–601, 649–51.

Suleski, Ronald. "The Rise and Fall of the Fengtien Dollar, 1917–1928: Currency Reform in Warlord China." *Modern Asian Studies* 13 (1979): 643–60.

Survey of International Affairs. London: Oxford University Press, various years.

Sutton, Donald S. *Provincial Militarism and the Chinese Republic: The Yunnan Army, 1905–25.* Ann Arbor: University of Michigan Press, 1980.

Takemoto, Toru. *Failure of Liberalism in Japan: Shidehara Kijuro's Encounter with Anti-Liberals.* Washington, D.C.: University Press of America, 1978.

Takeuchi, Tetsuji. *War and Diplomacy in the Japanese Empire.* New York: Doubleday, Doran, 1935.

T'ang Leang-li. *The Inner History of the Chinese Revolution.* New York: Dutton, 1930.

Taylor, A. J. P. *The First World War: An Illustrated History.* Harmondsworth, Middlesex, England: Penguin Books, 1966.

Tchou, Louis Ngaosiang [Zhu Aoxiang]. *Le Régime des Capitulations et La Réforme Constitutionnelle en Chine.* Cambridge, England: Cambridge University Press, 1915.

"The Living Tree: The Changing Meaning of Being Chinese Today" Special issue of *Daedalus* **120** (Spring 1991).

"This War." *The China Weekly Review* **30** (September 27, 1924), pp. 103–6.

Thomson, James C., Jr. *While China Faced West.* Cambridge, Mass.: Harvard University Press, 1969.

———, Stanley, Peter W., and Perry, John Curtis. *Sentimental Imperialists: The American Experience in East Asia.* New York: Harper & Row, 1981.

Thorne, Christopher. *The Limits of Foreign Policy: The West, The League and The Far Eastern Crisis of 1931–33.* New York: Putnam's, 1972.

———. *Border Crossings: Studies in International History.* Oxford: Basil Blackwell, in association with the East Asian Institute, Columbia University, 1988.

Todd, Oliver J. *The China That I Knew.* Palo Alto, Calif.: Oliver J. Todd, 1973.

Townsend, James R. "Nationalism and the Chinese Revolution Part One: the Culturalism to Nationalism Thesis." Unpublished manuscript.

Tozer, Warren W. "Response to Nationalism and Disunity: United States Relations with the Chinese Nationalists, 1925–1938." Ph.D. dissertation, University of Oregon, 1972.

Toynbee, Arnold J. *Survey of International Affairs 1923,* 2 vols. London: Oxford University Press, 1927.

———. *Survey of International Affairs 1926.* London: Oxford University Press, 1928.

Trani, Eugene P. "Woodrow Wilson, China, and the Missionaries, 1913–1921." *Journal of Presbyterian History* **49** (1971): 328–51.

Tsang, Chiu-sam. *Nationalism in School Education in China,* 2d ed. Hong Kong: Progressive Education Publishers, 1967.

Tung, William L. *The Political Institutions of Modern China.* The Hague: Martinus Nijhoff, 1964.

Tyau, Min-ch'ien T. Z. [Diao Minqian]. *The Legal Obligations Arising Out of Treaty Relations Between China and Other States.* Shanghai: Commercial Press, 1917.

———. *China's New Constitution and International Problems.* Shanghai: Commercial Press, 1918.

———. *China Awakened.* New York: Macmillan, 1922.

———. *Two Years of Nationalist China.* Shanghai: Kelly & Walsh, 1930.

U.S. Congress. *Conference on the Limitation of Armament. Senate Documents,* Vol. 9. 67th Congress, 2d Session 1921–1922, Document No. 126. Washington, D.C.: U.S. Government Printing Office, 1922.

U.S. Congress. *Conference on the Limitation of Armament. Senate Documents* Vol. 10, 67th Congress, 2d Session 1921–1922, Document No. 126. Washington, D.C.: U.S. Government Printing Office, 1922.

U.S. Department of State. *Report of the Commission on Extraterritoriality in China, Peking, September 16, 1926.* Washington, D.C.: U.S. Government Printing Office, 1926.

Ulam, Adam B. *A History of Soviet Russia.* New York: Praeger, 1976.

Usui, Katsumi. "The Role of the Foreign Ministry." In *Pearl Harbor as History,* pp. 127–48. Ed. Dorothy Borg and Shumpei Okamoto. New York: Columbia University Press, 1973.

Vamvoukos, Athanassios. *Termination of Treaties in International Law: The Doctrines of Rebus Sic Stantibus and Desuetude.* Oxford: Clarendon Press, 1985.

Van Meter, Robert H., Jr. "The Washington Conference of 1921–1922: A New Look." *Pacific Historical Review* 46 (1977): 603–24.

Van Slyke, Lyman P., ed. *The China White Paper, August 1949.* Stanford: Stanford University Press, 1967.

Vandervelde, Emile. *A travers la révolution Chinoise: Soviets et Kuomintang.* Paris: Alcan, 1931.

Varè, Daniele. *The Maker of Heavenly Trousers.* New York: Doubleday, Doran, 1936.

———. *Laughing Diplomat.* New York: Doubleday, Doran, 1938.

Varg, Paul A. *Missionaries, Chinese, and Diplomats: The American Protestant Missionary Movement in China, 1890–1952.* Princeton: Princeton University Press, 1958.

Vilensky, V. (Vilensky-Sibiriakov) *Wu Peifu: Kitaiskii militarizm* Giz. Moscow–Leningrad, 1925.

Vinacke, Harold M. *Modern Constitutional Development in China.* Princeton: Princeton University Press, 1920.

Vinson, John Chalmers. *The Parchment Peace: The United States Senate and the Washington Conference, 1921–1922.* Athens: University of Georgia Press, 1955.

Waldron, Arthur N. "Theories of Nationalism and Historical Explanation." *World Politics* 37 (April 1985): 416–33.

———. *The Great Wall of China: From History to Myth.* Cambridge, England: Cambridge University Press, 1990.

———. "The Warlord: Twentieth Century Chinese Understandings of Violence, Militarism, and Imperialism," *American Historical Review* 96 (October 1991): 1073–1100.

———. *How the Peace Was Lost: The 1935 Memorandum "Developments Affecting American Policy in the Far East."* Prepared for the State Department by Ambassador John

Van Antwerp MacMurray. Hoover Archival Documentaries. Stanford: Hoover Institution Press, 1992.

Wales, Nym. See Snow, Helen Foster.

Walker, Richard L. "Students, Intellectuals and 'The Chinese Revolution.'" In *The Strategy of Deception*, pp. 87–108. Ed. by Jeanne J. Kirkpatrick. New York: Farrar, Straus, 1963.

Walt, Stephen M. "Alliance Formation and the Balance of Power." *International Security* 9 (Spring 1985), 3–43.

Wang, Cheng-t'ing. "Looking Back and Looking Forward," unedited typescript memoir available in microform at the Rare Books and Manuscripts Library, Columbia University.

Wang, Gungwu. *China and the World since 1949: The Impact of Independence, Modernity and Revolution.* New York: St. Martin's, 1977.

Wang, Tseng-tsai. *Tradition and Change in China's Management of Foreign Affairs: Sino-British Relations 1793–1877.* Taipei: China Committee for Publication Aid and Prize Awards under the auspices of Soochow University, 1972.

Wang, Y. C. *Chinese Intellectuals and the West, 1872–1949.* Chapel Hill: University of North Carolina Press, 1966.

Ward, Harry F. "The White Boomerang in China: The Patronizing Superiority of the West That Is Firing China to End 'Special Privilege.'" *Asia* 25 (November 1925): 936–40.

Weale, Putnam. See Simpson, B. Lennox.

Weber, Eugen. *Peasants into Frenchmen: The Modernization of Rural France, 1879–1914.* Stanford: Stanford University Press, 1976.

"What's The Matter With China?" *China Weekly Review* 29 (June 7, 1924): 3–4.

Wheeler, W. Reginald. *John E. Williams of Nanking.* Old Tappan, N.J.: Fleming H. Revell, 1937.

———. *The Vanished Empire.* London: Macmillan, 1906.

Who's Who in China, 3d ed. Shanghai: China Weekly Review, 1925.

Who's Who in China, 4th ed. Shanghai: China Weekly Review, 1931.

Wieger, Léon. *Chine moderne*, vol. 6. "Le Feu Aux Poudres." Imprimerie de Hien-hien, 1925.

———. *Chine moderne*, vol. 5. "Nationalisme, xénophobie, anti-Christianisme." Imprimerie de Hien-hien, 1924.

———. *Textes Historiques: Histoire politiques de la Chinese depuis l'origine, jusqu'en 1929*, 2 vols. Hien-hien: Imprimerie de Hien-hien, 1929.

Wilbur, C. Martin. *Forging the Weapons: Sun Yat-sen and the Kuomintang in Canton, 1924.* Mimeograph. New York: East Asian Institute of Columbia University, 1966 (not seen by this author).

———. "Military Separation and the Process of Reunification under the Nationalist Regime, 1922–1937." In *China's Heritage and the Communist Political System*, vol. I, Book 1 of *China in Crisis*, pp. 203–63. Ed. Ping-ti Ho and Tang Tsou. Chicago: University of Chicago Press, 1968.

———. *Sun Yat-sen: Frustrated Patriot.* New York: Columbia University Press, 1976.

————. *The Nationalist Revolution in China, 1923–1928.* Cambridge, England: Cambridge University Press, 1983.

————, and How, Julie. Lien-ying, eds. *Documents on Communism, Nationalism, and Soviet Advisers in China 1918–1927; Papers Seized in the 1927 Peking Raid.* New York: Columbia University Press, 1956.

————. *Missionaries of Revolution: Soviet Advisers and Nationalist China, 1920–1927.* Cambridge, Mass.: Harvard University Press, 1989.

Willert, Sir Arthur. *Aspects of British Foreign Policy.* New Haven: Yale University Press for the Institute of Politics, 1928.

Williams, E. T., and Nicholls, C. S., eds. *Dictionary of National Biography 1961–1970.* Oxford: Oxford University Press, 1981.

Williams, John F. "The Permanence of Treaties: The Doctrine of Rebus Sic Stantibus, and Article 19 of the Covenant of the League." *American Journal of International Law* **22** (1928): 89–104.

Williams, Raymond. *Keywords: A Vocabulary of Culture and Society.* Rev. and exp. ed. London: Fontana, 1983.

Willoughby, Westel W. *Foreign Rights and Interests in China.* Baltimore: Johns Hopkins University Press, 1920.

————. *Constitutional Government in China.* Pamphlet Series of the Carnegie Endowment for International Peace, Division of International Law, No. 47. Washington: Carnegie Endowment, 1922.

Wilson, David A. "Principles and Profits: Standard Oil Responds to Chinese Nationalism, 1925–1926." *Pacific Historical Review* **46** (1977): 625–48.

Winkler, Max. *Foreign Bonds: An Autopsy. A Study of Defaults and Repudiations of Government Obligations.* Philadelphia: Swain, 1933.

Wood, Herbert J. "Nelson Trusler Johnson: The Diplomacy of Benevolent Pragmatism." In *Diplomats in Crisis,* pp. 7–26.

Woodhead, Henry George Wandesforde, ed. *The China Yearbook 1924.* Tientsin: Tientsin Press, 1924.

————. *The China Yearbook 1925–6.* Tientsin: Tientsin Press, 1925.

————. *The Truth About the Chinese Republic.* London: Hurst & Blackett, n.d.

————. *A Journalist in China.* London: Hurst & Blackett, 1934.

————. *Adventures in Far Eastern Journalism: A Record of Thirty-Three Years' Experience.* Tokyo: Hokuseido Press, 1935.

————[Saggitarius]. *The Strange Apotheosis of Sun Yat-sen.* London: Heath, Cranton, 1939.

————. Arnold, Julean, and Norton, Henry Kittredge. *Occidental Interpretations of the Far Eastern Problem (Lectures on the Harris Foundation 1925).* Chicago: University of Chicago Press, 1926.

Wou, Odoric Y. K. *Militarism in Modern China: The Career of Wu P'ei-Fu, 1916–39.* Folkestone, Kent, England: Dawson & Sons; also Canberra: Australian National University Press, 1978.

Wright, Mary Clabaugh, ed. *China in Revolution: The First Phase, 1900–1913.* New Haven: Yale University Press, 1968.

Wright, Stanley F. *China's Customs Revenue since the Revolution of 1911,* 3d ed.

Revised and enlarged with the assistance of John H. Cubbon. Shanghai: Inspectorate General of Customs, 1935.

Wright, Stanley F. *China's Struggle for Tariff Autonomy*. Shanghai: Kelly & Walsh, 1938.

"Writing 'Nationalism' Above the Open Door." *The Independent* (June 27, 1925), p. 714.

Yang, Dali. "Beiyang University, 1895–1912: Charles D. Tenney and the Politics of Educational Entrepreneurship." Paper presented to the Workshop on the History of Christian Higher Education in China, Yale University, February 1990.

Yen, Hawkling L. [Yan Heling] *A Survey of Constitutional Development in China*. Studies in History, Economics and Public Law. Ed. the Faculty of Political Science of Columbia University, vol. 40, no. 1. New York: Columbia University Press, 1911.

Yen, W. W. [Yan Huiqing]. *East–West Kaleidoscope, 1877–1946: An Autobiography*. New York: St. John's University, 1974.

Yip, Ka-che. "The Anti-Christian Movement in China, 1922–1927 with Special Reference to the Experience of Protestant Missions." Ph.D. dissertation, Columbia University, 1970.

Young, C. Walter. *The International Relations of Manchuria*. Chicago: University of Chicago Press, for American Council, Institute of Pacific Relations, 1929.

———. *Japan's Special Position in Manchuria*. Baltimore: Johns Hopkins University Press, 1931.

Young, Ernest P. *The Presidency of Yuan Shih-k'ai: Liberalism and Dictatorship in Early Republican China*. Ann Arbor: University of Michigan Press, 1977.

Young, John W., "The Hara Cabinet and Chang Tso-lin, 1920–1." *Monumenta Nipponica*, **27** pt. 2 (Summer 1972): 125–42.

Yu, George T., *Party Politics in Republican China: The Kuomintang, 1912–1924*. Berkeley: University of California Press, 1966.

Zhu, Aoxiang. *See* Tchou, Louis Ngaosiang.

Chinese and Japanese sources

Periodicals

Beiyang Zhengfu Gongbao, 《北洋政府公報》 ed. Zhongguo di er lishidangang-uan. Shanghai: Shanghai shudian, n.d.

Chenbao 晨報 [The Morning Post] (Beijing)

Dongfang zazhi 東方雜誌 [Eastern Miscellany]

Shenbao 申報 [The Shun Pao] (Shanghai)

Shengjing shibao 盛京時報 (Mukden)

Xiandai pinglun 現代評論

Books and Articles

Bai Jianwu 白堅武. "Di erci Zhi-Feng zhanzheng riji" "第二次直奉戰爭日記". *Jindaishi ziliao* 《近代史資料》 47 (1982): 100–12.

"Beijing zhengju de bianhua" "北京政局的變化". *Dongfang zazhi* 《東方雜誌》 21 (1924): no. 20, 1–3; no. 21, pp. 1–4.

Bi Keguan and Huang Yuanlin 畢克官、黃遠林. *Zhongguo manhuashi* 《中國漫畫史》. Beijing: Wenhua yishu chubanshe, 1986.

Cai Yiming 蔡一鳴. "Guanyu 'Jiang-Zhe zhanzheng de qianyin houguo' he 'Qilu zhi zhan jilue' de dingzheng" "關於'江浙戰爭的前因後果'和'齊盧之戰紀略'的訂正". In *Wenshi ziliao xuanji* 《文史資料選輯》, no. 51: 273–7. Beijing: Wenshi ziliao chubanshe, n.d.

Cai Zhongxing 蔡中興. *Diguo zhuyi lilun fazhan shi.* 《帝國主義理論發展史》. Shanghai: Shanghai renmin chubanshe, 1987.

Chang Cheng, ed. 常城編, *Zhang Zuolin* 《張作霖》. Shenyang: Liaoning renmin chubanshe, 1980.

———. "Fengxi junfa de 'zhinang' Yang Yuting" "奉系軍閥的'智囊'楊宇霆". *Shehui kexue zhanxian* (1984): 《社會科學戰線》 no. 1, 219–24.

Chen Changhe 陳長河. "Cong dangan kan Beiyang junfa tongzhi shiqi de lujun ji qi junfei" "從檔案看北洋軍閥統治時期的陸軍及其軍費". *Lishi jiaoxue* 《歷史教學》 (1983): no. 8, 39–40.

Chen Chongqiao 陳崇橋. "Fengxi junfa yu zhishi fenzi" "奉系軍閥與知識份子". *Liaoning daxue xuebao* 《遼寧大學學報》 (1986): no. 3, 80–5.

Chen Cungong 陳存恭. *Lieqiang dui Zhongguo de junhuo jinyun (Minguo ba nian – sh iba nian* 《列強對中國的軍火禁運（民國8年–18年）》. Zhongyang yanjiu yuan jindaishi yanjiusuo zhuankan 47. 中央研究院近代史研究所專刊 47. Taibei: Zhongyang yanjiu yuan, 1983.

Chen Fang zhi 陳芳芝. "Meiguo diguo zhuyi zai Huashengdun huiyizhong zaige Zhongguo de yinmo" "美國帝國主義在華盛頓會議中宰割中國的陰謀". *Beijing daxue xuebao* 《北京大學學報》 (1955): no. 2, 75–7.

Chen Guanxiong 陳冠雄. *Zhi Feng Zhanyun lu* 《直奉戰雲錄》. Tianjin: Tianjin Xinminyibao chubanshe 榮孟源、章伯鋒主編, 1922. In JDBH, vol. 5, 《近代稗海》第五輯, 3–187.

Chen Lunqing and Ma Kunjie. 陳倫慶、馬昆傑. *Wu Peifu jiangjun zhuan* 《吳佩孚將軍傳》. Hong Kong: n.p., n.d.

Chen Mingzhong 陳鳴鐘. "Duan Qirui churen linshi zhizheng de jige pianduan" "段祺瑞出任臨時執政的幾個片斷". *Lishi dangan* 《歷史檔案》 (1982): no. 2, 117–22.

Chen Shaoxian 陳劭先. "Xinhai geming hou Sun Xhongshan zai Guangdong de jiqi jiluo" "辛亥革命後孫中山在廣東的幾起幾落". *Wenshi ziliao xuanji* 《文史資料選輯》 no. 24 (1960–): 24, 1–16.

Chen Shiru 陳世如. "Cao Kun jiazu dui renmin de jingji lueduo he yazha" "曹錕家族對人民的經濟掠奪和壓榨". In *Tianjin wenshi ziliao xuanji*, no. 1, 99–112 《天津文史資料選輯》第一輯 pp. 99–112. Tianjin: Tianjin renmin chubanshe, 1978.

Chen Xizhang 陳錫璋. *Xishuo Beiyang* 《細説北洋》. Taibei: Zhuanji Wenxue chubanshe, 1982.

Chen Xiuhe 陳修和. "Feng Zhang shiqi he Ri wei shiqi de Dongbei binggongchang" "奉張時期和日偽時期的東北兵工廠". *Wenshi ziliao xuanji* 25 (1962): no. 1, 《文史資料選輯》第二十五輯 1962年, no. 1. 150–65.

Cheng Daode, Zheng Yueming, and Rao Geping, eds. 程道德、鄭月明、饒戈平編. *Zhonghua Minguo waijiaoshi ziliao xuanbian (1919–1931)* 《中華民國外交史資料選編, 1919–1931》. Beijing: Beijing Daxue chubanshe, 1985.

———, Zhang Minzheng, Rao Geping, and Liu Peihua, eds. 張敏孚、饒戈平、劉培華編朱憲、徐鶴雲 *Zhonghua Minguo waijiaoshi ziliao xuanbian (1911–1919)* 《中華民國外交史資料選編 (一), 1911–1919》. Beijing: Beijing Daxue chubanshe, 1988.

China. Waijiaobu danganzixunchu, ed. 外交部檔案資訊處編. *Zhongguo zhuwai ge da gong shiguan liren guanzhang xianming nianbiao.* 《中國駐外各大公使館歷任館長銜名年表》. Taibei: Taiwan Shangwu, 1969.

Deng Hanxiang 鄧漢祥. "Jiang Zhe zhanzheng de qianyin houguo" "江浙戰爭的前因後果". In *Wenshi ziliao xuanji*, no. 35, 34–40, 《文史資料選輯》Vol. 35, pp. 34–40. Beijing: Wenshi ziliao chubanshe, 1963.

———. "Wo suo liaojie de Duan Qirui" "我所了解的段祺瑞", in *Beiyang junfashi shiliao xuanji* 《北洋軍閥史史料選輯》. Ed. Du Chunhe, Lin Binsheng, and Qiu Quanzheng 杜春和、林斌生、丘權政編 Beijing: Zhongguo shehui kexue chubanshe, 1981, vol. 2, pp. 287–301.

Ding Wenjiang 丁文江, ed. *Minguo junshi jinji* 民國軍事近記, [1926] reprint ed. Taibei: Wenhai chubanshe, n.d.

"Dongbei zhanzheng de shengfu juedingle" "東北戰爭的勝負決定了". *Dongfang zazhi* 《東方雜誌》 21 (1924): no. 21, pp. 4–5.

"Dongnan zhanshi de liaojie" "東南戰事的了結". *Dongfang zazhi* 《東方雜誌》 21 (1924): no. 19, 1–6.

Du Chunhe, Lin Binsheng, and Qiu Quanzheng, eds. 杜春和、林斌生、丘權政編. *Beiyang junfashi xuanji* 2v. 《北洋軍閥史料選輯》. Beijing: Zhongguo shehui kexue yuan chubanshe, 1981.

Du Lianqing 杜連慶. "Dongbeijun kongjun shimo." "東北軍空軍始末" *Shehui kexue zhanxian* 《社會科學戰線》 (1988) No. 1, pp. 194–7.

Duan Yunzhang and Qiu Jie 段雲章、邱捷. *Sun Zhongshan yu Zhongguo jindai junfa* 《孫中山與中國近代軍閥》. Chengdu: Sichuan renmin chubanshe, 1990.

"Dujun chengbing yu fubi" "督軍逞兵與復辟". *Xin qingnian* 《新青年》, vol. 3, no. 6 (August 1917), 561–67.

"Feng-E xieding yu Zhongdonglu gaizu" "奉俄協定與中東路改組". *Dongfang zazhi* 《東方雜誌》 21 (1924): no. 19, pp. 9–13.

"Feng-E xieding cao'an" "奉俄協定草案". *Dongfang zazhi* 《東方雜誌》 21 (1924): no. 19, pp. 149–152.

Feng Yuxiang 馮玉祥. *Feng Yuxiang zizhuan* 《馮玉祥自傳》. Beijing: Junshi kexue chubanshe, 1988.

————. *Wo de shenghuo* 《我的生活》. Ha-er-bin: Heilongjiang chubanshe, 1981.

Fu Xingpei 傅興沛. "Di er ci Zhi Feng zhanzheng jishi" "第二次直奉戰爭紀實". *Wenshi ziliao xuanji*, no. 4, pp. 29–53. 《文史資料》 no. 4, pp. 29–53. Beijing: Wenshi ziliao chubanshe 1960.

Gao Dunfu 高敦复. "Feng Yuxiang yu junfa jituan" "馮玉祥與軍閥集團". *Zhongguo shehui kexueyuan yanjiushengyuan xuebao* 《中國社會科學院研究生院學報》 (1985), no. 6, pp. 71–7.

Gao Mingkai and Liu Zhengtan, eds. 高名凱、劉正埃編. *Xiandai Hanyu Wailaizi Yanjiu* 《現代漢語外來字研究》. Beijing: Wenzi gaige chubanshe, 1958.

Gao Zhennong 高振農. *Longhuasi* 《龍華寺》. Shanghai: Shanghai shehui kexueyuan chubanshe, 1989. 上海、上海社會科學院出版社, 1989.

Gensui Uehara Yūsaku denki hensan iinkai. 元帥上原勇作傳編纂委員會. *Gensui Uehara Yūsaku denki*. Tokyo: Gensui Uehara Yūsaku kankōkai, 1937. 東京元師上原勇作刊行會昭和 12.

Gu Tiaosun 古蕕孫. *Jiazi neiluan shimou jishi* 《甲子內亂始末紀實》. Shanghai: Zhonghua shuju 見榮孟源、章伯鋒主編, 1924. In JDBH, vol. 5, pp. 191–361.

————. *Yichou junfa bianluan jishi* 《乙丑軍閥變亂紀實》. Beijing: Heping yinshuaju, 1926. In JDBH, vol. 5, pp. 463–592. 見榮孟源、章伯鋒主編《近代稗海》, Vol. 5, pp. 463–592.

Gu Weijun 顧維鈞. *Gu Weijun Huiyilu* 《顧維鈞回憶錄》 5v. Beijing: Zhonghua shuju, 1983.

Guo Fu Quanji 《國父全集》. Taibei: Zhongyang wenwu gongyingshe, 1961.

Guo Jianlin 郭劍林. "Beiyang Zhengfu gechao gaishu". *Tianjin shizhvan xuebao* No. 4 (1983), pp. 54–58.

————. "Hunan shengxian yundong zhi kaocha" "湖南省憲運動之考察". *Nankai shixue* 《南開史學》 no. 1 (1984), pp. 189–215.

————. "Wu Peifu yu Riben" "吳佩孚與日本". In *Zhong Ri guanxishi yanjiu*, 中日關係史研究編輯組編 no. 3 pp. 217–34. 《中日關係史研究》. no. 3, pp. 217–34. Ed. Zhong Ri guanxishi yanjiu bianjizu. Shenyang: Dongbei diqu Zhong Riguanxishi yanjiuhui, 1984.

————. "Lue lun Xinan gesheng 'zizhi' chaoliu he 'feiducaibing' de husheng." In *Xinan junfashi yanjiu congkan*, "略論西南各省'自治'潮流和'廢督裁兵'的呼聲" no. 3, pp. 48–65. Ed. Xinan junfashi yanjiuhui. Kunming: Yunnan renmin chubanshe, 1985.

————. "Wusi shiqi de Wu Peifu" "五四時期的吳佩孚". *Xueshu yuekan* 《學術月刊》 (1985): no. 11, pp. 74–9.

————. "Zhi Feng Tianjin fenzang huiyi ji qi eguo" "直奉天津分贓會議及其惡果". *Tianjin shi yanjiu* 《天津史研究》 no. 2 (1985): pp. 22–33.

————. "Zhang Zuolin yu Wu Peifu." "張作霖與吳佩孚". *Dongbei difangshi yanjiu* 《東北地方史研究》 (1986): No. 2, pp. 53–8.

————. "Kangzhan shiqi de Wu Peifu" "抗戰時期的吳佩孚". *Xueshu yuekan* 《學術月刊》 (1987): no. 5, pp. 78–9.

————. "Liang ci Zhi Feng zhanzheng zhi bijiao" "兩次直奉戰爭之比較". *Lishi dangan* 《歷史檔案》 (1987), no. 3, pp. 108–12.

————. "Sun Zhongshan yu Wu Peifu" "孫中山與吳佩孚". *Xueshu yuekan* 《學術月刊》 (1987): no. 5, pp. 76–81.

————. "Sun Zhongshan yu junfa – jian da Hu Xianzhong tongzhi" "孫中山與軍閥——兼答胡顯中同志". *Xueshu yuekan* 《學術月刊》, No. 10 (1988), pp. 50–6.

————. "Yuan Shikai de 'shu'" "袁世凱的'術'" "*Minguo chunqiu* 《民國春秋》 (1988) No. 2, pp. 49–50.

————. "Huaijun – Zhongguo jindai junfa zhidu de fazhan" "准軍—中國近代軍閥制度的發展". *Zhongguo jindai junshishi yanjiu tongxun* 《中國近代軍事史研究通訊》 No. 1 (1989), pp. 14–16.

————. "Lue lun Sun Duan Zhang fan Wu san jiao lianmeng" "略論孫、段、張反吳三角聯盟". *Zhongguo jindai junshishi yanjiu tongxun* 《中國近代軍事史研究通訊》 No. 4 (1990), pp. 1–16.

————. "Sun Zhongshan yu Beiyang junfa" "孫中山與北洋軍閥". Sun Zhongshan yanjiu "孫中山研究" No. 2 (1990), pp. 73–89.

————. "Wu Peifu pingzhuan" "吳佩孚評傳". In *Jindai Zhongguo renwu* No. 2. pp. 504–48, 《中國近代人物》 No. 2. pp. 504–48. A special issue of *Jindaishi yanjiu* 《近代史研究專刊》.

————. *Wu Peifu da zhuan: yidai xiaoxiong* 《吳佩孚大傳—— 一代梟雄》. Tianjin: Tianjin daxue chubanshe, 1991. 2v.

Guo Jianlin and Hao Qingyuan 郭劍林、郝慶元. "Wu Peifu yu Xinan junfa" "吳佩孚與西南軍閥". In *Xinan junfashi yanjiu congkan* 《西南軍閥研究叢刊》, no. 5, pp. 1–17. Guangzhou: Guangdong renmin chubanshe, 1986.

Guo Jianlin and Wang Huabin 郭劍林、王華斌. "Zhi Wan zhanzheng de shehui lishi beijing" "直皖戰爭的社會歷史背景". *Hangzhou shiyuan xuebao* 《杭州師範學院學報》 1986 No. 3, pp. 88–94.

————. "Lu Yongxiang du Zhe shi zhi kaocha" "盧永祥督浙史之考察". *Hangzhou shifanxueyuan xuebao* 《杭州師範學院學報》 No. 1 (1988), pp. 99–103.

Guo Xipeng 郭希鵬. "Wo sui Fengjun sanjia Nankou zhanyi zhi huiyi" "我隨奉軍參加南口戰役之回憶". In *Wenshi ziliao xuanji* 《文史資料選輯》 No. 51, pp. 114–22. Beijing: Wenshi ziliao chubanshe, 1962.

Guo Xuyin and Chen Xingtang, eds. 郭緒印、陳興唐. *Aiguo jiangjun Feng Yuxiang* 《愛國將軍馮玉祥》. Henan renmin chubanshe, 1987.

Guoli Zhongxing Daxue lishixi Zhongguo tongshi jiaoxue yantaohui, 國立中興大學歷史系中國通史教學研討會編 ed. *Zhongguo xiandaishi lunwen xuanji* 《中國現代史論文選輯》. Tainan: Jiuyang chubanshe, 1985.

Han Hongtai 韓宏泰. "Beiyang junfa shiqi de Jiaotong yinhang" "北洋軍閥時期的交通銀行". *Wenshi ziliao xuanji* No 《文史資料選輯》. 88 [hedingben, collected ed.], vol. 30, pp. 90–110.

Hata Ikuhiko, 泰郁彥 ed. Senzenki Nihon Kanryōsei no seido, soshiki jinji, 戰前期日本官僚制の制度，人事組織. Tokyo: Tokyo University Press, 1981.

He Ben Da Zuo [Kawamoto Daisaku] 河本大作者.武育文譯. "Wo sha le Zhang Zuolin" "我殺了張作霖". Trans. Wu Yuwen. *Jindaishi ziliao* 《近代史資

料》 No. 47. Beijing: Zhongguo shehui kexue yuan chubanshe, 1982, pp. 113–23.

He Xiya 何西亞. "Jiazi dazhanhou quanguo jundui zhi diaocha" "甲子大戰後全國軍隊之調查". *Dongfang zazhi* 《東方雜誌》 22(1925) no. 1, pp. 103–12; no. 2, pp. 34–57; no. 3, pp. 69–83.

Hu Chunhui 胡春惠. *Minchu de difang zhuyi yu liansheng zizhi.*《民國的地方主義與聯省自治》. Taibei: Zhengzhong shuju, 1983.

Hu Menghua 胡夢華. "Zhongguo junfa zhi she de xushu" "中國軍閥之史的敍述". In *Zhongguo xiandaishi lunwen xuanji* 《中國現代史論文選輯》, pp. 235–83.

Hu Shi 胡適. "Guojizhong de Zhongguo" [1922] "國際中的中國" [1922]. In *Hu Shi Zuopinji* 見《胡適作品集》, 9: 89–95. Taibei: Yuanliu, 1986.

Huang Yingqian, Chen Zuwu, and Liu Kejun 黃應乾、陳祖武、劉克俊. "Wu Peifu liuyu Sichuan wunianzhong de yinmou huodong" "吳佩孚流寓四川五年中的陰謀活動". *Wenshi ziliao xuanji* 《文史資料選輯》, No. 41, pp. 193–209.

Huang Zheng, Chen Changhe, Ma Lie 黃征、陳長河、馬烈. *Duan Qirui yu Wanxi junfa* 《段祺瑞與皖系軍閥》. Zhengzhou: Henan renminchubanshe, 1990.

Ikei Masaru 池井優 "Dainiji Hōchoku sensō to Nihon." 第二次奉直戰爭と日本. In *Tai-Manmō seisakushi no ichimen: Nichi-Ro sengo yori Taishōki ni itaru*, 對滿蒙政策的一面:日露戰後より大正期にいたる. Ed. Ken Kurihara 栗原健. Tokyo: Hara Shobō, 1966.

Japan. Gaimushō 外務省, comp. *Nihon gaikō Nempyō Narabini Shuyō Bunsho* 日本外交年表重要文書. Tokyo: Nihon Kokusai rengō Kyokai, 1955.

Japan. Gaimushō 外務省, comp. *Nihon Gaikō bunsho* 日本外交文書. Tokyo: Ministry of Foreign Affairs, 1949.

Japan. Gaimushō gaikō shiryokan 外務省外交史料館, comp. *Nihon gaikōshi jiten* 日本外交史辭典. Tokyo: Okurashō, 1979.

Ji chen ju shi 寄塵居士, ed. *Zhi Feng Da Zhan shi* 《奉直大戰史》. Shanghai: Shanghai weiyi tushuguan, 1922.

Ji Di 吉迪. "Beiyang junfa zhengke zichan jiwen" "北洋軍閥政客資產紀聞". *Jindaishi ziliao* 《近代史資料》 No. 36 (1978), pp. 163–75.

Jia Zi Feng Zhi zhan shi 《甲子奉直戰史》. Shanghai: Hongwen tushuguan, 1924.

Jian Youwen 簡又文. "Feng Yuxiang zhuan" "馮玉祥傳". *Zhuanji wenxue* 《傳記文學》 37.2 pp. 132–40; 37.3, pp. 133–40.

Jiang Changren 江長仁. *San Yiba canan ziliao huibian* 《三•一八慘案資料匯編》. Beijing: Beijing chubanshe, 1985.

Jiang Duo 姜鐸. "Lue lun jiu Zhongguo san da caituan" "略論舊中國三大財團". *Shehui kexue zhanxian* 《社會科學戰線》 1982, No. 3, pp. 186–99.

Jiang Duo 姜鐸. "Lue lun jiu Zhongguo sanzhong zibenzhuyi" "略論舊中國三種資本主義". *Shehui kexue zhanxian* 《社會科學戰線》 1986, no. 2, pp. 175–83.

Jiang Ming 姜鳴. "Sanyang haijun kaobian – jian lun Qing zhengfu fazhan jindai haijun de gouxiang he shishi" "三洋海軍'考辨'——兼論清政府發展近代海軍的構想和實施". *Xueshu yuekan* 《學術月刊》 (1986), no. 10, pp. 66–70.

Jiang Zhe zhan shi 《江浙戰史》. Shanghai: Hongwen tushuguan 1924.

Jiang Zuobin 蔣作賓. "Jiang Zuobin huiyilu." "蔣作賓回憶錄" *Jindai Zhongguo* 《近代中國》, no. 35 (1982), pp. 145–56.

Jiaotong yinhang 交通銀行編, ed. *Jiaotong yinhang qishi nian* 《交通銀行七十年》. Jiaotong yinhang: Taibei, 1982.

Jin Baohua 金保華. "Feng Yuxiang yu Beijing zhengbian" "馮玉祥與北京政變". *Lishi jiaoxue* 《歷史教學》 (1983), No. 12, pp. 29–40.

Jin Liang 金梁. "Yu bian riji" "遇變日記". In *Wenshi ziliao xuanji* 《文史資料選輯》, (1960–) 30, 94–111.

Jin Sheng 金聲. "Di er ci Zhi Feng zhanzhengzhong Feng Wang miyi dao Zhi de shi hedi" "第二次直奉戰爭中馮王密議倒直的時和地". *Lishi dangan* 《歷史檔案》 (1982), no. 1, p.129.

Jin Yan 金研, "Guanyu Jincheng yinhang de ruogan shiliao" "關於金城銀行的若干史料". *Xueshu yuekan* 《學術月刊》 (1962), No. 19, pp. 30–8.

Jin Youyan 荊有岩. "Di er ci Zhi Feng zhan Jiumenko zhangdou de huiyi" "第二次直奉戰九門口戰鬥的回憶". In *Wenshi ziliao xuanji* 《文史資料選輯》, No. 3, pp. 40–51. Shenyang: Liaoning renmin chubanshe, 1963.

Kabashima Tadao 樺島忠夫. *Meiji Taishō shingō zokugo jiten* 明治大正新語俗語辭典. Tokyo: Tokyōdō, 1985.

Kong Jingwei 孔經緯. "Guanyu Zhongguo de zibezhuyi xingcheng he zichanjieji xingcheng" "關於中國的資本主義形成和資產階級形成". *Shehui kexue zhanxian* 《社會科學戰線》 1985 No. 4, pp. 153–56.

Kurihara Ken 栗原健, ed. *Tai-Manmō seisakushi no ichimen: Nichi-Ro sengo yori Taishōki ni itaru.* 對滿蒙政策の一面:日露戰後より大正期にいたる. Tokyo: Hara Shobō, 1966.

Laijiang zhuowu 瀨江濁物. *Wu Peifu zheng zhuan* 吳佩孚正傳. Shanghai: Zhongyang guoshi bianjishe, 1920.

Lai Xinxia 來新夏, ed. *Beiyang junfa* 《北洋軍閥》 5 vols. Shanghai: Shanghai renmin chubanshe, 1988–1993.

Lai Xinxia, Guo Jianlin, and Jiao Jingyi 來新夏、郭劍林、焦靜宜. "Lue lun Beiyang junfa shi yanjiu zhong de jige wenti" "略論北洋軍閥史研究中的幾個問題". *Xueshu yuekan* 《學術月刊》 (1982), No. 4, pp. 58–63.

———. *Beiyang junfa shigao* 《北洋軍閥史稿》. Hubei renmin chubanshe, 1983.

Lan Changyun 藍長雲. "Jindai fandi aiguo yundongzhong de Tianjin shanghui – dui 'Tianjin shanghui dangan shiliao huibian' yi shu suo if Tianjin shanghui canyu jindai fandi aiguo yundong shiliao de pingjie" "近代反帝愛國運動中的天津商會——對《天津商會檔案史料匯編》一書所輯天津商會參與近代反帝愛國運動史料的評介". Zhongguo shanghui yu zichanjieji xueshu taolun hui lunwen《中國商會與資產階級學術討論會論文》. Tianjin: Tianjin shi danganguan, 1986.

Li Bingzhi 李炳之. "Wu Peifu zhi zaiqi yu baikuei" "吳佩孚之再起與潰敗". In *Wenshi ziliao xuanji* 《文史資料選輯》 No. 41, pp. 162–77. Beijing: Wenshi ziliao chubanshe, 1963.

Li Chengyi 李誠毅. *Sanshinian lai jiaguo—Zhonguo jindai yi shi* 《三十年來家國——中國近代逸史》. 2 vols. Hong Kong: Zhenghua chubanshe, 1962.

Li Jun 李軍. "Di er ci ZhiFeng zhanzhengzhong Zhixi shibai de yuanyin" "第二次直奉戰爭中直系失敗的原因". *Jindaishi yanjiu* 《近代史研究》 (1985) No. 2, pp. 158–70.

Li Taifen 李泰芬. *Guominjun shigao* 《國民軍史稿》. Reprint ed. Taibei: Wenhai, n.d.

Li Xin 李新, "Junfa lun." "軍閥論" *Shixue yuekan* 《史學月刊》 (1985) No. 1, pp. 90–4.

Li Xianke 李憲科. *Zhongguo junshi zhi zuijian shuo* 《中國軍史之最簡説》. Jinan: Shandong renmin chubanshe, 1989.

Li Zaolin 李藻麟. "Er ci ZhiFeng zhan Zhanzheng zhong Shanhaiguan zhanyi qinliji." "二次直奉戰爭中山海關戰役親歷記" *Wenshi ziliao xuanji* 《文史資料選輯》 No. 4, pp. 38–53. Beijing: Wenshi ziliao chubanshe, 1960.

Li Zhongsan 李仲三. "Guominjun dao Cao zhi zhenxiang." "國民軍倒曹之真相" In *Wenshi ziliao xuanji* 《文史資料選輯》 No. 51, pp. 53–4. Beijing: Wenshi ziliao chubanshe, 1962.

Li Zongying 李宗穎. "Lue shu Dongbei daxue." "略述東北大學" In Liaoning wenshi ziliao 《遼寧文史資料》 No. 8, pp. 65–85. Shenyang: Liaoning renmin chubanshe,1984.

Liaoning sheng danganguan 遼寧省檔案館, ed. "Beiyang zhengfu zhenya Fengtian shengyuan wu-sa yundong handian xuan." "北洋政府鎮壓奉天聲援五州運動函電選" *Lishi dangan* 《歷史檔案》 (1984) No. 1, pp. 51–60.

———. *Zhonghua Minguo shi ziliao conggao – diangao—Fengxi junfa midian di yi ce* 《中華民國史資料叢稿——電稿——奉系軍閥密電第一冊》. Beijing: Zhonghua shuju, 1984.

———. *Zhonghua Minguo shi ziliao conggao – diangao—Fengxi junfa midian di er ce* 《中華民國史資料叢稿——電稿——奉系軍閥密電第二冊》. Beijing: Zhonghua shuju, 1985.

———. *Zhonghua Minguo shi ziliao conggao – diangao—Fengxi junfa midian di sance* 《中華民國史資料叢稿——電稿——奉系軍閥密電第三冊》. Beijing: Zhonghua shuju, 1986.

———. *Zhonghua Minguo shi ziliao conggao – diangao – Fengxi junfa midian di si ce* 《中華民國史資料叢稿——電稿——奉系軍閥密電第四冊》. Beijing: Zhonghua shuju, 1986.

———. *Zhonghua Minguo shi ziliao conggao – diangao – Fengxi junfa midian di wu, liu ce heji* 《中華民國史資料叢稿——電稿——奉系軍閥密電第五、六冊合集》. Beijing: Zhonghua shuju, 1986.

Lin Zhenhui 林貞惠. "Feng Yuxiang yu beifa qianhou de Zhongguo zhengju (Minguo 13–17 nian)." 《馮玉祥與北伐前後的中國政局（民國13–17年）》 Master's thesis, National Chengchi University 國立政治大學歷史研究所碩士論文指導教授:張玉法, 1980.

Lin Xiuhua 林秀華. "Zhong Rih liangguo waijiaoshi jiebiao." "中日兩國外交使節表" *Jindaishi ziliao* 《近代史資料》 (1958) No. 9, pp. 145–8.

Liu Bo, Shi Yin, and Xu Wei 劉波、石英、徐偉. "Beijing zhengjuan jiaoyisuo jianshi." "北京證券交易所簡史" *Beijing dangan shiliao* 《北京檔案史料》 No. 8 (1987), pp. 57–63.

Liu Guiwu 劉桂五. "'Jiaotong xi shulun." "'交通系'述論" *Shehui kexue zhanxian* 《社會科學戰線》 1982 No. 3, pp. 174–85.

Liu Huairong 劉懷榮. "Beiyang zhengfu lijie neige zhiguan yange." "北洋政府歷屆內閣職官沿革" *Beijing Dangan Shiliao* 《北京檔案史料》 (1988), no. 1, pp. 51–8; no. 2, pp. 52–61; no. 3, pp. 56–60.

Liu Jingfu 劉景富. "Guojiazhuyi pai ji qi zai dageming shiqi de huodong." "國家主義派及其在大革命時期的活動." In *Zhongguo xiandaishi dashi jishi benmo (1919—1949).* Ed. Wang Weili, vol. 1, pp. 271–8. 見王維禮主編.《中國現代史大事紀事本末(1919–1949)》. Ha-er-bin: Heilungjiang renmin chubanshe, 1987.

———. "'Xiandai Pinglun' yu Lu Xun dui ta de pipan." "'現代評論'與魯迅對它的批判" In *Zhongguo xiandaishi dashi jishi benmo (1919–1949)*. Ed. Wang Weili, vol. 1, pp. 288–93. 見主維禮主編《中國現代史大事本末(1919–1949)》. Ha-er-bin: Heilungjiang renmin chubanshe, 1987.

Liu Peiqian 柳培潛. *Da Shanghai zhinan* 《大上海指南》. Shanghai: Zhonghua shuju, 1936.

Liu Qingmin and Bai Shulan 劉慶旻、白淑蘭, eds. "Feng xi junfa Zhang Zongchang huo Lu zhi zuizhuang." "奉系軍閥張宗昌禍魯之罪狀" *Beijing Dangan shiliao* 《北京檔案史料》 (1988) No. 3, pp. 25–34.

Lou Xiangzhe 婁向哲. "Yue Feng Wan 'San jiao tongmeng' qianxi." "粵奉皖'三角同盟'淺析" *Tianjin shida xuebao* 《天津師範大學學報》 (1984) No. 2, pp. 39–44.

———. "Zhixi junfa zhengquan de caizheng pochan ji qi qingfu." "直系軍閥政權的財政破產及其傾覆" *Xueshu yuekan* 《學術月刊》 (1984) No. 2, pp. 76–81.

———. "Lun di er ci Zhi Feng zhanzheng," "論第二次直奉戰爭" Master's thesis, Nankai University, 1985.

Lu Hai jun Dayuanshuai Dabenying Gongbao 《陸海軍大元帥大本營公報》. In *Zhonghua Minguo shiliao congbian* 見《中華民國史料叢編》, series 3, no. 1, 12 vols. 1922–25. Reprint: Taibei: Committee for the Compilation of Material on Party History, Central Executive Committee of the Chinese Guomindang, 1969.

Lu Hesong 盧鶴松. "Beiyang junfa shiqi de juanshui jiazheng yu JinZhi shangmin dizhi keshui de douzheng." "北洋軍閥時期的捐稅加征與津直商民抵制苛稅的鬥爭" *Zhongguo shanghui yu zichanjieji xueshu taolun hui lunwen* 《中國商會與資產階級學術討論會論文》. Tianjin: Tianjin shehui kexue yuan lishi yanjiusuo, 1986. 見天津社會科學院歷史研究所.

Lü Weijun 呂偉俊. *Zhang Zongchang* 《張宗昌》. Jinan: Shandong renmin chubanshe, 1980.

———. *Han Fuju* 《韓復榘》. Jinan: Shandong renmin chubanshe, 1985.

Lu Zhonglin 鹿鐘麟. "Sun Zhongshan xiansheng beishang yu Feng Yuxiang." "孫中山先生北上與馮玉祥" *Wenshi ziliao xuanji* 《文史資料選輯》 (1960-), 89, 150-78.

Luo Jialun 羅家倫. *Guofu pidu moji* 《國父批牘墨跡》. Taibei: Guomindang shiliao biancuan weiyuanhui, 1955.

Luo Jinghuan 羅靖寰. "Wo suo zhidao de Zhang Zuolin de dui Ri waijiao." "我所知道的張作霖的對日外交" In *Tianjin wenshi ziliao xuanji* 《天津文史資料選輯》 No. 2, pp. 21-52. Tianjin: Tianjin renmin chubanshe, 1979.

Luo Wengan 羅文幹. "Waiguo zhidu yu Zhongguo." "外國制度與中國" *Dongfang zazhi* 《東方雜誌》 21 (1924) No. 22, pp.143-7.

Ma Baoxing 馬葆珩. "Qi Lu zhi zhan jilue." "齊盧之戰紀略" *Wenshi ziliao xuanji* 《文史資料選輯》 No. 35, pp. 41-55.

Ma Bingnan 馬炳南. "Er ci ZhiFeng zhanqian Zhang Zuolin yu Feng Yuxiang de lalong." "二次直奉戰前張作霖與馮玉祥的拉攏" In *Wenshi ziliao xuanji* 《文史資料選輯》 No. 4, pp. 54-7. Beijing: Wenshi ziliao chubanshe, 1960.

Ma Lie 馬烈. "Beiyang 'guaijie' Xu Shuzheng." "北洋'怪傑'徐樹錚" *Minguo chunqiu* 《民國春秋》 (1988) No. 2, pp. 39-44.

Ma Wenyan 馬文彥. "Hu Jingyi jiangjun zai 'Beijing zhengbian' qianhou de huodong." "胡景翼將軍在'北京政變'前後的活動" In *Wenshi ziliao xuanji* 《文史資料選輯》 No. 9, pp. 205-11. Beijing: Zhongguo wenshi chubanshe, 1987.

Matsushita Yoshio 松下芳男. *Meiji no guntai* 明治の軍隊. Tokyo: Shibundo, 1963.

Mao Jinling 毛金陵. "Beiyang Zhixi jundui zhi yanjiu." 《北洋直系軍隊三研究》 Ph.D. dissertation, National Taiwan University, 1987.

Meng Xingkuei 孟呈魁. "Zhixi junfa dalianhe de yunniang he shibai jingguo." "直系軍閥大聯合的醞釀和失敗經過" In *Wenshi ziliao xuanji* 《文史資料選輯》 No. 35, pp. 98-102. Beijing: Wenshi ziliao chubanshe, 1963.

Mo Shixiang 莫世祥. *Hufa yundongshi* 《護法運動史論(1917-1923)》. Guangxi: Guangxi renmin chubanshe 華中師範大學博士學位論文1987, 1991.

Nan Shi 南史. "Tianjin de wu sanshi fandi yundong." "天津的五卅反帝運動" *Lishi jiaoxue* 《歷史教學》 (1965), May, pp. 37-9.

Ning Wu 寧武. "Sun Zhongshan yu Zhang Zuolin lianhe fan Zhi jiyao." "孫中山與張作霖聯合反直紀要" *Wenshi ziliao xuanji* 《文史資料選輯》, No. 41, pp. 115-21.

Niu Dayong 牛大勇. "Beifa zhanzheng shiqi Meiguo fenhua zhengce yu MeiJiang guanxi de xingcheng." "北伐戰爭時期美國分化政策與美蔣關係的形成" *Jindaishi yanjiu* 《近代史研究》 (1986) No. 6, pp. 187-212.

Okano Masujirō 岡野增次郎. *Go Haifu* 吳佩孚 [Wu Peifu]. Tokyo: Banseikaku, 1939.

Pan Chenglu 潘承祿. "Cao Kun he Wang Chengbin de guanxi diandi jianwen." "曹錕和王承斌的關係點滴見聞" *Wenshi ziliao xuanji* 《文史資料選輯》 (1960-) 35, 72-5.

————. "Wu Peifu baitui Tianjin suoji." "吳佩孚敗退天津瑣記" In *Wenshi ziliao xuanji* 《文史資料選輯》 no. 41, pp. 158–61. Beijing: Wenshiziliao chubanshe, 1963.

Pan Xiting 潘喜廷. "Zhang Zuolin yu Riben de guanxi." "張作霖與日本的關係" *Xuexi yu tansuo* 《學習與探索》 (1980) no. 2, pp. 136–42.

Peng Ming 彭明. "Beiyang junfa (yanjiu gangyao)." "北洋軍閥（研究綱要）" *Jiaoyu yu yanjiu* 《教學與研究》 (1980) no. 5, pp. 33–7; no. 6, pp. 31–8.

————, gen. ed. *Zhongguo xiandaishi ziliao xuanji*, 5 vols. 《中國現代史資料選輯》 5 Vols. Beijing: Zhongguo renmin daxue chubanshe, 1988.

Pu Jia 溥佳. "1924 nian Pu Yi chugong qianhou suoji." "1924 年溥儀出宮前後瑣記" *Wenshi ziliao xuanji* 《文史資料選輯》 No. 35, pp. 246–76.

Qi Qingchang and Sun Zhisheng 齊慶昌、孫志昇. *Zhi-Feng Dazhan* 《直奉大戰》. Beijing: Shehui kexue wenxian chubanshe, 1993.

Qian Shifu 錢實甫. *Beiyang zhengfu shiqi de zhengzhi zhidu*, 2 vols. 《北洋政府時期的政治制度》 2 vols. Beijing: Zhonghua shuju, 1984.

————, with Huang Qinggen 黃清根整理. *Beiyang zhengfu zhiguanbiao* 《北洋政府職官年表》. Shanghai: Huadong Shifan Daxue chubanshe, 1991.

Qin Weihua 秦衞華. "Feng Yuxiang Beijing zhengbian de yuanyin ji lishi zuoyong." "馮玉祥北京政變的原因及其歷史作用" *Shixue yuekan* 《史學刊》 (1985) no. 4, pp. 114–16.

Rong Mengyuan and Zhang Baifeng, eds. 榮孟源、章伯鋒主編. *Jindai Baihai* 《近代稗海》, 13 vols. Chengdu: Sichuan renmin chubanshe, 1985.

Sang Bing 桑兵. "Xuesheng yu jindai Zhongguo." Ph.D. 《學生與近代中國》博士論文. dissertation, Huazhong Normal University, 1987. 華中師範大學, 1987.

Shan Bao 單寶. "Beiyang junfa zhengfu de gongzhai." "北洋軍閥政府的公積" *Shixue yuekan* 《史學月刊》 (1987) no. 1, pp. 96–8.

Shanghai shehui kexue yuan lishi yanjiusuo, ed. 上海社會科學院歷史研究所編. *Wusa yundong shiliao*, vol. 2. 《五卅運動史料》 Vol. 2. Shanghai: Shanghai renmin chubanshe, 1986.

Shanghai tongshe, ed. 上海通社編. *Shanghai yanjiu ziliao* 《上海研究資料》. Shanghai: Zhonghua shuju, 1936.

Shen Weibin 瀋渭濱. "Lun Zhongguo jindai junshishi de yanjiu duixiang yu fenqi." "論中國近代軍事史的研究對象與分期" *Xueshu yuekan* 《學術月刊》 (1986) no. 10, pp. 58–70.

Shen Yu 瀋予. "Lun Beifa zhanzhneg zhiqi Meiguo duihua zhengce." "論北伐戰爭時期美國對華政策" *Jindaishi yanjiu* 《近代史研究》 (1986) no. 3, pp. 258–82.

Shen Zhenrong 瀋振榮. "Dong sansheng binggongchang." "東三省兵工廠" *Liaoning wenshi ziliao* No. 8 (Shenyang: Liaoning renmin chubanshe, 1984), pp. 47–64. 《遼寧文史資料》 no. 8, pp. 47–64.

Shi Xuancen and Zhao Mingzhong, eds. 施宣岑、趙銘忠 主編. *Zhongguo di er lishidanganguan jianming zhinan* 《中國第二歷史檔案館簡明指南》. Beijing: Dangan chubanshe, 1987.

Shi Kang 石康. "Ji Feng Yuxiang Gubeikou daoge zhi yi." "記馮玉祥古北口倒戈之役" *Yiwen zhi* 《藝文誌》 no. 14 (1975) pp. 14–16.

"Shishi rizhi." "時事日誌" *Dongfang zazhi* 《東方雜誌》 21(1924) no. 19, pp. 165–7; no. 20, pp. 147–50; no. 21, pp. 147–50; no. 22, pp. 157–60; no. 23, pp. 139–43; no. 24, pp. 117–20.

Shi Yazhen 石雅貞. "Jiang Zhe zhi zhan." "江浙之戰" In *Zhongguo xiandaishi dashi jishi benmo (1919–1949)*. Ed. Wang Weili. 見王維禮編《中國現代史大事紀事本末(1919–1949)》, vol. 1, pp. 259–61. Ha-er-bin: Heilungjiang renmin chubanshe, 1987.

———. "Di er ci Zhi Feng zhanzheng yu Beijing zhengbian." "第二次直奉戰爭與北京政變" In *Zhongguo xiandaishi dashi jishi benmo (1919–1949)*. Ed. Wang Weili. 見王維禮編《中國現代史大事紀事本末(1919–1949)》. vol. 1, pp. 261–66. Ha-er-bin: Heilungjiang renmin chubanshe, 1987.

———. "Feng Yuxiang yu Guominjun." "馮玉祥與國民軍" In *Zhongguo xiandaishi dashi jishi benmo (1919–1949)*. Ed. Wang Weili. 見王維禮編《中國現代史大事紀事本末(1919–1949)》, vol. 1, pp. 278–283. Ha-er-bin: Heilungjiang renmin chubanshe, 1987.

———. "Sun Zhongshan beishang yu Guomin huiyi yundong." "孫中山北上與國民會議運動" In *Zhongguo xiandaishi dashi jishi benmo (1919–1949)*, 見王維禮編《中國現代史大事紀事本末(1919–1949)》 Ed. Wang Weili. vol. 1, pp. 284–7. Ha-er-bin: Heilungjiang renmin chubanshe, 1987.

———. "Duan Qirui yu Shanhou huiyi." "段祺瑞與善後會議" In *Zhongguo xiandaishi dashi jishi benmo (1919–1949)*. Ed. Wang Weili. 見王維禮編《中國現代史大事紀事本末(1919–1949)》, vol. 1, pp. 297–300. Ha-er-bin: Heilungjiang renmin chubanshe, 1987.

———. "Zhe-Feng zhanzheng." "浙奉戰爭" In *Zhongguo xiandaishi dashi jishi benmo (1919–1949)*. Ed. Wang Weili. 見王維禮編《中國現代史大事紀事本末(1919–1949)》, vol. 1, pp. 338–41. Ha-er-bin: Heilungjiang renmin chubanshe, 1987.

Song Meiyun 宋美雲. "Beiyang junfa shiqi Tianjin minzu gongye gaikuang." "北洋軍閥時期天津民族工業概況" *Zhongguo shanghui yu zichanjieji xueshu taolun hui lunwen* "中國商會與資產階級"學術討論會論文. Tianjin: Tianjin shehui kexue yuan lishi yanjiusuo, 1986.

Song Zheyuan, as told to Zhao Geng 宋哲元（口述）、兆庚（記錄）. "Xibeijun zhilue." "西北軍志略" *Jindaishi ziliao* 《近代史資料》 (1963) no. 4, pp. 114–29.

Song Yunbin 宋雲彬. *Zhongguo jinbainan shi* 《中國近百年史》. Shanghai: Xinzhi shudian, 1948.

Su Xilin 蘇錫麟. "Wo zai Zhang, Wu hezuozhong de qinshen jingli." "我在張、吳合作中的親身經歷" In *Wenshi ziliao*《文史資料選輯》 No. 51, pp. 82–8. Beijing: Wenshi ziliao chubanshe, 1962.

Su Zhenshen, ed. 蘇振申 編. *Zhong Ri guanxi shishi nianbiao* 《中日關係史事年表》. Taibei: Huagang, 1977.

Sun Dasheng 孫達生. "Wo suo zhidao de Zhang Zuolin he Zhang Xueliang."

"我所知道的張作霖和張學良" In *Liaoning wenshi ziliao* 《遼寧文史資料》 no. 8, pp. 131-45. Shenyang: Liaoning renmin chubanshe, 1984.

Sun Zhongshan 孫中山. "Beifa xuanyan." "北伐宣言" In *Sun Zhongshan xuanji* 《孫中山選集》. Beijing Renminchubanshe,: 1956, vol. 2, pp. 873-5.

Sun Zhongshan junshi sixiang yu shijian bianxiezu, ed. 《孫中山軍事思想與實踐》編寫組. *Sun Zhongshan junshi sixiang yu shijian* 《孫中山軍事思想與實踐》. Beijing: Junshi kexue chubanshe, 1989.

Tan Zhiqing 譚志清. "Wo suo zhidao de Jin Yunpeng he Jin Yun'e." "我所知道的靳雲鵬和靳雲鶚" *Wenshi ziliao xuanji* 《文史資料選輯》 (1960-) 35, 226-45.

Tao Juyin 陶菊隱. *Beiyang junfa tongzhi shiqi shihua* 《北洋軍閥統治時期史話》. 8v. Beijing: Sanlian shudian, 1959.

——— 陶菊隱. *Beiyang junfa tongzhi shiqi shihua* 《北洋軍閥統治時期史話》, rev. ed. 3v. Beijing: Sanlian, 1983.

Tao Shangming and Guan Genqin 陶尚銘、關根勤. "Zhang Zuolin he ta de Riben guwen." "張作霖和他的日本顧問" *Wenshi ziliao xuanji* 《文史資料選輯》 (1960-) 51, 175-185.

Tōa dōbunkai 東亞同文會. Taishi kaikoroku 對支回顧錄. Tokyo: Hara Shobō, 1968-1973.

Tian Ziyu and Liu Dejun, eds. 田子瑜、劉德軍 編. *Zhongguo jindai junfashi cidian* 《中國近代軍閥史辭典》 Beijing: Dangan chubanshe, 1989.

Tianjinshi danganguan, ed. 天津市檔案館 編輯. *Beiyang junfa Tianjin dangan shiliao xuanbian* 《北洋軍閥天津檔案史料選編》. Tianjin: Tianjin Guji chubanshe, 1990.

Tianjinshi danganguan 天津市檔案館, Tianjin shehui kexue yuan lishi yanjiusuo 天津社會科學院歷史研究所, Tianjinshi gongshangye lianhehui, eds. 天津市工商業聯合會 編. *Tianjin shanghui dangan huibian (1903-1911)* 《天津商會檔案匯編(1903-1911)》. Tianjin: Tianjin renmin chubanshe, n.d.

Ugaki Kazushige 宇垣一成. *Ugaki nikki* 宇垣日記. Tokyo: Asahi shimbunsha 1956.

Usui Katsumi 臼井勝美. *Nitchō gaikō: hokubatsu no jidai* 日中外交北伐の時代. Tokyo: Hanawa shobō,1971.

———. *Nihon to Chūgoku: Taishō jidai* 日本と中國:大正時代. Tokyo: Hara Shobō, 1972.

Wang Chuqing 王楚卿. "Duan Qirui gonguan jianwen." "段祺瑞公館見聞" *Wenshi ziliao xuanji* 《文史資料選輯》, no. 41, pp. 236-74.

Wang Ermin 王爾敏. *Qingji binggongye de xingqi* 《清季兵工業的興起》. Taibei: Zhongyang yanjiuyuan, jindaishi yanjiusuo, 1963.

Wang Hanming 王翰鳴. "Zhang Zongchang xingbai jilue." "張宗昌興敗紀略" *Wenshi ziliao xuanji* 《文史資料選輯》, No. 41, pp. 210-35.

Wang Hongyong 王紅勇. "Beijing zhengbian xingzhi yu yuanyin xintan." "北京政變性質與原因新探" *Xueshu yuekan* 《學術月刊》 (1986) no. 7, pp. 70-6.

Wang Jianmin 王健民. *Zhongguo Gongchandang Shigao* 中國共產黨史稿. Taibei: n.p., n.d.

Wang Ling 王玲. "Beijing diwei bianqian yu Tianjin lishi fazhan." "北京地位變遷與天津歷史發展" *Tianjin shehui kexue* 《天津社會科學》 (1986) No. 1, pp. 92–6; No. 2, pp. 74–5,

Wang Tan 王坦. "Cao Kun luxuan zongtong shimo." "曹錕賄選總統始末" *Wenshi ziliao xuanji* 《文史資料選輯》 (1960–) 35, 21–33.

Wang Tiehan 王鐵漢. "Dongbei junshi shilue." 2 parts "東北軍史略" 2 parts. In *Dongbei wenxian* 《東北文獻》 2.1(1971), pp. 35–47; 2.2(1971), pp. 37–46.

Wang Weicheng 王維成. "1926 nian Wu Peifu de chongfan Luoyang." "1926年吳佩孚的重返洛陽" In *Wenshi ziliao xuanji* 《文史資料選輯》 no. 41, pp. 179–82. Beijing: Wenshi ziliao chubanshe, 1963.

———. "Zhi xi de fenlie he er ci zhi feng zhan zhi xi de shibai." "直系的分裂和二次直奉戰爭的失敗" In *Beiyang junfa shiliao xuanji*, 2 vols. Ed. Du Chunhe, Lin Binsheng, and Qiu Quanzheng 杜春和、林彬生、丘權政 編. Beijing: Zhongguo shehui kexue chubanshe 《北洋軍閥史料選輯》, 1981, vol. 2, pp. 92–105.

Wang Weili, ed. 王維禮 編. *Zhongguo xiandaishi dashi jishi benmo (1919–1949)* 《中國現代史大事紀事本末(1919–1949)》 2v. Ha-er-bin: Heilungjiang renmin chubanshe, 1987.

Wang Yunwu 王雲五 編, ed. *Yunwu shehui kexue da cidian* 《雲五社會科學大辭典》. Taibei: Taiwan Shangwu, 1974. Vol 6: *Falüxue*, ed. Liu Jihong.

Wang Zhuoru 王倬如. "Feng Yuxiang jiangjun tan junfa wenti." "馮玉祥將軍談軍閥問題" In *Wenshi ziliao xuanji* 《文史資料選輯》 No. 9, pp. 198–200. Beijing: Wenshi ziliao chubanshe, 1987.

Wei Fuxiang 魏福祥. "Lun Fengpiao maohuang ji qi shuailou." "論奉票毛荒及其衰落" *Shehui kexue zhanxian* 《社會科學戰線》 1986 no. 3, pp. 239–43.

———, Zhang Wei and Cui Can 魏福祥、張偉、崔燦. "Zhang Zuolin yu chafeng tianhe shengshang hao yi an." "張作霖與查封天合盛號一案" *Liaoning daxue xuebao* 《遼寧大學學報》 1986 no. 4, pp. 72–4.

Wei Ming 魏明. "Lun Beiyang junfa guanliao de siren zibenzhuyi jingji huodong." "北洋政府官僚與天津經濟" *Jindaishi yanjiu* 《天津社會科學》 1985, no. 2, pp. 66–110.

———. "Zhang Zuolin jingji huodong pingshu." "張作霖經濟活動評述" *Shehui kexue zhanxian* 《社會科學戰線》 1986 no. 3, pp. 234–8.

———. "Beiyang zhengfu guanliao yu Tianjin jingji." "北洋政府官僚與天津經濟" *Tianjin shehui kexue* 《天津社會科學》 (1986) no. 4, pp. 87–93.

Wei Xijiu 韋錫九. "Dongbei bianye yinhang shimo ji." "東北邊業銀行始末記". In *Wenshi ziliao xuanji* 《文史資料選輯》 no. 35, pp. 177–195. Beijing: Wenshi ziliao chubanshe, 1963.

Wei Yisan 魏益三. "Di erci ZhiFeng zhanzheng Zhang Zuolin goujie Rihben de liangjian shi." "第二次直奉戰爭張作霖勾結日本的兩件事" *Jindai shi ziliao* 《近代史資料》 (1978) no. 2, pp. 178–79.

魏益三. "Wo you fan Feng dao tou Feng tou Wu tou Jiang de jingguo." "我由反奉到投馮、投吳、投蔣的經過". In *Wenshi ziliao xuanji* 《文史資料選輯》

no. 51, pp. 215–51. Beijing: Zhongguo wenshi chubanshe, n.d.

Wen Gongzhi 文公直. *Zuijin sanshi nian Zhongguo junshi shi* 《最近三十年中國軍事史》, reprint ed., Taibei: Wenhai, n.d.

Wu Hao 伍豪. See Zhou Enlai 周恩來.

Wu Jiezhang, Su Xiaodong and Cheng Zhifa, eds. 吳桀章、蘇小東、程志發主編. *Zhongguo jindai haijunshi* 《中國近代海軍史》. Beijing: Jiefangjun chubanshe, 1989.

Wu Liao Zi 無聊子. *Beijing zhengbian ji* 《北京政變記》. Shanghai: Gonghe shuju, 上海. 共和書局. 1924. In JDBH, vol. 5, pp. 365–457 見榮孟源、章伯鋒主編 《近代稗海》 vol. 5. pp. 365–457.

———. *Di er ci Zhi Feng da zhan ji* 《第二次直奉大戰記》. Shanghai: Gonghe shuju, 1924.

———. *Xiandai zhi Wu Peifu* 《現代之吳佩孚》. (not seen)

———. *Wu Peifu chuzhou hou Zhongguo zhi jianglai* 《吳佩孚出走後中國之將來》. (not seen)

Wu Xiqi 吳錫祺. "Feng Yuxiang, Guo Songling lianhe fandui Zhang Zuolin de jingguo." 郭松齡聯合反對張作霖的經過. "馮玉祥 In *Wenshi ziliao xuanji* 《文史資料選輯》 (1960–) 35, 168–76.

———. "Songshi Xiaolang [Matsumoro Kōtarō] he Feng Yuxiang de yiduan guanxi." "松室孝良和馮玉祥的一段關係" *Wenshi ziliao xuanji* 《文史資料選輯》 (1960–) 186–92.

Xi Wuyi 習五一. "Sun Zhongshan yu Fengxi junfa." "孫中山與奉系軍閥" *Jindaishi yanjiu* 《近代史研究》 1986, no. 6, pp. 74–93.

Xie Benshu 謝本書. "Beiyang junfa tongzhi shiqi Beijing zhengquan yuanshou, guowuzongli, gengxuan biao." "北洋軍閥統治時期北京政權元首，國務總理更迭表" *Lishi jioaxue* 《歷史教學》 (1962), no. 6, pp. 51–2.

Xie Xueshi 解學詩. "Riben diguo zhuyi yu dongbei meitie gongye." "日本帝國主義與東北煤鐵工業" *Shehui kexue zhanxian* 《社會科學戰線》 1983, no. 4, pp. 193–200.

Xie Zongtao 謝宗陶. "Di er ci Zhi Feng zhanzheng suijun jianwen." "第二次直奉戰爭隨軍見聞" In *Wenshi ziliao* 《文史資料選輯》 no. 41, pp. 141–57. Beijing: Wenshi ziliao chubanshe, 1963.

Xin Peilin 辛培林. *Junfa liezhuan* 《軍閥列傳》. Ha-er-bin: Heilongjiang renmin chubanshe, 1987.

Xiong Jianhua 熊建華. "Cong 'Min bao' kan Feng Yuxiang dui wu-sa yundong de taidu. "從'民報'看馮玉祥對五州運動的態度" *Jindaishi yanjiu* 《近代史研究》 (1986) no. 5, pp. 215–18.

Xu Cangshui 徐滄水, ed. *Shanghai yinhang gonghui shiye shi* 上海銀行公會事業史 Shanghai yinhang zhoubao, 1925.

Xu Nianhui 許念暉. "Shanghai zhengjuan jiaoyisuo gaikuang." "上海證券交易所概況" *Wenshi ziliao xuanji* 《文史資料選輯》, no. 24, pp. 154–72.

Xu Youchun and Wu Zhiming 徐友春、吳志明, eds. *Sun Zhongshan Fengan Dadian* 孫中山奉安大典 Beijing: Huawen chubanshe, 1989.

Yang Daxin 楊大辛, "Fengxi ZhiLu lianjun huo Jin shimo" "奉系直魯聯軍禍津始末" *Tianjin shizhi* 《天津史志》 (1988), no.1, pp. 41–4.

———. 楊大辛主編. *Beiyang zhengfu zongtong yu zongli* 《北洋政府總統與總理》. Tianjin: Nankai Daxue chubanshe, 1989.

Yang Hao and Ye Lan 楊浩、葉覽, eds. *Jiu Shanghai fengyun renwu* 《舊上海風雲人物》. Shanghai: Shanghai renmin chubanshe, 1989.

Yang Peixin 楊培新. "Lun Zhongguo jinrong zichang jieji de fengjianxing." "論中國金融資產階級的封建性" *Jindaishi yanjiu* 《近代史研究》 1985 no. 2, pp. 41–65.

Yang Xuefeng 楊雪峯. "Guofu gei Xu Qian jifeng weijian fabiao de handian." "國父給徐謙幾封未見發表的函電" *Zhuanji wenxue* 《傳記文學》 41.5 (1982), pp. 10–13.

Yang Yinbo, (楊蔭溥) ed. *Shanghai jinrong zuzhi gaiyao* 《上海金融組織概要》. Shanghai, ca. 1929.

———, ed. *Shanghai jinrong zuzhi gaiyao* 《上海金融組織概要》. In *Zhongguo zhi yinhang shiliao sanzhong* 見《中國之銀行史料三種》. Taibei: Xuehai chubanshe, 1972.

"Yijiuersi nian Beijing zhengbian." "一九二四年北京政變" In *Zhongguo gemingshi yanjiu huicui (1911–1949)*, pp. 104–13. Ed. Zhai Zuojun and Wu Zhenghong 見翟作君、鄔正洪主編《中國革命史研究薈萃》. Shanghai: Huadong shifan daxue chubanshe, 1986.

Yoshizawa Kenkichi 芳澤謙吉. *Gaikō rokujū nen* 外交六十年. Tokyo: Jiyū Ajiasha, 1958.

"Yuguan dazhan." "榆關大戰" *Dongfang zazhi* 《東方雜誌》 21 (1924) no. 19, pp. 6–9.

Yu Guifen 于桂芬. "Wusa yundong de fasheng yu fazhan." "五卅運動的發生與發展" In *Zhongguo xiandaishi dashi jishi benmo* (1919–1949) 見王維禮編《中國現代史大事紀事本末(1919–1949)》 vol. 1, pp. 311–16. Edited by Wang Weili. Ha-er-bin: Heilungjiang renmin chubanshe, 1987.

Yu Jianxin 虞建新. "Song Hu hujunshi Lu Yongxiang." "淞滬護軍使盧永祥" In *Jiu Shanghai fengyun renwu* 《舊上海風雲人物》, pp. 135–43. Ed. Yang Hao and Ye Lan 楊浩、葉覽編. Shanghai: Shanghai renmin chubanshe, 1989.

Yu Liyan 于立言. "Zhang Zuolin tongguo Duan Qirui wajie Zhixi de neimu." "張作霖通過段祺瑞瓦解直系的內幕" In *Wenshi ziliao xuanji* 《文史資料選輯》 no. 51, pp. 49–52. Beijing: Wenshi ziliao chubanshe, 1962.

Yu Xuezhong 于學忠. "Wo zai Beiyang shiqi yu Zhixi Fengxi de guanxi." "我在北洋時期與直系奉系的關係" In *Wenshi ziliao xuanji* 《文史資料選輯》 no. 51, pp. 193–214. Beijing: Wenshi ziliao chubanshe, n.d.

Zeng Fanxiu and Liu Xiaohui 曾凡秀、劉曉暉. "Wu sanshi yundong zai dongbei." "五卅運動在東北" *Dongbei shida xuebao* 《東北師範大學學報》 (1981), no. 3, pp. 96–101.

Zhai Zuojun and Wu Zhenghong 翟作君、鄔正洪編. Zhongguo gemingshi yanjiu huicui (1911–1949) 《中國革命史研究薈萃(1911–1949)》. Shanghai: Huadong shifan daxue chubanshe, 1986.

Zhang Bofeng and Li Zongyi 章伯鋒、李宗一, eds. *Beiyang junfa* 《北洋軍閥》. 6 vols. Wuhan: Wuhan chubanshe, 1990.

————. *Wanxi junfa yu Riben* 《皖系軍閥與日本》. Chengdu: Sichuan renmin chubanshe, 1988.

Zhang Guochen 張國忱. *"Zhang Zuolin fuzi dangquanshi dui Sulian guanxi he Zhongdong tielu neimu."* "張作霖父子當權時對蘇關係和中東鐵路內幕" In *Tianjin wenshi ziliao xuanji* 《天津文史資料選輯》 no. 2, pp. 1–20. Tianjin: Tianjin renmin chubanshe, 1979.

Zhang Junsheng 張俊聲. "Feng Yuxiang Beijing zhengbianzhong de yimu." "馮玉祥北京政變中的一幕" In *Wenshi ziliao xuanji* 《文史資料選輯》 no. 51, pp. 57–62. Beijing: Wenshi ziliao chubanshe, 1962.

Zhang Keming 張克明, comp. "Beiyang zhengfu chajin shuji, baokan, chuandan mulu (xu)." "北洋軍閥查禁書籍報刊傳軍目錄" *Tianjin shehui kexue* (1982) no. 6, pp. 65–71.

Zhang Pumin 張樸民. *Beiyang zhengfu guowu zongli liezhuan* 《北洋政府國務總理列傳》. Taibei: Shangwu yinshuguan, 1984.

Zhang Xia, Sun Baoming and Chen Changhe, eds. 張俠、孫寶銘、陳長河編. *Beiyang lujun shiliao and 1912–1916* 《北洋陸軍史料1912–1916》. Tianjin: Tianjin renmin chubanshe, 1987.

Zhang Xianwen 張憲文, ed. *Zhonghua Minguo shigang* 《中華民國史綱》. Henan renmin chubanshe, 1985.

————, Chen Xingtang, and Zheng Huixin, eds. 張憲文、陳興唐、鄭會欣編. *Minguo dangan yu Minguoshi xueshu taolunhui lunwenji* 《民國檔案與民國史學術討論會論文集》. Beijing: Dangan chubanshe, 1988.

Zhang Yichun 張義純. "Zang Zhiping, Yang Huazhao zi Min tuwei ru Zhe ji." "藏致平、楊化昭自關突圍入浙記" *Wenshi ziliao xuanju* 《文史資料選輯》 no. 35, pp. 56–66.

Zhang Yueting 張樾亭. "Guominjun Nankou zhanyi qinliji." "國民軍南口戰役親歷記" In *Wenshi ziliao xuanji* 《文史資料選輯》 no. 51, pp. 100–13. Beijing: Wenshi ziliao chubanshe, 1962.

Zhang Zisheng 張梓生. *Feng Zhi zhanzheng jishi*, reprint ed: 《奉直戰爭紀事》 reprint ed. Taibei: Wenhai chubanshe,1967.

Zhao Hengti, ed. 趙桓愓 ed. *Wu Peifu xiansheng ji* 《吳佩孚先生集》. 1939. Reprint ed.,Taibei: Wenhai, 1971.

Zhao Xiaotian 趙曉天. "Feng Yuxiang Beijing zhengbian xintan." "馮玉祥北京政變新探" *Xibei daxue xuebao* 《西北大學學報》 (1988) no. 3, pp. 1–6.

Zheng Tingxi 鄭廷璽. "Wo suo zhidao de Wang Zhanyuan." "我所知道的王占元" In *Wenshi ziliao xuanji* 《文史資料選輯》 no. 51, pp. 252–68. Beijing: Wenshi ziliao chubanshe, n.d.

————. "Zhixi de fenhua ji shibai." "直系的分化及失敗" In Tianjin wenshi ziliao xuanji, no. 23.

"Zhi Feng bingli zhi bijiao." "直奉兵力之比較" *Dongfang zazhi* 《東方雜誌》 21 (1924) no. 19, pp. 152–62.

Zhi Xin 稚心. "Feng Yuxiang yu Sun Zhongshan." "馮玉祥與孫中山" *Liaoning daxue xuebao* 《遼寧大學學報》 (1988) no. 1 pp. 15–16.

Zhonggong Tianjin shiwei dangshi ziliao zhengji weiyuanhui 中共天津市委黨史資料征集委員會, Tianjin shi zonggonghui gongyunshi yanjiushi 天津市總工

會工運史研究室, Tianjinshi lishi bowuguan 天津市歷史博物館, eds. *Wusa yundong zai Tianjin* 《五州運動在天津》. Beijing: Zhonggong dangshi ziliao chubanshe, 1987.

Zhongguo da baikequanshu junshijuan bianshenshi, comp. 中國大百科全書軍事卷編審室, comp. *Zhongguo da baikequanshu: junshi, qiangxie huopao, tanke, danyao fence* 《中國大百科全書:軍事,槍械火砲,坦克,彈藥分冊》. Beijing: Junshi kexue chubanshe, 1987.

Zhongguo di er lishi danganguan, ed 中國第二歷史檔案館編. *Zhonghua Minguo shi dangan ziliao congkan–Beiyang junfa tongzhi shiqi de bingbian* 《中華民國史檔案資料叢刊——北洋軍閥統治時期的兵變》. Nanjing: Jiangsu renmin chubanshe, 1982.

———, ed. 中國第二歷史檔案館, 編. *Shanhou huiyi* 《善後會議》. Beijing: Dangan chubanshe, 1985.

Zhongguo junshishi bianxiezu, comp. 中國軍事史編寫組. *Zhongguo junshishi*, vol. 1 《中國軍事史》 Vol. 1. *binggi* 《兵器》. Beijing: Jiefangjun chubanshe, 1983.

Zhongguo shehui kexue yuan jindaishi yanjiusuo fanyishi, comp. 中國社會科學院近代史研究所翻譯室, comp. *Jindai laihua waiguo renming cidian* 《近代來華外國人名辭典》. Beijing: Shehui kexue chubanshe, 1981.

Zhongguo renmin yinhang, Shanghai branch, ed. 中國人民銀行, 上海分行. ed. *Shanghai qianzhuang shiliao* 《上海錢莊史料》. Shanghai: Renmin chubanshe, 1960.

Zhongguo renmin yinhang, Shanghai branch, ed. 中國人民銀行, 上海分行. ed. *Jincheng yinhang shiliao* 《金城銀行史料》. Shanghai: Renmin chubanshe, 1983.

Zhongguo renmin zhengzhi xieshang huiyi quanguo weiyuanhui, wenshi ziliao yanjiu weiyuanhui, ed. 中國人民政治協商會議全國委員會,文史資料研究委員會, ed. *Wenshi ziliao xuanji* 《文史資料選輯》 hedingben (collected edition). Beijing: Zhongguo wenshi chubanshe, n.d.

Zhongguo shehui kexue yuan Shanghai jingji yanjiusuo and Shanghai shehui kexue yuan jingji yanjiusuo, eds 中國社會科學院上海經濟研究所、上海社會科學院經濟研究所, 編. *Shanghai jiefang qianhou wujia ziliao huibian* 《上海解放前後物價資料匯編》. Shanghai: Shanghai renmin chubanshe, 1958.

Zhou Dai 周玳. "Er ci zhi feng zhan shi Yan Xishan yu zhi feng wan junfa de gouxin doujiao." "二次直奉戰爭時閻錫山與直奉皖軍閥的勾心鬥角" In *Wenshi ziliao xuanji* 《文史資料選輯》 no. 41, pp. 122–40. Beijing: Wenshiziliao chubanshe, 1963.

Zhou Enlai [Wu Hao] 周恩來[伍豪]. "Junfa tongzhi xia de Zhongguo." "軍閥統治下的中國" *Jindaishi yanjiu* 《近代史研究》 1979, no. 2, pp. 1–4. [1924]

Zhou Yuhe 周玉和. "Wuli tongyi yu liansheng zizhi yundong." "武力統一與聯省自治運動" In *Zhongguo xiandaishi dashi jishi benmo (1919-1949)* 王維禮編 《中國現代史大事紀事本末(1919-1949)》, vol. 1, pp. 51-5. Ed. Wang Weili. Ha-er-bin: Heilungjiang renmin chubanshe, 1987.

———. "Jin falang an." "金法郎案" In *Zhongguo xiandaishi dashi jishi benmo*

(1919–1949) 王維禮編《中國現代史大事紀事本末(1919–1949)》, vol. 1, pp. 300–3. Ed. Wang Weili. Ha-er-bin: Heilungjiang renmin chubanshe, 1987.

Zhu Chuanyu, ed 朱傳譽主編. *Feng Yuxiang zhuanji ziliao.* 5 vols 《馮玉祥傳記資料》. 5 vols. Taibei: Tianyichu chubanshe, 1981.

Zhu Chunfu 祝淳夫. "Beiyang junfa dui Tianjin jindai gongye de touzi." "北洋軍閥對天津近代工業的投資" In *Tianjin wenshi ziliao xuanji* 《天津文史資料選輯》 no. 44, pp. 146–62. Tianjin: Tianjin renmin chubanshe, 1979.

Zou Guiwu 鄒桂五. "Feng Yuxiang jiangjun chuangban de Xibei lujun ganbu xuexiao." "馮玉祥將軍創辦的西北陸軍幹部學校" In *Wenshi ziliao xuanji* 《文史資料選輯》 no. 9, pp. 191–5. Beijing: Wenshi ziliao chubanshe, 1987.

Zou Lu 鄒魯. *Zhongguo Guomindang shigao* 《中國國民黨史稿》. Shanghai: Commercial Press,

Glossary

Andong　安東
Anfujun　安福軍
Anfuxi　安福系
Anhui　安徽
Anminzhai　安民寨
Ao Jingwen　敖景文
Araki　荒木

Ba Jin　巴金
Bai Baoshan　白寶山
baihua　白話
Bai Jianwu　白堅武
Baoding　保定
Baoding lujun sucheng xuetang　保定陸軍速成學堂
Baokang　保康
Baoshan　寶山
baqi　八旗
bawang　霸王
Beidaihe　北戴河
Beifa　北伐
Beijing　北京
Beijing weishu zongsiling　北京衞戍總司令
Beijing zhengbian　北京政變
Beijing zhengjuan jiaoyisuo　北京證卷交易所
Beipiao　北票
Beiyang dachen　北洋大臣
Beiyang zhengfu　北洋政府
Beiyangjun　北洋軍
Beizhen　北鎮
Bengbu　蚌埠
Bian Shoujing　邊守靖
Biaohujiang　裱糊匠

Bohai　渤海
Boshan　博山

Cai Benping　蔡本平
Cai Chengxun　蔡成勛
Cai Hesen　蔡和森
Cai Yuanpei　蔡元培
Cangkou Huaxin　滄口華新
Cangzhou　滄州
Cao Kun　曹錕
Cao Linsheng　曹麟（霖）生
Cao Rui　曹銳
Cao Shijie　曹士桀
Cao Ying　曹媖
Caojia huayuan　曹家花園
Cen Chunxuan　岑春煊
Chaha'er　察哈爾
Chang Desheng　常德盛
Changchun　長春
Changguanshui　常關稅
Changli　昌黎
Changxindian　長辛店
Changxing　長興
Changshan　常山
Changzhou　常州
Chaoyang　朝陽
Chen Duxiu　陳獨秀
Chen Guangyuan　陳光遠
Chen Jiamou　陳嘉謨
Chen Jiongming　陳炯明
Chen Diaoyuan　陳調元
Chen Leshan　陳樂山
Chen Xingya　陳興亞
Cheng Ke　程克
Chengde　承德
Chengziyu　城子峪
Chifeng　赤峯
Chongwenmen jiandushu shui　崇文門監督署稅
Chougang　臭港
Chu Yupu　褚玉璞
Chuanmin　船民
Chufafei　出發費
Chun, Prince　醇親王
Chuzhou　滁州
Chuyu　楚豫

Cixi　慈禧

Dabeiying　大北營
dageming　大革命
Dagu　大沽
Dagulu　大沽路
Dalinghe　大凌河
Daming　大名
Dan Duyu　但杜宇
dayang　大洋
dashuai　大帥
dayuanshuai　大元帥
Dayunhe　大運河
dazongtong　大總統
dan　石
Danyang　丹陽
Dangshan　碭山
"daole qianxian, gei ta fang liang qiang, jiu suan duideqi ta."　"到了前線給他放兩槍就算對得起他。"
dedaozhe duozhu, shidaozhe guazhu　得道者多助，失道者寡助
Debuchi Katsuji　出淵勝次
Deng Baoshan　鄧寶珊
Deng Hanxiang　鄧漢祥
Deyu　德餘
Dezhou　德州
dian che　電車
Di er ci Zhi-Feng Zhanzheng　第二次直奉戰爭
Di yi ci Zhi-Feng Zhangzheng　第一次直奉戰爭
Ding Changfa　丁長發
Doihara Kenji　土肥原賢二
Dongge　東葛
Dong Zhengguo　董政國
Dongmen　東門
Dongjiang diqu　東江地區
Dongsansheng binggongchang　東三省兵工廠
Dongsansheng Minbao　東三省民報
Dongta nongye shiyanchang　東塔農業試驗場
Dou Lun　竇倫
Du Xigui　杜錫珪
Duan Qirui　段祺瑞
Duan Zhigui　段芝貴
duban　督辦
dujun　督軍
duli　督理

Erlangmiao　二廊廟

ershiyitiao　二十一條

fatong　法統
Fa zujie　法租界
Fan Yuling　範毓靈
Fan Zhongxiu　樊鍾秀
fandi feiyue, zhichi Sun Zhongshan zhaokai guomin huiyi　反帝廢約，支持孫
　中山召開國民會議
fan diguo zhuyi da tongmeng　反帝國主義大同盟
fandui youdai qingshi datongmeng　反對優待清室大同盟
Fang Benren　方本仁
Fei Baoyan　費保彥
fen　分
Feng Delin　馮德麟
Feng Guozhang　馮國璋
Feng Yurong　馮玉榮
Feng Yuxiang　馮玉祥
Feng Ziming　馮子明
Fengpiao　奉票
Fengrun　豐潤
Fengtai　豐台
Fengtian　奉天
Fengtian junxiechang　奉天軍械場
Fujian　福建
Funatsu Tatsuijirō　船津辰一郎

gansidui　敢死隊
Gao Lingwei　高凌霨
Gaoqiao　皋橋
Gaozi　高資
Ge Yinglong　葛應籠
geming shouduan　革命手段
Giga Masaya　儀我咸也
Gong Bangduo　宮邦鐸
Gong Hanzhi　龔漢治
gongshituan　公使團
Gong Debai　龔德柏
Gong Xinzhan　龔心湛
gonggong zujie　公共租界
Gongxian　鞏縣
Gongxian binggongchang　鞏縣兵工廠
gourou jiangjun　狗肉將軍
Gu Weijun　顧維鈞
Gu Zhenghong　顧正紅
Guan Yu　關羽

guanyu　關余
Guangdong　廣東
Guangxu　光緒
Guangzhou　廣州
guantie　官貼
guanyu　關余
Gubeikou　古北口
guiyuan　規元
Guo Moruo　郭沫若
Guo Songling　郭松齡
Guo Yingzhou　郭瀛洲
guochi huapu　國恥畫譜
guohunzhou　國魂舟
guomin huiyi　國民會議
guoshi　國事
guowu zongli　國務總理

Ha-er-bin　哈爾濱
Haichou　海籌
Haihe　海河
Haiji　海吉
Hainan dao　海南島
Hairong　海容
Haiqi　海圻
Hamamoto　濱本少佐
Han Guojun　韓國鈞
Han Linchun　韓麟春
Han Yukun　憨玉昆
hangkongchu　航空處
Hanjiang　漢江
Hankou　漢口
Hanyang　漢陽
Hanyeping gongsi　漢冶蘋公司
Hanzhuang　韓莊
Hayashi Gonsuke　林權助
He Fenglin　何豐林
Henan　河南
Heishanyao　黑山窰
Heishiguan　黑石關
honghuzi　紅胡子
hongqianghui　紅槍會
Honjō Shigeru　本莊繁
Hu Hanmin　胡漢民
Hu Jingyi　胡景翼
Hua Fei　華飛

333

huabao　畫報
Huaijun　淮軍
Huairouxian　懷柔縣
Huang Fu　黃郛
Huang Wennong　黃文農
Huangdu　黃渡
Huanghe　黃河
Huangpujiang　黃浦江
Huangtuling　黃土嶺
Huanzhang　煥章
huaqi ying　花旗營
Hubei　湖北
Hubei diwu hunchenglu　湖北第五混成旅
Huhang tielu　滬杭鐵路
Huzhou　湖州
Huifeng yinhang　匯豐銀行
Huludao　葫蘆島
Hunan　湖南
hunchenglu　混成旅
hunchengtuan　混成團
hunzhan　混戰
hutong　胡同
Huxian junzhengfu　護憲軍政府
Huzhou　湖州

Inukai Tsuyoshi　犬養毅

Ji Jinchun　汲金純
Jiading　嘉定
Jia Deyao　賈德耀
Jia Shancong　嘉善從
Jianchang　建昌
Jiang Hongyu　蔣鴻遇
Jiang Dengxuan　姜登選
Jiang Fangzhen　蔣方震
Jiang-Zhe Zhanzheng　江浙戰爭
Jiang Zuobin　蔣作賓
Jiangnan chuanwu　江南船塢
Jiangnan zhizaoju　江南制造局
Jiangsu baoan zongsiling　江蘇保安總司令
Jiangsu junshi shanhou gongzhai　江蘇軍事善後公債
Jiangsu junwu duli jian Songhu hujunshi　江蘇軍務督理兼淞護軍使
Jiangshan　江山
Jianguo dagang　建國大綱
jiangwutang　講武堂
Jiangxi　江西

Jianping 建平
Jianshanzi 尖山子
jiao 角
jiaofei 剿匪
Jiaoshan 角山
Jiaoshansi 角山寺
Jiao Yitang 焦易堂
Jiaoshansi 角山寺
Jiaotongxi 交通系
Jiawu zhanzheng 甲午戰爭
Jiazi 甲子
Jiazi zhiyi 甲子之役
Jiazhuang 賈莊
Jiazi 甲子
Jielingkou 界嶺口
Jieyan 戒嚴
jin 斤
Jinan 濟南
Jin-Chao gonglu 錦—朝公路
Jin-Pu tielu 津浦鐵路
Jin Yun'e 靳雲鄂
Jin Yunpeng 靳雲鵬
Jing-Han tielu 京漢鐵路
Jing-Shen tielu 京沈鐵路
Jingbei zhuangtai 警備狀態
Jinrong 金融會
jinshi 進士
Jinxi 錦西
Jinzhou 金州
Jinzhou 錦州
Jiuguantaimen 九關臺門
jiuguo 救國
jiuliu 九六
Jiumenkou 九門口
junfa 軍閥
Junliangcheng 軍糧城
Junshi shanhou mijuan 軍事善后米捐
Junxu shanhou mijuan 軍須善后米捐
Junzi zhijiao danrushui 君子之交淡如水
Juren 舉人
Juren tang 居仁堂
jurong 句容
jutou 巨頭

Kaifeng 開封

kaihuadan　開花彈
Kailu　開魯
Kailuan　開灤
Kaiping　開平
Kan Chaoxi　闞朝璽
kanglongyouhui　亢龍有悔
Kangxi　康熙
Kiyoura Keigo　清浦奎吾
Kokuryūkai　黑龍會
Kong Xiangxi　孔祥熙
Korenaga Shigeo　是永重夫
Kou Yingjie　寇英桀
Kunshan　昆山
Kuomintang [Guomindang]　國民黨

Langfang　廊房
Laolongtou　老龍頭
Laozha　老閘
Lengkou　冷口
li　里
Li Dazhao　李大釗
Li Dingxin　李鼎新
Li Dequan　李德全
Li Guishan　李桂山
Li Guoyi　利國驛
Li Hongzhang　李鴻章
Li Jichen　李濟臣
Li Jinglin　李景林
Li Jingrong　李竟容
Li Liejun　李烈鈞
Li Lisan　李立三
Li Mingyang　李明揚
Li Mingzhong　李鳴鍾
Li Shaobai　李少白
Li Shiceng　李石曾
Li Shuangkai　李爽
Li Sihao　李思浩
Li Shucheng　李書城
Li Yanqing　李彥青
Li Yuanhong　黎元洪
Li Yuying　李煜瀛
Li Zonghuang　李宗黃
Liang Hongzhi　梁鴻志
Liang Qichao　梁啟超
Liang Shiyi　梁士怡

Lianzhipai　聯治派
Lianghu jingbei zongsilingbu　兩湖警備總司令部
LiangHu xunyueshi　兩湖巡閲使
LiangJiang zongdu　兩江總督
Liaodongwan　遼東灣
Liguoyi　利國驛
lijin　釐金
Lincheng　臨城
Lin Jianzhang　林建章
Lincheng　臨城
Linshi zongzhizheng　臨時總執政
Lingyuan　凌源
liti zhan　立體戰
Liu Cunhou　劉存厚
Liu Fuyou　劉富友
Liu Xianghan　劉祥漢
Liu Ji　劉驥
Liu Jun　劉軍
Liu Ruming　劉汝明
Liu Yufen　劉郁芬
Liu Yuncheng　劉允丞
Liu Zhenhua　劉鎮華
Liu Zhizhou　劉治洲
Liuhezhen　瀏河鎮
Liuhe　柳河
Liujiang　柳江
Liulihe　琉璃河
liutongjuan　流通卷
Liuyuan　柳園
Longhai tielu　龍海鐵路
Longhua　龍華
Longhua yamen　龍華衙門
Longyu　隆裕
Lu Hongtao　陸洪濤
Lu Jin　陸錦
Lu Xiangning　盧香寧
Lu Xiangting　盧香亭
Lu Xiaojia　盧小嘉
Lu Yongxiang　盧永祥
Lu Zhonglin　鹿鍾麟
Lujun jianyueshi　陸軍檢閲使
Luanhe　灤河
Luanping　灤平
Luanxian　灤縣
Luanzhou chezhan　灤州車站

337

Luo Wengan　羅文乾
Luodian　羅店
Luoyang　洛陽
Lutai　蘆臺
Lüzhang　旅長
Luying　綠營

Ma Bingnan　馬炳南
Ma Hongkui　馬鴻逵
Ma Liang　馬良
Ma Lianjia　馬聯甲
Ma Xulun　馬敍倫
Ma Yuren　馬玉仁
Machino Takema　町野武馬
Machang　馬場
Mao Dun (Shen Yanbing)　茅盾（沈雁冰）
Maofeng qianzhuang　茂豐錢莊
Matsui Nanao　松井七夫
Matsumoro Takayoshi　松室孝良
Meiguo gongshiguan　美國公使館
Meng Zhaoyue　孟昭月
Mi Zhenbiao　米振標
Min　閩
Min-Zhe xunyueshi jian Jiang-Zhe junwu duli　閩浙巡閱使兼江浙軍務督理
Miyun　密雲
mu　畝

naisei fukanshō　內政不干涉
NanBei zhi zheng　南北之爭
Nanhai　南海
Nanjing　南京
Nanjing tiaoyue　南京條約
Nanjinglu　南京路
Nanxiang　南翔
Nanyang　南陽
Nanyanglu　南陽路
Nanyuan　南苑
Ning Wu　寧武
Niu Huisheng　牛惠生
Niu Yongjian　紐永建
Nogi Maresuke　乃木希典

Okano Masujirō　岡野增次郎
Ouyang Zhen　歐陽振

Pan Fu　潘復
Pan Guogang　潘國綱

Pan Hongjun　潘鴻鈞
Peng Shouxin　彭壽辛
Penglai　蓬萊
pingmin xuexiao　平民學校
Pingquan　平泉
Puyi　溥儀

Qi Enming　奇恩銘
Qi Jiguang　戚繼光
Qi Xieyuan　齊燮元
qian　錢
Qian Duansheng　錢端升
Qiananxian　遷安縣
Qianlong　乾隆
Qianmen　前門
Qianye gonghui　錢業公會
Qianzhuang　錢莊
Qin Dechun　秦德純
Qin Guang　秦
Qingdao　青島
Qingfeng　慶豐
Qinghe　清河
Qingpu　青浦
Qingshan　青山
Qinhuangdao　秦皇島
Quanluan　拳亂
Quzhou　衢州

Rehe　熱河
Ribenren ganshe Shandong shijian　日本人干涉山東事件
rujiang　儒將
runyu　潤余

sabishi　寂
Sandaoguan　三道關
Sanjiao lianmeng　三角聯盟
Sanxingtun　三姓屯
Shaanxi　陝西
Shaanxi dujun　陝西督軍
Shahe　沙河
Shaji　沙基
Shamian　沙面
Shandong　山東
Shandong haohan　山東好漢
Shanghai de beiju　上海的悲劇

339

Shanhaiguan　上海關
Shanghai nanzhan　上海南站
Shanghai zongshanghui　上海總商會
shangtuan　商團
Shanhou huiyi　善後會議
Shanyangzhai　山羊寨
Shao Piaoping　邵飄萍
Shaoguan　韶關
Shen Bochen　沈泊塵
Shenshang　紳商
Shenyang　沈陽
Shengyihui　省議會
Shengyuan　生員
Shengyuehan daxue　聖約漢大學
Shidehara Kijūrō　幣原喜重郎
Shisheng tongmeng　十省同盟
Shi Zhaoji　施肇基
Shikan gakkō　士官學校
Shimenzhai　石門寨
Shinise　老舖
Shōkin gintō　正金銀行
Shuangshijie guomin taocao youxing dahui　雙十節國民討曹游行大會
Shunyi　順義
Sichuan　四川
sigang　死港
Siping　四平
SongHu hujunshi　淞滬護軍使
Song Hanzhang　宋漢章
Song Zheyuan　宋哲元
Songjiang　松江
Song Jiuling　宋九齡
Suidong　綏東
Suizhong　綏中
Suren zhi Su　蘇人治蘇
Sun Baoqi　孫寶琦
Sun Chuanfang　孫傳芳
Sun Ke　孫科
Sun Liangcheng　孫良誠
Sun Liechen　孫烈臣
Sun Runyu　孫潤宇
Sun Yixian　孫逸先
Sun Yue　孫岳
Sun Zhongshan　孫中山
Sunzi　孫子
Suzhou　蘇州

Taihe　太和

Taihu　太湖

Taimingfu　太名府

Taiping Tianguo　太平天國

Tan Qinglin　譚慶林

Tan Yankai　譚延凱

Tang Jiyao　唐繼堯

Tang Shaoyi　唐紹儀

Tang Yi　湯漪

Tang Yulin　湯玉麟

Tanggu　唐沽

Tangshan　康山

Tao Jingwu　陶經武

Tao Zhiping　陶治平

taobing　逃兵

taofa mingling　討伐命令

Taolinkou　桃林口

Taonijun　討逆軍

Teranishi Hidetake　寺西秀武

Tian Weiqin　田維勤

Tian Xiongfei　田雄飛

Tian Yuhao　田玉浩

Tianjin　天津

Tianjin huiyi　天津會議

Tianjin tiaoyue　天津條約

Tianjin wubei xuetang　天津武備學堂

Tianxia diyiguan　天下第一關

tiaoyueguo　條約國

Tieshizi hutong　鐵獅子胡同

Tō gunbatsu　倒軍閥

Tōgō Heihachirō　東鄉平八郎

Tongguan　潼關

Tongxian　通縣

Tōyama Mitsuru　頭山滿

Uehara Yūsaku　上原勇作

Ugaki Kazushige　宇垣一成

waichong guoxin　外充國信

Wang Chengbin　王成斌

Wang Chonghui　王寵惠

Wang Huaiqing　王懷慶

Wang Jingwei　汪精衛

Wang Jinyu　王金鈺

Wang Jiuling　王九齡

Wang Kemin　王克敏

Wang Naibin　王乃斌
Wang Pu　王普
Wang Rongbao　汪榮寶
Wang Shizhen　王士珍
Wang Tao　王韜
Wang Tan　王坦
Wang Weicheng　王維城
Wang Xianchen　王獻臣
Wang Yitang　王揖唐
Wang Yongjiang　王永江
Wang Zhanyuan　王占元
Wang Zhengting　王正廷
Wanjiatun　萬家屯
Weichi jinrong hui　維持金融會
Wen De　文德
Wen Gongzhi　文公直
Wen Shude　温樹德
Wenhua dageming　文化大革命
Wu Changzhi　吳長植
Wu Chaoshu　伍朝樞
Wu Guangxin　吳光新
Wu Hengzan　吳恆瓚
Wu Jinglian　吳景濂
Wu Junsheng　吳俊陞
Wu Peifu　吳佩孚
Wu Tingfang　伍廷芳
Wu Xiang　吳翔
Wu Xintian　吳新田
Wuli tongyi　武力統一
WuSi　五四
Wuhan　武漢
Wuqing　武清
Wusong　吳淞
Wuweijun　武衞軍
Wuxi　無錫

Xia Chao　夏超
Xia Zhaolin　夏兆麟
Xiamen　廈門
xian　縣
Xi'an　西安
Xiang fang　象房
Xianfeng huangdi　咸豐皇帝
Xiangcheng　項城
Xianggang　香港

342

Xiangyu qianzhuang　祥裕錢莊
Xianxialing　仙霞嶺
Xianzhishi　縣知士
Xiao Yaonan　肖耀南
Xiaoxian　簫縣
xiaoyang　小洋
Xie Hongxun　謝鴻勛
Xie Zongtao　謝宗陶
Xifengkou　喜峯口
Xinan　新安
Xinchou tiaoyue　辛丑條約
Xing Shilian　刑士廉
Xingcheng　興城
Xinhai geming　辛亥革命
Xinhuamen　新華門
Xinjiang　新疆
Xiong Kewu　熊克武
Xu Guoliang　徐國樑
Xu Lanzhou　許蘭洲
Xu Qian　徐謙
Xu Shichang　徐世昌
Xu Shiying　許世英
Xu Shuzheng　徐樹錚
Xu Yongchang　徐永昌
Xuchang　許昌
Xujiahui　徐家匯
Xuzhou　徐州

Yamanashi Hanzō　山梨半造
Yan Huiqing　顏惠慶
Yan Tingrui　閻廷瑞
Yan Xishan　閻錫山
Yan Zhitang　閻治堂
Yang Chisheng　楊池生
Yang Huazhao　楊化昭
Yang Qingchen　楊清臣
Yang Ruxuan　楊如軒
Yang Shukan　楊庶堪
Yang Shuzhuang　楊樹莊
Yang Wenkai　楊文愷
Yang Yinpu　楊陰溥
Yang Yuting　楊宇霆
Yangcun　楊村
yangli　洋厘
Yantai　煙臺

yanyu　鹽余

Yao Zhencao　姚震草

Ye Baishou　葉柏壽

Ye Gongchuo　葉恭綽

Yifeng qianzhuang　益豐錢莊

Yijing　易經

Yijun　毅軍

Yinhang gonghui　銀行公會

Yingkou　營口

Yingrui　應瑞

Yingtai　瀛臺

yi tui wei jin　以退為進

Yixing　宜興

Yiyuan　義園

Yizhou　義州

Yongchang　永昶

Yongchun　永春

Yongle huangdi　永樂皇帝

Yongxiang　永翔

Youdai qingshi tiaojian　優待清室條件

"you duoshao qian bian da duoshao zhang"　"有多少錢便打多少仗"

Yoshida Shigeru　古田茂

Yoshioka Kensaku　吉岡顯作

Yoshizawa Kenkichi　芳澤謙吉

Yuguan　榆關

Yu Liyan　于立言

Yu shuai　玉帥

Yu Sun　裕孫

Yushan　虞山

Yu Youren　于右任

Yu Zhen　于珍

Yuan Shikai　袁世凱

Yue Fei　岳飛

Yue Weijun　岳維峻

Yuezhou　岳州

Yushan　玉山

Yu shuai　玉帥

Yuxian　禹縣

Zang Zhiping　臧致平

Zaoqiang　棗強

zei　賊

Zeng Yujun　曾毓雋

Zhabei　閘北

Zhang Bi　張壁

344

Zhang Dianru　張殿如
Zhang Fangyan　張方嚴
Zhang Fulai　張福來
Zhang Guotao　張國濤
Zhang Guowei　張國威
Zhang Huaibin　張懷斌
Zhang Ji　張繼
Zhang Jingrao　張敬堯
Zhang Liantong　張連同
Zhang Lin　張林
Zhang Muhan　張慕韓
Zhang Qihuang　張其煌
Zhang Shizhao　章士釗
Zhang Weixi　張維璽
Zhang Wanru　張萬嚴
Zhang Xiluan　張錫鑾
Zhang Xueliang　張學良
Zhang Xun　張勛
Zhang Yaozeng　張耀曾
Zhang Yinghua　張英華
Zhang Yunming　張允明
Zhang Zaiyang　張載揚
Zhang Zhidong　張之洞
Zhang Zhigong　張治公
Zhang Zhijiang　張之江
Zhang Zongchang　張宗昌
Zhang Zuolin　張作霖
Zhang Zuoxiang　張作相
Zhangjiakou　張家口
Zhangjia huayuan　張家花園
Zhantansi　旃檀寺
Zhao Erxun　趙爾巽
Zhao Hengti　趙恆惕
Zhao Jie　趙桀
Zhao Ti　趙倜
Zhejiang　浙江
Zheng liu　整六
Zheng Qian　鄭歉
Zheng Shiqi　鄭士琦
Zhengjin yinhang　正金銀行
Zhengwu weiyuanhui　政務委員會
Zhengzhou　鄭州
Zhenjiang　鎮江
Zhenshoushi　鎮守使
Zhenweijun　鎮威軍

Zhili　直隸
Zhili zongdu　直隸總督
Zhixi　直系
Zhi, Lu, Yu sansheng xunyueshi　直，魯，豫三省巡閱使
Zhongdong tielu　中東鐵路
Zhongguo yinhang　中國銀行
Zhonghua minguo guominjun　中華民國國民軍
Zhonghua minguo linshi zhizhengfu　中華民國臨時執政府
Zhongnanhai　中南海
Zhou Ziqi　周自齊
Zhu Peide　朱培德
Zhu Shengguang　朱聲廣
Zhuozhou　涿州
Zijincheng　紫禁城
Zongtong yin　總統癮
Zoudaonali chidaonali　走到那里吃到那里

Index

347

355